Sacrifice Unveiled

Sacrifice Unveiled:

The True Meaning of Christian Sacrifice

ROBERT J. DALY

t&t clark

Published by T&T Clark International
A Continuum imprint
The Tower Building, 11 York Road, London SE1 7NX
80 Maiden Lane, Suite 704, New York, NY 10038

www.continuumbooks.com

British Library Cataloguing-in-Publication Data
A catalogue record for this book is available from the British Library

ISBN-10: HB: 0-567-03420-8
PB: 0-567-03421-6
ISBN-13: HB: 978-0-567-03420-5
PB: 978-0-567-03421-2

Typeset by RefineCatch Limited, Bungay, Suffolk
Printed and bound in Great Britain by CPI Antony Rowe, Chippenham, Wiltshire

To My Parents,
My Brothers and Sisters,
My Jesuit Brothers,
and to all My Teachers, Mentors, Colleagues and Students
from Whom and with Whom
I Have Been Learning How to Offer
Christian Sacrifice

CONTENTS

FOREWORD

'Sacrifice' is perhaps the most massively misunderstood word and concept in all of Christian theology. What many people think is sacrifice is often not only not particularly Christian; it is all too often an aberration of authentic Christianity. Even the mere titles of a number of recent books give eloquent witness to the problem we are facing: S. Mark Heim's *Saved from Sacrifice*,[1] Stephen Finlan's *Problems with Atonement*,[2] Erin Lothes Biviano's *The Paradox of Christian Sacrifice*,[3] and the book whose title inspired my title: Gil Bailie's Violence Unveiled.[4] The *'Unveiled'* in my title indicates the twofold nature of my task: to expose the mistaken ideas of Christian sacrifice, and to unveil what it really is.

However much this may be a scholarly work, it would be disingenuous to pretend that it is not also autobiographical.[5] Its remote personal background is my early years of growing up in the 1930s and 40s as one of seven siblings in the almost ghetto-like atmosphere of second-generation immigrant (Irish, French-Canadian and Italian) Catholic family life in south-suburban Boston. It was there that I began to learn what it meant to be Roman Catholic, there that I grew up dreaming of becoming a priest, even a heroic missionary. Eventually, however, having completed high school at age seventeen, and no longer sure what kind of priest I wanted to be, I cast my lot with the Jesuits, assuming that they would find something useful for me to do. Having subsequently grown to maturity within the Jesuit seminary system, I was ordained; I became a priest, daily offering what Catholics traditionally call the Sacrifice of the Mass.

During those formative years, I had also discovered that I had a mind and that I was destined to spend my life happily using it, and not, as I had originally thought, as a priest-physicist, nor, as I subsequently thought, as a scholar in English literature, but, as I discovered in my 4 years of basic theology from 1960 to 1964, those

---

1   S. Mark Heim, *Saved from Sacrifice: A Theology of the Cross* (Grand Rapids, Mich.: Eerdmans, 2006).
2   Stephen Finlan, *Problems with Atonement; The Origins of, and Controversy about, the Atonement Doctrine* (Collegeville, Minn.: Liturgical Press, 2005). For many Christians, as Finlan points out, 'atonement' is almost synonymous with 'sacrifice'.
3   Erin Lothes Biviano, *The Paradox of Christian Sacrifice*, A Herder and Herder Book (New York: Crossroad, 2007).
4   Gil Bailie, *Violence Unveiled: Humanity at the Crossroads* (New York: Crossroad, 1995).
5   I will use the autobiographical motif in much greater detail as a means of organizing my summary conclusion in Part Three of this book.

heady years when the Second Vatican Council was being called into session, in theology itself. In those years, Father Philip Donnelly, S.J. showed me how exciting good theology could be, and Father Edward J. Kilmartin, S.J. how scholarly and critical it also needed to be. Kilmartin was, in fact, the one who introduced me to the work of the Würzburg professor, Johannes Betz who, shortly thereafter, became my dissertation director.

This brought me to 1965, the year that I began work on a dissertation then entitled 'Sacrifice in Origen', a project so ambitious that, 6 years later, I had completed only its prolegomena. But that was sufficient for my dissertation on *Christian Sacrifice*.[6] My lifelong study of this topic, now into its fifth decade, had been launched. Upon completion of the dissertation in the early 1970s, I formulated the grandiose plan of producing a series of historical-doctrinal studies on Christian sacrifice from its biblical origins up to the present day, and then, finally, of producing a culminating *magnum opus* that brought it all together in a definitive study of Christian sacrifice. Reality, however, in the form of multiple teaching, administrative and editorial responsibilities, intervened. I never even got to write the sacrifice-in-Origen book, although I did publish some half-dozen articles on various aspects of that subject.

Subsequently, by the late 1980s, two further changes had taken place in my academic life. The first of these was my discovery that I was called to be, primarily, a liturgical rather than a dogmatic or systematic theologian. This meant that, in addition to other theologians, the colleagues from whom I most learned tended to be members of the North American Academy of Liturgy or the international Societas Liturgica rather than members of the biblical or patristic associations. The second important change that took place at this time was my discovery of René Girard and the international group that studies mimetic theory, the Colloquium on Violence and Religion (COV&R). These new discoveries began to give me a sense, in phenomenological and anthropological terms, of how sacrifice actually works.

A decade later, in the mid 1990s, the last great change in my grandiose plans began to take shape. Instead of a whole series of historical-doctrinal monographs to be completed before the culminating theological *magnum opus*, the now more humbly realistic plan was to produce just one part of that ambitious project: a comparative study of Christian sacrifice in the Greek and Latin patristic traditions, using the major figures of Origen and Augustine as typical representatives of their respective Greek and Latin traditions. But that plan, too, turned out to be illusory. In 1994, Edward Kilmartin, S.J., my first great mentor in these matters, prematurely died, leaving behind the rough draft of *The Eucharist in the West*.[7] To me fell the task of preparing this work for publication.

---

6   This dissertation was later published as: Robert J. Daly, S.J., *Christian Sacrifice: the Judaeo-Christian Background before Origen* (Studies in Christian Antiquity, 18; Washington, D.C.: The Catholic University of America Press, 1978). A somewhat adapted, much abbreviated, and much more widely read version of it also appeared as: *The Origins of the Christian Doctrine of Sacrifice* (Philadelphia, Fortress Press, 1978).
7   Edward J. Kilmartin, S.J., *The Eucharist in the West: History and Theology* (ed. Robert J. Daly, S.J.; Collegeville, Minn.: Liturgical Press, 1998).

I had sensed that getting Kilmartin's last work published would end up being more important than the implementation of my own research plans. That turned out to be true in a way that, at the outset, I could not have imagined. What was at first a kind of self-sacrificing task of *pietas* for a beloved teacher – it consumed one whole precious sabbatical year – turned out, to my delighted astonishment, to be a revelation into the essential Trinitarian reality of Christian sacrifice. Until then, I had been naively oblivious of this. Had I gone ahead with my *magnum opus* without this controlling, overarching insight, I could not possibly, as I now realize, have even begun to do justice to the mystery of Christian sacrifice.

In the meantime, as the years passed, other developments put me in a position to do possibly much more, or at least much better, than what I could have done had I been able to carry out what had been envisaged in my earlier ideal plans. For in addition to the overarching liturgical-theological perspective that I now have, I also have the experience of having written and spoken on aspects of this theme for a variety of audiences and from a variety of theological perspectives: biblical, patristic, historical, doctrinal, ethical, and, more recently, also pastoral and homiletic. Theologically, I had become a jack of all trades, not the best stance from which to produce rigorous scholarly studies, but perhaps a very good position from which to produce this particular book.

My hope is that *Sacrifice Unveiled*, when I have finally put it to bed, will have become a book that is not just a 'must-read' for the scholar and theologian, but also a 'can read' for the intelligent and determined non-specialist, sufficiently insightful and revelatory for the one, and sufficiently reader-friendly for the other. The book will have three high points connected together by two bridge sections.

The opening high point, Part One, will lay out the central Trinitarian insight into, and begin to indicate the attendant implications of, authentic Christian sacrifice. The following bridge section will outline in three stages the general religious context and the biblical and patristic origins and background of this central insight. The second, middle high point, Part Two, keeping in mind our central Trinitarian insight, will expound the coming-to-crisis of Christian sacrificial ideas, first in the flawed development and unhappy implications of Western Christian atonement theories, and then in the disastrous reformational consequences of these flawed sacrifice and atonement theories. Following this, the second bridge section, again in three stages, will deal with the post-Reformation distortions, the contrasting poles at play in the unfolding of modernity, and the new seeds beginning to grow in the more recent developments in ecumenism, liturgical renewal and mimetic theory. Finally, the culminating high point, Part Three, building on all that has gone before, will suggest how the unveiling of Christian sacrifice will begin to make possible a phenomenology of authentically Christian redemptive sacrifice, and begin to deal with the homiletic and pastoral aspects of that revelatory unveiling.

PART ONE

TO UNVEIL SACRIFICE

Chapter I

The Many Meanings of Sacrifice

Few ideas or concepts are more central to Christian life and more thought than that of sacrifice. However, as we pointed out in our Foreword, and whether by Catholics or by Protestants, there is hardly anything that is more massively misunderstood than sacrifice. A brief anecdote can begin to illustrate the challenge we face.

> 'Have you found out what sacrifice is?' asked the pastor when the children, after having been segregated from the grownups for the Liturgy of the Word, had clambered back into their places in the front pews 'Yes!' triumphantly answered the religious education teacher. 'Sacrifice means giving up what you love.' The pastor clucked approvingly, added a few more words, and then (as I was restraining my urge to stand up and shout: 'No! No! You've got it all wrong!') moved to the altar to begin celebrating the specifically sacrificial part of the Sacrifice of the Mass. The first reading, on that Second Sunday of Lent, had been the account of the sacrifice of Isaac from Chapter 22 of the Book of Genesis.

Although this actually happened in a parish church in Germany a few years ago, it could have happened in any number of churches throughout the world. It strikingly illustrates the theological and pastoral challenges we face, even from the Church's own pastors and teachers, when we talk about 'sacrifice'. It is overwhelmed with negative connotations. For if we are correct, as this book will claim, in seeing the essence of Christian sacrifice as our participation, through the Spirit, in the transcendently free and self-giving love of the Father and the Son, and if Christian sacrifice is our inchoative, but already real, entering into the fullness of the totally free, self-giving, loving personal life of God, then it is obvious that the common understanding of 'sacrifice' with all its negative baggage – giving up what you love, destruction of a victim, doing something you'd rather not have to do, etc., etc. – does more to veil than it does to reveal this reality.

I can quickly list at least six meanings, any one of which, or almost any combination of them, can be what different people are thinking of when they hear or read the words 'sacrifice' or 'offering'.

A. SECULAR MEANING

First, there is the general secular meaning of the word: giving up something in order to get something else that is thought to be more valuable. What is given up could be almost anything, as long as it is considered to be of at least some value to the one making the sacrifice. The sacrifice is constituted by some kind of personal separation from the object of the sacrifice. The sacrifice is *by* somebody, *of* something, and *for* something, but never *to* anybody. Because of the deprivation factor, there is always some sadness or misfortune connected with it. In other words, sacrifice is something generally to be avoided, or at least to be kept as small as possible. Thus, there is almost always some 'calculation' involved, at least to make sure that the good obtained is higher in value than what is sacrificed. In some usages the associations are extremely negative, as, for example, in the Germanic languages where the same word, *Opfer*, means both 'sacrifice' and 'victim'. These secular connotations are pervasive and so deeply rooted in the way we think and talk and feel that it is almost impossible to avoid them. It is not prudent to pretend that they are not there.

B. General Religious Meaning

Then, overlaid on this secular meaning is the general religious meaning in which sacrifice is understood as the offering of something valuable to God. It can be defined as a gift presented to God in a ceremony in which the gift is destroyed or consumed. It symbolizes the internal offering of commitment and surrender to God. The purpose is primarily for the offerers to acknowledge the dominion of God, but also to bring about the reconciliation of themselves (and possibly others) with God, to render thanks for blessings received, and to petition for further blessings for oneself and others. One can see here the obvious distinction between internal and external sacrifice that Thomas Aquinas pointed out.[1] But this general religious meaning is something that is common to many religions. It is not yet specifically Christian.[2]

C. Sacrifice in the Hebrew Scriptures

Christian sacrifice, of course, has its roots in, and also draws much of its theology from the sacrificial practices of Ancient Israel. What eventually became the specifically Christian concept of sacrifice was already beginning to develop deep in the Old Testament in the early pages of the Book of Genesis where, in Chapter 4, we read about the sacrifices of Cain and Abel, and in Chapter 8 about the sacrifice of Noah after the flood.

For even here, in these early material sacrifices of animals and food, we find the sacred writers explicitly insisting on the vital importance of the religious dispositions with which one offers sacrifice. From the outset, it is clear that God alone decides what an 'acceptable sacrifice' is. But this was not an arbitrary decision. For in God's progressive self-revelation to our Jewish forebears, especially through the prophets, God made increasingly clear that living up to the covenant require-

---

1 *Summa Theologica*, II-II, q. 85, a. 2.
2 A quick overview of the vast variety of meaning that we are depicting with these few broad brush strokes can be gained, for example, from Jeffrey Carter, ed., *Understanding Religious Sacrifice: A Reader* (London/New York: Continuum, 2003).

ments of justice and mercy are absolute requirements for offering sacrifice pleasing to God and, by implication, for any proper religious act.

The next major development in pre-Christian Judaism that also became an essential part of the earliest Christian idea of sacrifice was, *first*, the identification of sacrifice with atonement and reconciliation, and *then* the awareness that what actually brought about reconciliation, atonement and communion with God was not so much the actual performance of a sacrifice, but the fact that it was performed *according to the law*, that is, in accordance with the will of God.

Finally, stimulated by the situation in which many Jews could not get to the Temple – remember, the Temple had eventually become accepted as the only place where sacrifice could be offered – there arose in Judaism the explicit awareness that prayer and the virtuous works of mercy and of service (i.e., living and acting according to the will of God) brought about precisely what rightly offered sacrifice in the Temple used to bring about, namely, reconciliation, atonement and communion with God.

It is fascinating to see how the earliest Christians, while rejecting material sacrifice in a temple, learned from and took over this Jewish spiritualized idea of sacrifice. But in doing so, they, so to speak, 'Christologized' it. For this is what was being referred to in Romans 12.1: '. . . present your bodies as a living sacrifice, holy and acceptable to God, which is your spiritual worship', and in those several other New Testament passages that speak about Christian sacrificial activity, i.e., sacrifices that Christians offer.[3]

D. General Christian Meaning

This is the biblical background of the general Christian, or at least the general Catholic Christian understanding of sacrifice as offering something to God. This offering can be something quite valuable as, for example, the dedication of one's life to priestly service, or to religious life with the vows of poverty, chastity and obedience. It can also be in the offering of something much less costly, like simply giving up something for Lent. But, as we learn from Jesus' praise for the widow's tiny offering in Mark 12.43 and Luke 21.3, 'size' is not the issue. The range of sacrificial significance or 'sacrificial awareness' can also vary considerably. There is, on the one hand, the profound and sometimes deeply heroic level of personal self-giving/self-offering that characterizes a life specially dedicated to the service of God.

But on the other hand there can be very little of this, as, for example, in a child who is conditioned by pious family custom to 'give up something' for Lent, and only later comes to appropriate such a practice as an aspect of personal self-giving in union with Christ. Thus there can be considerable variation in the extent to which these sacrificial actions are more or less merely external actions that Christians do or perform, or are genuinely Christological or Trinitarian in their inner inspiration.

---

3   Rom. 15.16; 1 Peter 2.4–10; Hebrews 10.19–25; 13.10–16. Comment on these passages will be a prominent feature of our treatment of sacrifice in the New Testament hereafter in Bridge 1 B: Sacrifice in the New Testament (below, pp. 51–74).

E. SPECIFICALLY CATHOLIC UNDERSTANDING

Then there is the very specifically Catholic Christian understanding of the sacrifice of Christ/the sacrifice of Jesus on the Cross and its relationship, almost one of identity, with the Sacrifice of the Mass. Although this has been understood and taught in different ways, and has sometimes been a point of bitter controversy as in the debates accompanying the Protestant Reformation, the fact of this most intimate and unique relationship has been a constant and central point of Catholic faith and teaching from the time of the Fathers of the Church right up to *Sacramentum Caritatis*, the recent Post-Synodal Apostolic Exhortation of Pope Benedict XVI.

However, this most central point of Catholic faith has also been one around which there have been massive misunderstandings, by Catholics as well as by Protestants, that have at times veiled rather than revealed what the sacrifice of Christ, and what authentic Christian sacrifice is really all about. For example, Christians generally agree that everything in the Old Testament finds its fulfilment in the New Testament, and most specifically in the Christ-event. But we often have difficulty in recognizing the really radical nature of the Christ-event. For, although that event did not do away with God's covenant with Israel, it did very much do away with sacrifice in the history-of-religions sense of the word. But with neither side at the time of the Reformation being aware of that, Catholics argued aggressively for the idea of the Mass as sacrifice, and Protestants argued bitterly against it. As we will explain a few pages hereafter in Section III. The Sacrifice of the Mass, both sides made the same fatal methodological mistake of not looking first to the Trinitarian Christ-event to ask what it was that the early Christians were groping to express when they began to refer to the death of Christ and to the Eucharist in sacrificial terms.

Further, helpful and sad illustrations of this problem are supplied by some of the classical Christian atonement theories, for problems with atonement usually end up also being problems with sacrifice. As we will expound in greater detail hereafter in Part II of this book, traditional Western atonement theory includes, or ultimately reduces to something like the following: (1) God's honour is damaged by sin; (2) God demanded a bloody victim to pay for this sin; (3) God is assuaged by the victim; (4) the death of Jesus the victim functioned as a payoff that purchased salvation for us.[4] Such an atonement theory, when absolutized, as it often is (witness the reactions to Mel Gibson's film *The Passion of the Christ*) and when pushed to its 'theo-logical' conclusions and made to replace the Incarnation itself as the central doctrine of Christianity, ends up turning God into a 'sacrifice demander' and Jesus into a 'punishment bearer'. It turns God into some combination of a great and fearsome judge, or offended lord, or temperamental spirit.

Without any further belabouring of the obvious, sacrifice is a word laden with anything but happy connotations and implications. These are inevitably called to mind by the mere mention of the word 'sacrifice'. However, skirting the problem

---

4   See Stephen Finlan, *Problems with Atonement: The Origins of, and Controversy about, the Atonement Doctrine* (Collegeville, Minn.: Liturgical Press, 2005), p. 1. Much of what I say in this book about 'problems with atonement' is gleaned from Finlan's book. In addition, much of what I learned from Finlan has been incorporated into my recent article: 'Images of God and the Imitation of God: Problems with Atonement', *Theological Studies* 68 (2007), pp. 36–51.

by simply refusing to use the word does not seem to be a viable option either. The word is simply too closely identified with central Christian faith and practice. The Roman Catholic tradition, all the more so from the perspective of its historical development, cannot simply prescind from words and concepts like the 'Sacrifice of the Mass', or the 'Holy Sacrifice', and still think of itself as Catholic. And for Christians generally, not just for Catholics, if you take away the 'sacrifice of Christ' you take away Christianity itself. The so-to-speak 'problems with sacrifice' have to be faced and dealt with. But how? If a direct approach does not seem to be good homiletic strategy, how can we be sure that some other indirect approach will truly lead us to the authentic heart of the matter?

For most of the 40-plus years that I have been thinking and writing about Christian sacrifice, I did not have a good answer to this question. But recently, from the work of Father Edward Kilmartin, S.J., I am beginning to get a better sense of what authentic Christian sacrifice is. It can be cautiously formulated in a specifically Trinitarian way, in a way that begins to allow us to make sense of all these problems and challenges. Because, when we now, as Christians, are confident that the Spirit has been guiding our growing understanding of the faith, ask what is the essence of sacrifice, i.e., the internal essence of specifically Christian sacrifice, we can come up with something like the following:

F. Authentic Christian Sacrifice

First of all, Christian sacrifice is not some object that we manipulate, nor is it something that we do or give up. It is first and foremost, a mutually self-giving event that takes places between persons. It is, in fact, the most profoundly personal and interpersonal event that we can conceive or imagine. It begins, in a kind of first 'moment',[5] not with us but with the self-offering of God the Father in the gift of the Son. It continues, in a second 'moment', in the self-offering 'response' of the Son, in his humanity and in the power of the Holy Spirit, to the Father and for us. And it continues further in a third 'moment' – and only then does it begin to become Christian sacrifice – when we, in human actions that are empowered by the same Spirit that was in Jesus, begin to enter into that perfect, en-Spirited, mutually self-giving, mutually self-communicating personal relationship that is the life of the Blessed Trinity.[6] In a nutshell, this is the whole story. Anything less than this, and especially anything other than this, is simply not *Christian* sacrifice. This cannot be overemphasized. It might be something that Christians do, or it might be something that some Christians think is sacrifice, but if it is not Trinitarian in this sense, it is not *Christian* sacrifice.

---

5 As I explain in detail in a few pages hereafter (below, pp. 8–9), I put 'moment' in scare quotes in order to alert the reader to how profoundly metaphorical is the use of this word, for there can be nothing of the temporal in the inner Trinitarian relationships (the Immanent Trinity).
6 See my expansion of this Trinitarian view of sacrifice in a few pages hereafter, and the source of it in Edward Kilmartin referenced below in Note 14.

Chapter II

A Trinitarian View of Sacrifice

Since sacrifice, in one form or another, has been an important part of practically every major religion, studies on sacrifice have typically begun by looking first to the various religions of the world. Then, having extracted from them some basic idea of sacrifice, they would then proceed to see how this idea is verified in the biblical and Christian practice and understanding of sacrifice. This is an eminently logical, scholarly, even scientific way of proceeding. Who could be against that? For us, however, such an approach is fatally flawed: flawed in its assumption that Christian sacrifice legitimately fits into the general category of sacrifice; and flawed as well in its failure to recognize that the Christ-event did away with sacrifice in the history-of-religions sense of the word. And, from this failure to recognize what Christian sacrifice clearly is not, comes the concomitant failure to recognize what it really is, namely, a profoundly Trinitarian event, the beginning of our personal entering into the life of Father, Son and Spirit.[7] Consequently, the typical scholarly approach to sacrifice establishes a bias that effectively veils from both the preacher and the scholar as well as from the general, run-of-the-mill Christian the specifically Christian concept of sacrifice. As a result, many think it is best to avoid even using the word.

A helpful illustration of this is Keenan's recent study, *The Question of Sacrifice*.[8] Impressively appropriating the insights of Hegel, Nietzsche, Kristeva, Levinas, Irigaray, Lacan, Derrida and others, he identifies the present 'moment in the genealogy of sacrifice' as one that calls for the 'sacrifice of sacrifice'.[9] It is in this light that he comes in his final chapter to treat 'The Sacrifice *of* the Eucharist'. Keenan has quite correctly seen that the ideal of Christian sacrifice is, and indeed must be, '*an*economical', i.e., not looking for a reward. And he is also correct in pointing out that this ideal, even in the very preaching of Jesus, seems to be sublated by an economical understanding of sacrifice, albeit that the reward promised by Jesus is celestial rather than terrestrial.[10] However, he does not take the further step of looking more deeply into the development of the Christian tradition to see how a more profound Trinitarian viewpoint, a Trinitarian understanding of sacrifice, something that is not even on his radar screen, sublates his whole approach. However, Keenan, the philosopher, cannot fairly be faulted for this since Christian theologians themselves are only beginning to take this further step.

---

7   In the course of this work, especially towards the end of it as we attempt to point out the implications of an authentic concept of Christian sacrifice, we will be claiming that what we are describing in specifically Christian Trinitarian terms is, in fact, also a universal human – and indeed uniquely humanizing – phenomenon, namely, responding to love with love.

8   Dennis King Keenan, *The Question of Sacrifice* (Bloomington: Indiana University Press, 2005).

9   Keenan, p. 1.

10   See, e.g., Mt. 6.3. 6. 17.

Thus, our attempt to take this further step, to expound – 'point towards' would be a more modest claim – the mystery of Christian sacrifice will begin from inside rather than from outside Christianity. We will begin with the Christ-event itself. We will look at this Christ-event from a specifically Trinitarian perspective. We will then follow this up by seeing how it is confirmed by a careful reading of the classical Eucharistic Prayers of the Christian tradition. The practical and pastoral implications of our findings will then be indicated, but only briefly, leaving the more extensive treatment of these implications for the final pages of this book.

It is important to note that an attempt such as this cannot be made on the basis of biblical data alone. Such an explanation was not possible, and did not become even theoretically possible, before the so-called 'golden age' of patristic theology that began in the late fourth century.[11] For the theological vision we are attempting to expound presumes the maturation not just of Christology, but also of the theology of the Trinity and of the Holy Spirit, and then, in confirmation thereof, the appropriation of that theology in the classical Eucharistic Prayers of the Church. In other words, the traditional *lex orandi lex credendi* axiom – i.e., the attempt to educe the doctrine of the Church from its life of prayer – is in full play here. But theology's attempt to do this has a curious history. First, the Trinitarian theology we are applying in this book became possible, theoretically at least, some fifteen hundred years ago. But then practically, and in actual fact, it was not universally understood and applied. For it did not *actually* become the basis of a mature liturgical theology – something that is still not universally accepted – until the late twentieth century. The relative novelty of how we are now able to use that Trinitarian theology is indicated by Bernhard Meyer's comment that Edward Kilmartin was the first to attempt a full-scale liturgical theology from a Trinitarian perspective.[12]

Beginning with the New Testament, at first somewhat hesitantly, but then ever more explicitly, Christians referred not only to the Christ-event but also to their primary celebration of that event, the Eucharist, in sacrificial terms.[13] What was it, then, that the early Christians were pointing towards, groping to express. Put theoretically, what is the prime analogate or core reality of Christian sacrifice? Edward Kilmartin answers with a singular directness:

> Sacrifice is not something that, in the first instance, begins as an activity of human beings directed to God and then, in the second instance, become something that reaches its goal in the response of divine acceptance and bestowal of divine

---

11 See Robert J. Daly, S.J., 'Eucharistic Origins: From the New Testament to the Liturgies of the Golden Age', *Theological Studies* 66 (2005), pp. 3–22.

12 'In our opinion no book of similar scope has yet appeared that on the basis of the theological tradition of East and West offers such a systematic, consistently structured Trinitarian theology of Christian worship and sacrament' – Hans Bernhard Meyer, S.J., 'Eine trinitarische Theologie der Liturgie und der Sakramente', *Zeitschrift für katholische Theologie* 113 (1991), pp. 24–38 (37), as quoted/translated by Michael A. Fahey, S.J., 'In Memoriam: Edward J. Kilmartin, S.J., (1923–1994)', *Orientalia Christiana Periodica* 61 (1995), pp. 5–35 (17–18). Meyer is referring to Edward J. Kilmartin, S.J., *Christian Theology: Theology and Practice*. Part I *Systematic Theology of Liturgy* (Kansas City: Sheed & Ward, 1988).

13 See Robert J. Daly, S.J., *Christian Sacrifice: The Judaeo-Christian Background before Origen* (Studies in Christian Antiquity, 18; Washington: Catholic University of America, 1978) and *The Origins of the Christian Doctrine of Sacrifice* (Philadelphia: Fortress, 1978).

blessing in the cultic community. Rather, sacrifice in the New Testament understanding – and thus in its Christian understanding – involves, so to speak, three
'moments.' The first 'moment' is the self-offering of the Father in the gift, the
sending, of his Son. The second 'moment' is the unique 'response' of the Son, in
his humanity and in the Spirit, to the Father and for us. The third 'moment' – and
only then does Christian sacrifice begin to become real in our world – consists in
the self-offering of believers in union with Christ by which they share in his covenant relation with the Father. The radical self-offering of the faithful is the only
spiritual response that constitutes an authentic sacrificial act according to the
New Testament (Romans 12.1). In other words, Christian Sacrifice is a profoundly
personal, eschatological, and trinitarian event, an event in which we Christians, in
the power of the same Spirit that was in Jesus, and in *our* concrete humanity, begin
to do in this world what will be able to do completely only in the next: we begin,
namely, to enter into that perfectly self-giving and self-communicating relationship of Father and Son.[14]

This is the central reality and meaning of Christian sacrifice. The three
'moments' of this reality that, following Kilmartin we will now expound, are the
respective self-offerings of the Father, of the Son and of the Christian faithful.
These are not totally separate actions; they flow into each other forming one
unifying dynamic.

Theologically, this may be as close as we can come in our efforts to reach out
and touch this central mystery of our Christian lives. It is, I think, what Trent was
groping towards, but was unable to express clearly, when it declared the Mass to be
a true and proper *(verum et proprium)* sacrifice.[15] As Einstein is reported to have
said, 'I want to know the thoughts of God; everything else is just details'. But, as
another popular saying goes: 'The love of God is in the details'. And it is in and
through the details that we, humans, experience the love of God. Unpacking these
details that constitute the religious history and personal reality of Christian sacrifice is the purpose of this book.

But before we move on, let me call attention to the 'scare quotes' I have used
around the words 'moment(s)' and 'response'. These are examples of how words
can veil as well as reveal. For, there is no before and after in the Blessed Trinity of
Father, Son and Spirit; nor, strictly speaking, are there any 'moments' in their
relationship with each other. They are coequal and coeternal. However, all the
words we use about God are human words, affected, as God is not, by the limitations of time and space. So, with only human words at our disposition, we use scare
quotes as a handy reminder of their limitations. That is why 'response' is also in
scare quotes. 'Response' suggests a certain amount of otherness, or tension, or

---

14   As expanded from the words of Edward J. Kilmartin, *The Eucharist in the West: History and
Theology* (Collegeville: Liturgical Press, 1988), pp. 381–83.
15   See Canon 1 (DS 1751) of the AD 1562 twenty-second session of the Council of Trent. With
'sacrifice' *(offerre)*, as Kilmartin points out (ibid., p. 198), Trent referred both to the transcendent
Christ-event, the self-offering of Christ, and 'the liturgical-ritual sacrificial act of the Eucharistic
celebration' which it tended to see in history-of-religions types of categories, This confusion was
resolved for the worse in the post-Tridentine Protestant and Catholic polemics, as we noted in the
introduction to this article and will develop further below in Part II of this book.

some element of 'over-against', of which there is absolutely nothing in the inter-relationship of divine Father and Son.

Now that we have laid out for all to see the specifically Christian perspective or bias from which we are attempting to unveil Christian sacrifice, this is a good place for us to give some attention to those more typical approaches that actually do this veiling. Whether explicitly or implicitly, we will throughout this book be in constant dialogue or argument with these approaches. The ordinary commonsense ideas of sacrifice that usually come to mind when one hears the word 'sacrifice' can be described as follows:

> [Sacrifice] describes some sort of renunciation, usually destruction, of something valuable in order that something more valuable may be obtained. One may sacrifice duty for pleasure or pleasure for duty, or honesty for gain or gain for honesty. One may sacrifice an eye or a limb or a life for one's country or for some other country. One may even sell stocks 'at a sacrifice'.[16]

These modern, secular connotations associated with 'sacrifice' can be analysed further: (1) The thing sacrificed may be material (money, a limb) or immaterial (pleasure, fidelity, honour). (2) It must be of some value to the one making the sacrifice. (3) The sacrifice is constituted by the sacrificer *renouncing* or *giving up* the valuable thing of which he or she is henceforth deprived. (4) The sacrifice is *by* somebody, *of* something and *for* something, but never *to* anybody; it is only a coincidence if the thing sacrificed comes into someone else's possession. (5) Because of the deprivation factor, sacrifice always denotes sadness or misfortune; it is to be avoided, if possible, or at least kept as small as possible. (6) Because one wants to obtain as much as possible for as little as possible, one often compares the cost of the sacrifice with the value of the good obtained. (7) The good for which the sacrifice is made is higher in value than what is sacrificed (e.g., the baseball batter 'gives up' his chance for a crowd-pleasing hit in order to enhance his team's chance of winning). If the one sacrificing happens to share in its benefits, we think of him/her as particularly fortunate. In the 'supreme sacrifice' the one sacrificing gives up everything and obtains, for him/herself at least, nothing. (8) In some usages the meaning is totally negative; no recompense is received or higher value served by the deprivation (The problem is even more acute in languages such as German which, as we have already noted, has just one word, *Opfer*, for both 'sacrifice' and 'victim'.[17]

The pervasive, 'veiling' influence of this general, secular idea of sacrifice – what automatically comes to mind when one hears the word – can also be seen even in specifically Christian-theological definitions of sacrifice. For example, in the kind of definition characteristically given at the beginning of articles on sacrifice in theological dictionaries and encyclopaedias one will find something like

---

16 Royden Keith Yerkes, *Sacrifice in Greek and Roman Religions and Early Judaism* (New York: Scribner's, 1952/London: A&C Black, 1953), p. 2.
17 Dependent extensively on Yerkes, this paragraph, with some modifications, is taken mostly from Robert J. Daly, S.J., *The Origins of the Christian Doctrine of Sacrifice* (Philadelphia: Fortress Press, 1978), p. 2.

Sacrifice is a gift presented to God in a ceremony in which the gift is destroyed or consumed. It symbolizes the internal offering of commitment and surrender to God. The purpose is primarily for the offerers to acknowledge the dominion of God, but also to bring about the reconciliation of themselves (and possibly others) with God, to render thanks for blessings received, and to petition for further blessings for oneself and others.

In terms of most people's religious idea of what sacrifice is, this is not a bad description. But in terms of introducing what authentic Christian sacrifice is, a profoundly Trinitarian event, or in terms of what people should have in mind when thinking of the Eucharist as sacrifice, it is defective in the extreme. It asks the wrong question. It approaches the matter completely backwards, in a completely upside-down way. It disastrously assumes that one should look to the religions of the world, and to the characteristics of sacrifice derived from them, in order to find out what we mean when we speak of the 'Sacrifice of Christ', the 'Sacrifice of the Mass', or 'Christian sacrifice'. In contrast to this, the right way, as we have been insisting, and as we will now proceed to point out in some detail, is to look first to the Christ-event, and *primarily from the perspective of that Trinitarian event*, rather than primarily from the practices of other religions, to try to understand sacrifice. This detailed explanation will be arranged in accord with the three 'moments' of Trinitarian Christian sacrifice: the self-offering of the Father, the 'response' of the Son, and the responding self-offering of the believers.

A. THE SELF-OFFERING OF THE FATHER

In attempting to understand Christian sacrifice, our focus is not on a concept or theory, but on a personal event. This event, consonant with the authentic notion of atonement revealed in the Hebrew Scriptures, is not a God-directed action of human beings, nor is it something that fits comfortably into broad history-of-religions categories. Rather, it is an event that begins with the initiative of God the Father; it begins with the self-offering of the Father in the gift of his Son. This will help us to avoid repeating a whole series of misconceptions that in the past have led to serious theological, ecumenical and pastoral dead ends. For the originating reality of sacrifice is not just the *initiative* of the Father, but the Father's *self-offering* initiative in the gift of his Son whose 'response', in turn, is also a self-offering. In plain terms – and this is something that cannot possibly be emphasized too much – sacrifice is not something that the Father does to the Son. It is not something that the Father demands from the Son. It is not something that is required of the Son or that is imposed upon the Son as upon some 'other'. The unity of the Trinity prohibits that kind of thinking. Thus, since all authentic Christian sacrifice begins here, authentic Christian sacrifice can never be something that someone does to or demands from someone else.

We find one very obvious example or illustration of this in the way that feminists typically reject sacrifice because of the way that traditional patriarchal Christian society has often used sacrificial rhetoric and exhortation as a means of keeping women in positions of subservience. In what they are rejecting – as long as the

whole baby doesn't get thrown out with the dirty water – the feminists are absolutely right. For what they are rejecting is not *Christian* sacrifice but an aberration
of it.[18]

At its core, then, true sacrifice, absent the negative implication of a 'loss of self',
is *self*-offering/*self*-gift – in the Father, and in the Son, and in us. In theological
terms, we are attempting to say something about the central, core event of the
economic Trinity, the action of the triune God outside of God, i.e., in our human
world of existence. We are talking about the Christ-event, the simultaneously
historical *transitus* and eternally transcendent en-Spirited relationship of Christ to
the Father, and how we are invited into that reality.

We can find, on this point, a helpful analogy with the traditional scholastic
distinction between *actus hominis*/the act of a human being (i.e., the act of someone who happens to be a human being, e.g., sleeping) and *actus humanus*/a
human act (i.e., the act of a human being precisely qua human being, e.g., choosing to forgive). So, to beat up on this almost dead horse, not all sacrifices that
happen to be performed by Christian human beings are actually also authentic
Christian sacrifices.

This runs stunningly counter to the 'theo-logical' implications of some New
Testament statements such as, for example, 'He who did not withhold ("spare" is
the word used in some translations) his own Son, but gave him up for all of us'
(Romans 8.32). And it also seems to contradict the theo-logical implications of
some of the Pauline atonement metaphors; and to contradict some of the – not just
patristic and medieval – atonement theories that have been built on these metaphors. Yes, indeed it does! But, as I have begun to and will continue to point out,
some of these interpretations, some of these atonement *theories* – as opposed to the
transcendent incarnational mystery of the Atonement – however popular they may
have been and, for many, may still be, are fundamentally un-Christian.

B. THE SELF-OFFERING 'RESPONSE' OF THE SON

We are speaking here of the unique response of the Son to the Father, in his
humanity and, of course, in and through the Holy Spirit. *In his humanity* refers
specifically to the human living of Jesus – his life, works, death, resurrection (and
subsequent sending of the Spirit) – as (so Aquinas) the instrumental cause of our
salvation or (so the Church Fathers) the 'hinge of our salvation'. Within this series
of events as constituting the 'historical' Christ-event, the death of Christ is usually
seen as constituting the central sacrificial moment. Thus, the term 'sacrifice of
Christ' is generally taken as referring specifically, and perhaps exclusively, just
to his death on the cross. In its tendency to turn the whole life of Christ into just

---

18   The recent work of Erin Lothes Biviano, *The Paradox of Christian Sacrifice: The Loss of Self, The
Gift of Self* (New York: The Crossroad Publishing Company, 2007) provides a helpful way to review
the substance and significance of the well-known feminist critique of sacrifice. See esp. her second
chapter, 'The Feminist Critique of a Distorted Idea of Sacrifice' (pp. 71–118). Most helpful is the
way she, while defending the integrality of sacrifice to authentic Christian living, astutely unpacks
the paradoxical tensions between self-sacrifice as 'the loss of self' and the transcending fulfillment
of genuinely free self-giving as 'the gift of self'.

a prelude to the Passion, and in its tendency to overlook the resurrection and sending of the Spirit, this can be too narrow a view. But even after all correctives, the cross remains ineluctably central to what Christians mean by (1) the Christ-event, (2) the sacrifice of Christ and (3) the Sacrifice of the Mass.

This requires some careful distinguishing, nuancing, and balancing, not least because of the long Catholic tradition of bringing together, even identifying, these three 'moments' or aspects of the Son's response to the Father. First, we must make sense of, and not be methodologically overwhelmed or led astray by the fact that in the crucifixion of Christ are found most of the essential elements or characteristics of a history-of-religions concept of sacrifice: (1) the sacrificial *material* to which something is done, (2) the *agents* of the sacrificial action, (3) the *recipients* of the sacrificial action, (4) the *purpose* for which the sacrificial action is performed. Keeping in mind the traditional 'identification' of the sacrifice of Christ and the Sacrifice of the Mass, let us see what happens when we try to 'apply' these four history-of-religions elements to the way in which the Christ-event is present in the Eucharistic celebration.

(1) In terms that are reminiscent of human sacrifice and of the various material offerings found in the religions of the world, the *sacrificial material*, the victim in other words, is the bodily person of the human Jesus offered/destroyed on the Cross. Fixation on this aspect led to the fruitless polemics of the post-Tridentine arguments about whether the Mass is a sacrifice, with the Catholics attempting to find, and Protestants attempting to deny a 'destruction of the victim' in the celebration of the Mass that Catholics saw identified with the sacrifice of Christ. Ironically, the two sides were in agreement primarily in making the same methodological mistake. Instead of looking to the Christ-event, they first looked back to the Old Testament and to the other religions of the world in order to find a 'basic idea' of sacrifice that they then could apply to the Mass. They found that common, basic, and therefore seemingly essential element of sacrifice in the destruction of a victim, and then tried to prove the presence or absence of that in the celebration of the Mass that, in 1562, the Council of Trent had defined to be a 'true and proper sacrifice' (DS 1751). Since Christians from as far back as the third century saw Christ as both the priest and the victim in his one unique sacrifice, and since all Christians knew that Christ, now risen in glory, was beyond all suffering, the Protestants easily won most of the debating points.

But what would be the 'material' of the offering when we look at Christ's death as a central 'event' in the working of the economic Trinity? This 'material' now becomes, first and foremost, the perfectly free, responsive self-giving, self-communicating, en-Spirited love of the Son to the Father – and also to and for us. (Note that this could begin to serve as a definition of the second Person of the Trinity.) This is the transcendent essence of the sacrifice of Christ. This is its transhistorical or eschatological reality. This is, then, what is clearly present in the Sacrifice of the Mass. It is at the heart of what theologians through the ages have sought to express by speaking of the presence of the sacrifice of the cross in the Mass as 'unbloody', 'sacramental', 'metahistorical', etc. But while this transcendent essence of the sacrifice of Christ must be kept central in our focus, along with it must also be kept, in equally central focus, the concrete, historical, incarnational dying and rising of Christ.

(2) In categories accessible to history-of-religions analysis, the *agents of the sacrifice* are, for the death of Jesus, the Roman government of Judea and its soldiers, certain Jewish religious authorities, and even, in some views, Jesus himself 'staging' his own death. (And if one extends history-of-religions analysis to the New Testament text: 'He who did not withhold/spare his own Son' – Romans 8.32, the agent can even seem to be God the Father sacrificing his Son.) For the Eucharistic celebration, the agents are the priest(s) or ministers (and – with liturgical renewal – participating assembly) who are ritually celebrating the Eucharist.

But if one's point of view is the 'transcendent essence of the sacrifice of Christ' mentioned in the previous paragraph, the 'historical' agents become more secondary. The sacrificial death of Christ becomes the hinge-point of the *magnalia Dei*, the turning point of salvation history. It is something that, with full due given to its human actors, is primarily the saving action of God brought about through the instrumentality of the human living, dying and rising of Jesus. From this same transcendent viewpoint, the Eucharist becomes the action of the Church, the Body of Christ and of a particular assembly of that Body, that is acting in the power of the Holy Spirit, the same Spirit that was in Jesus,[19] actualizing the most intimate relationship with her divine partner of which the two are capable – i.e., entering eschatologically and proleptically into that event in which the self-offering initiative of the Father in the gift of his Son is, in the Spirit, responded to in the mutually self-communicating love of the Son.

(3) When we ask about the *recipient(s) of the sacrificial action*, still more nuance is required. For the history of religions (or its historical and philosophical antecedents in the ancient world) probably would not have seen the death of Christ as sacrificial (to the outside world it was just a public execution) were it not for the witness of the New Testament and subsequent Christian reflection on that witness. But on the basis of that witness (see esp. Romans 8.32)[20] one could think of God the Father as the recipient of the sacrifice, until one recalls that Greek philosophy had already established the illusory absurdity of trying to offer anything bodily or material to a spiritual god. Some of the Church Fathers also speculated about the devil being the one to whom the sacrifice was offered, but that, for obvious theological reasons never really caught on in authentic Christian circles. To whom, then, is the sacrifice of Christ – let alone its commemoration or re-presentation in the Sacrifice of the Mass – offered? If authentic sacrifice is 'in the first place the self-offering of the Father in the gift of his Son ... etc.' as pointed out earlier, there really is no proper recipient either of the sacrifice of Christ or of the

---

19   One cannot say 'that the Father is in the strict sense one and the same in the Son, in the Holy Spirit, and in us. The Holy Spirit, however, is, in the strictest sense, one and the same in the Father, in the Son, in the human nature of Jesus, and in us!' – Heribert Mühlen, *Una mystica persona. Die Kirche als das Mysterium der Identität des heiligen Geistes in Christus und den Christen: Eine Person in vielen Personen*, (Munich – Vienna: Schöningh, 2nd rev. edn, 1967), §§ 11.70–11.82 (11.77). See also Kilmartin, *The Eucharist in the West*, pp. 357–58.
20   For details on the New Testament witness, see the works cited above in Note 6 of the Foreword.

Sacrifice of the Mass. In authentic Christian sacrifice, no *thing* is being given. What is *happening* is that persons, in full freedom are giving/communicating themselves to each other. All the more reason to question the appropriateness of beginning a treatment of Christian sacrifice with the history of religions.

(4) Analysis of the *purpose for which the sacrifice is performed* offers more interesting results. The affirming, the deepening, or the setting aright of the relationship between God and human beings describes, if one must do so in a few words, the purpose of sacrifice in the Hebrew Bible and, analogously, in the other sacrificial religions of the world. It seems clear that the New Testament refers to Christ as the Lamb of God, Passover Lamb and sin offering, and the overall thesis of the Epistle to the Hebrews shares in this view. In this instance, a history-of-religions approach seems to be neutral. It does not help much, but neither does it get in the way, as long, of course, that it does not try to exclude from consideration data or claims that transcend its own limits.

C. THE SELF-OFFERING OF BELIEVERS

As we have already pointed out, authentic Christian sacrificial activity does not begin with human beings, and then get accepted or rejected by God; it is a responsive, interpersonal, self-communicative activity that has begun with the initiative of the Father. It is, in Christians, a self-offering 'response', just as was the self-offering response of the Son with which it is in union. It is a response that explicitly commits Christians to emulate and to make their own the virtuous dispositions of the human Jesus in his response to the Father. And finally, it is a response that believers make, and indeed are enabled to make, only in the power of the Holy Spirit, the same Spirit that was in Jesus[21] and that empowered his perfect loving response. This empowering of the Holy Spirit is what enables the faithful to share in Jesus' covenant relation with the Father. Hence Kilmartin's conclusion (quoted earlier) that 'the radical self-offering of the faithful is the only spiritual response that constitutes an authentic sacrificial act'.

This is the basic reality, and thus the foundation of the basic concept, of Christian sacrifice. The rest, to return again to Einstein's famous saying, is just details. But since there, in the details, is precisely where the love of God is to be found, we can't just stop; we have to go on talking our talk and writing our books, hoping that we are unveiling rather than veiling the mystery.

Chapter III

The Sacrifice of the Mass

One of the principal sources or confirmations of the concept of Christian sacrifice that we have been developing is theological reflection on the Eucharist. This is to

---

21   See above, Note 19.

be expected not only because Christians, even in the New Testament, had begun to refer to the central moments of the Christ-event as the sacrifice of Christ, but also because, soon after that, they began to refer to their liturgical commemoration of that event in sacrificial terms and eventually, in its Catholic development, as the Sacrifice of the Mass. To begin to understand this development, we again take our cue from Edward Kilmartin. With regard to the key source for an adequate theology of the Eucharist, he writes

> If the law of prayer, the Eucharistic Prayer, determines and explicates the law of belief, and if this is indeed the doing of theology, then the voice of the Church should be heard when she speaks to her divine partner in that moment of maximum relative tension of which the one and the other are capable.[22]

We are now in a position to see more clearly why it is proper to call the Eucharist a sacrifice. We look primarily to the Eucharistic Prayer in its classical patristic formulations. These prayers provide the basic models for practically all the developed Eucharistic Prayers[23] that have come to be used in the Christian churches. They have also already provided the basis for an astonishing convergence in Eucharistic theology among the main-line sacramental Christian churches. The full context of our analysis must be, of course, not just the Eucharistic Prayer but the whole liturgical celebration, and that, in turn, cannot be isolated from context of the whole of Christian life in the world. In addition, in order not to get totally lost in details, we are attempting to step back and at least begin this analysis from a transtemporal and transtraditional point of view. For while some actual Eucharistic celebrations in some contexts may tend to obscure rather than unveil the reality being celebrated, we are still trying to keep our analysis recognizably faithful to the various ways in which Christians have celebrated the Eucharist both across the ages and across the cultures and traditions. At the same time, modern hermeneutics keep reminding us of the relative impossibility of ever stepping out of our own time and culture. It is in full awareness of all these caveats that we now focus our attention on the ritually celebrated Eucharistic Prayer of the Christian assembly, specifically from the Dialogue Preface through to the Communion of the Assembly. Keeping in mind both the (theological) Trinitarian reality of authentic Christian sacrifice as well as the kinds of (scientific) issues raised by the history of religions, we now do this by attending to three questions: Who is doing what? Who is saying what? What is taking place?

A. WHO IS DOING WHAT?

When we examine the Eucharistic Prayer on its own terms; when, independent of preconceived notions, we look to what, in that ritual context, is being said and done, it is clear that the primary ritual agent and speaker (i.e., what is being said

---

22 Kilmartin, *The Eucharist in the West*, p. 324.
23 By 'developed' I am intending to exclude those instances where the prayer is reduced to just a proclamation of the words of institution.

and done in this here-and-now time and space) is the liturgical assembly. As an example, we can take the currently used Eucharistic Prayers of the Roman Catholic Church. Except for some 'private prayers of the priest' that have crept in here and there, the presider or priest celebrant never speaks in his own voice or for himself alone. This is entirely consistent with the internal logic of the Eucharistic Prayer in which the presider, qua presider proclaiming the Eucharistic Prayer, never speaks as one above or apart from the assembly. Nor does the presider speak or act as a mediator between God or Christ and the assembly. It is vitally important to emphasize this because some misunderstandings of the special role of the priest tend to veil the fact that Jesus Christ and he alone is the one, unique mediator. The presider's words and actions are never spoken in his own name, or from his own power, but always in the first person plural, as one of the assembly. To my knowledge, the same can be said about all the fully developed Eucharistic Prayers used by the main Christian church bodies.

Notice how different this is from the popular Roman Catholic idea of personal 'priestly power' that reigned from the Middle Ages and still dominates much traditional Catholic thinking. In the post-Vatican-II revision of the rite of ordination, the laying on of hands and the invocation of the Holy Spirit is now seen as the central ordaining 'moment'. But before that revision, the central act of the ordination ceremony was taken to be the moment when the ordaining bishop handed over the chalice and paten (*traditio instrumentorum*) to the deacon being ordained with the words: 'Receive the power of offering sacrifice for the living and the dead'. This illuminates the precise problem point in the famous medieval case about the renegade priest who consecrates all the bread in a bakery. Since it was assumed that the bread was indeed consecrated – there was little argument about that – the 'problem' tended to focus on issues of justice: the baker was not allowed to sell what was no longer bread but was now the Body of Christ.

B. Who is Saying What?

The Eucharistic Prayer is a prayer addressed by the assembly to God the Father.[24] It gives praise and thanks for the gifts of creation and salvation history, and most especially for the coming into our world of the Son who, the night before he died, took bread, etc. . . . At this point, the presider breaks out of the first-person-plural mode of discourse to quote a conflation of the four New Testament accounts of Jesus instituting the Eucharist. The presider does not speak these words in his own voice, nor, if remaining true to the logic and dynamic of the prayer and the rubrics (which are very precise at this point), does the presider speak them as if he were acting out the role of Jesus. And finally, these words of institution, or 'consecration' as the Catholic tradition calls them, are definitely not performative. The transformation of bread and wine does not take place 'by the action of the priest' as, until recently, a popular Catholic Eucharistic hymn used to put it. Rather, the Eucharistic words of institution have a decidedly epicletic or, if you

---

24   Some, mostly very early, Eucharistic Prayers, but also a few contemporary ones as, e.g., in the Maronite Church, at variance with what has become the common rule, are addressed to Jesus.

will, petitionary cast.[25] In the dynamics and structure of the Eucharistic Prayer, the instituting words of Jesus are an 'embolism', i.e., an insertion into an already existing prayer structure that is a basically Jewish, but now Christianized, table prayer of blessing. As such, the words of institution not only constitute the key element that gives specifically Christian meaning to what is fundamentally a Jewish prayer, they also take their meaning from their place and function within that prayer.

But can an analysis like this be done in a way that remains faithful to the Christian tradition, even the Roman Catholic tradition, at least as it is broadly understood? For, our analysis is not particular to just part of the tradition. The whole range of classical Eucharistic Prayers, both those from antiquity as well as their widely used contemporary progeny, supports an interpretation of the words of institution as primarily epicletic or petitionary rather than as performative. The most significant point of difference in all of these is between Eucharistic Prayers that place an epiclesis over the gifts to be sanctified *before* the Words of Institution (like the current prayers of the Roman Rite), and those that place the epiclesis *after* the Words of Institution (like most of the Eastern and modern Protestant Eucharistic Prayers). But this difference does not affect the fact that the Words of Institution are always primarily epicletic.

The Roman Eucharistic Prayer I, a translation/adaptation of the *Canon Missae*, the Eucharistic Prayer of the historical Mass of the Roman Rite, has only an implicit invocation of the Holy Spirit just before the Words of Institution when it prays: 'Bless and approve our offering; make it acceptable to you, an offering in spirit and in truth. Let it become for us the body and blood of Jesus Christ, your only Son, our Lord.' Then, after the Institution Narrative and the ensuing Memorial Prayer, and before the prayers for the living and the dead, there is an even 'softer', i.e., much less explicit Epiclesis over the assembly: 'Then, as we receive from this altar the sacred body and blood of your son, let us be filled with every grace and blessing.' The (1969/70) Missal of Pope Paul VI with its new Eucharistic Prayers, taking its lead from the classical patristic Eucharistic Prayers still in use in the Eastern Churches, made these epicleses fully explicit. For example, in Eucharistic Prayer II, just before the Institution Narrative we pray: 'Let your Spirit come upon these gifts to make them holy, so that they may become for us the body and blood of our Lord, Jesus Christ'. Then, after

---

25   The *Epiclesis* is the place in the Eucharistic Prayer where the assembly appeals to the Holy Spirit to come and sanctify the gifts and the assembly. In most of the Eastern Eucharistic Prayers, whose validity is unchallenged by the Western Roman Church, this Epiclesis takes place *after* the recitation of the words of institution. In some of these prayers the order is reversed: the Spirit is invoked to come and 'sanctify us and these gifts'. This demolishes the traditional Western 'moment-of-consecration' theology which assumed that the Eucharist and the presence of the sacrifice of Christ was essentially complete as soon as the priest pronounced the words of institution. Cesare Giraudo has suggested that what may be most effective in helping Roman Catholicism to break out of its theologically debilitating fixation on the 'moment of consecration', and thus move towards a more fully catholic Eucharistic theology, might be the official adaptation of a Eucharistic Prayer which has the Epiclesis in the classical Antiochene position *after* the words of consecration. See 'Anafore d'Oriente per le Chiese d'Occidente', in Robert F. Taft, ed., *The Christian East, Its Institutions & Its Thought, A Critical Reflection: Papers of the International Scholarly Congress for the 75th Anniversary of the Pontifical Oriental Institute*, Rome, 30 May–5 June 1993 (Rome: Pontificio Istituto Orientale, 1996), pp. 339–51.

the Institution Narrative and as the conclusion of the Memorial Prayer, the presider prays: 'May all of us who share in the body and blood of Christ be brought together in unity by the Holy Spirit'. Explicit epicleses of this kind, first before the Words of Institution over the gifts, and then after the Words of Institution over the assembly are clear features in all the new Roman Eucharistic Prayers. Overall, however, this 'split epiclesis' is an exception to the more common rule.

In most Eastern Eucharistic Prayers, the structure of the prayer is different but the fundamental meaning is the same. For here we find a unified Epiclesis, over both the Assembly and the gifts, after the Memorial-Offering Prayer that follows the Words of Institution, and before the Solemn Prayers for the Church (i.e., in the place where the Roman Eucharistic Prayers have an Epiclesis over just the Assembly). In the Byzantine form most commonly used in the Orthodox Churches of the East, the assembly, through the voice of its presiding priest, prays more or less in these words (here, as adapted for use in modern Eucharistic Prayers such as the Methodist Great Thanksgiving):

> Pour out, holy God, your Spirit on us and on these gifts of bread and wine. Make them be for us the body and blood of Christ, that we, through them, may be his true body, redeemed by his blood. Look, then, upon this offering of your Son. Look upon this body which your Spirit has made us. Hear us as we pray that we may be more fully one with Christ in his sacrifice, and with each other, and in service to all the world.[26]

In each case the assembly, in words solemnly proclaimed by the presider, prays for the Holy Spirit to come and sanctify these gifts and make them become for us the Body and Blood of Christ. Thus, *it is not the presider who consecrates*. The presider, speaking solemnly in the name of the assembly, petitions the Holy Spirit to consecrate the assembly and the Eucharistic gifts – notice the *order* – so that we the assembly may become the true Body of Christ offering ourselves, with Jesus (for the force of this prayer is to make us one with and part of Jesus' self-offering) to the Father. It can hardly be overemphasized that the transformation of bread and wine is not the primary focus. As we will shortly expound further, the primary focus, indeed the very purpose of the transformation of the bread and wine, is the transformation of the assembly.

C. WHAT IS TAKING PLACE?

One can tie all this together by attending to the third question: 'What is taking place?' We can answer on three interpenetrating but distinguishable levels: (1) the here-and-now level of human ritual action, (2) the transcendent level of divine action and (3) the eschatological level that combines these two levels in the already/not yet of the Eucharistically celebrated Christ-event.

---

26 *The United Methodist Book of Worship* (Nashville, Tenn.: The United Methodist Publishing House, 1992), p. 57 and passim.

(1) On the *here-and-now level of human ritual action,* it is clear that the one speaking and acting is the Church, specifically a particular local assembly of the Church, speaking and acting under the 'presidency' of one chosen (ordained) by the Church to lead the assembly in this its central prayer and action. This needs to be particularly stressed in the Roman Catholic tradition because of its strong traditional emphasis, especially since the twelfth century, on the 'prayer and action of the priest'. A narrow understanding and application of the *in persona Christi* axiom tended to exacerbate this overemphasis because of the frequent neglect of the completion of the axiom: *capitis ecclesiae.* The full axiom sees the presiding priest acting not just *in the person of Christ* but *in the person of Christ the head of the Church.* This points to the ecclesiological fullness of the Eucharistic celebration as the prayer and action not just of the priest but of a particular assembly of the Body of Christ. The role of the priest is not that of a mediator between Christ and the Church, the role of the priest is embedded in the Christ–Church relationship that brings about the Eucharist.

(2) The picture becomes clearer when we look to – or at least look towards – *the transcendent level of divine action.* In faith we know that the Church is speaking to her divine partner, which it can do because her members have already been empowered to do so in baptism. Indeed the Church herself, both from previous Eucharistic celebrations and from ages of practical Eucharistic living, is already experienced in being partner to the divine. The Church praises and thanks God the Father for all the gifts of creation and salvation history, past, present and still to come. At the heart of this praising and thanking, it recalls the central events of the Christic Paschal Mystery, but it does this in a particular and unique way. The Church, in supreme confidence – it knows that it is already the Body of Christ, indeed the Bride of Christ – asks God the Father to send his Holy Spirit to sanctify the Eucharistic gifts and the Eucharistic assembly, in order to make them, together, the true Body of Christ. Then, continuing in its supreme confidence that God/the Holy Spirit has indeed done, and is actually doing this, the Church then goes on to pray for the needs of all the people of God and all the members of the human family. The Church does this, it seems, with the same kind of confidence that Mary apparently had at Cana when she told the servants to follow the instructions of her Son (John 2.1–11). Then, after the concluding doxology, the members of the Body come forward to receive sacramentally that which by virtue of their baptism they already are: the Body of Christ.

But, in our attempt to look ever more deeply we can ask: What, on the transcendent level of divine action, is actually happening? There are two interrelated transformational happenings: (1) the Eucharistic elements of bread and wine become, by divine action, the body and blood of Christ; (2) the participating faithful become, also by divine action, more fully members of the Body of Christ. Both of these happen, indeed happen ontologically, *in* space and time; but each of them is, strictly, a 'divine' rather than a space–time event. They are not events that are capable of detection and analysis by human, this-worldly means. God is the principal cause but not the only agent in the Eucharistic event. The Eucharistic celebration involves both eternity and time; it is a conjoined divine/human operation.

When we go on to ask *why* these events are taking place, a very important fact becomes strikingly clear: one of these transformational events is clearly subordinated to the other. That the bread and wine are to become the Body and Blood of Christ present on this or that altar is not an end in itself, not the final purpose of the Eucharistic transformation. The transformation that brings about the Eucharistic presence happens *for us*, that *we* may become more fully and more truly the Body of Christ. *The whole purpose is the eschatological transformation of the participants.* Take that away and the Eucharist becomes (even blasphemously) meaningless. Remembering that modern philosophical thinking tends to identify meaning with reality, this seems to suggest that if the transformation of the Eucharistic elements is not having its effect in the virtuous dispositions of the participants, if the participants are not at least beginning to be transformed, at least beginning to appropriate the self-offering virtuous dispositions of Christ, then there is no Eucharistic presence. We must examine this conclusion closely, for it seems to be, on the one hand, 'theo-logically' impeccable, and, on the other hand, at odds with solemn Catholic teaching on the Eucharist.

Historically, this is a revisiting of the traditional question of the relationship between the sacrifice of the cross and the sacrifice of the Mass. The *fact* of the real, ontological 'presence' of the one to the other is not what is in question – at least not in what I understand to be Catholic approaches to the understanding of the Eucharist. The *how* is the question. How, *precisely*, is the historical sacrifice of the cross present in/related to the sacramental sacrifice of the Church? If, by 'precisely' we mean a clearly achieved doctrinal and theological position that is held in peace by the Church and its theologians, there is no clear answer. Within the sacramental traditions of Christian theology there seem to be two basic approaches. The first and most common approach is to see *the sacrifice of Christ as made present to the faithful.* The second approach is to see *the faithful as made present to the sacrifice of Christ.*[27] Each approach supports the core Catholic belief of the real ontological 'presence' to each other of the sacrifice of the cross and the Sacrifice of the Mass. The delicacy of the theological problem is that many see the first approach as the only theological position that can do justice to traditional Catholic faith, while some see the second approach as the only one that can adequately begin to do theology's job of trying to understand the faith.

The first approach, that sees the sacrifice of Christ as (somehow, but in any case really, e.g., transhistorically or metahistorically) made present in the celebration of the Eucharist, now seems to hold pride of place in Catholic theology and much contemporary high-church theology. Since the last half of the twentieth century, because of the gradual acceptance in the sacramental churches of the main tenets of the 'mystery theology' of Odo Casel, this presence has come to be understood not merely as a psychological remembering of the sacrifice of Christ (against a spiritualizing reductionism), but also not as a repeating or re-enacting of the unique and unrepeatable historical sacrifice of Christ (against a naïve realism),

---

27   For example, Giraudo, followed by Kilmartin, points out that it is more reasonable to say that the Church is represented liturgically to the sacrifice of Christ through the medium of the Eucharistic Prayer – Cesare Giraudo, *Eucaristia per la chiesa. Prospettive teologiche sull'eucaristia a apartire dalla 'lex orandi'* (Rome: Gregorian University/Brescia: Morcelliana, 1989), pp. 563–64; Kilmartin, *The Eucharist in the West*, p. 176.

but rather as a making present, a 're-presentation' (from the German *Vergegen-wärtigung*) of the perfect, once-for-all (as the Epistle to the Hebrews emphasizes) sacrifice of Christ.

This theological theory constituted a major theological and ecumenical advance in the twentieth century. It has the merit not just of being amenable to many Protestant theologians, but also of strongly supporting the doctrine of real presence as understood in traditional Catholic teaching. But it also has some notable weaknesses that suggest to theologians that they must continue to search for a better theory. First, it is not particularly supported by nor required by biblical revelation. Second, although aspects of it may be found in this or that Father of the Church, it does not rest on any significant convergence of patristic teaching. Third, significant support for it cannot be found in Thomas Aquinas, or in scholastic teaching generally, right up to and including Pius XII's 1947 encyclical, *Mediator Dei*. And finally, it is an explanation that itself requires a further explanation that does not seem to be forthcoming. For theologians and philosophers are unable to come to agreement on just how a past historical act can become present in another age and time.[28] There is no denial that this is within the miraculous power of God. But there is a strong tradition, not just in Catholic theology but in mainline Christian theology generally, that avoids appealing to miracles for explanations when other possible theological explanations have not yet been fully explored.

The second approach, that sees the participating faithful as being made present to the sacrifice of Christ, has been proposed by several Catholic theologians in the final years of the twentieth century. It is much more reasonable, Kilmartin points out, in agreement with Giraudo and Meyer, to say that the Church is represented liturgically to the sacrifice of Christ through the medium of the Eucharistic Prayer.[29] Philosophically and theologically, this is a more satisfying approach. It does not postulate a philosophically questionable transporting of a past historical event to later times. It is also much more respectful of Thomistic metaphysics in locating the effect of the divine action – i.e., the most important transformation that now takes place in the Eucharist – precisely where it belongs: in the participating faithful. In other words, Christ is not changed, God is not changed, *we* are changed. In addition, but without going into detail, this way of thinking is much more consistent with basic Catholic doctrine and theology in the other major areas of theology: prayer, spirituality and grace, Christology, soteriology, pneumatology and Trinitarian theology. In other words, consonant with our Trinitarian understanding of Christian sacrifice, this way of thinking *totally excludes that sacrifice can mean that something is done to something or, even worse, that something is done to someone. It sees sacrifice as a totally personal – indeed the person-constituting event par excellence – interpersonal event.* The claim can be made that, theologically, this is the most satisfying approach to an adequate and faithful Catholic understanding of the Eucharist. But the matter is far from settled for, in comparison with the first

---

28 See Kilmartin, *The Eucharist in the West*, pp. 268–76.
29 Ibid., p. 176. Kilmartin is here following the lead of Giraudo, *Eucaristia per la chiesa*, pp. 563–64. Hans Bernhard Meyer also agrees and acknowledges his debt to Giraudo in *Eucharistie: Geschichte, Theologie, Pastoral – Gottesdienst der Kirche. Handbuch der Liturgiewissenschaft*, Teil 4 (Regensburg: Pustet, 1989), pp. 448–49.

approach, it is not as supportive of traditional Catholic teaching regarding the real transformation (transubstantiation) of the Eucharistic gifts, regarding the real presence of Christ in the Eucharist, and regarding traditional devotional Eucharistic practices.

(3) Attending to *the eschatological level of this Christ-event* can help reveal more clearly the different interrelationships of the divine and the human, the eternal and the temporal in this event that we call the 'Sacrifice of the Mass'. As already noted, two transformations take place in the Sacrifice of the Mass, the transformation of the gifts and the transformation of the participating faithful, the former subordinated to the latter. This subordination, however, does not imply unimportance of the one in relation to the other; for the transformation of the gifts is the real foundation and condition of the transformation of the participants. Nevertheless, the relationship between the two transformations is not, in every respect, necessary or absolute. For most human beings, their transformation (i.e., ultimately, saying yes to the self-giving love of God in their lives) has obviously neither been preceded by nor accompanied by participation in the Eucharist. But does, on the other hand, the transformation of the Eucharistic gifts always result in the transformation of the participants? The transformation of those who actually participate in real faith is not in question. But in the hypothetical case of a Eucharist celebrated without at least an initial transformation of at least some participants, can one claim that the transformation of the gifts has taken place? This question has to be raised in both postmodern and premodern traditional terms. A Eucharist without transformation of participants is a Eucharist without meaning; and in postmodernity, where there is no meaning there is no reality. But this way of understanding the Eucharistic transformations can also be seen as quite consistent with the premodern, traditional Christian Trinitarian perspective outlined near the beginning of this article. If Christian sacrifice means the conjoined self-offerings of the Father, the Son and human beings, can the sacrifice of Christ be present if there is not at least an inchoative self-offering 'response' from the human side?

This is precisely where an *eschatological* understanding of the Eucharistic event, the Sacrifice of the Mass, is of critical importance. The transformation of a human being, and therefore of participants in the Eucharist, can only begin and never be complete in this life. Of the three interrelated self-offerings (Father, Son and human beings), the first two, as divine actions, are essentially perfect and complete; but the third, clearly, is not. The liturgical assembly is praying for and beginning to appropriate in itself the self-offering virtuous dispositions of Christ. This is a process that can begin now but can be completed only on the Last Day. The beginning of this appropriation is something that has a unique symbolic intensity as well as actual reality in the worthy celebration of the Eucharist. And unless one chooses to follow the theologically dubious path of postulating radically different ontological paths to salvation for those outside the Christian communion, this inchoative transformation of participants is found analogously, but also really, in all situations where human beings respond positively to self-giving love. All this is sacrifice in the authentic sense of the word.

Chapter IV

Conclusion

At the end of this Part I, so that it might to some extent stand by itself as an initial presentation of the whole, we will begin to do what we will do in greater detail at the end of this book: i.e., spell out the implications of this Trinitarian understanding of Christian sacrifice. In contrast to what might constitute an effective *pastoral* response to inadequate or false understandings of Christian sacrifice, something that we will struggle with more extensively at the end of this book, a proper *theological* response, however challenging, has now become relatively easy. For the basic approach to a Trinitarian understanding of Christian sacrifice that is at the heart of this book has now become relatively accessible, at least to theologians. So too, our explanation of the real but still inchoative actualization of this understanding in the Eucharistic celebration of the Christian assembly is similarly accessible. Thus, whether or not all the nuances of our presentation, or all the theological implications and consequences that we have begun to suggest turn out to be valid, the basic theological trajectory we are pursuing seems to be sound and also to have been recognized as sound by other theologians.

But that is still just the relatively easy part of the task. For it is in the area of the pastoral that the challenges are the most formidable. There is so much negativity connected with 'sacrifice' that some suggest that the best pastoral strategy is to avoid using the word altogether. For even when it refers to the most gloriously admirable acts of generous of self-giving, we are still talking about something that everyone would have preferred to avoid. Even Jesus' crucifixion can veil, as much as it in faith unveils, his divinity. But the pastoral challenge has to be faced. Let me suggest the following as a possible way to begin.

As we will spell out in more detail in the concluding Part III of this book, every human being who has had some, however fleeting, experience of genuine human happiness, has already experienced Christian sacrifice or, more precisely perhaps, the essential reality of what we have been referring to as Christian sacrifice. From parents and spouses, from caregivers, co-workers, friends and teachers, in other words from other human beings who have played a constructive role in their lives, most people have at least occasionally experienced totally free, totally loving, totally self-giving love. They could not have otherwise even begun to become half-decent human beings. However transitory these experiences might have been, they are real enough that they can be evoked in people's memory, imagination and longing. (Witness the almost universal appeal of a really good love story! And, of course, this is what Augustine was referring to with the unforgettable 'Our hearts are made for thee . . .' with which he opens his *Confessions*). When these experiences are evoked in people, they have begun, totally independent of technical theology, to understand and to know Christian sacrifice.

Pastorally, this would seem to be an obvious starting point from which preaching and teaching about sacrifice could take off. Such an approach also enables us to put the suffering and negativity that characteristically accompanies sacrifice in a more positive perspective. Growing up as a human being means coming to know what mature people already know from experience, namely that genuine self-giving love is not without its costs, costs that are sometimes terribly dear. Mature human beings already know, without having to hear St. Paul tell them again in 1 Cor. 13, that it is love and not suffering that is the defining, eternal reality that will save them and that will never pass away. And in that knowledge, they also know that suffering, however subordinate to the defining reality of love, is still somehow 'necessary', as Jesus proclaimed on the road to Emmaus (Luke 24.26).

We are attempting to 'unveil' Christian sacrifice. To the extent that we may be succeeding, we will also have been describing the universally human path of salvation. It is a path that transcends the lines separating nations, cultures and religions from each other. For it is the path of personal self-giving response to one's personal experiences of receiving self-giving love from others. As is obvious, and as recent discussions and controversies have painfully shown, Christian theology in general and Catholic magisterial teaching in particular has only just begun to try to make sense of this in terms both of its own traditions and the traditions of the other religions of the world.

THE ORIGINS AND EARLY DEVELOPMENT OF THE IDEA OF CHRISTIAN SACRIFICE

In Part One, we laid out the central thesis of this book, namely that Christian sacrifice is primarily a Trinitarian reality and event. We then went on to point out how that Trinitarian understanding of sacrifice is fundamental to the basic theological content and dynamic of the Eucharistic Prayers of the Church, past and present, East and West. Finally, we briefly indicated what we will develop in greater detail in Part Three at the end of the book: the practical-pastoral implications of this theology. We turn now in this three-part bridge section to the historical details that form the early background for this view of Christian sacrifice. First, in Bridge 1 A, we look briefly at the practice of sacrifice in the ancient world, and to what scholars call the general theory of sacrifice. We then attend in somewhat greater detail to the practice and the implicit understanding of sacrifice that can be found, first in the Hebrew Scriptures, and then in the period of transition from the Hebrew Scriptures to the Christian Scriptures. Next, in Bridge 1 B, we attend carefully to the pluriform witness to sacrificial themes in the Christian Scriptures of the New Testament. Finally, in Bridge 1 C, we examine how these sacrificial themes are taken up and developed in the early Christian writers, the Fathers of the Church.

Bridge 1 A

Sacrifice in the Ancient World and in the Hebrew Scriptures

Chapter I

Sacrifice in the Ancient World[1]

In contrast to the predominantly negative associations connected with sacrifice in the modern world, much more positive features usually characterize it in the ancient world. In the ancient Greco-Roman and Semitic-Hebrew civilizations the following characteristics are generally present. (1) The words describing sacrifice generally have no secular significance; they are used to describe strictly religious rites and objects. (2) These words generally do not connote reluctance, sadness, or deprivation, but rather, joy, festivity or thanksgiving. Sacrifices are usually performed gladly as expressions of the attitudes of human beings towards their God or gods. (3) Proper sacrifices are always as large as possible. Quite in contrast to common modern attitudes, the larger the sacrifice the greater the accompanying joy or festivity. (4) Sacrifices are offered *by* human beings *to* their god or gods. The emphasis is on the *giving*, not on the giving up. (5) Sacrifices are offered both to secure boons and to express thanksgiving for boons received. (6) In Old Testament animal sacrifice, the death of the animal is only a necessary prerequisite or condition for the sacrificial action. *No significance is attached to the death of the animal. Its death, in itself, effects nothing.* Ignorance of this has been the point of departure for some common but erroneous theories of sacrificial atonement that emphasize the suffering and death of the victim or the destruction of the material being offered. Such theories, that are the source of some serious theological and pastoral problems are, in this respect, totally without scriptural foundation.

The differences between the ancient (mostly biblical) and the modern (mostly secular) concepts of sacrifice, and the specifically Christian (Trinitarian) idea of sacrifice can be compared and contrasted in Table 1. Notice how different, and by contrast with the others how seemingly irrelevant, are the Christian entries. Despite the unavoidable oversimplifications, such a chart graphically supports our assertion that Christian sacrifice is radically different, and that the Christ-event did away with sacrifice in the history-of-religions sense of the word.

---

1   The material in this section is taken, with some modifications, from Robert J. Daly, S.J., *The Origins of the Christian Doctrine of Sacrifice* (Philadelphia: Fortress Press, 1978), pp. 2–3. This reproduces to a large extent what is found in Royden Keith Yerkes, *Sacrifice in Greek and Roman Religions and Early Judaism* (New York: Scribner's, 1952/London: A&C Black, 1953), pp. 1–7.

Table 1 Sacrifice: ancient, modern, Christian

	ANCIENT	MODERN SECULAR	CHRISTIAN/ TRINITARIAN
Field of use	Wholly religious, never secular	Almost wholly secular; used religiously by transference	All of genuinely human reality and activity
Purpose	Solely a cultic act	Never a cultic act	Self-communication/ fulfillment
Size of the sacrifice	As large as possible	As small as possible	Irrelevant, since it is the actualization of an interpersonal relationship
Recipient	Always offered to a god, thus indicating a recognition of superiority	Never offered to anyone	Not applicable, since sacrifice is, ultimately, self-communicating fulfillment
Performance and accompanying emotions	Generally performed with joy; came to be identified with thanksgiving	Generally performed with regret accompanied with sadness	Associated/identified with a free, loving, joyous, self-giving act
Significant emphasis	Emphasis on giving and action. Deprivation, while a necessary fact, as with all giving, is never a constituent factor in the sacrifice	Emphasis always on giving up, and on deprivation	Self-communicating participation in Trinitarian life
Death or destruction of the thing sacrificed	Wholly incidental and never with any inherent or significant meaning; a fact, but never a factor in the sacrifice	Signifies the 'supreme sacrifice'; a regretted but necessary factor in all sacrifice	Irrelevant or contradictory; for sacrifice is the ultimate fulfillment of personal life

Chapter II

General Theory of Sacrifice[2]

Since the late nineteenth-century, flowering of the disciplines of the history of religions or comparative religion, there have been numerous attempts to isolate or abstract the *essential idea* common to all sacrifice.[3] Such attempts generally focused

---

2   The material in this section reproduces, with some modifications, Daly, *The Origins*, pp. 4–6.
3   Of the many things written on this subject, one of the most perceptive and readily intelligible is George Buchanan Gray, *Sacrifice in the Old Testament: Its Theory and Practice* (Oxford: Clarendon

on the question: What element in the idea of sacrifice is the primary element (it was usually presumed that there was a primary element) from which the numerous forms, concepts, and practices derive? The most common suggestions for this primary element have been: (1) the gift of the human being to the deity, or (2) the homage of the subject to the lord, or (3) the expiation of offenses, or (4) *communion* with the deity, especially in the sacrificial banquet, or (5) *life* released from the victim, transmitted to the deity, and conferred upon the worshippers. However, even for a relatively well-defined group like the ancient Hebrews of biblical times, the practice of sacrifice was too complicated for it to be reduced to a single radical element.[4]

For example, one major aspect of Israel's religious and cultural background is its nomadic experience. The sacrificial offering of a nomad is naturally something from his flocks, usually a lamb or a goat. A nomad feels close to the animals in his flocks; they share his existence and his struggle for life in the inhospitable desert. The nomad is also aware that his animals share with him the same life-principle bestowed on them by the deity. Thus it is only natural that the communion and life concepts of sacrifice seem to dominate in Israel's nomadic background. This seems to be confirmed by the findings of history and archaeology that indicate that the holocaust form of sacrifice (the burning up of the whole sacrificial animal) was not practiced among the early Semitic nomads. An animal was too sacred and too valuable to be disposed of in this way. In early communion and life sacrifices, the animal (except for the blood, and perhaps also the liver, kidneys and intestinal fat) was totally eaten, probably in the manner still practiced into modern times in the celebrations of the desert bedouins.[5]

However, another major aspect of Israel's cultural background is agricultural. For the Israelites were descendants not merely of the desert wanderers but also of the sedentary Canaanite tillers of the soil who were gradually assimilated into Jewish life and religion after the settlement of the Exodus remnants in the Promised Land. The offering of a sedentary farmer is, naturally, not taken from a flock but from the fruits of the earth. In this context, the *gift* and *homage* ideas of sacrifice tend to dominate. The sacrifices of Cain ('fruit of the ground') and Abel ('firstlings of his flock') in Genesis 4.3–7 illustrate the difference between the sacrifice of the farmer and the nomad, while also suggesting the tension that often existed between them.

These examples by no means exhaust the considerable variety in Israel's cultural and religious background. Only at the price of oversimplification might one claim to find a clearly dominant central idea in ancient Israelite sacrifice. Never-

Press, 1925). Recent scholarship, however, more aware of the great variety of sacrificial practices and attitudes throughout the world, and also influenced by post-modernity's suspicion of master narratives, is far less optimistic that any overarching theory of sacrifice is possible. See, for example, the recent collection of essays assembled and edited by Jeffrey Carter, *Understanding Religious Sacrifice: A Reader* (London/New York: Continuum, 2003).

4   Almost any general treatment of sacrifice in the Hebrew Scriptures will now point this out; it has been common, consensual knowledge for some time. See, for example, John McKenzie, 'Sacrifice', in *Dictionary of the Bible* (Milwaukee: Bruce, 1965), p. 754.

5   See especially William Robertson Smith, *Lectures on the Religion of the Semites: The Fundamental Institutions* (3rd ed., with an Introduction and Additional Notes by S.A. Cook; London: A&C Black, 1927 [1st ed., 1889; repr. New York: Schocken, 1973]).

theless, if any idea can approach to being basic or central in ancient Israel's practice of sacrifice as presented in the Hebrew Scriptures, it is the *gift* idea. What was given or offered in sacrifice, whether from the field or the flock, was some form of food or drink.

In some of the more primitive stages, traces of which can be found in the account of Noah's sacrifice in Genesis 8.20–21, food was given to the gods for them to eat. (See the second-century BCE Jewish polemic against this belief in the story of Bel and the Dragon related in chapter 14 of the Book of Daniel.) Traces of this crassly anthropomorphic and materialistic view of sacrifice can be found in some older layers of the Bible. But overall, the Hebrew Scriptures, if we are interpreting them correctly, actually portray the gradual purification or elevation or 'spiritualization' (see the Excursus below, pp. 69–74) of the idea of sacrifice. An example of this is the development of the phrase 'pleasing odor/appeasing fragrance/sweet odor' (see Genesis 8.21). Originally signifying the pleasure that the gods take in smelling the sweet odor of sacrifice offered to them, it developed into a technical term signifying the acceptability of sacrifice in God's eyes, an acceptability that is due not to the material richness of the sacrifice but to the proper internal or spiritual dispositions of those offering the sacrifice.

The highest or most purely 'spiritualized' expression of this gift-theory of sacrifice from the pre-Christian Jewish tradition is found in the works of Philo of Alexandria (ca. 13 BCE to AD 45/50). There we find a mature expression of the idea that sacrifice is only a returning to God of what God has first given us; that it is not *what* we give that is of primary importance, but rather the *dispositions* with which we give; and that ultimately the only gift or sacrifice worthy of God is that of a pure mind and soul offering itself to God. Thus, much of what Philo had to say about sacrifice gives witness to the spiritual and spiritualizing developments in late biblical and early rabbinic Judaism that formed the foundation of the primitive Christian theology of sacrifice.[6]

Chapter III

Sacrifice in the Hebrew Scriptures[7]

Sacrifice can be described as the central religious institution of ancient Israelite religion or, as Christians call it, the Old Testament. Orthodox or main-stream Christianity, especially after surviving the early Christian gnostic movements that wanted to have it otherwise, saw itself as the 'New Temple', or the 'New Covenant'.

---

6   For more attention to Philo, see hereafter in Bridge 1 C, pp. 85–87.
7   See the opening chapters of Robert J. Daly, S.J., *Christian Sacrifice: The Judaeo-Christian Background before Origen* (Studies in Christian Antiquity, 18; Washington: Catholic University of America, 1978). Here we follow closely the more brief presentation of this material in Chapter Two of Daly, *The Origins of the Christian Doctrine of Sacrifice*.

Christians gradually came not only to call their Scriptures the 'New Testament', they also began to speak of their own particular founding event, the Christ-event, in sacrificial terms. Thus, no treatment of Christian sacrifice can ignore its background in the biblical religion of the Hebrews.

A. THE PROBLEM AND THE METHOD

Since the Hebrew Scriptures took the shape in which we now know them in a process that extended over a span of some 900 years up to about 100 BCE, and since they at times concern 'events' that took place long before they were written down in a biblical book, in some cases long before any recorded human history, one cannot avoid asking how reliable they are as historical sources.

The whole question becomes vastly more complex when we note that the biblical text, especially the first five books, the Pentateuch (Genesis, Exodus, Leviticus, Deuteronomy, Numbers) underwent repeated revisions in which the thinking and attitudes of later periods were projected back into earlier periods. For example, the first seven chapters of Leviticus are called 'The Law(s) of Sacrifice' and are presented as coming from the mouth of Moses who lived about 1500 BCE., give or take a few centuries. But most scholars agree that these chapters were written down in the form in which we now have them some thousand years after the time of Moses by the so-called 'Priestly Writers' who projected their own concerns and issues back into the time and mouth of Moses.

A further complicating factor is that we – those writing and reading this book – are theoretical and theological in a way that the ancient Israelites were not. Quite in contrast to the way that we are constantly, even 'instinctively' forming ideas about the nature and the meaning – i.e., the 'philosophy' and 'theology' of sacrifice, that was not much of a concern for the original authors and hearers/readers of the Hebrew Scriptures. The meaning, the implicit theology that we will be making explicit in the next few pages is not something that the ancient biblical writers paid much attention to; it is much more something that we conclude or educe from what they wrote.

Excursus 1

The Sources of the Pentateuch[8] and Source Criticism of the Hebrew Bible

There are four distinct major literary sources for the Pentateuch, the first five books of the Bible. (1) The **J** source or Yahwist, from about the time of King Solomon, or a bit later, in the late tenth century, called 'J' because writings

---

8   Libraries of books have been written about this since it was first presented by Julius Wellhausen in the nineteenth century. Most critical scholarship of the Hebrew Scriptures go along, more or less, with the basic sketch that we outline here.

from this source generally call God *Jahwe* – German for Yahweh. From this source come the vivid stories of the creation, temptation, and sin of Adam and Eve in Genesis 2–3, and the Noah saga in Genesis 8–9. One of its main concerns seems to be to lead up to the founding of the royal house of David in the Southern Kingdom of Benjamin and Juda. (2) Then there is the **E** source, so called because it uses the name *Elohim* for God. This comes from a bit later, probably from the ninth century. The covenant between God and Abram/ Abraham (Genesis 15) and the sacrifice of Isaac (Genesis 22) come from this source. This source seems to have come from the Northern Kingdom, the ten northern tribes that broke off from the Southern Kingdom of Benjamin and Juda after the reign of Solomon. Its underlying historical and theological concerns are, thus, quite different from those of **J**, the Yahwist. (3) The third source, **D** (*Deuteronomist*) comes from the period just before the Babylonian Exile in the seventh century. Most of the 'historical' material found in the books of Judges, Samuel and Kings comes from this source. These writings update the Law and illustrate Israel's rocky covenant history. (4) However, all that we have from these sources has passed through the censoring and editing hands of **P**, the *Priestly Writers* who, with an eye for enhancing the institutional, legal, and ritual significance of the material, not only compiled, but also significantly edited and shaped the various traditions into the basic form in which we now know the Hebrew Scriptures.

END OF EXCURSUS 1

Fundamentalists and biblical literalists generally reject source theory and attempt the hopeless task of reading these writings as literal history. But that is only the beginning of the complexity. For no one in antiquity, including all the human authors of the Christian Scriptures and the early Christian writers who commented on them, had any real understanding of this variety of literary sources. Their only refuge from the sometimes bizarre absurdities that came from a literal reading of Scriptures was to escape into typology or allegory, or to seek for a deeper, spiritual meaning hidden beneath a problematical historical meaning.

Modern scientific historical criticism however, allows us, if we use it judiciously, to unravel, to unveil to a significant extent, the complex processes through which the biblical texts as we now have them actually came about. It also allows us to recover some knowledge, sometimes extensive knowledge, of the historical situations in which the biblical texts took shape, and sometimes even some knowledge of the historical events behind the texts. All this, but without getting lost in the details, we will be bringing to bear as we attempt to unveil the Israelite and Jewish background of the idea of Christian sacrifice. At the risk of oversimplification, most of our exposition will revolve around two main types of sacrifice: first the burnt offering or holocaust, and second, the sin offering.

B. THE BURNT OFFERING AND THE DIVINE ACCEPTANCE OF SACRIFICE

The burnt offering or 'holocaust' (= 'whole burnt offering')[9] is the most frequently mentioned type of sacrifice in the Hebrew Scriptures. More than any other kind of sacrifice, it fulfilled a broad variety of functions and it contained or suggested a richness of meaning – adoration, praise, thanksgiving, atonement, petition, etc. – that later exercised great influence on the Christian idea of sacrifice. Characteristically, the whole offering, usually an animal, sometimes grain, was *wholly* burned on the altar (see Leviticus 1–2) as distinguished from offerings in which only *part* was burned on the altar, with the rest being consumed by the people (Leviticus 3) or by the priests. This was the kind of sacrifice that was in play in the story of Cain and Abel, that Noah offered after the flood, that Abraham was about to use in sacrificing Isaac, and that had pride of place in all the great festive occasions in which sacrifices were offered.

1. The divine acceptance of sacrifice

Very closely associated with the burnt offering was the 'theology – i.e., as we reconstruct it – of the divine acceptance of sacrifice. Especially in the middle and later periods of Israelite history, and as religious understanding become more refined, the value or effectiveness of any sacrifice was understood as being wholly dependent on its being accepted by Yahweh. Also connected with this was the general idea behind sacrifice (i.e., the idea of sacrifice that saw it primarily as gift) namely that whoever accepts a gift is bound by particular ties of favour to the giver of the gift (see, e.g., the reconciliation scene between Jacob and Esau in Genesis 33.9–11). The most important technical term used to express this divine acceptance is that of '*rêach nichoach* – pleasing odor/pleasing fragrance/odor of sweetness', phrases that also later became popular in Christian devotion.[10]

This 'odor of sweetness' idea is obviously metaphoric. Its original sense was that the deity was literally placated or pleased by smelling the sweet fragrance of the burning sacrifice. Concrete traces of this primitive meaning remain in Noah's sacrifice where we read that 'Noah . . . offered burnt offerings on the altar. And when the Lord smelled the pleasing odor, the Lord said in his heart, . . .' (Genesis 8.20–21). Another clear example is found in David's perplexed question or complaint to King Saul who had been trying to kill him: 'If it is the Lord who has stirred you up against me, may he accept an offering' (literally: 'smell a sacrifice' –

---

9   This is the primary meaning of 'holocaust'. Since the 1950s it has come to be applied absolutely ('The Holocaust') to the Nazi persecution of and eventual attempt at the total extermination of European Jews from 1933 to 1945.

10   For example, a common phrase found in the traditional vow formulas of religious profession read: 'May the Lord accept this holocaust [of the vows and religious life] in an odor of sweetness'. This outmoded and – to modern ears – bizarre way of speaking has been removed from many modern versions of religious vow formulas, sometimes thereby eliminating the notion of sacrificial self-giving. This is quite understandable if one thinks of sacrifice in the negative terms outlined earlier; but it is unfortunate if all reference to or allusion to the Trinitarian idea of sacrifice is also being eliminated.

1 Sam. 26.19).'[11] However, in the later texts of the Hebrew Scriptures, especially those from **P** (the Priestly Writers), the meaning of the phrase *rêach nichoach*, which occurs some 40 times, is wholly metaphorical. Quite possibly, the later writers were not even aware of its original, physical meaning.

The third-century BCE translation of the Hebrew Bible into Greek, the 'Septuagint' (abbreviated as LXX) suggests a further development of the theology of sacrifice that is connected with this phrase. First, it emphasizes that God's acceptance of the sacrifice is a totally free act. God, in other words, is 'bound' to accept something from human beings only to the extent that God freely chooses to do so. But second, the sacrifice is really expected, somehow, to reach God; it is expected to 'make an impression' on or 'arouse an effect' in God. This apparent contradiction is the same paradox that is implicit in the traditional theology of prayer. Prayer 'works'; prayer is effective; but God, nevertheless, remains totally free, transcendent, immutable.

This theology of acceptance, even if with different levels of sophistication, is found, beginning with Cain and Abel in Genesis 4,[12] at all levels of the Bible. Except perhaps for the abuse of sacrifice against which the prophets vehemently railed (see Excursus 2), divine acceptance was never seen as automatic. God is free to accept or reject: and rejection is a disaster. Generally, acceptance of the offering is implicitly identified with acceptance of the one offering or with at least a favourable divine attitude towards that person. But it is not an arbitrary God that is being revealed. Implicit in the acceptance/non-acceptance of the sacrifices of Cain and Abel is the idea that was later powerfully preached by the whole prophetic tradition that the good conduct and good intentions of the offerer are of paramount importance.

Excursus 2

The Prophetic Critique of Sacrifice

It has often been assumed or claimed that the prophets rejected sacrifice. However, upon close examination, we find that their sometimes fierce denunciations make use of the traditional cultic technical terms that signify God's acceptance or rejection of sacrifice. Phrases like 'Your burnt offerings are not acceptable' (Jer. 6.20), or 'Their sacrifices shall not please him' (Hos. 9.4), or 'I will not accept them' (Amos. 5.22) are actually negative

---

11   This phrase 'accept an offering' (NRSV translation) is a good example of how modern translations frequently mask or betray the full meaning of the original text. The **D** (Deuteronomist) writer of this passage remembers/records David as saying, literally, 'smell a sacrifice'. David lived at a time when the primitive, physical, anthropomorphic idea that God/the gods were pleased/placated by smelling the fragrance of burnt offerings was still very much alive.

12   This is from the earliest literary level, the **J**/Yahwist: 'And the Lord had regard for Abel and his offering, but for Cain and his offering he had no regard. So Cain was angry and his countenance fell. The Lord said to Cain, "Why are you angry, and why has your countenance fallen? If you do well, will you not be accepted?" ' (Genesis 4.4–7).

formulations of precisely the same technical ritual formulas used by the sacrificing priest in the temple to declare that this or that sacrifice was being offered in the right way and, therefore, was accepted by God. Thus, the very criticism of the prophets assumes the existence of and the 'effectiveness' of the sacrificial system.

END OF EXCURSUS 2

What is being taught, therefore, and more and more forcefully as Israel grows into deeper understandings of its relationship with God, is that what really counts is not the material size of the offering but the dispositions of the offerer. That this was not just an ideal teaching but something that was, at least at times, actually carried out is indicated by the following Jewish narrative that dates from the beginning of the Christian era:

> Simeon the Just stated that he had never eaten of the guilt-offering of the defiled Nazirite, and only once he had no hesitation to do so [the priests eating part of a sacrifice was a sign that it was 'accepted']. It was when a Nazirite from the Darom came to the Temple to have his hair shaved; he had beautiful eyes, was of good looks and had magnificent curls. I asked him, 'My son, what made thee undertake to destroy thy beautiful hair?' He replied, 'I was in my town my father's shepherd, and when I one day went to draw water from a well and saw mine image in the water, my impulse seized me and strove to drive me out from the world; but I said, Thou, wicked, why boastest thou of what is not thine and will once turn into maggots and worms? I swear that I shall cut thee of in honor of God!' I kissed him on his head, and said to him, 'My son, may many like thee be Nazirites in Israel.'[13]

Towards the chronological end of the Hebrew biblical tradition, but well before the beginning of the Christian era, in a development that became very important for a religiously mature idea of sacrifice, sacrifice came to be looked upon less and less as the precise performance of a ritual act, and more and more as an act of obedience to the will of God. This was the maturation of a spiritualizing process that was of critical importance, though in different ways, for Jews as well as for Christians. For Jews, it allowed escape from a terrible dilemma. For them, atonement had come to be identified with the process of offering sacrifice.[14] But, towards the end of the pre-exilic period, as Israelite religion became increasingly centralized, sacrifice could be offered only in the Jerusalem Temple. Thus, for Jews in the Diaspora, and for Jews generally after the destruction of the Temple in 70 CE, ritual sacrifice had become impossible. For Christians, this development allowed them to flow into and continue the processes of 'spiritualization' they inherited from their Jewish origins, and to transform that spiritualization into a

---

13   Quoted from Adolf Büchler, *Studies in Sin and Atonement in the Rabbinic Literature of the First Century* (Library of Biblical Studies; New York: KTAV, 1967 [original edition 1927]), p. 419.
14   This 'identification' was also found in the thinking of at least some of the earliest Christians, as is attested by the following statement from the New Testament Epistle to the Hebrews: 'Without the shedding of blood [i.e., in animal sacrifice] there is no forgiveness of sins' (Hebrews 9.22).

'Christologization' – a theological development by which Christians could look upon the various activities of Christian living, and the Christian life itself, as sacrificial.[15]

C. Sin Offering and Atonement

The history, the experience and the concepts of sin and atonement are central to the religious history and religious identity of both Jews and Christians. However their various understandings of this have been at times very different and often quite confusing. Mistaken understandings of atonement have been part of mistaken understandings of sacrifice. Our first and the most basic task here is to sketch out, as clearly as possible, the central Hebrew-scriptural understanding of sin and atonement. The concept of atonement that we have found to be central to the Hebrew Scriptures is as follows: Atonement is *the process whereby the positive creature-Creator relationship, after having been weakened, disturbed, or violated (by the creature) is restored by the Creator to its proper harmony.*

After the Babylonian Exile in the sixth century, this atoning process, previously associated with sacrifice in general, came to be primarily associated with one type of sacrifice, the sin offering, and especially with a particular part of that sacrificial ceremony, the blood rite, the ritual manipulation of blood by the priests.

Interestingly, but also typically as I have mentioned, the Hebrew Scriptures do not explain the meaning of *kipper*, the common word for atonement that occurs 91 times in the Hebrew Scriptures. Literally (or etymologically) *kipper* means 'to cover'. Its basic functional meaning is *to carry out an atoning action*. What then, was ancient Israel's idea of sin. What was Israel's idea of the condition needing to be remedied by *kipper*? Sin seems to have been any kind of an act or offence against a sacred ordinance, and hence against God and the majesty of God, *whether or not the sinning subject was aware of its sinfulness*. It is something that could happen in all phases of life, and it was, by nature, a social reality, never something strictly private. The idea was that, by sin, an evil had been set loose that, unless atoned for, would return to plague the individual and/or the individual's community or children. Ancient Israel conceived of itself as a holy camp surrounded by a massive, threatening evil force. What sin did was to set loose some of this force that, unless neutralized by atonement, would eventually wreak its havoc on the land and its people.

Behind this was an intensely synthetic view of life in which there is an intense correspondence between a deed and its consequences, between the temple, and the land, and the people. Coupled with this is a pervasive materiality in ancient Israel's idea of the holy. Evil/sin, was perceived to be intensely contagious, intensely contaminating. Contact with sin and evil inevitably contaminated what was clean and pure, making necessary some atoning (or purifying) ceremony to restore a contaminated person's (or object's) proper relationship to God.

Looking ahead, it is precisely here we find what seems to be one of the more significant differences between biblical Judaism and Christianity. Jesus seemed to

---

15   See our extended treatment of 'spiritualization' hereafter in Excursus 3 at the end of BRIDGE 1 B, pp. 69–74.

go out of his way to touch sinners, or to let sinners touch him, confident of his power, that he also handed on to his disciples, to reverse the contamination process into one of cleansing, healing and forgiving.[16]

1. The process of atonement

There was a twofold function, positive and negative, in the process of atonement. There was the *positive* function of making persons or objects 'acceptable' to Yahweh, of preserving them in this condition, of making them eligible to participate in Israel's religious life and sacrificial cult. There was the *negative* (apotropaic) function of interrupting or averting the course of evil set in motion by sin or transgression, whether knowing or unknowing.[17] The words *propitiation, expiation* and *forgiveness*, often used as general words for the process of atonement, can also refer to specific aspects of this process.[18]

Actions of propitiation soothe the anger or ill will of the deity and/or secure the deity's favour. (I use 'deity' instead of 'God' or 'Yahweh' to indicate that I am not, or not necessarily, talking about only the God of Israel.) This idea, still alive in the minds of many people, originates in a primitive notion of an arbitrary deity who had to be 'bought off' or somehow kept happy, or at least favourable. The fundamental dynamic of propitiation, understood in this way, is that of a *God-directed action* of the creature.

Actions of expiation restore the order between creature and Creator that had been disturbed by sin or transgression. In contrast to propitiation, the basic dynamic here is that of a creature-directed action in which God is the ultimate subject or agent. Things as well as persons can be the objects of expiation, as we see in the original liturgy of Yom Kippur in Leviticus 16.

Forgiveness was God's ultimate gift of personal favour. It follows (at least conceptually) upon and is thus distinguished from the atoning actions of expiation. See, for example, the forgiveness granted to David after he repents of Uriah's murder (2 Sam. 12.13).

But since the Hebrew Scriptures themselves were not wholly consistent in its understanding and terminology, some confusion is inevitable. What we are doing here is attempting to provide some guidelines for an orderly understanding by trying to focus on the reality or the dynamic to which the words refer. For the Hebrew Scriptures were not wholly consistent in viewing atonement as, ultimately, a creature-directed dynamic originating in God; and we modern people inherit a long tradition which has often (and often disastrously) viewed atonement as a penitential action by which we 'earn' or make ourselves worthy of God's forgiveness.

---

16 St Paul clearly grasped this in his teaching that the non-Christian spouse does not contaminate but rather is sanctified by marital union with his/her Christian spouse (see 1 Cor. 7.12–16).
17 See Levitcus 10.6; Num. 1.53; 17.11; 18.5.
18 There is, unfortunately little consistency in the use and meaning of the rich and varied terminology of atonement. I have assigned meanings that seem to be most consistent with the trajectory of research and understanding that grounds this study. But one cannot assume that our meanings and definitions are followed by all other scholars.

2. The sin offering

After the exile, the sin offering was developed by the Jerusalem priesthood into the dominant ritual means of atonement. The ceremony had the following parts:

1. *Bringing the sacrificial material to the altar.* This was, if the offerers could afford it, an animal previously examined to make sure that it was without blemish.
2. The *laying on of hands.* This may have come into the ritual from what happened in the original Yom Kippur liturgy in Leviticus 16.21–22. The meaning of this ritual gesture remains uncertain, but there is general agreement that it signifies a certain connection or identification between the offerer and the animal victim. To see this rite as signifying the penal substitution of the animal victim in place of the human offerer is an over-interpretation, though an understandable one, that comes from contexts and situations that are strong in substitutionary ideas.
3. *Confession.* See Leviticus 16.21 for the background. By the time of Christ, good practice required the priest to inquire about the purpose of the sacrifice and the dispositions of the one offering it. See the story of Simeon just quoted. See also the instruction of Jesus in Matthew 5.23 instructing us to make sure that we are reconciled with others before we attempt to offer sacrifice.
4. The *slaughtering* of the animal victim was originally carried out by the offerer, and in later times by Levites or other cultic officials. It is extremely important to note that the Hebrew Scriptures never attached much importance to the slaughtering of the victim; it was just the necessary means of obtaining sacrificial flesh and, above all, sacrificial blood.
5. The *blood rite* was the cultic manipulation of sacrificial blood (see hereafter). It was an action strictly reserved to the priests, in which action it was generally seen that atonement took place.
6. A *declaratory formula* was spoken by the priest (on behalf of God) to affirm that the sacrifice had been carried out according to the Law, and that God had accepted it and effected the atonement.
7. The *eating* by the priests or the *burning* of the flesh of the animal sacrificial victim was the final act of the ritual.

3. Sacrificial blood

In the early rabbinic Judaism out of which Christianity grew, some atoning function had become associated with almost every kind of sacrifice. But in particular, the blood rite of the sin offering had become practically identified with the process of atonement. This also had a strong influence on primitive Christianity as is witnessed by the recurring phrase and idea found in Paul and the Book of Revelation: 'redeemed by/in the blood of Christ'. See also Hebrews 9.22: 'Without the shedding of blood there is no forgiveness of sins'.

Comparative religion points out that in the Ancient Near East, sacrificial blood had four functions: (1) life-giving or fortifying, (2) cathartic or apotropaic, (3) 'sacramental', (4) nutritive. The first three of these figures are also in Israel's cultic history. But beyond this, comparative religion is of little help in understanding Israelite practice. Four instances or types of instances of the use of sacrificial blood stand out in the Hebrew Scriptures: (1) the Exodus 12 Passover blood rite, (2) the Exodus 24.3–8 covenant sacrifice, (3) the atonement rituals of Leviticus 4 and 16, and (4) the legislation regarding the use (actually prohibition against any non-cultic use of blood) of sacrificial blood in Leviticus 17.11 and 14 and in Genesis 9.4.

Blood could be ritually handled in different ways: (1) by throwing, (2) by pouring it out at the base of the altar, (3) by sprinkling and (4) by applying or smearing. The latter two rites, the ones used in sin offerings, seem originally to have had the function of dedicating, consecrating, purifying and atoning for sacred *things*, and then later to have taken on the function of making atonement for *people*.

We can sum this up in three points. First, although the primary purpose of these blood rites was apotropaic, the warding off of evil, the ultimate goal remained that of rendering both objects and persons eligible to take part in Israel's public life of worship. Second, the various words: 'atone', 'purify', 'consecrate', 'shall be forgiven', etc. and their counterparts: 'sin', 'transgression', 'uncleanness', etc. seem to be basically synonymous. Finally, the atoning effect (assuming, especially in later times, the appropriate dispositions of those offering) was attributed to the correct performance of the whole sacrificial ritual, but especially the blood rite.

4. Leviticus 17.11 and the significance of sacrificial blood

Only three texts, all of them prohibitions against consuming blood, suggest anything about the underlying meaning of the connection between blood and atonement: Genesis 9.4, Deuteronomy 12.23, and Leviticus 17.11 and 14. The most complete is Leviticus 17.11, quoted here in four modern English translations:

> For the *life* of the flesh is in the blood; and I have given it for you upon the altar to make atonement for your *souls*; for it is the blood that makes atonement, by reason of the *life*.
>
> RSV

> For the *life* of the flesh is in the blood; and I have given it to you for making atonement for your *lives* on the altar; for, as *life*, it is the blood that makes atonement.
>
> NRSV

> The *life* of the flesh is in the blood. This blood I myself have given you to perform the rite of atonement for your *lives* at the altar; for it is blood that atones for a *life*. [or: 'by reason of the *life* (which is in it)']
>
> Jerusalem Bible

> For the *life* of the flesh is in the blood, and I have assigned it to you for making expiation for your *lives* [or: 'to serve as ransom for your *lives*'] upon the altar; it is the blood, as *life*, that effects expiation.
>
> Jewish Study Bible

First note that behind the italicized (my italics) words is always the Hebrew word *nephesh* that means *soul, living being, life, self, person, desire, appetite, emotion, passion,* etc. The phrase 'for your souls/for your lives' basically means 'for you', or 'for your person'. The other two uses of this word in Leviticus 17.11 means, simply, 'life', or 'seat of life'. It definitely does not mean 'soul' (Greek *psychê*) as something distinct from the body.

The verse first explains why eating blood is prohibited: the life of the flesh is in the blood and *only* the Lord has dominion over life. By solemn divine decree, the one use to which blood may be put is to make atonement with it on the altar. Finally, the blood does this because of the *nephesh* contained in it. In other words, *The blood of the sacrificial animal atones by means of and by power of the (God-given) life (b'nephesh) contained in this sacrificial animal.*

Most important to note here is that the Hebrew of Leviticus 17.11 simply does not speak of substitution, despite the predilection of many translators, and many Christians, to see substitution in this text. There are, indeed, at least overtones of substitutional atonement in the New Testament. This idea became stronger in some of the early Fathers of the Church. It was assumed as doctrinal in the Anselmian idea of satisfaction. And, as we shall see hereafter in Part Two of this book, it has, especially since Anselm of Canterbury (1033–1109), and more for the worse than for the better, dominated the theology of Christian sacrificial atonement, eventually achieving creedal or quasi-creedal status in most mainline Christian theologies.

5. Passover[19]

The laws about consecrating or 'redeeming' the firstborn or the first fruits are usually found in a Passover context. The blood of the original Passover lambs in Exodus 12 was the sign that saved Israel's firstborn. This inevitably suggests ideas of substitution, but there is no evidence to suggest that the Hebrew Scriptures considered the sacrifice of the Passover lamb to be an atoning death in the sense of vicarious or substitutionary penal suffering. There was no attention paid to the death, as such, or to the suffering, if any (as, for example, there is in some Hindu sacrificial rituals) of the sacrificial animal.

6. Vicarious suffering and death

The idea of the vicarious intercession of a mediator, along with at least the suggestion of the idea of vicarious atonement, is present in a number of instances, for example, when the people intercede for Jonathan (1 Sam. 14.45), and when Abraham intercedes for Sodom (Genesis 18.22–33), and when Moses stands between the people and God's chastising wrath (Exodus 32.30–32). The account of this particular intervention of Moses may have been the model for a similar prayer of David for his plague-threatened people (2 Sam. 24.17).

By the time we come to early rabbinic Judaism, the idea of a/the just man

---

19   Here we consider Passover only from the point of view of 'substitution'. For the fuller treatment of Passover, see shortly hereafter in Chapter IV. From the Old Testament to the New, pp. 42–43.

atoning vicariously for Israel had become common, especially in relation to the figures of Moses and Isaac. Then, by the third century of the Christian era, whatever soteriological significance the Christians were claiming for Jesus, the Jews were, in turn, claiming for Moses or Isaac. Pre-Christian Judaism, however, had apparently been unfamiliar with the idea of a suffering, atoning Messiah. This helps explain the initial resistance of Jesus' disciples to this idea. But this, presumably in the aftermath of the resurrection, quickly changed. The Fourth Servant Song of Isaiah 52.13–53.12 was read quite early by Christians as pointing to Jesus, the suffering Messiah.

7. Martyrdom

Two Maccabees (first century BCE) and 4 Maccabees (first century CE) are clear pre-Christian sources for the idea of the vicarious and even atoning suffering and death of the martyrs. For example, Eleazar prays: 'Be merciful to your people, and let our punishment suffice for them. Make my blood their purification, and take my life in exchange for theirs' (4 Macc. 6.28–29). The idea of atoning substitution is increasingly strong near the end of biblical Judaism. However, there is no evidence to support the idea (or claim) that the whole sacrificial system is based on the idea of the death of an animal substituting for that of a person.

But the idea of penal substitution did not get invented out of whole cloth. It seems to have come, in large part, from the influence of the (obviously erroneous) third-century BCE. Greek (Septuagint – LXX) translation of *b'nephesh* in Leviticus 17.11 as 'in place of the soul' instead of 'by reason of the life' (as we explained a few pages ago). The Christian writers of the New Testament looked upon this Greek translation, which was the way they knew the Hebrew Scriptures, as authoritative, if not actually inspired. The mistranslation of this particular text seems to have been a contributing source for some serious theological problems such as the suggestion that God is wrathful, punishing, jealous and avenging. It became a primary source for those exaggerated theories of penal substitution that many Christians – in the past as well as in the present – have erroneously thought to be expressive of the central teaching of Christian sacrificial soteriology.

Chapter IV

From the Old Testament to the New

For the earliest Christians, the Bible was not the Gospels or the other New Testament writings – they did not yet exist – but the Hebrew Scriptures, what Christians have traditionally called the Old Testament. Furthermore, the writers of the Christian Scriptures did not know the Bible in the same way that we know it. On the one hand, they knew and understood it far better than we do because of their proximity to the times and cultures from which it came. But on the other hand, modern scholars have far greater technical knowledge of the Bible than was possible to anyone living in New Testament times. The Late Temple Judaism in which Jesus and the very first Christians grew up had become quite different from the earlier Judaism that had produced most of the books of the Bible. It seems fairly clear that the language that Jesus spoke was Aramaic, basically a Hebrew dialect. Presumably he knew some Greek (the lingua Franca of the ancient Mediterranean world) and some Hebrew (the language the Scriptures), but how much, we simply don't know. Whether or not he knew any Latin is a matter of sheer conjecture. The first Christian sacred or theological language was Greek, and primarily, it seems, the Greek of the Septuagint. In other words, as contemporary scholarship has come to recognize, the original matrix of Christianity was not precisely the Hebrew Scriptures, but rather the religious Judaism of the post-biblical, intertestamental period.

A. The Septuagint

The Septuagint (LXX or 'Seventy') established the Greek religious and cultic language and terminology used by the New Testament writers. It was not a super-precise, scientific translation, but a translation that provided a living interpretation to serve the religious needs of third- and second-century BCE Greek-speaking Jews in Alexandria, Egypt and elsewhere in the diaspora.[20] Primitive anthropomorphisms were generally eliminated in this translation. For example, the 'hand' of God becomes the 'power' of God. Shifts in meaning also take place, as when *chesed* (loving kindness) becomes *eleos* (mercy), or *sedeq* (righteous or righteousness) becomes *dikaiosynê (justice)*. And, as we have already pointed out, there was, regarding Leviticus 17.11, at least one serious mistranslation.

B. Covenant Sacrifice

The act of making or 'cutting' a covenant was a sacrificial ceremony, as can be seen with God making covenants with Noah (Genesis 8.20–9.17) and with Abraham (Genesis 15), and especially with the Mosaic covenant sacrifice in Exodus 24.3–8. Along with the sacrifice of Isaac (Genesis 22), the Passover in Egypt (Exodus 12), and the sacrifice of the Great Day of Atonement (Leviticus 16), this Mosaic covenant sacrifice in Exodus 24 is one of the major foundational sacrificial events in the Hebrew Scriptures. As recorded, it was a unique and unforgettable event. Moses, who was not a priest, here acts as a priest (for only priests could carry out a

---

20   The *Letter of Aristeas* (late second century BCE) contains the legend that this translation was produced in miraculously identical copies by seventy-two Jewish elders, hence the name 'Septuagint', meaning seventy. To some extent because of this legend, it was popularly thought to be a God-inspired translation. See Claude Cox, 'Septuagint (LXX)', in *Encyclopedia of Early Christianity*, 2 vols., ed. Everett Ferguson (New York/London: Garland, 1997), pp. 1048–49; see also 'Septuagint ("LXX")', in *The Oxford Dictionary of the Christian Church*, 3rd ed. (Oxford: Oxford University Press, 1997), pp. 1483–84.

sacrificial blood rite) when he throws half of the sacrificial blood against the altar and the other half upon the people as they ratify the covenant that the Lord has just made with them.

Both of these actions, Moses acting as a priest, and blood being thrown upon people, are absolutely unique occurrences. This is one of the reasons why Jesus' Eucharistic words 'This cup is the new covenant in my blood' are so powerfully evocative. This did not become a type of sacrifice that was regularly repeated. Rather, ideas associated with covenant and blood tended to become associated with the blood rite of any sacrifice, especially where the blood was *tossed* or *thrown*. This was part of a general development in late biblical and early rabbinic Judaism in which the ideas (and technicalities) traditionally associated with this or that particular type of sacrifice were more and more associated with any and all sacrifices. Chapter 9 of the Epistle to the Hebrews, for example combines and runs together ideas and images from several different (kinds of) sacrifices.[21]

C. THE PASSOVER

As witnessed by what is basically a throwaway line by Paul, 'Our paschal lamb, Christ, has been sacrificed (1 Cor. 5.7), the first Christians looked upon the Christ-event as a Passover event. Historically, Passover began as a family sacrifice feast (see Exodus 12). By the time Deuteronomy 16 has been written, shortly before the Exile in the sixth century BCE, the Passover has been combined with the Feast of Unleavened Bread, and has also become a great pilgrimage feast to be celebrated each year in Jerusalem. By the time of Christ, it has become what Christians referred to as 'the Passover of the Jews' (Jn 2.13). Its celebration began with the lamb being slaughtered by priests in the temple, with an elaborate rite of *tossing* or *throwing* the blood at the altar with the strong covenantal associations noted in the previous section.

The Christian Gospels explicitly place the Lord's Supper in the context of the Passover feast. Whether or not it was an actual Passover meal,[22] all the Gospels see it as a Passover event. As such, the three temporal dimensions are present and operative (as they also are for Christians now celebrating the Eucharist): the past, the present and the future.

The past is obviously present because Israel consistently historicized the Passover into a memorial of the Exodus. The sentiments of Deuteronomy 16.1–6 and Exodus 13.8 are expanded in the Mishnah (and indeed remain present in the way that Jews of today still celebrate the Passover as a family feast):

> In every generation a man must so regard himself as if he came forth himself from out of Egypt, for it is written, And thou shalt tell thy son in that day saying, It is because of that which the Lord did for me when I came forth out of Egypt.

---

21 The Day of Atonement (Leviticus 16), the Exodus 24.3–8 covenant sacrifice, the rites of sprinkling with the waters of purification (Numbers 19), and the vicarious atonement of the suffering Servant (Isaiah 53).
22 Because of the conflicting chronologies in the Gospels, this cannot be decided, one way or the other, with historical certitude.

Therefore we are bound to give thanks, to praise, to glorify, to honor, to exalt, to extol, and to bless him who wrought all these wonders for our fathers and for us. He brought us out from bondage and from darkness to great light, and from servitude to redemption.[23]

The *present* is also operative because the participants also believed that they were part of a salvific action taking place with them and upon them right here and now. For the Passover celebration was not just a memorial, but also a living sacrificial action, as can be seen, for example, from the following late-second-century BCE text:

And do thou command the children of Israel to observe the Passover throughout their days, every year, once a year on the day of its fixed time, and it shall come for a memorial well pleasing before the Lord, and no plague shall come upon them to slay or to smite in that year in which they celebrate the Passover in its season in every respect according to His command.

(*Jubilees* 49.15)

The *future.* Israel saw the original Passover as the archetype of the eschatological event to come at the last day.[24] The Passover celebration became the occasion or anticipation of the future final salvation event now also seen as a Passover event.[25]

Almost without exception, the lamb was the preferred sacrificial animal. For Passover, a one-year-old male without blemish was prescribed, the same as prescribed for the daily morning and evening burnt offering. The animal did not have to be a firstborn animal. But, significantly, all the regulations regarding the dedication or redemption of a firstborn are actually found in a Passover context. This has the effect of bringing together ideas of redemption and ransom with those of vicarious atonement. This provides background for the special predilection for the firstborn or first fruits as the best material for sacrifice. This – connected with the New Testament idea of Christ's vicarious ('for us') sacrificial death – was enthusiastically taken over by the Christian Church Fathers. It is still alive today in Catholic devotion, for example, in the special value pious Catholics put on a priest's first Mass and first blessing.

In the New Testament, the evangelists, especially John who places Jesus' death at the time when the Passover lambs were being slaughtered in the temple, took explicit pains to highlight Christ's death as a Christian Passover sacrifice.

D. The Blood of Circumcision

By New Testament times, the initiation rite of circumcision had, along with Sabbath observance, become one of the principle signs of the covenant in post-exilic

---

23 *Pesah* 5.1–7; 8.3 in Herbert Danby, *The Mishnah* (Oxford: Oxford University Press, 1933), pp. 141–42, 147. The *Mishnah* is the early 3rd-century BCE codification of Jewish Law. In Judaism, its authority is second only to that of the Scriptures. It is generally regarded to reflect fairly accurately Jewish religious understanding at the time of Jesus.
24 See Isa. 31.5; Hos. 2.16; Jer. 23.7; 31.31–32; Isa. 40–45.
25 See Isa. 25.5; 30.29 along with 2 Chron. 30.21–27; 35.1–19.

Judaism. Also, because of the close association often made with Passover blood, especially in the Palestinian Targums,[26] circumcision also began to take on a strong sacrificial or atoning significance. This can be seen in the targumic development (that was beginning as early as the second century BCE) of the mysterious verses in Exodus 4.24–26 when Zipporah, Moses's wife, after circumcising her son, touches Moses's 'feet' (i.e. penis) with the blood of that circumcision and exclaims (in the Palestinian targumic expansion): 'Now may the blood of this circumcision atone for the guilt of my husband'; and 'How beloved is the blood of [this] circumcision which has saved my husband from the hand of the angel of Death [Destroying Angel]'.

In addition, both the Hebrew Scriptures and the Haggadah (non-legal, devotional Jewish literature) have a strong tendency to associate circumcision with Passover. This is especially true in the development of the 'legend of the two bloods', i.e., that the blood of circumcision was mingled with the [saving] blood of the first Passover lambs. This is made explicit in one of the targums (the *Targum Pseudo-Jonathan* on Exodus 12.13):

> You shall mix the blood of the Passover sacrifice and of circumcision and make of it a sign to put on the houses where you live; I will see the merit of the blood and will spare you.

Among numerous other references to this theme, the most interesting one seems to be a passage from the *Targum on the Canticle of Canticles* (which was read at Passover time):

> At the time when the glory of Yahweh was manifested in Egypt on the night of the Passover in order to kill the first-born . . . he protected the house where we were, lay in wait by the window, watched by the trellis, and saw the blood of the Passover sacrifice and the blood of the circumcision stamped on our doors. . . . He looked down from the height of the heavens and saw the people eating the sacrifice of the feast and he spared them and he did not give power to the Destroying angel to destroy us[27]

Thus the idea, concept, etc. of the 'blood of circumcision' has great theological significance, because of its association with atonement in general, and with Passover and covenant in particular. Much of the Pauline and Deutero-Pauline theology of baptism, not merely as initiation and purification, but above all as a participation in the sacrificial death and resurrection of Christ, even as a 'circumcision' of Christ as in Colossians 2.11, seems indebted to this background. See Romans 6.3–4

---

26 The Targums were Aramaic interpretative translations of and expansion on the Scriptures which were used in Jewish community (synagogue) worship. As texts, they date from the early centuries of the Christian era; in content, they are generally thought to reflect religious ideas possibly as early as the period in which the Christian Scriptures were being written.

27 *Targum Pseudo Jonathan* I on Exodus 12.13. See Roger Le Deaut, *La Nuit Pascale: Essai sur la signification de la Paque juive à partir du Targum d'Exode XII.42* (Analecta Biblica, 22; Rome: Pontifical Biblical Institute, 1963), p. 211.

and Colossians 2.11–12 with this in mind. But Paul's radical Christologizing of it seems also to dispense with its basic Jewish meaning: 'In Christ Jesus neither circumcision nor uncircumcision is of any avail, but faith through love' (Gal. 5.6; see also Phil. 3.3).

E. QUMRAN: THE COMMUNITY AS TEMPLE

The Dead Sea Scrolls, a fairly extensive body of texts and fragments discovered in the years following 1947 in some dozen caves west of the Dead Sea, apparently represent the library of a breakaway Jewish sect that did not survive the Jewish-Roman War of 66–70 CE. These texts constitute the single most important non-biblical source for the background of the early Christian idea of sacrifice:

> The Qumran texts contain a consistent temple symbolism, in which the community is represented as the new temple, and in which the true sacrifice is seen as being spiritual in character, offered in the holy and pure lives, the praise and the prayer of the members of the community. No direct parallel to this temple symbolism has been traced in Judaism.[28]

What precipitated or at least accelerated the development of this temple theme was the particular religious situation of the Qumran community. They, more than most, were aware both of both God's transcendent holiness and of human sinfulness and need for atonement. Atonement at that time was still centred in ritual sacrifice that could be offered only in the Jerusalem temple. But the Qumran sectarians believed that what was going on in the Jerusalem temple was invalid because of tampering with the sacred calendar and with the membership rolls of the priests. This intolerable situation forced them to find surrogates for ritual sacrifice while eagerly awaiting, as the *War Scroll* (*1QM* 2.1–6) shows, the full restoration of the true cult.

Several passages in the Qumran *Community Rule*, often referred to as the *Manual of Discipline* (*1QS*) offer clear witness to this community-as-temple idea. The clearest of these is probably in the eighth column of the scroll:

> It [the council of the Community] shall be an everlasting Plantation, a House of Holiness for Israel, an Assembly of the *Holy of Holies* for Aaron. They shall be witnesses to the truth at the Judgment, and shall be the elect of Goodwill who shall *atone for* the land and pay to the wicked their reward. It shall be that tried wall, that precious cornerstone, whose foundations shall neither rock nor sway in their place (Isa. 28.16). It shall be a *Holy of Holies* for Aaron, with everlasting knowledge of the covenant of justice, and shall offer up sweet fragrance (*reach nichoach*). It shall be a House of Perfection and Truth in Israel that they may establish a

---

28   Bertil Gärtner, *The Temple and Community in Qumran and the New Testament: A Comparative Study in the Temple Symbolism of the Qumran Texts and the New Testament* (Society for New Testament Studies Monograph Series, 1; Cambridge: University Press, 1965), p. 47.

Covenant according to the everlasting precepts. And they shall be an agreeable offering, *atoning for* the land.[29]

Thus the community not only sees itself as performing the atoning functions of the temple, it also *sees itself as the very sacrifice* offered in this spiritual temple. The next column of the scroll makes clear that it is indeed the whole community that is seen as the atoning temple:

> When these [the ordinary members of the community] become members of the community in Israel according to all these rules, they shall establish the spirit of holiness according to everlasting truth. They shall atone for guilty rebellion and for sins of unfaithfulness that they may obtain lovingkindness for the land more than from the flesh of burnt offerings and the fat of sacrifice. And an offering of the lips rightly offered shall be an acceptable fragrance of righteousness and perfection of way as a delectable free-will offering.
>
> (*1QS* 9.3–5)

An (apparently later) text from Cave 4 makes this temple spiritualization even more explicit:

> And he proposed to build him a Sanctuary of men (or among men) in which should be offered sacrifices before him, the works of the law.
>
> (*4Qflor* 1.6–7)

Only Christology separates these passages from a new Testament passage such as 1 Peter 2.4–10 where Christians are exhorted to be living stones being built up into the holy temple, in which spiritual sacrifices are offered to God, and of which Christ is the cornerstone.

F. The Akedah (Sacrifice of Isaac)

One of the more fascinating developments in all of religious history is the post-biblical and early rabbinic development of the story of the sacrifice of Isaac. The basic story in Chapter 22 of the Book of Genesis is simple. Abraham is told by God to go and sacrifice his only son, Isaac, the one born miraculously to him in his and Sara's old age. As he is about to carry out the command, God (the angel of the Lord) stops him and says, basically, OK, you've passed the test, and I now repeat my promise to make of your descendants a great nation of many people.

We can only conjecture at the historical origins of this story. We know of it only from the Elohist **E** writing in the ninth century BCE., some eight centuries after the time of Abraham. The Elohist frames the story around the ritual of the burnt offering of his own day. Three theological themes stand out: (1) the rejection – at least as we now read the story – of human sacrifice, (2) the identification of the site

---

29   *1QS* 8.5–10. Translation by Geza Vermes, *The Dead Sea Scrolls in English*, 2nd ed. (Harmondsworth/Baltimore: Penguin Books, 1965).

(in tradition it is Mt. Moriah) with that of the Jerusalem temple, (3) the theological heart of the story: Abraham's faith–obedience relationship with God and God's renewal of the promise of future blessings. The imaginative embellishment of this story in the Jewish Haggadah (devotional literature as contrasted with the Halakah, the legal literature, the Law) supplies the single most important piece of background we have for the sacrificial soteriology of the New Testament.

In this haggadic literature, the Palestinian Targums are the richest source, and within them the 'Poem of the Four Nights' stands out as the mother lode. This poem, a commentary on Exodus 12.42,[30] sees salvation history as focused on four 'nights': (1) creation, (2) the Genesis 15 covenant with Abraham and his Genesis 22 sacrificing of Isaac, (3) the Passover and (4) the final night at the end of the world. The major, theologically significant developments or embellishments that go beyond the Genesis 22 narrative are (a) the Akedah is seen as the actual source of the efficacy of the Passover, (b) Isaac is portrayed as a mature man, 37 years old, and voluntarily acquiescing in the sacrifice, (c) Isaac is spoken of as actually having been sacrificed – one hears of the 'ashes' and the 'blood' of Isaac, or hears him being called 'the Lamb of the burnt offering', (d) Isaac, not Abraham, is the one who experiences a vision, (e) Abraham prays – and in some versions in an explicitly expiatory way – that his obedience and Isaac's covenant will be *remembered* by God for the benefit of their descendants.

A wide range of Jewish literature in the centuries just before, during, and after the time of Christ develops this theme. The location of the event was identified as Mt. Zion, the place on which the Temple was built. Abraham and Isaac are portrayed (sometimes in Stoic terms) as lofty heroes acting in complete harmony with the divine will as they carry out the sacrifice. They become models for the Jewish martyrs whose atoning power derives implicitly from that of the Akedah. Josephus, the Jewish historian writing in Greek at the end of the first Christian century, bathes the event in a liturgical atmosphere, portraying it as the returning of a gift to God. Pseudo Philo (mid-first century of the Christian era) emphasizes the unique position of this sacrifice – with Isaac being conscious of being the type of sacrifice God desires – both as a memorial of past sacrifices and as something performed in expiation for future generations.

Thus, by New Testament times, this Haggadah on the Akedah contained a fairly well-developed soteriology, as if made to order for Christian use: (1) Isaac's self-offering was seen as a true sacrifice in its own right. Isaac's free consent overcame the great (typological) weakness of traditional sacrifice, the passive role of the animal victim. (2) The effects of the Akedah were seen as redemptive. (3) The Akedah had a special causal relationship to the atoning efficacy of all other sacrifices. (4) The liturgical *Sitz im Leben*–'situation in life' of the Akedah Haggadah is the Passover feast.

---

30   'That was for the Lord a night of vigil, to bring them out of the land of Egypt. That same night is a vigil to be kept for the Lord by all the Israelites throughout their generations' (Exodus 12.42). The Targums, in Aramaic, were exhortatory, devotional, homiletic expansions on the biblical text that took place in synagogue services. The texts that we now have come from a few centuries after Christ, but, as we have already noted, they are generally considered to reflect the kinds of things that were being said in synagogue services at the time of Christ.

1. Clear references to the Akedah in the New Testament

Hebrews 11.17–20 speaks as if the sacrifice had actually occurred, then goes on to speak of God's power 'even to raise someone from the dead' (Hebrews 11.19). James 2.21 also speaks of the sacrifice as accomplished. The faith-works theology of James also evokes the haggadic tendency to view the Akedah as the meritorious achievement *par excellence*. Romans 8.32 'He who did not withhold (spare) his own Son' evokes the Septuagint Greek of Genesis 22.18. The continuation of Romans 8.32 'but gave him up for all of us' supports the allusion to the Akedah. Similar uses of 'to give, to give up' in Galatians 1.4 and 2.20, Ephesians 5.2 and 25; Titus 2.14 and 1 Timothy 2.6 to express Christ's loving act of self-immolation also recall the targumic portrayal of Isaac's self-immolation.

2. Probable references to the Akedah in the New Testament

John 3.16: 'God so loved the world that he gave his only Son, so that everyone who believes in him may not perish but may have eternal life' seems to be an obvious allusion. Mark 1.11 and 9.7 and their synoptic parallels (the voice from heaven in the baptism and transfiguration stories): 'You are my Son, the Beloved; with you I am well pleased' almost certainly allude to the Septuagint wording of Genesis 22.2 'Take your son, your only son Isaac, whom you love'. These baptism and transfiguration stories are also permeated with other Akedah motifs, notably that of theophany. The theophany motif, one of the oldest elements of the baptism and transfiguration stories, is also at the very heart of the Akedah, as we can see in this passage from the targumic 'Poem of the four Nights':

> The heavens were let down and descended
> and Isaac saw their perfection . . .
> On the fourth night, . . . Moses shall come out of the wilderness
> and the King of Messiah out of Rome.
> The one shall be led upon a cloud
> and the Word of the Lord shall lead between them
> and they shall go forward together.[31]

The thematic affinity with the baptism and transfiguration theophanies is unmistakable, but not such as to allow us to decide the question of literary source or literary analogue. In respect to 1 Corinthians 15.4, 'raised on the third day in accordance with the scriptures', countless exegetes have struggled to find where previous Scripture might have mentioned resurrection on the third day, not realizing that this scripture fulfilment refers not to 'raised' but to 'on the third day'. For it was 'on the third day' (Genesis 22.4) that Abraham came to the place for sacrificing Isaac. In the accounts of Israel's salvation history, the 'third day' was a characteristic time (some thirty instances of it in the Hebrew Scriptures make it practically a code word) for salvation achieved or disaster averted. Since, in the

---

31   Geza Vermes, 'Redemption and Genesis XXII' in *Scripture and Tradition in Judaism* (Studia Postbiblica, 4; Leiden: Brill, 1964), p. 216.

religious consciousness of New Testament times, the Akedah was one of the most notable of these 'third day' events, an allusion to it in 1 Corinthians 15.4 seems plausible.[32] Finally, Galatians 3.14 'That in Christ Jesus the blessing of Abraham might come to the Gentiles' appears to be a paraphrase of Genesis 22.18.

3. Possible references to the Akedah in the New Testament

Possible New Testament references to the Akedah are numerous. Galatians 1.4 and 2.20; Ephesians 5.2 and 25; Titus 2.14; 1 Timothy 2.6, in their use of the verb 'to give' to express Christ's self-giving strongly evoke the Akedah gift motif of Philo, Josephus and Pseudo-Philo. Typical of this group of texts is Galatians 1.3–4 '. . . the Lord Jesus Christ, who gave himself for our sins to set us free . . .' In Matthew 12.18, '. . . my beloved, with whom my soul is well pleased' and in the similar text of Mark 12.6 the Greek *agapêtos* (beloved) seems to be influenced by the similar Septuagint translation of the Hebrew *yahid* in Genesis 22.2, 12, 16. The pre-election of the sacrificial lamb referred to in 1 Peter 1.19–20, is an Akedah motif. John 1.29, 'The lamb of God who takes away the sin of the world', recalls Abraham addressing Isaac as 'the lamb of the burnt offering' in the *Neofiti Targum* to Genesis 22.8. Finally, the Eucharistic inaugurative command in 1 Corinthians 11.24–25 and Luke 22.19, 'Do this in remembrance of me', reminds us how the Akedah portrays God as 'remembering' the merits of Isaac's sacrifice at the moment of the daily offering of lambs, at specific moments in Israel's salvation history, and at the moment of the first Passover in Egypt.

4. The Akedah: A full expression of Jewish sacrificial soteriology

To sum up: the Genesis 22 account of the sacrifice of Isaac was so richly elaborated by the Haggadah that, by New Testament times, the Akedah had developed into a full expression of Jewish sacrificial soteriology. The sacrifice to which the mature Isaac consented was looked upon as if actually consummated. It was God's remembering of the Akedah that caused him to deliver and bless Israel at the first Passover and at the other moments of deliverance and blessing in its history. More specifically, the sacrificial cult was thought to be effective because it reminded God of the Akedah, the sacrifice par excellence. Admittedly, we cannot advance much beyond probabilities in determining relationships to specific New Testament texts; the classifications given earlier must be seen as provisional and, to some extent, conjectural. I would, nevertheless, submit that it is now proven not only that such relationships exist, but also that the sacrificial soteriology of the New Testament can no longer be adequately discussed apart from the Akedah.

---

32   See Karl Lehmann, *Auferweckt am dritten Tag nach der Schrift: Früheste Christologie, Bekenntnisbildung und Schriftauslegung im Lichte von 1 Kor. 15,3–5*, (Quaestiones Disputatae, 38; Freiburg/ Vienna: Herder, 1968), pp. 176–81; 262–90.

Chapter V

Conclusion

In our brief treatment of sacrifice in the ancient world, we found little correlation with what we have laid out as a Christian, Trinitarian understanding of sacrifice. In our equally brief discussion of attempts to establish a 'general theory of sacrifice' that might be helpful to us, we found at least some correlation in the gift theory of sacrifice. But it was only when we looked at sacrifice in the Hebrew Scriptures that background correlations to an eventual Trinitarian understanding of sacrifice began to be significant. The close association, if not identification, of sacrifice with atonement, the (esp. prophetic) emphasis on proper ethical dispositions as a condition for God accepting sacrifice and granting its atoning effects, and finally, the late biblical (at least implicit) theological developments associated with Passover, circumcision and the Akedah (sacrifice of Isaac) effectively set the stage for the central revelation of a Christological and eventually Trinitarian understanding of sacrifice in the writings and in the worship of the New Testament and early Christian periods.

Sacrifice in the New Testament

Considering how prominent sacrifice and sacrificial themes are throughout the Hebrew Scriptures, it seems at first surprising that the New Testament says relatively little about this theme. Part of the reason may be that Jesus and his first Jewish followers were more closely associated with the Pharisees and their emphasis on the law than with the priest and Sadducees and their emphasis on ritual observance. Another likely reason is that, in the minds of the early Christians, sacrifice was what pagans and Jews did, not what followers of Jesus did. Exceptions to this relative reticence about sacrifice are two writings that come from the late New Testament period (and that are also untypical in comparison with the rest of the New Testament): the book of Revelation and the epistle to the Hebrews. However, even should one prescind from these, there would still be enough in the rest of the New Testament to provide an ample foundation for a Christian theology of sacrifice.

Methodologically, we cannot avoid the complexity that now characterizes New Testament Studies. The Gospels, which provide practically the only detail we have about Jesus, belong to the middle to late New Testament period. They were written some four or more decades after the death of Jesus, and also primarily as faith documents rather than as historical records. The epistles of Paul which (together with some later epistles dependent on Paul) are our richest biblical source for a Christian theology of sacrifice were written several decades earlier. But Paul also depends on the early Christian preaching that only later on took the precise written form of the Gospels. Making our task still more complex is the fact that very few people in the New Testament period, if any at all, had any inkling of the historical and technical complexity behind the writing of the biblical books. As a result, no approach can completely evade the charge of circularity, for we inevitably project our own order into what we find. Nevertheless, our approach and the order and nature of our discussion will try to combine not only the systematic and theoretical with the chronological, but also the historical-scientific with the theological and the faith-based, and also to do that in a way that respects the authenticity of the data.

Chapter I

The Synoptic Gospels [1]

The infancy narratives in Matthew and Luke, which actually come from the middle to the later stage of New Testament writing, some 50 or more years after the time of Christ, seem to reflect a positive attitude toward the sacrificial cult. Technical sacrificial terms are used to describe some of the gifts of the Magi in Matthew 2.11. And in the Lukan infancy narrative, Zechariah's vision about the future birth of his son, John the Baptist, occurred while he, a priest, was performing the morning incense offering (Luke 1.8–23).

The rest of the Synoptic Gospels, on the other hand, seem to be at times favourable and at other times critical of sacrifice. Implying a mostly favourable attitude toward sacrifice are texts like Matthew 5.23 that instruct us to be first reconciled with others before offering sacrifice; or Mark 1.44 parr that instruct the cured leper to offer the prescribed sacrifice for his cleansing; or Jesus' praise of the poor widow's offering (Mark 12.41–44 par); or his sharp criticism of the abuse of 'Corban' (Mark 7.9–13 parr). Such texts make sense only in the context of a basically positive attitude toward the sacrificial cult.

But other texts express or at least imply criticism of sacrifice. Jesus' defence of his disciples plucking grain on the Sabbath implies his superiority over the temple, or at least relativizes the importance of the temple. The accounts of Jesus cleansing the temple (one of the relatively few events found in all four Gospels) suggest primarily zeal for the purity of the temple, but they also suggest that Jesus may have regarded the temple more as a place of prayer than as a place of sacrifice. More sharply critical, are the numerous – *there are six of them!* – New Testament versions of the saying, '. . . destroy this temple that is *made with hands*, and in three days I will build another, *not made with hands*' (Mark 14.58 par). The term 'made with hands – *cheiropoiêtos*' was a term normally used by Jews to describe the idols of wood and stone that were so abhorrent to Jewish religious sensitivity. The use of this term is, in effect, calling the temple a place of idolatrous worship. Likewise critical, but more by implication, is the Lukan (10.29–37) Parable of the Good Samaritan. For the priest and the Levite, had they been in contact with someone who died on their hands, would, to the chagrin of their communities, have been rendered 'impure', i.e. incapable of participating in public religious worship.

---

1 The Synoptic Gospels, Mark, Matthew and Luke follow a basically similar order and arrangement in their accounts of the teaching and activity of Jesus. Almost all the material in Mark is also found in Matthew and Luke, almost all of it in the same order as in Mark, and much of it even in the same words. The abbreviations 'par' and 'parr' indicate that there is a parallel passage in one (par) or both (parr) of the other two Synoptic Gospels. Matthew and Luke also have in common more than 200 verses of Jesus' teaching that is not in Mark; in addition, Matthew and Luke each have material – for example, the infancy narratives – that is unique to just that one Gospel.

One of the great sacrificial sayings of Jesus and of the whole New Testament is Mark 10.45 (par Matthew 20.28) – 'The Son of Man came not to be served but to serve, and to give his life [as] a ransom for many.' The 'for many' suggests Isaiah 53.10–12, hence Servant of God, sacrifice, and martyrdom. 'To give his life' evokes the many ways in which this implicitly sacrificial motif is present in the Gospel of John (Chapters 10, 11, 15, 17). It also evokes the numerous Pauline texts that speak of Christ's sacrificial self-giving. Luke's relocation of this saying to the Last Supper, immediately after the institution of the Eucharist, and John's (Chapter 13) symbolic presentation of the same in the Washing of the Feet, the opening scene of the Last Supper, connect it all unmistakably with the Servant themes of Eucharistic institution.

All four accounts of the Institution of the Eucharist (Mark 14.12–27; Matthew. 26.17–29; Luke 22.7–20; 1 Cor. 11.23–26) present it as an integral part of the passion narrative, affirming the basic identity between Jesus' last meal and his death. Taken together, the themes of Passover sacrifice, covenant sacrifice and sin offering cannot be separated from the way the New Testament remembers and witnesses to the institution of the Eucharist.

In the end, however, and at the most profound level, it is Servant Christology that dominates the primitive kerygma about the Eucharist and supplies its deep theological context. The phrases 'shed for many' and 'given up for many', and Paul's 'on the night when he was betrayed' leave no doubt about that; they are both verbal and thematic allusions to the fourth and culminating Servant Song in Isaiah 53. The Eucharistic terms 'body' and 'blood' find their fullest meaning in this Servant-of-God framework. They point not to the death of a passive victim, but to the free and voluntary character of Jesus' death as an act of self-giving. This, and this alone, is the full meaning of 'body' in the Eucharistic texts. To sum up:

> It is not the idea of cultic sacrifice in which the body is seen as a separable part of the sacrifice, but rather that of a martyr's offering which signifies the offering of one's body as the self-giving of one's whole person. Thus the sacrificial idea is also contained in the words over the bread; but this idea should not be seen in the understanding of the term *soma* as isolated sacrificial flesh separated from the blood; it must rather be looked for in the whole participial phrase and seen in its martyrological coloring.[2]

It is from this background, along with the Trinitarian understanding of Christian sacrifice outlined in Part One that we can now safely speak of the Eucharist, or the historical Lord's Supper, as Christ's personal self offering. For it cannot be emphasized too often or too much that Christ's death is the Father-initiated, but absolutely free, totally voluntary self-offering of Christ the Servant in the Holy Spirit. Consequently, as we repeatedly emphasized in Part One, our sacrifice –

---

2 Translated from Johannes Betz, *Die Eucharistie in der Zeit der griechischen Väter* 2nd edn (Freiburg/Vienna: Herder, 1964), II/1, pp. 40–41. A summary of Betz's Eucharistic theology can be found in 'Eucharist, I. Theological' in *Sacramentum Mundi*, vol. 2, (New York: Herder, 1968), pp. 257–67.

Christian sacrifice – is authentically Christian only to the extent that it enters into and becomes part of this economic Trinitarian dynamic.[3]

To relate this to what we spoke of at the end of Bridge 1 A, the most sublime ideas of perfect sacrifice and perfect dispositions for sacrifice found or suggested in the figure of the Suffering Servant, and above all in the Akedah (sacrifice of Isaac), find their fullest expression and fulfilment in the New Testament doctrine of the sacrifice of Christ.

Chapter II

The Acts of the Apostles

The evangelist Luke was obviously familiar with the Christological Servant-theme. Although this theme is also found in Acts (see Philip's explanation to the Ethiopian eunuch in Acts 8.26–40; see also Luke 24.25–27, 48), Luke, as author of Acts does not seem to emphasize the atoning character of Jesus' death. The temple, does, however, receive special attention.

The first Christians pray in the temple and Peter and John perform a miracle there (Acts 2–3); and Paul was apparently praying in the temple when he received, in a vision, his mission to the Gentiles (Acts 22.17–21). This indicates that the basic attitude of Acts is favourable to the temple. But it also implies that the temple belongs to Jesus, and that connection, joined with Paul's mission to the Gentiles, implies the beginning of the end for the prerogatives of the temple. This anti-temple position becomes more than an implication in the fierce temple criticism of the deacon, Stephen, the first martyr. In his speech, just before getting stoned, he implies that idolatry is at the very root of Jewish sacrificial practice. He commits the (to traditional ears) blasphemy of calling the temple (as Jesus also provocatively did at his trial) '*cheiropoiêtos* – made with hands'. In other words, he is calling the temple an idolatrous human artifact. It would have been a miracle if Stephen had not been stoned.

Chapter III

The Pauline Theology of Sacrifice

In the Pauline letters we find a fairly well-rounded outline of a biblical theology of Christian Sacrifice. It is on the one hand thoroughly Jewish in most of its basic

---

3 In common theological terminology, the 'immanent' Trinity refers to the inner life of God, the intra-divine relationships between Father, Son and Spirit. The 'economic' Trinity, on the other hand refers to the 'relationship' of the Trinity to things outside of God, i.e., creation and salvation history.

ideas, but on the other hand, and at the same time, quite profoundly and incarnationally Christological. It was, however, not yet a Trinitarian theology of sacrifice such as we outlined earlier in Part One. There are three major themes: (1) the sacrifice of Christ, (2) the Christians as the new Temple, (3) the sacrifice of (i.e. by) the Christians.

A. THE SACRIFICE OF CHRIST

Paul is the earliest Christian witness to the idea of the sacrifice of Christ.[4] Paul clearly associates this idea, this reality, with the two particular types of sacrifice that the Jewish people of his time most associated with redemption and forgiveness: the Passover sacrifice and the sin offering. The association with the Passover is witnessed in one unique, but also uniquely eloquent and powerful text: 'Our paschal lamb, Christ, has been sacrificed' (1 Cor. 5.7).

The significance of this text comes from the fact that, in its context, it is not something that Paul is teaching, or trying to prove; it is almost a throw-away line. It is something that Paul and his readers obviously take for granted, and that can be appealed to in order to support some other point in his argument. In other words, this is a powerful indication that the earliest Christians, at least in the Pauline communities, looked upon the death of Christ as a Passover event, a Passover sacrifice.

Paul is also our earliest witness to the idea of Christ as a sin offering. Among the numerous texts that indicate this, three stand out:

> For our sake he [God] made him [Christ] to be *sin* [i.e. a sin offering] who knew no *sin*, so that in him we might become the righteousness of God.
>
> (2 Cor. 5.21)

> Christ redeemed us from the curse of the law by becoming a curse for us – for it is written, 'Cursed is everyone who hangs on a tree' – in order that in Christ Jesus the blessing of Abraham might come to the Gentiles, so that we might receive the promise of the Spirit through faith.
>
> (Gal. 3.13–14)

> For God has done what the law, weakened by the flesh, could not do: by sending his own Son in the likeness *of sinful flesh*, and to deal with *sin* [or: 'for sin' or 'as a sin offering'], he condemned sin in the flesh.
>
> (Rom. 8.3)

We have here another instance where translations badly miss the full meaning of the text. In the first and third of these texts, the italicized word *sin* and the phrase

---

4 In itself this is not significant, since Paul's letters are by far the earliest extant Christian writings in which this witness could have been recorded. But it is significant how extensive the theme of the sacrifice of Christ is at this earliest level, as well as at the later level, of New Testament epistolary writing (2 Cor. 5.14–15, 21; Rom. 3.24–25; 5.6–11; 8.3, 23, 32; Gal. 2.20; 3.13; Ephesians 5.2, 25; Col. 1.24; 1 Tim. 2.5–6; Tit. 2.13–14; 1 Jn 3.16; etc.).

of sinful flesh [my emphasis] are all attempting to translate the same Greek word: *harmartia. Harmartia*, as Paul the Jew presumably well knew, was the ordinary translation of the Hebrew word *chattat*. This Hebrew word had a double meaning. It meant both *sin* and *sin offering*. Paul is obviously playing on this double meaning, thus powerfully proclaiming that Christ is the offering for our sins.

B. CHRISTIANS AS THE NEW TEMPLE[5]

Paul freely (and astutely!) mixes metaphors as he strives to express the mystery of God's presence in our lives. He speaks of us, the Christian community, as a plant, then, in almost the same breath, as a building, all the while reminding us that we are the temple of God or of the Spirit:

> Do you not know that you are God's temple and that God's Spirit dwells in you? If anyone destroys God's temple, God will destroy that person. For God's temple is holy, and you are that temple.
>
> (1 Cor. 3.16–17)[6]

But not only does Paul mix metaphors, he also (purposely it seems) leaves us guessing as to whether he is talking about the individual or the whole community. And he presumes that his readers understand that there is a connection between the community and/or individual as temple and the indwelling in us of the Holy Spirit.[7] The fullest 'Pauline'[8] expression of this theology and what develops from it is found in the deutero-Pauline writings:

> So then you are no longer strangers and aliens, but you are citizens with the saints and also members of the household of God, built upon the foundation of the apostles and prophets, with Christ Jesus himself as the cornerstone. In him the whole structure is joined together and grows into a holy temple in the Lord; in whom you also are built together spiritually into a dwelling place for God.
>
> (Ephesians 2.19–22)

The best guidelines for interpreting this passage are the already mentioned in 1 Cor. 3.5–17, and also Ephesians 4.11–16 texts that expresses the same message while using only the metaphor of the body. This passage in Ephesians 2 is addressed to Gentile converts who are now full members of God's household. The image of Christ as the cornerstone marvellously complements the image of Christ

---

5 The Jewish background of this theme was treated above in Bridge 1 B (pp. 45–46) under the heading: 'Qumran: the Community as Temple'.
6 See the full context in 1 Cor. 3.6–15; 6.15, 19; 2 Cor. 6.16.
7 This understanding provides background for the many texts that speak of or allude to the indwelling of the Spirit, for example, Rom. 5.5; 8.9, 11, 15–16; 1 Thess. 4.8; 1 Cor. 2.10–16; 2 Cor. 1.22. This theology is also found in the Pastoral Epistles: 1 Tim. 3.15; 2 Tim. 2.20–22; Tit. 2.14.
8 The epistle to the Ephesians is generally considered to have been written, in Paul's voice, by someone later than Paul.

as head of the body,[9] and then the idea of growth strikingly bursts the limits of the building image. The image of living stones that we will see in 1 Peter 2:5 brings still more richness to this theme. Two deeply significant theological insights are communicated or revealed here: (1) the mode of existence of the Christian community, both moral and ontological, is that of an *inner process of growth* toward holiness, and (2) this is a *continuous* process.

C. Sacrifice of (i.e. by) the Christians

In numerous texts, Paul clearly compares, even identifies, the life and death of the Christian with the sacrificial death of Christ. For example:

(Quoting Ps. 44.23) 'For your sake we are being killed all day long; we are accounted as sheep to be slaughtered.'

(Rom. 8.36)

. . . always carrying in the body the death of Jesus, so that the life of Jesus may be made visible in our bodies. For while we live, we are always being given up to death for Jesus' sake, so that the life of Jesus may be made visible in our mortal flesh.

(2 Cor. 4.10–11)

I have been crucified with Christ; and it is no longer I who live, but it is Christ who lives in me.

(Gal. 2.19–20)

I am now rejoicing in my sufferings for your sake, and in my flesh I am completing what is lacking in Christ's afflictions for the sake of his body, that is, the church.

(Col. 1.24)

From these and other texts it is clear that Paul viewed his own apostolic life and impending death in the same way that he viewed Christ's, i.e., as a personal self-offering (see Phil. 2.17; 2 Tim. 4.6). In brief, there is no doubt that the Pauline literature speaks of the life of apostleship, and of the Christian life in general, as sacrificial, as is witnessed in the following key texts.

I appeal to you therefore, brothers and sisters, by the mercies of God, to present (*parastanai*) your bodies (*sômata*) as a living sacrifice, holy and acceptable to God, which is your spiritual (*logikên*) worship. Do not be conformed to this world, but be transformed by the renewing of your minds, so that you may discern what is the will of God – what is good and acceptable and perfect.

(Rom. 12.1–2)

---

9   Ephesians 1.22; 2.16; 3.6; 4.4, 11–16; 5.23–24.

For our theme, the location of these verses is strategic. They mark the end of the first doctrinal teaching part of Paul's letter to the Romans and the beginning of the second, practical-application part of the letter. At this critical juncture, and in this obviously key sacrificial text, Paul combines in a uniquely striking way two incompatibles. He uses the spiritualizing language of 'spiritual worship' that comes from Hellenistic religious philosophy that had long been pointing out the unreasonableness of trying to offer material worship to a spiritual deity. But in the same breath Paul exhorts us to do precisely that: to offer our *bodies* as a living sacrifice to God. Behind this is, first, the Hebrew understanding of *body*. As it does in Jesus' Eucharistic Words of Institution, body signifies the total person in his/her physical, bodily, as well as spiritual state of being. Second, and even more importantly, this also reflects the specifically Christian, incarnational way of looking at things: 'The Word became flesh and lived (literally "pitched his tent" among us' (Jn 1.14). This combining of the most elevated ethical and spiritual ideas of the Greeks with the somatic ideas of his Jewish and Christian experience enables Paul to reject the Hellenistic mistrust of matter and emphasize the two cardinal points of Christian faith: the goodness of creation and the reality of the incarnation.

> On some points I have written to you rather boldly by way of reminder, because of the grace given me by God to be a minister (*leitourgos*) of Christ Jesus to the Gentiles in the priestly service (*leitourgein*) of the gospel of God, so that the offering of the Gentiles may be acceptable, sanctified by the Holy Spirit.
>
> (Rom. 15.15–16)

Paul sees his apostolic life and mission as a 'priestly – i.e. sacrificial – service', as a liturgy of life. The 'grace' of this that Paul speaks of comprises (1) the offering up of Jesus Christ, through God, and for us, (2) the 'priestly/sacrificial service' of a life of preaching the Gospel, and (3) the obedience of faith in giving oneself to God for the sake of one's neighbour. Altogether it constitutes a comprehensive service involves the founding, the building up and the maintaining of the Church.[10]

1 Peter 2.4–10 is the richest single source for a New Testament theology of sacrifice. It takes up and amplifies the Pauline ideas of the community as temple and the sacrificial nature of Christian life, while holding the idea of the sacrifice of Christ implicitly in the background:

> [4]Come to him, a living stone, though rejected by mortals yet chosen and precious in God's sight, and [5]like living stones, let yourselves be built into a spiritual (*pneumatikos*) house, to be a holy priesthood, to offer spiritual sacrifices (*pneumatikas thusias*) acceptable to God through Jesus Christ. [6]For it stands in scripture: 'See, I am laying in Zion a stone, a cornerstone chosen and precious; and whoever believes in him will not be put to shame.'[7] To you then who believe, he is precious; but for those who do not believe, 'The stone that the builders rejected has become the very head of the corner,'[8] and 'a stone that makes them stumble, and

---

10   This line of interpretation seems to be emphatically reinforced by 2 Cor. 2.14–17.

a rock that makes them fall.' They stumble because they disobey the word, as they were destined to do. ⁹but you are a chosen race, a royal priesthood, a holy nation, God's own people, in order that you may proclaim the mighty acts of him who called you out of darkness into his marvelous light. ¹⁰Once you were not a people, but now you are God's people; once you had not received mercy, but now you have received mercy.

Verses 4 and 5 are the richest two biblical verses for a theology of sacrifice. *Come to him* uses the same verb that describes the approach of the Jewish priest to the altar of sacrifice. *Living stone* = Christ; *living stones* = the Christians, recalling the *living sacrifice* of Rom. 12.1. This leads directly into the community-as-temple theme. The combination in this one phrase of images from building construction and plant growth develops what we saw begin in Paul and emphasizes further both the importance of internal dispositions and the fact that true Christian sacrifice means putting oneself totally, both body and soul, at the disposition of God and neighbour. The *house* (= temple) to be built of these *living stones* is *pneumatikos* (spiritual), the opposite of the idolatrous 'made with hands'.[11] It is the dwelling place of God's Spirit, the place where *spiritual* (= Christian) *sacrifices* are to be offered to God through Jesus Christ. Compactly but powerfully emphasized are three important themes: (1) the Christian form of cultic spiritualization, (2) the theology of acceptance and (3) the mediatorship of Christ.

This passage is also a focal point for the often-controverted doctrine of universal priesthood. Since the Second Vatican Council in the 1960s, this doctrine has recovered its rightful place in Catholic thinking. Before that, Catholic polemical thinking usually considered it to be 'Protestant' because of the way it was used to counter the Catholic over-emphasis on the power of the ordained priesthood. Note how this passage, along with the others we have been examining, emphasizes the practical, Gospel-preaching, and ethical, rather than the specifically cultic, nature of Christian sacrifice. Just like Hebrews 13.16, as we will see hereafter (p. 63), it clearly identifies *spiritual sacrifices acceptable to God* with active commitment to living the Christian life.

Chapter IV

The Temple as Community in Qumran and the New Testament

There seems to have been an early stratum of Christian thought that had some connection with Qumran. This can be shown by juxtaposing, as in Table 2, the text of 1 Peter 2.5–6 with some texts from the Qumran Dead Sea Scrolls.

---

11 See our treatment of this made-with-hands theme earlier in the chapter on the Acts of the Apostles (p. 54).

Table 2 1 Peter 2.5–6 and Qumran

1 PETER 2.5–6	QUMRAN
and like living stones be yourselves built into a spiritual house	(cf. *4Qflor* 1.6): to build him a sanctuary of [or: 'among'] men a House of Holiness for Israel (*1QS* 8.5; cf. 5.6; 9.6) a House of Perfection and Truth in Israel (*1QS* 8:9)
to be a holy priesthood	it shall be a Holy of Holies for Aaron (*1QS* 8.9) an assembly of the Holy of Holies for Aaron (*1QS* 8.9)
to offer spiritual sacrifices	shall offer up sweet fragrance (*1QS* 8.9)
acceptable to God	they shall be an agreeable offering pleasing to God (*1QS* 8.6)
through Jesus Christ. For it stands in scripture	it shall be that tried wall (*1QS* 8.7)
Behold, I am laying in Zion a chosen stone A precious cornerstone	that precious cornerstone (*1QS* 8.7)
and he who believes in him will not be put to shame	whose foundation shall neither rock nor sway (*1QS* 8.8)

The likelihood that we have here a specifically Christian reworking of Qumran ideas is supported by Paul's words in Second Corinthians:

> What agreement does Christ have with Belial? Or what does a believer share with an unbeliever? What agreement has the temple of God with idols? For we are the temple of the living God.
>
> (2 Cor. 6.15–16)[12]

The evidence, therefore, is quite strong that among the many things that Christianity owes to its Jewish origins is the idea of the community as temple of God.

Chapter V

The Epistle to the Hebrews

Among the things that make the epistle to the Hebrews unique among the New Testament writings is its emphasis on sacrifice. Both in general, and in particular, with regard to sacrifice, the overriding message is the inadequacy of the old and the perfection of the new covenant.

---

12   Some exegetes suspect that these words are not those of Paul, but an interpolation. But if so, this reinforces even more the likelihood that we have here a common early Christian theme.

For if the blood of goats and bulls, with the sprinkling of the ashes of a heifer sanctifies those who have been defiled so that their flesh is purified, how much more will the blood of Christ, who through the eternal Spirit offered himself without blemish to God, purify our conscience from dead works to worship the living God.

(Hebrews 9.13–14)

When he said above, 'You have neither desired nor taken pleasure in sacrifices and offerings and burnt offerings and sin offerings' (these are offered according to the law), then he added, 'See, I have come to do your will.' He abolishes the first in order to establish the second. And it is by God's will that we have been sanctified through the offering of the body of Jesus Christ once for all.

(Hebrews 10.8–10)

Within that message, the sacrificial ministry of Jesus the high priest and the liturgy of the Day of Atonement constitute the central themes and provide the basic structure of the letter. However, since it is quite unlike any other New Testament writing, it is not wise to give it a dominant, controlling position in establishing a New Testament theology of sacrifice, especially since the substance of what it teaches is also found elsewhere, especially in Paul[13] who also gives a much broader view of a Christian theology of sacrifice.

A. THE SACRIFICE OF CHRIST THE HIGH PRIEST

The Epistle to the Hebrews sees Christ the high priest prefigured in the mysterious Melchizedek figure from the time of Abraham. From the first Melchizedek passage we read:

In the days of his flesh, Jesus offered up prayers and supplications, with loud cries and tears, to the one who was able to save him from death, and he was heard because of his reverent submission. Although he was a Son, he learned obedience through what he suffered; and having been made perfect, he became the source of eternal salvation for all who obey him, having been designated by God a high priest according to the order of Melchizedek.

(Hebrews 5.7–10)[14]

The allusion to the theme of the Suffering Messiah is unmistakable. So too is the proclamation of the physical reality of the redemptive incarnation of Jesus: 'For we do not have a high priest who is unable to sympathize with our weaknesses, but we

13 Although some traditional lectionaries insist on naming Paul as the author of the Epistle to the Hebrews – and much of the thought in the epistle is indeed Pauline – the earliest and best opinion, while listing it as among the inspired books, states that we simply do not know who the author was.

14 The main Melchizedek passages are Hebrews 5.5–10 (which quotes Psalm 110.4) and 7.1–10. They refer, of course to the mysterious priest-king figure in Genesis 14.17–20 who brought out bread and wine and blessed Abraham.

have one who in every respect has been tested as we are, yet without sin.'[15] The central message is that Jesus redeemed us by offering himself to God as a sin offering in the full, realistic, biblical sense of the word. In the new cult, Jesus the high priest is both the offering (victim) as well as the one doing the offering in a sacrifice carried out perfectly, once-for-all, and superseding all other sacrifices, physically as well as spiritually.

B. THE SACRIFICE OF/BY THE CHRISTIAN

A principal purpose of Hebrews is to encourage us – i.e. all Christians – as follows: Since Christ the high priest offered himself *for our sakes*,[16] we should not hesitate to *draw near/approach*. This is a technical term signifying the priestly action of approaching the altar to offer sacrifice. The following themes are being power-fully emphasized: (1) that, despite the once-for-all reality of Christ's sacrifice, sacrificial redemption in us remains a continuing process; (2) the theme of uni-versal priesthood; (3) the spiritualization of sacrifice. Strikingly, the same struc-tural function that Rom. 12.1–2 exercises in moving the reader from the earlier doctrinal to the later exhortatory part of the letter is served by the following passage in this letter:

> [19]Therefore, my friends, since we have confidence to enter the sanctuary by the blood of Jesus, [20]by the new and living way that he opened for us through the curtain (that is, through his flesh), [21]and since we have a great high priest over the house of God, [22]let us approach with a true heart in full assurance of faith, with our hearts sprinkled clean from an evil conscience and our bodies washed with pure water. [23]Let us hold fast to the confession of our hope without wavering, for he who has promised is faithful. [24]And let us consider how to provoke one another to love and good deeds, [25]not neglecting to meet together, as is the habit of some, but encouraging one another, and all the more as you see the Day approaching.
>
> (Hebrews 10.19–25)

If we are reading this letter as Pauline in theme, and therefore aware of the implication that Christian sacrifice is the practical living out of the Christian life, the next verse becomes stunningly powerful:

> [26]For if we willingly persist in sin after having received the knowledge of the truth, there no longer remains a sacrifice for sins, [27]but a fearful prospect of judgment.
>
> (Hebrews 10.26–27)

---

15 Hebrews 4.15. See also 9.26 and 13.12. These texts also reflect the same abasement-exaltation theme as Phil. 2.5–11 and Luke 24.26. Like Paul, the author of Hebrews, in focusing on the big picture and his central message, had little concern for accuracy of technical detail regarding the Hebrew-biblical rites which he mentions.
16 Hebrews 2.9; 5.1; 6.20; 7.25; 9.24; 10.12.

In other words, the only sacrifice that is real – i.e. effective for the forgiveness of sins – is the practical living out of the Christian life! This is powerfully confirmed by the final explicitly sacrificial text in Hebrews:

> [10]We have an altar from which those who officiate in the tent have no right to eat. [11]For the bodies of those animals whose blood is brought into the sanctuary by the high priest as a sacrifice for sin are burned outside the camp. [12]Therefore Jesus also suffered outside the city gate in order to sanctify the people by his own blood. [13]Let us then go to him outside the camp and bear the abuse he endured. [14]For here we have no lasting city, but we are looking for the city that is to come. [15]Through him, then, let us continually offer a sacrifice of praise to God, that is, the fruit of lips that confess his name. [16]Do not neglect to do good and to share what you have, for such sacrifices are pleasing to God.
>
> (Hebrews 13.10–16)

But just before this is a powerful passage in which the barriers between heaven and earth seem to be dismantled, giving the impression that the sacrificial activity of Christians, even now, is already part of the heavenly liturgy:

> [18]You have not come to something that can be touched, a blazing fire, and darkness, and gloom, and a tempest, [19]and the sound of a trumpet, and a voice whose words made the hearers beg that not another word be spoken to them. [20](For they could not endure the order that was given, 'If even an animal touches the mountain, it shall be stoned to death.' [21]Indeed so terrifying was the sight that Moses said, 'I tremble with fear.') [22]But you have come to Mount Zion and to the city of the living God, the heavenly Jerusalem, and to innumerable angels in festal gathering, [23]and to the assembly of the firstborn who are enrolled in heaven, and to God the Judge of all, and to the spirits of the righteous made perfect, [24]and to Jesus, the mediator of a new covenant, and to the sprinkled blood that speaks a better word than the blood of Abel.
>
> (Hebrews 12.18–24)

There is a similar structure or pattern in each of the three major Christian-life-as-sacrifice texts in Hebrews: (1) the idea of the OT cult being superseded by the New Testament cult in which the believer is exhorted to take part, (2) the exhortatory supportive argument is presented in the context of expectation of the parousia (second coming of Christ) and (3) direct exhortation to offer spiritual sacrifices. This pattern seems to represent a characteristic way of preaching in the primitive Church.

Chapter VI

The Gospel and First Letter of John

Tradition has often assumed that these two works come from the hand of John the Apostle. Although critical exegesis is unable to confirm that this is indeed the case, exegetes do generally agree that they at least come from the same hand.[17]

A. TEMPLE THEMES

The theme of the Christian community as the new temple, although not as developed as in Paul, is much more developed, at least implicitly, than it is in the Synoptic Gospels. 'The Word . . . dwelt (literally "pitched his tent") among us' (Jn 1.14) evokes the desert tent of meeting which became, later, the Most Holy Place of the temple. John's account of the cleansing of the temple (Jn 2.13–22) occurs at the first of John's three Passovers, and explicitly mentions the animals used for sacrifice. Further, Jesus' mention of true worship 'in spirit and in truth (Jn 4.23–24) seems both to be liberating sacrificial worship from location in a particular place (the temple) and also to be implicitly introducing a Christologizing spiritualization of sacrifice'.

In addition there are two striking texts that make sense only in the context of the centrality of the temple theme in John:

> On the last day of the festival, the great day, while Jesus was standing there [in the temple], he cried out, 'let anyone who is thirsty come to me, and let the one who believes in me drink. As the scripture has said, "Out of the believer's heart shall flow rivers of living water" '.
>
> (Jn 7.37–38)

> But when they came to Jesus and saw that he was already dead, they did not break his legs. Instead, one of the soldiers pierced his side with a spear, and at once blood and water came out. (He who saw this has testified so that you also may believe. . . . These things occurred so that the scripture might be fulfilled, 'None of his bones shall be broken.'
>
> (Jn 19.33–36)

In the Hebrew religious imagination at the time of Jesus, the source of life-giving water is under the rock on which the temple is built. That rock was also seen and revered as the first solid thing that emerged from the watery chaos out of which

---

17 See Raymond E. Brown, *The Gospel According to John* (Anchor Bible, 29, 2 vols; New York: Doubleday, 1966–1970) and Rudolf Schnackenburg, *Das Johannesevangelium* (HTKNT, IV/1–3; 3 vols; Freiburg/Vienna: Herder, 1967–75); idem, *Die Johannesbriefe.* (HTKNT, XIII/3; Freiburg/Vienna: Herder, 1953).

God created the earth. This was what was behind Ezekiel's striking vision of 'water flowing from below the threshold of the temple' (Ezek. 47.1). In the first passage, Jesus is pointing to himself, and to those who are one with him, as the new source of life-giving water. In the second passage, which evokes the memory of the first, the extraordinary emphasis of the Evangelist regarding the water as well as the blood flowing from Christ's side, and the allusion to the non-breaking of the bones of the Passover lambs, deeply emphasize the temple/sacrifice theme.

B. SACRIFICIAL SELF-GIVING

The same intimate association found in Paul and Hebrews between the sacrifice of Christ and the sacrifice of (i.e. by) Christians is also richly witnessed to in the Johannine writings. This is found first in the numerous (at least implicitly sacrificial) 'for you/for us' themes and statements, including the unforgettable 'God so loved the world that he gave his only Son, so that everyone who believes in him may not perish but may have eternal life (Jn 3.16), and the Good Shepherd laying down his life for his sheep (Jn 10.11, 15). In the washing-of-the-feet, the opening event of Jesus' Last-Supper discourse, Jesus exhorts us, as he did in the Synoptic Gospels, that we should do for others what he has done for us. The first letter of John makes sure that we don't miss the point:

> We know love by this, that he laid down his life for us – and we ought to lay down our lives for one another.
>
> (1 Jn 3.16; see also 4.10–11)

C. SIN OFFERING AND ATONEMENT THEMES

These themes figure prominently in John's first letter. A typical passage (that also shows similarity with Paul on this theme) is:

> My little children, I am writing these things to you so that you may not sin. But if anyone does sin, we have an advocate with the Father, Jesus Christ the righteous; and he is the atoning sacrifice for our sins, and not for ours only but also for the sins of the whole world.
>
> (1 Jn 2.1–2)

Even more emphatically than do the Synoptic Gospels, John sees Christ's death as a Passover event. It takes place, for example, at the precise time when the Passover lambs were being slaughtered in the Temple for the third of the three Passovers that frame this Gospel.[18] In addition the branch of hyssop lifted to the mouth of the dying Jesus in Jn 19.29 recalls the blood rite of the first Passover in Egypt.

---

18   This means that, according to the chronology of John's Gospel, the Last Supper itself, though obviously taking place within the framework of the Passover celebration, could not have been a Passover meal. The chronology of the Synoptic Gospels is different. Opinion is divided as to whether the Last Supper was an actual Passover supper, or simply a religious meal taking place within the framework of the Passover celebration.

Finally, the comparison with the Passover lambs, 'None of his bones shall be broken' (19.36) is explicit.

Chapter VII

The History-of-Religions Context of 'Worship in Spirit and in Truth'

The uniquely central passage for this theme is in Jesus' words to the Samaritan woman in Chapter 4 of the Gospel of John:

> But the hour is coming and is now here, when the true worshipers will worship the Father in spirit and truth, for the Father seeks such as these to worship him. God is spirit, and those who worship him must worship in spirit and truth.
>
> (Jn 4.23–24)

At first glance, and especially if taken out of context, one could think that this was coming from the Greek-philosophical concept of spiritualization and the idea that religions are more pure the more they are separated from the material and the bodily. But this would be a massive misunderstanding of John's antidocetic, incarnational, sacramental Christology. The main point being made is not just that the temple is passé, but primarily that true worship is in no sense something that can be done 'in the flesh', i.e., by merely human means, but only 'in the Spirit' (i.e., in Christ).

Chapter VIII

The Book of Revelation

From the beginning of Chapter 4 through to the beginning of the epilogue in Revelation 22.8, this book is a series of visions of the heavenly sanctuary seen after the model of the Jerusalem temple. The narrator finds himself, in his visions, looking into the Most Holy Place where the throne of God is situated, from a position – not unlike the position from which Isaiah had his famous temple vision (Isaiah 6) – that was apparently in the vicinity of the altar of sacrifice (which he does not mention). This is at least the starting point for all the visions in the Book of Revelation (see Table 3):

Table 3 Temple topography in the Book of Revelation

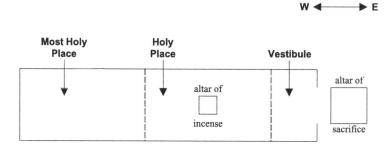

A. THE THRONE OF GOD

The throne of God – in the visions, this would be 'located' in the Most Holy Place – almost identified with God himself, as was also the case in Hebrews 4.16, 8.1, and 12.2, is the centre of the visions. Many have remarked on the parallel between what Jesus says at the (Lukan) Last Supper and here in Revelation 3.21:

> You are those who have stood by me in my trials; and I confer on you, just as my Father has conferred on me, a kingdom, so that you may eat and drink at my table in my kingdom, and you will sit on thrones judging the twelve tribes of Israel.
>
> (Luke 22.28–30)

> To the one who conquers I will give a place with me on my throne, just as I myself conquered and sat down with my Father on his throne.
>
> (Revelation 3.21)

But even more striking is how thoroughly Johannine this is in teaching that Jesus' followers are given the same mission, power, and glory that Jesus shares with the Father.[19]

B. THE LAMB

The most frequent Christological title given to Jesus in the book of Revelation is 'the Lamb' (28 times). The several references to the Lamb as slain and to the 'blood of the Lamb' leave no doubt that the Lamb of the Apocalypse/book of Revelation is the crucified and glorified Lord who appears now in heaven in the form of a sacrificial lamb. These references suggest sin offering and/or Passover sacrifice, but the most significant background likelihood seems to be that of the Lamb as Servant of God from Isaiah 53; for only here do we have a personal title capable of carrying the full breadth of Christological meaning associated with the title: the Lamb.

---

19 See Jn 6.57; 13.12–15; 17.7–10, 20–26; 20.21–23.

C. The Incense Offering

Despite the fact that the heavenly temple is the scene for the whole Book of Revelation, only one specific Jewish sacrificial ceremony is mentioned: the incense offering:

> When he ['a Lamb standing as if it had been slaughtered'] had taken the scroll, the four living creatures and the twenty-four elders fell before the Lamb, each holding a harp and golden bowls full of incense, which are the prayers of the saints.
>
> (Revelation 5.8; see also 8.1–4)

This shows, among other things, the Jewish origin of the early Christian close association of incense/altar of incense with the prayers of the souls of the martyrs and saints.[20]

Revelation uses the same basic imagery of the heavenly liturgy as Hebrews. But the similarity ends there. Hebrews is a very down-to-earth, this-worldly book, never moving far from the practical concerns of the Christian life. Revelation however, never descends from the heavenly sanctuary except, at the end, to speak of the New Jerusalem 'coming down out of heaven from God' (Revelation 21.2) at the end of time. Thus, the final book of the Christian Bible actually adds very little to the Christian theology of sacrifice.

Chapter IX

Summary of New Testament Teaching on Christian Sacrifice

Here in Bridge 1 B we have laid out the biblical evidence that underlies the specifically Christian or Trinitarian understanding of sacrifice with which we began in Part One of this book. In laying out this evidence, we claim to have proven two main, culminating points. First, the full New Testament and, by implication, Christian, and thus, implicitly and ultimately, Trinitarian theology of sacrifice can be helpfully arranged under what we found to be the threefold Pauline division: (1) the sacrifice of Christ, (2) Christian(s) as the new temple, (3) the sacrifice(s) offered by Christians. The second and no less important main point is that modern critical exegesis can demonstrate beyond reasonable doubt that the primary idea of Christian sacrifice that is revealed in the New Testament – i.e. of sacrifices that Christians offer – is not liturgical or ritual but first and foremost ethical and practical. This is, in other words, anything but just homiletic exagger-

---

20 See also Phil. 2.17 and 2 Tim. 4.6

ation or pious rhetoric. It is a scientific exegetical conclusion that flows quite simply and directly from reading in context, as we have done, those five New Testament passages that speak of sacrifices that are offered by Christians: Rom. 12.1–2; Rom. 15.15–16; 1Peter 2.4–10; Hebrews 10.19–25; Hebrews 12.18–13.16. Christian sacrifice is a liturgy of life.

Excursus 3
Spiritualization and Institutionalization

Spiritualization is a term that is open to a great variety of meanings. Some of its common synonyms, listed in random alphabetical order, are *dematerializing, deepening, ethicizing, humanizing, interiorizing, rationalizing, sublimating, symbolizing*, etc. None of these is adequate, nor are they adequate even when taken cumulatively. And some of them, such as 'dematerializing', can be positively misleading. A rationalist approach, for example, that builds narrowly on what can be learned from the discipline of comparative religions, tends to assume that cultic worship is imperfect to the extent that it is material, and perfect to the extent that it is immaterial. Someone working from that approach will tend to think of 'true' sacrifice in terms of a radical dematerialization of it. But such an understanding of spiritualization is clearly at odds both with the Christian Scriptures and with the incarnational thinking of the founding figures of Christian theology: Paul, Barnabas, Irenaeus, Hyppolytus, the two Clements, Origen, Augustine, etc. Right from the outset, Paul, seems to go out of this way to make this clear:

> I appeal to you, therefore, brothers and sisters, by the mercies of God, to present your bodies as a living sacrifice, holy and acceptable to God, which is your spiritual worship.
>
> (Rom. 12.1)

In this pivotal passage, as we have already pointed out (pp. 57–58), the incarnational-sacrificial implications of the phrase *present your bodies as a living sacrifice* are strikingly contrary to any anti-material interpretation. Then, to speak of this as *spiritual worship* (language used by Greek religious philosophy to describe the worship proper to a purely spiritual deity) is telling. It is indeed spiritualized sacrifice that Paul is talking about, but also and most emphatically sacrifice that is embodied in practical, incarnational, en-Spirited Christian living. A dematerializing understanding of spiritualization thus cannot be the meaning we attribute to it in this study.

The much broader sense in which we are using the term includes all those tendencies within Judaism and Christianity that attempted to emphasize the true meaning of sacrifice: the inner, spiritual or ethical significance of the cult over against the merely material or merely external understanding of it.

Included are such different things as: (1) the effort by Jews to make their material sacrifice an expression of an ethically good life; (2) the prophets' criticism of the sacrificial cult; (3) the philosophically influenced doubts about the sense or propriety of offering material sacrifice to a spiritual God; (4) the necessity of finding substitutes for material sacrifice when participation in the sacrificial cult of the Jerusalem temple was not possible, as in Qumran, or in the diaspora, or after the destruction of the temple; (5) and of course we also include with special emphasis the various practices in the areas of cult and worship, and in their practical understanding of the 'liturgy of life,' in which Christians understood that the old economy of salvation had been sublated into something radically new.

All of these had in common a certain shift in emphasis from the material to the spiritual. But their attitudes towards and understanding of this shift could vary greatly. For example, Philo's typically Platonic disesteem of things material was in deep contrast to the incarnational thought of Christians who, even in their most Platonizing moments, could never forget that God had come to them in Jesus Christ, in the flesh, and that they were called, as Paul put it, to offer their bodies as spiritual worship (Rom. 12.1).[21]

A. SPIRITUALIZATION IN THE EARLY CHURCH[22]

If we are tempted to try to avoid completely any use of the language of sacrifice on the grounds that we do not offer animals or other material gifts in sacrifice, and still less believe that the forgiveness of sins is tied up with certain sacrificial blood rites, we have to remind ourselves that the early Christians also did not offer animals or other material gifts in sacrifice. They too did not believe that the forgiveness of sins was tied up with sacrificial blood rites. Nevertheless, despite their fierce rejection of pagan and Jewish sacrifice, a rejection that caused many of their religious neighbours to think of them as irreligious, the early Christians continued to speak not only of the sacrifice of Christ but also of themselves as the 'new temple'. They spoke in sacrificial terms of their lives, as members of the Body of Christ and as 'living stones' in this new temple. In Part One we sketched out in Trinitarian and incarnational terms what we believe that the early Christians were groping to express when, hesitatingly at first, but then ever more explicitly, they used sacrificial terms to speak of themselves, their lives, and their religious celebrations. Our task now is to portray in broad brush strokes how this came about.

A sweeping overview uncovers two distinct trends in the origin and development of the Christian concept of sacrifice. There is a primary, spiritualizing trend that begins deep in the Hebrew Scriptures and culminates in the Christ-

---

21   Philo was a Greek-speaking Jewish religious philosopher who lived in Alexandria (the 'second Athens') in the first half of the first Christian century. He exercised great influence (ironically more influence than on Jewish thinking) on Christian theological thinking in the first few centuries. Platonism and/or Neoplatonism provided the philosophical toolbox for much early Christian theology, much in the same way that Aristotelianism later did for the theology of Thomas Aquinas.

22   See Daly, *The Origins*, pp. 135–40.

event. Within that dynamic we can distinguish three significant phases. Then, beginning in early Christian times, and at least partially in tension with this primary, spiritualizing trend, there is a secondary, institutionalizing trend. This trend, at times, seems to be a reinstitutionalizing trend.

(1) The *first phase* of the spiritualizing trend begins deep in the Hebrew biblical tradition. The tenth-century Yahwistic (J) accounts of Noah's sacrifice (Genesis 8) and the sacrifices of Cain and Abel (Genesis 4) insist implicitly – quite explicitly if we consider the full biblical context – on the importance of the religious dispositions with which one offers sacrifice. This spiritualizing trend is clearly at work in the dynamic of *the divine acceptance of sacrifice*,[23] especially in the insistence that it is God and not the human being who decides what is acceptable. At a first reading, the reason why God does or does not accept a particular sacrifice may seem to be arbitrary. But as salvation history progresses, this reason does not remain concealed in the inscrutability of the divine will. It is progressively revealed not only in the covenant theology of the Deuteronomists who, in the historical books, are the primary narrators of Israel's off-again, on-again love affair with Yahweh. It is also revealed in the sometimes quite fierce criticism of the prophets who point out that sacrifices by those failing to live up to the demands of justice and mercy are simply 'not acceptable', to God, and indeed even 'hateful' in God's eyes.

Despite the conclusions of some modern scholars who have read this criticism of sacrificial practice as a direct attack on sacrifice itself, this first phase of spiritualization clearly does not do away with the material sacrificial system, but, rather, continues to assume its validity. The clear lesson, however, is that the system of material sacrifice – and, by powerful implication, all external religious observance – has no validity, has no meaning, or simply does not 'work', without the proper religious and ethical dispositions of its participants.

(2) In the *second phase* of the spiritualizing trend, largely a post-exilic development, the dynamic center of sacrifice – i.e. what makes it 'work' – clearly shifts away from the external ceremony and to the internal dispositions. An obvious catalyst for this shift was the experience of exile, of diaspora, or, as in the case of Qumran, of sectarian separation. Increasing numbers of Jews, increasingly the great majority of them, and finally, after the destruction of the temple in 70 CE, all members of the Jewish religious community who continued to believe in the necessity of material sacrifice for the restoration of and maintenance of their good relationship with God, were prevented from participating in ritual sacrifice. For the temple in Jerusalem had come to be seen as the only place where valid sacrifice could be offered. In response to this desperate situation, the notion increasingly took hold that what made sacrifice 'work' for reconciliation, atonement and union with God was not the

---

23 See the section under this title earlier in Bridge 1 A. [MS pp. 11–13]

actual performance of the sacrifices, but the fact that they were performed *according to the Law*, i.e., in accordance with the will of God.

This, for example, is what made it possible, and indeed psychologically necessary, for the members of the Qumran community to see themselves, their community, and their individual good works as the temple and the sacrifices that achieved atonement. It also helped make it possible for the religion of Judaism to survive the loss of the temple. Once the value and effectiveness of sacrifice was seen to be precisely in its dynamic as an act of obedience, it was a logical, 'natural' step towards seeing other acts of obedient piety as being able to accomplish that which, previously, could have been accomplished only by ritual sacrifice.

In this context, Philo, a mid-first-century contemporary of St. Paul, writing in diaspora Alexandria, grants only symbolic significance to the external action or ceremony. His basically Platonistic philosophy helps explain the extremity of this position. Some of this antimaterial bias and susceptibility to dualistic thinking that was very much in the air at that time also affected some of the early Christian thinkers. But they, except perhaps for some of the heretical Gnostics, were generally protected from its extremes by their belief in the goodness of God's material creation and in the historical, physical reality of the incarnation of the Logos. Their fundamental incarnational faith led them to know with comfortable certitude that Christian sacrifice, both in its perfect realization in Jesus Christ and in its imperfect realization in the followers of Christ, is both a spiritual *and* a bodily reality.

(3) The *third and culminating phase* of the spiritualization trend in the overall dynamic of Christian sacrifice is, thus, specifically Christian. It is incarnational, and might even be called a 'Christologization' of sacrifice. This incarnational spiritualization takes up and moves beyond the initial phase where dispositions are emphasized while ceremonial action remains central. It also takes up and moves beyond the second phase where ceremonial action becomes almost superfluous. And then it moves beyond that to a third and culminating phase where, to the vital importance of proper dispositions is now added the importance of embodying/incarnating proper dispositions in human action: the performance of down-to-earth, practical, diaconal, ministerial and apostolic works of the Christian life. That this is much more than just a possible interpretation; and that it identifies what is at the heart of authentic Christian sacrifice, is verified by the fact, as we have pointed out several times, most recently in the summary section just preceding this Excursus, that all five of the New Testament passages that seem to talk about Christian sacrificial activity do so in practical, ethical terms.

(4) Nevertheless, however complete this may sound, we still don't have a theologically mature *concept* of Christians sacrifice. That requires the recognition and appropriation of sacrifice as a *Trinitarian* event. This, as one can gather from Part One, requires recognition that authentic Christian sacrifice begins with the self-offering of the Father in the gift of the Son, and requires the self-offering response of the Son in his humanity and in the power of the

Holy Spirit, and requires, finally, that Christians, in the power of the same Spirit that was in Jesus, enter by their life of self-giving into that Trinitarian Father–Son relationship. That, of course, was what was actually happening in Christian sacrificial activity long before this Trinitarian theology had been worked out by the Fathers of the Church, and long, long before the twentieth century when theologians like Edward Kilmartin could make the connections and explicitly articulate a Trinitarian theology of Christian sacrifice. Ultimately, then, taking seriously God's universal salvific will, the fundamental reality of Christian sacrifice – i.e., that which really makes it 'work' – has been practiced from human time immemorial. For, it has actually been happening whenever human beings have genuinely given themselves to each other in love. For all love is from God, and there is only one God and one Spirit of God.

B. Institutionalization in the Early Church[24]

However, somewhat in tension with this primary spiritualizing trend in the early Church, there is also a secondary, institutionalizing trend. The significance of this fact is not only for its value in terms of the historical record, but also in terms of its contribution to an understanding of contemporary developments in the Church, all the more so since it is in the early development of the *Eucharist* that this institutionalizing trend is located. We have already shown that the primitive Church saw the Eucharist as sacrificial.[25] Can we recover with any precision what concept or concepts of sacrifice might have been operative in these early Christian Eucharistic celebrations?

First, the texts of these celebrations seem to assume without question and without exception what we have just described as the first two phases of the spiritualization process. Second, what we have described as the third, Christian-incarnational phase of the spiritualization process is also supported in these texts by considerable evidence. For when we asked of these texts what concept of 'sacrificial action' seemed to be operative in the celebration of the Eucharist, we found that it did not appear to be, at least not primarily and not solely, the actual performance of the ceremony or the ritual action of the bishop or president of the assembly. It seemed to be primarily the *prayer* of the presider or of the assembly. Prayer was, of course, one of those actions that, in the spiritualization process, had come to be seen as replacing material sacrifice.

But then, in Justin, Irenaeus, and especially Hippolytus, one can detect growing evidence of an institutionalizing trend which not only tends to institutionalize Christian Eucharistic worship, it also begins to reintroduce what

---

24   See Daly, *The Origins*, pp. 135–40.
25   We are painting here in very broad brush strokes; 'Eucharist' in the primitive Church was anything but a univocal concept. For example, just within the Christian Scriptures (New Testament) alone, one can identify as many as six different ways of celebrating table fellowship, celebrations we commonly label as Eucharists. See Robert J. Daly, S.J., 'Eucharistic Origins: From the New Testament to the Liturgies of the Golden Age', *Theological Studies* 66 (2005), pp. 3–22.

seems to have been superseded at least initially in the second, but certainly and definitively in the third phase of the spiritualizing trend: namely the idea that the performance of the ritual action is a sacrifice. Strongly sacramental traditions such as Roman Catholicism have resonated vibrantly with this and tend to find in such texts early evidence for their traditional theology of the Sacrifice of the Mass.

The full history of the tension between these institutionalizing and spiritualizing trends cannot yet be written. The whole matter is still being thrashed out, ecumenically, between the Christian churches and, theologically, within many of the individual Christian confessions. Ironically, and quite in contrast to the situation of several decades ago, tension on the ecumenical level has, at least theologically, abated considerably. There is an impressively growing ecumenical convergence on the theological understanding of the Eucharist and of the Eucharist as sacrifice. Within the different churches however, and especially, it seems, within Roman Catholicism in the early years of the twenty-first century, the tension between theologians supporting and contributing to this ecumenical convergence and theologians wishing to maintain exclusivist traditionalist approaches seems to be growing.

END OF EXCURSUS 3

Bridge 1 C

Sacrifice in the Fathers of the Church

The faith, the practice and the writings of the early Christians have traditionally been considered to be normative models for the faith and practice of later Christians. While this remains basically true, we are now much more aware of plurality and diversity in early Christianity. For example, historically informed theologians no longer assume that there is a clear line of doctrinal development from the New Testament and the early Fathers[1] to the great councils of the fourth and fifth centuries. Nor, in this ecumenical age, do theologians search the patristic period only for those teachings that support a particular confessional position. Thus, although post-modern sensitivity makes us instinctively suspicious of 'great stories' or overarching explanations, our abiding Christian sensitivity nevertheless makes us confident of the fundamental truth of the 'Christian story'. And although more hermeneutically suspicious than our forbears, we remain confident that there are important continuities between the past and the present. It is with all this in mind that we will be looking to see whether and to what extent the scheme that enabled us to get some sense of the overarching unity of New Testament teaching on sacrifice, the Pauline triple division of sacrificial themes – sacrifice of Christ, the new temple and Christian sacrificial activity – can provide a helpful focus for our reading of the patristic data.

Chapter I

The Early Writings

The *Didache*, Clement of Rome, Ignatius of Antioch, the Shepherd of Hermas and Polycarp of Smyrna[2] are the earliest of the post-biblical Christian writings. They all have something to say about sacrifice.

---

1 The term 'Fathers of the Church' refers to those early Christian teachers – up to John of Damascus in the East (d. 749) and Gregory the Great in the West (d. 604) – who established the foundations of orthodox Christian doctrine. The term 'patristics' or 'patristic period' refers more broadly to all that was going on at this time.
2 The *Didache* is a brief, anonymous Greek document, a primitive church order that, theologically at least, antedates the gospels. Clement of Rome, Pope (ca. 96) is recognized as the author of two Epistles to the Corinthians. Ignatius (ca. 37–ca. 107), bishop of Antioch, is the author of seven letters written while being brought by military guard to Rome for martyrdom. *The Shepherd of Hermas* is a somewhat moralizing allegorical work from the mid-second century that was highly regarded in early Christianity. Polycarp (ca. 69–155), bishop of Smyrna, is the author of an *Epistle to the Philippians*.

As for the *Didache*, the earliest extant document on 'church order', there is little agreement about the precise time and place of its provenance. However, recent scholarship[3] tends to date it earlier, perhaps even prior to the gospels, rather than later. The theologically and christologically 'primitive' prayers in Chapters 9 and 10 are referred to as 'Eucharist', and the act of praying them as 'eucharistizing'. It is likely, but not certain, that this is what is being referred to when chapter 14 refers to the liturgy of the Sunday assembly as 'your sacrifice' (14.1), before which there must be confession of sins and fraternal reconciliation 'so that your sacrifice may be pure' (14.2). Then, the rephrasing of Malachi 1.11 as a divine command rather than as a prophecy, 'In every place and time, offer to me a pure sacrifice' (14.3) suggests that the author is at home with the idea of the Eucharist as sacrifice. However, apart from the obvious implication that 'sacrifice' is something that Christians do in their weekly gathering, there is no further indication of what is meant by this.

Clement, Bishop of Rome (ca. 96) emphasizes, as did the Hebrew Scriptures and the Jewish tradition before him, that true sacrifice is according to the will of God. He also spiritualizes sacrifice by a strategic use of some of the spiritualizing Psalm texts. But also, in a manner unique among the early Fathers, his startling reformulation of Malachi 1.11 manifests a concern to institutionalize sacrifice (apparently meaning the Eucharist) within the liturgical life of the Church: 'Not in every place, brethren, are the daily sacrifices offered, . . . but in Jerusalem only. And even there they are not offered in any place, but only at the altar before the temple' (*1 Clement*, 41.2). Clement sees offering sacrifice as the characteristic function of the priestly office (*1 Clement*, 44.3–4). However, similar to the *Didache*, he leaves it unclear precisely what he means by 'sacrifice'; nor is it clear why, almost three decades after the AD 70 destruction of the Temple, he continues to speak of temple worship in the present tense.

With Ignatius of Antioch a decade later,[4] the threefold Pauline division begins to become a helpful point of reference. The idea of the sacrifice of Christ is implicit throughout his letters. When he addresses the Ephesians 'as being stones in the temple of the Father',[5] he gives the temple theme from 1 Peter 2.4–10 a further and specifically ecclesiastical development by seeing the 'one altar' or the state of being 'within the altar' as symbols of church unity.[6] As for Christian sacrificial activity, in contrast to the way Paul seemed to think of this as expressing the broad range of Christian life, Ignatius seems to be thinking, more narrowly, just of martyrdom. But the graphically realistic way in which he does look ahead to his martyrdom is unforgettable. Remove the (implicitly Eucharistic) Christ-mysticism from these words and they can strike the modern reader as almost masochistic:

---

3 For example, see Aaron Milavec, *The Didache: Faith, Hope, & Life of the Earliest Christian Communities* (New York/Mahwah, NJ: Newman Press, 2003); Huub van de Sandt, ed., *Matthew and the Didache: Two Documents from the Same Jewish-Christian Milieu* (Assen: Royal Van Gorcum/ Minneapolis, MN: Fortress, 2005).
4 Although they are close to each other in time, there is no indication that Clement and Ignatius actually knew each other or each other's works.
5 Ignatius, *Letter to the Ephesians*, 9.1.
6 Cf. Ignatius, to the *Ephesians*, 5.2; *Philadelphians*, 4; 7.2; *Trallians*, 7.2; *Magnesians*, 7.2.

I am the wheat of God, and let me be ground by the teeth of the wild beasts that I may be found the pure bread of Christ . . . then shall I truly be a disciple of Christ, when the world shall not see so much as my body. Entreat Christ for me, that by these instruments I may be found a sacrifice [to God].

(*Rom.*, 4.1–2)

The *Shepherd of Hermas* speaks of fasting as sacrifice (*Sim.*, 5.3). This author also may be alluding to the living-stones temple image when he speaks of the Church as a tower under construction (*Vis.*, 3.2–4.3; 7.6). When we come to Polycarp, we find that he mostly just repeats already current stock phrases of Christian piety. The one exception is that, when he calls widows 'the altar of God' (*Polycarp to the Philippians*, 4.3), he may have been the first Christian writer to take up the idea, prominent in Philo, of the individual person as an altar.

Chapter II

The Apologists: Justin and Athenagoras

Justin Martyr[7] is the first Christian writer to treat sacrifice as a theological question. The clear, 'up-front' purpose of this theology is a fierce polemical rejection of both pagan and Jewish sacrifice, often unfairly identifying the latter with the former. This polemic included not just the common philosophical argument regarding the impropriety of offering material sacrificed to the spiritual God, but also the specifically religious condemnation of sacrifice (even Jewish sacrifice) as an idolatry inspired by evil spirits. This fierce anti-Judaism, however, does not prevent him from taking from the Jewish cult much of its implicit theology, especially the theology of the divine acceptance of sacrifice (*1 Apology*, 37–39; *Trypho*, 12.3; 15.4; 28.5; 40.4), and the idea that atonement is the purpose of sacrifice (*Trypho*, 22.1; 40.4; 41.1; 111.3–4; 112.1–2).

Reference to the Pauline triple division is helpful, but precisely because of the total absence of the *temple theme*. Since this theme would have been very congenial to Justin, its absence suggests that he did not know Paul's letters. As for theme of the *sacrifice of Christ*, Justin adds to its development both in the way that he sees Christ as the typological fulfillment of the Passover sacrifice (*Trypho*, 40.1–2; 72.1; 111.3), and in the way that he continues to develop the tradition of seeing Christ as an offering for sin (*Trypho*, 40.4; 111.4).

In view of Justin's anti-sacrifice polemic, one might expect him to be reserved on the theme of *Christian sacrificial activity*. But no; he aggressively appropriates it

---

7 Justin Martyr lived from ca. 100–ca. 165. His three writings, two *Apologies* and a *Dialogue with Trypho the Jew* come from the last decade of his life when he was living in Rome.

for his Christian view of life. Toward the end of the *Dialogue with Trypho*, we find Justin's most important statement on sacrifice.

> And so, anticipating all the sacrifices which we offer through this name, and which Jesus the Christ commanded us to offer, i.e., in the Eucharist of the bread and the cup, and which are presented by Christians in every place throughout the world [cf. Mal. 1.10–12], God himself bears witness that they are pleasing to him. But he utterly rejects the sacrifices presented by you and by those priests of yours, saying, 'And I will not accept your sacrifices at your hands; for from the rising of the sun to its setting my name is glorified among the Gentiles (he says); but you profane it' [Mal. 1.10–12]. Yet even now in your love of contention you assert that God does not accept the sacrifices of those who then dwelt in Jerusalem and were called Israelites. But you say that he is pleased with the prayers of the individuals of that nation then dispersed, and you call their prayers sacrifices. Now, that prayers and giving thanks, when offered by worthy men, are the only perfect and pleasing sacrifices to God, I also admit. For such sacrifices are what Christians alone have undertaken to offer; and they do this in the remembrance effected by their solid and liquid food whereby the suffering endured by the Son of God is brought to mind.
>
> (*Trypho*, 117.1–3)

'Sacrifices which we offer' (117.1) indicates that Justin is not speaking of something abstract, but of a concrete, familiar action. He claims that these sacrifices were commanded by Jesus Christ, and identifies them with the Eucharist. Here, as elsewhere in *Trypho* (esp. 4.13), it is clear that Justin is indeed speaking of the Eucharist and is speaking of it as sacrificial. For Justin, Christian sacrifice is the Eucharist. But what, precisely, does he mean by this? The key to the answer is in this passage (specifically in 117.2) that leaves no doubt that Justin's idea of sacrifice by Christians is primarily what we have already found it to be in the New Testament: the spiritualized sacrifice of prayer, especially in the Eucharistic celebration. There is no evidence, however, to suggest that Justin extended his notion of sacrifice – or that it even occurred to him to consider doing so – to include the ritual (or consecratory) action over the gifts of bread and wine.

Justin's fellow apologist, Athenagoras of Athens (ca. AD 177)[8] adds little to what we find in Justin except for what is possibly the earliest use of the term 'bloodless sacrifice' that became so prominent in some of the Church's later Eucharistic Prayers. After repeating the common religio-philosophical insight that God has no need of material sacrifice, Athenagoras adds:

> What need have I of holocausts of which God has no need? – though we do indeed need to offer a bloodless sacrifice and spiritual [or reasonable] worship (*anaimakton thusian . . . logikên . . . latreian.*
>
> (*Plea for the Christians*, 13)

---

8   There is no indication that Athenagoras actually knew the work of Justin.

Chapter III

Irenaeus of Lyons

Just as the Jews were the 'foil' for Justin's theology of sacrifice, for Irenaeus[9] it was the Gnostics. Thus, while repeating the cult criticism of both the Hebrew prophets (*Adv. Haer.*, 4.26.1; 4.29.1–4) and of the philosophers and poets (3.12.11; 4.31.2 and 5), and while reminding us that sacrifices were in fact ordained by God for our benefit (4.31.5), he departs decisively from the position taken by Justin; he sees Old Testament sacrifices not as something rejected by God, but as a providential preparation for Christian sacrifice (4.31.1). For, with the Gnostics in mind, his overriding concern was to stress the unity of and continuity between the two Testaments. Not surprisingly, in a body of work as extensive as that of Irenaeus, the threefold Pauline division of the theology of sacrifice is richly verified.

The idea of the *sacrifice of Christ* pervades his work, though often only implicitly. It comes through loud and clear as in the following passage that can be character-ized as summing up Irenaeus's Christology and soteriology. It portrays the physic-ally real sacrifice of Christ as the very purpose of the Incarnation.

> Thus he united man with God and brought about a communion between them, for we would otherwise have been unable to share in incorruptibility if he had not come to us. For incorruptibility, invisible and imperceptible as it is, would be no help to us; so he became visible that we might be taken up into full communion with incorruptibility. Because we are all connected with the first formation of Adam and were bound to death through disobedience, it was just and necessary that the bonds of death be loosed by him who was made man for us. Because death had established its dominion over the body, it was just and necessary that man who was once defeated by the body, should henceforth be free of its oppres-sion. Thus *the Word was made flesh* [Jn 1.14] in order that sin, destroyed by means of the same flesh through which it had gained its mastery and dominion, should no longer live in us. Thus did our Lord take up the same first formation [as Adam] in his incarnation, in order that he might offer it up in his struggle on behalf of his forefathers, and thus overcome through Adam what had stricken us through Adam.
>
> (*Proof of the Apostolic Preaching*, 31)

Behind this passage, of course, are Irenaeus's well-known theories of 'recapitula-tion' and 'exchange', i.e., the word of God, our Lord Jesus Christ, because of his boundless love became what we are in order to make us what he is.[10] It is not

---

9   Irenaeus (ca. 130–ca. 200), originally from Asia Minor, but eventually bishop of Lyons, thus bridging both East and West, was Christianity's first great theologian. His major work, the five books *Adversus Haereses*, written in Greek, is known to us mostly via a literal Latin translation.
10   See *Adv. Haer.*, 3.18.1; 3.19.1, and bk. 5, Preface.

difficult to recognize here an early articulation of what the later Fathers of the Church will call *theosis* ('divinization' or 'deification').

The *temple theme* is also prominent. But interestingly – and this may be an indication of how early Irenaeus is – he seems to have picked up from Paul only the idea of the individual, but not – at least not explicitly[11] – that of the community, as the new temple. He expands on 1 Cor. 3:16–17 and 6:13–15, and also brings in John 2.19 and 21 to emphasize – obviously against the Gnostics – that our *body* is the temple not merely of God but also of Christ (*Adv. Haer.*, 5.6.2). A pervasive sense of concrete, physical realism that is consistent with his anti-Gnostic concerns is also reflected in his realistic understanding of Eucharistic presence: 'How can they say that the flesh, which is nourished with the body of the Lord and with his blood, goes to corruption, and does not partake of life? . . . But our opinion is in accordance with the Eucharist, and the Eucharist in turn establishes our opinion' (*Adv. Haer.*, 4.31.3). Irenaeus, in pointing out how Jesus (Luke 6:1–5 parr) defends his disciples for plucking grain on the Sabbath by arguing that they too are priests, equivalently continually serving the Lord in the Temple, joins to the temple theme the ideas of universal priesthood and of continual sacrifice (*Adv. Haer.*, 4.17). In effect, Irenaeus, in a way that was not open to Justin because of his anti-Jewish polemic, was giving a further development to the dominical argument which implicitly made the Levitical priesthood a partial model for the Christian priesthood.

As for *Christian sacrificial activity, Adversus Haereses* 4.29.1–32 stands as the most extensive treatment of sacrifice from any second-century Christian source. Within what could stand as a mini treatise on the subject, we read:

> But when he was instructing his disciples to offer to God the first-fruits of his creatures, not as if God needed this but that they themselves might be neither unfruitful nor ungrateful, he took that created thing, bread, and gave thanks, saying: 'this is my body'. And likewise the cup, which is part of that creation to which we belong, he confessed to be his blood, and taught the new oblation of the new covenant. This is what the church, receiving from the apostles, offers to God throughout the whole world, to him who gives for our subsistence the first fruits of his own gifts in the New Testament. This is what Malachi, one of the twelve prophets, thus foretold: 'I have no pleasure in you, says the Lord almighty, and I will not accept sacrifice at your hands. For from the rising of the sun unto its setting my name is glorified among the nations, and in every place incense is offered to my name, and a pure sacrifice; for my name is great among the nations, says the Lord Almighty [Mal 1.10–12]. By this he indicates in the plainest manner that the former people shall indeed cease to make offerings to God, but that in every place sacrifice, indeed pure sacrifice – will be offered to him, and that his name will be glorified among the nations.
>
> (*Adv. Haer.*, 4.29.5)

---

11   *Adv. Haer.*, 4.17, a little further on, does suggest that he was at least open to this idea.

Without doubt, the Eucharist is the sacrifice now offered by Christians throughout the world. But just as with Justin, when we ask precisely what this means, and when we bring this question to the full range of Irenaeus's writings, including when he writes of the 'offering of the church – *ecclesiae oblatio*' in 4.31.1, we find that he is not thinking just of the Eucharist. For him as for those who went before him, the Eucharistic sacrifice itself seems to be primarily one of prayers of praise and thanksgiving.

Irenaeus is basically following, but also helping to establish, main-line Christian tradition in seeing not only the sacrifice of Christ as the purpose of the Incarnation, but also in seeing atonement as the general purpose of sacrifice. But a number of passages, unfortunately available only in Latin translation (thus making it impossible to detect the precise nuance intended by Irenaeus) present the idea of sacrifice as propitiatory, i.e., as a human action designed to have an effect on God. Irenaeus speaks of Jesus 'propitiating God for men – *propitians pro hominibus Deum*' (*Adv. Haer.*, 4.16). He speaks of the true sacrifice 'by offering which they shall appease God – *quod offerentes propitiabuntur Deum*' (*Adv. Haer.*, 4.29.2). These Latin phrases, quite possibly a massive misrepresentation of Irenaeus's original theology, contributed mightily to the establishment in Western Christian thought of at least the language, if not also the idea, of propitiation: the erroneous idea that human beings must somehow placate the divine anger, somehow repair the injury done to God by sin.

Chapter IV

Hippolytus of Rome

We have little information about the facts of the life of Hipolytus (ca. 176–ca. 236), an ecclesiastical writer and Doctor of the Church. He was largely neglected in the West, probably because of his schismatic activities – though he was reconciled to the Church before his death – and because of the fact that he wrote in Greek. It has been traditionally assumed that he was the author of the *Apostolic Tradition*, a work that is known to us primarily from its redaction and inclusion in the fourth-century church order called the *Apostolic Constitutions*. This provenance and dating makes it easier for us to explain the apparent anachronism of the relatively mature Trinitarian theology and Eucharistic euchology of the so-called 'Anaphora of Hippolytus', the Eucharistic Prayer contained in Book VIII of the *Apostolic Constitutions*.

Hippolytus was less polemical than Justin and Irenaeus, but perhaps even more than the latter, he had an intensely realistic, physical conception of the self-offering of the Word Incarnate. In fact, the connection between Incarnation and sacrifice can be called the leitmotif of Hippolytus's theology of sacrifice. For example, he writes:

I am not the one who says this, but he who has come down from heaven attests it; for he says: 'no one has ascended into heaven but he who descended from heaven, the Son of Man who is in heaven (Jn 3:13). What then can he seek except what is proclaimed? Will he say that flesh was not in heaven? Yet there is the flesh that was presented by the Word of the Father as an offering, the flesh that came from the Spirit and the Virgin and was shown to be the perfect Son of God. It is evident, therefore, that he offered himself to the Father. Before this there was no flesh in heaven. Who then was in heaven but the Word Incarnate who was sent to show that he was both on earth and also in heaven?[12]

Hippolytus is obviously very much at home with the by now traditional idea of the sacrifice of Christ. But he also adds to this traditional view by combining incarnational Christology and soteriology with the gift idea of sacrifice in such a way as to produce a new moment in the development of the idea of Christian sacrifice: i.e., the eternal Word of God became human in order to be able to rise again to heaven and there offer to the eternal Father not only his flesh, his own humanity, but also humanity itself. This offering to the Father, implying a theme of divinization, enables us also to share what the Father has granted to the Son.

Chapter V

The Early Treatises on the Passover

We begin with two second-century works: the *Peri Pascha* (*PP* – *On the Passover*) of Melito of Sardis,[13] and the anonymous, apparently Quartodeciman, *In S. Pascha* (*IP* – *On the Holy Passover*).[14] They represent a genre of basically liturgical or homiletic compositions that give a specifically Christian development to the Jewish Passover haggadah on Exodus 12. Two major themes intertwine: (1) the Eucharist and the Passion of Christ as the Christian Passover, and (2) the 'spiritual Passover'. Regarding the first of these themes, we encounter some of the same theological richness that we have seen in Hippolytus:

---

12   *Against Noetus*, 4. Translated from Eduard Schwartz, *Zwei Predigten Hippolyts* (München: Verlag der Bayerischen Akademie der Wissenschaften, 1936), 8. For a full English translation, see *The Ante Nicene Fathers*, vol. 5 (10 vols; repr., Grand Rapids, MI: Eerdmans, 1965), 223–31. *The Refutation of all Heresies* 10.33.17 (GCS 26 [III], pp. 291.29–292.5 and ANF, vol. 5, p. 152) is a sacrifice text equally explicit in its incarnational realism.
13   Othmar Perler, *Méliton de Sardes sur la Paque* (SC, 123; Paris: Cerf, 1966). The date and authenticity of this work is well established.
14   Pierre Nautin, *Homélies Paschales I: Une Homélie Inspirée de Traité sur la Paque d'Hippolyte* (SC, 27; Paris: Cerf, 1950). Raniero Cantalamessa, *L'Omelia 'In S. Pascha' dello Pseudo-Ippolito di Roma* (Milan: Vita e pensiero, 1967), appears to have fairly well demonstrated the Quartodeciman (second-century Jewish-Christian communities in Asia Minor) origins of this work and its close kinship with Melito's treatise.

This was the Pasch that Jesus desired to suffer for us [cf. Lk. 22.15]; by suffering he freed us from suffering, and by death he conquered death, and through the visible food he won for us his immortal life. This was the saving desire of Jesus, this his totally spiritual love, to prove the types to be types, and, in their place, to give his sacred body to his disciples: 'Take, eat, this is my body; take, drink, this is my blood, the new covenant, that is to be shed for many for the forgiveness of sins' For this reason his desire to eat was not as great as his desire to suffer, in order to free us from the suffering incurred by eating.

(IP, 49)

The second theme, spiritual Passover, is given a profoundly Christological meaning, keyed especially to the Greek noun *logos* – 'word' and adjective *logikos* – 'spiritual' or 'reasonable'. From earliest Christianity, these words were used to refer to Christ (Jn 1.14) and to describe that worship, i.e., that sacrifice, that is specifically Christian (cf. Rom. 12.1 and 1 Pet. 2.5). 'In order that we might be fully fed by the Word (*logos*)', we are exhorted, 'not with earthly but with heavenly nourishment, let us also eat the Passover of the Word [or spiritual Passover – *to logikon pascha*] with that spiritual desire with which the Lord himself desired to eat it with us when he said: [Luke 22.15] 'with desire have I desired to eat this Pasch with you' (*IP*, 4). So overwhelmingly Christological is the meaning of these Greek words that it is misleading to translate them into modern English with 'reasonable', or even 'spiritual'. For the ultimate full meaning of *logikos* in this context is 'of Christ' or simply 'Christian'.

The recent discovery and availability of Origen's *Peri Pascha* (*PP*) *Treatise on the Passover* written a half century later (ca. 245) adds a new wrinkle.[15] After chiding his Christian predecessors for their erroneous etymological association of the Greek word *pascha* with the Greek noun *pathos* (suffering) and verb *paschein* (to suffer) in order to emphasize the identification of Passover/*pascha* with the suffering/*pathos* of Christ, Origen goes on to explain that he wants to save Christians from the ridicule of 'Hebrew people' who know that *pascha* comes from the Hebrew *fas/fasek* that means not suffering but *diabasis* or *hyperbasis*, i.e., 'passage' or 'passing over'.

But Origen is concerned not just to correct his brethren and save them from ridicule. He is primarily concerned with teaching the true, i.e., spiritual meaning of the Passover. It is not just something that happened back then, it is something that is still happening now:

> Since the sacred ceremony of the Passover was already carried out in mystery (*mystêriôdôs*) in the time of Moses according to God's orders for the salvation of the first-born of the sons of Israel because of *the wrath of God inflicted* (cf. Rom. 3.5) on Pharaoh and on those who under his leadership disobey the word of God, we now raise the question whether it is only in that time of its concrete celebration that it is carried out, or whether we might not have to admit that it is also carried

---

15   *Origen: Treatise on the Passover* and *Dialogue of Origen with Heraclides and His Fellow Bishops on the Father, the Son, and the Soul*, trans. and ed. Robert J. Daly, S.J.; Ancient Christian Writers, 54 (New York/Mahwah, NJ: Paulist Press, 1992).

out in a different manner in our own time, the time of fulfillment – *upon whom the end of the ages has come* (1 Cor. 10.11).

(PP, 39.9–23)

Origen goes on, explaining with great emphasis that it is not so much what happened in the past, but what is now happening in the present that is of utmost importance, i.e., the transformation, the 'passing over' in and with Christ that is now taking place in the lives of the faithful and on the altar of their souls.

Chapter VI

The Second-Century Acts of the Martyrs

When one sees Christ's death as sacrificial and with that Christian life as an imitation of Christ, the idea of martyrdom as sacrificial naturally follows. This idea permeates the seven Acts of the Martyrs that come to us from different places in the Roman empire in the last half of the second century. A typical expression of it is in the description of Polycarp's martyrdom:

> And he, with his hands bound behind him, like a choice ram taken from a great flock for sacrifice, an acceptable whole burnt offering prepared for God, looked up to heaven and said: '. . . I bless you for making me worthy of this day and hour, that I should take part among the numbers of the martyrs in the cup of your Christ . . . among whom may I be accepted before you today as a rich and acceptable sacrifice'.

(Mart. Pol., 14.1–2)

The cause of the martyr's constancy, a recurrent theme, is not so much Stoicism, as might be suggested by the language used to describe it, but a kind of Christ-mysticism. For example, in witnessing her martyrdom, the companions of Blandina 'even with the eyes of the flesh saw in the person of their sister Him who was crucified for them' (*Letter of the Churches of Vienne and Lyons*, 41). Felicitas, in the pains of childbirth, protests to those mocking her suffering: 'Now I suffer what I suffer: but then another will be in me who will suffer for me, because I too am to suffer for Him' (*Passion of SS. Perpetua and Felicitas*, 15.3). Allusions to a Suffering Servant Christology are also found in this literature, as is also the idea of martyrdom as an athletic or gladiatorial combat. (Connected with this latter idea we can also detect some early suggestions of Pelagianism and hagiographical embellishment.)

Finally, we also find here some instances of the idea of *spiritual sacrifice*. For example, Apollonius, in defending himself, preaches a concept of Christian sacrifice that seems to be realized not in cultic worship but in the practical living of the Christian life:

> It was my hope, proconsul, that these religious discussions would help you and that the eyes of your soul would have been illumined by my defense, so that our heart would bear fruit and worship God the maker of all; and that to him alone, day by day and by means of almsgiving and brotherly love, you would offer your prayers, an unbloody and pure sacrifice to God.
>
> (*Acts of Apollonius*, 44; see also 8)

Chapter VII

The Alexandrian Tradition I: The Antecedents: Philo and Barnabas

Alexandria, the 'second Athens' of the ancient world, can be described as the one place where, more than in any other, early Christianity discovered its intellectual life. Already the place that, in the third and second century BCE, saw the first translation of the Hebrew Bible into another language, the Greek Septuagint, it was also the home of Philo (ca. 20 BCE–ca. 50 CE). This great Jewish religious philosopher, especially by way of his development of the allegorical method of interpreting Scripture, exercised great influence on Christian thought, especially through the writings of the early giants of the so-called Christian Alexandrian school: Clement of Alexandria and Origen.

A. PHILO OF ALEXANDRIA

Philo does not treat systematically of sacrifice in any one place, but spread across some three dozen extant works that are more or less equally divided among (1) philosophical works, (2) exegetical writings on the Pentateuch, and (3) historical and apologetic writings, are hundreds of passages in which he mentions or treats of sacrifice. From these it is possible to cull out a highly developed theology of sacrifice that in early antiquity was surpassed in richness and depth only by Origen, and in overall influence on Christian theology possibly only by the Scriptures themselves. Following the Alexandrian allegorical method of which he is the major mediator to us, Philo believed that a biblical passage could either (1) be literally true or (2) be literally true but also have an allegorical meaning, or (3) be true only in an allegorical sense, or (4) be doubtful in its literal sense but certain in its allegorical meaning. He was constantly looking not just for 'the meaning of the words' but also for 'the deeper meaning'. Combining Greek philosophy and Hebrew faith, his favourite moral on the subject of sacrifice was that – in a maxim that became foundational in the Christian idea of sacrifice – *we can only give to*

God what God has first given to us.[16] His overriding intent was to write an allegorical account of the human soul in its progress toward God. We can summarize his teaching on sacrifice in the following seven points, all of which became significant elements in the subsequent development of the Christian theology of sacrifice.

1. *The Passover is a symbol of the soul's progress.* The soul offers the Passover sacrifice when it begins to give up the pursuits and disorders of youth, and when the mind changes from ignorance and stupidity to education and wisdom.
2. *True sacrifice is an offering of the whole self – the soul, the mind and the heart.* Philo has numerous texts that, like the Pauline writings, see true oblation as the devotion of a soul to God, and that begin to see life itself as sacrificial. But unlike the consciously incarnational New Testament writings, Philo has a typically Platonic bias against matter.
3. *The acceptance of sacrifice and the primacy of dispositions* becomes increasingly important for Philo as he shifts attention from the ritual itself to the spiritual meaning.
4. *The purpose of sacrifice* is, first, to honour God and, second, to benefit the worshiper, and that either by obtaining blessings or obtaining release from evil. In contrast to most of rabbinic Judaism, there is a strong 'gnostic intention' in Philo, for the purpose of sin offerings is more in education than in atonement, and atonement itself is primarily an affair of the mind, a matter of knowledge, especially self-knowledge.
5. *The high priest.* Philo oscillates between a Jewish idealization and Hellenistic spiritualization of the idea of priesthood, as he raises the high priest to a more than human level, almost equating him with the Logos, thus providing an essential part of the background of at least the language and imagery of the Christian Alexandrians in their theology of Christ, the Divine Logos, High Priest and universal Mediator, not only on behalf of he whole human race but also for the rest of creation.
6. *The idea of universal priesthood* is one of the pillars of Philo's theology. He associates it with the Passover when the whole nation carried out the priestly functions in harmony. Christians could easily substitute baptism for Passover. But most important, in terms of later influence, he insisted that it was primarily ethical purity that confers priesthood.
7. *The temple, sanctuary, and altar* are realities around which Philo tended to centre his most characteristic statements on the theology of sacrifice. They are also the statements that had the most influence on Christian thinkers. The following two texts are characteristic:

> There are, as is evident, two temples of God: one of them this universe, in which there is also as high priest his First-born, the divine Word, and the other the rational soul, whose priest is the real man; the outward and visible image of

---

16   'Whatsoever you bring as an offering, you will offer God's possessions and not your own' (*On the Sacrifices of Cain and Abel*, 97).

whom is he who offers the prayers and sacrifices handed down from our
fathers, to whom it has been committed to wear the aforesaid tunic.

> (*On Dreams*, 1.215. Cf. also *On Noah's Work as a Planter*, 50,
> and *Who Is the Heir?*, 75)

This puts in context what Philo has to say about the soul-temple as the true
place of worship:

> The true altar of God is the thankful soul of the Sage, compacted of perfect
> virtues unsevered and undivided, for no part of virtue is useless. On this soul-
> altar the sacred light is ever burning and carefully kept unextinguished, and
> the light of the mind is wisdom, just as the darkness of the soul is folly. For
> knowledge is to the reason what the light of the senses is to the eye: as that
> gives the apprehension of material things, so does knowledge lead to the
> contemplation of things immaterial and conceptual, and its beam shines for
> ever, never dimmed nor quenched.
>
> (*On the Special Laws*, 1.287–88)

Although the imagery may not be totally consistent with his thought, what Philo is
affirming is fairly clear. His ideas of the soul as God's temple, and of the soul as the
altar of that temple, stand in the service of his ethics. But the ethical life is not
the goal; it is merely a preparation for mystical contemplation: 'the contemplation
of things immaterial and conceptual'. The similarities and contrasts with subsequent Christian thinking is striking. In Philo, ethics is the mere propaedeutic of
worship conceived in terms of nonmaterial contemplation. However enticing that
was for Christian thinkers, they – usually, at least – did not lose sight of the fact that
Christian worship *essentially* involves the ethical, and of the fact that, however
important contemplation may be, Christian worship in this life is realized not so
much in contemplation as in the living out of an incarnationally inspired life of
service.

B. Epistle of Barnabas

Shining through the ardour of the fiercely anti-Jewish polemic of this influential
work – for a time it was considered to be part of the inspired Scriptures – are some
of the foundational insights of the early Christian theology of sacrifice. Barnabas's[17] allegorical interpretation of Scripture owes much to Philo, but his basic
principle of interpretation is radically different: for Barnabas, everything points to
Christ. Literal interpretation, specifically as relates to Old Testament sacrifices, is
rejected as the typical Jewish error influenced by 'an evil angel' (*Barnabas, 9.5*).
Expressed positively, the central core of Barnabas's theology of sacrifice is his faith
in the physical reality of the Incarnation and of Christ's passion and death.

---

17   Coming from the second quarter of the second century, and actually more of a treatise than a
letter, the author of this work, though formerly thought by some to be the Barnabas associated
with St. Paul in the Acts of the Apostles, is actually unknown.

For example, in describing the Incarnation, he uses the word 'flesh' (*sarx*) a dozen times in this relatively brief work

When we come to the sacrificing activity of Christians, the temple theme is central. But it is not the anti-material, radically spiritualizing temple theology of Philo that is operative; that provides only the structural bones of the allegory. What is central is the incarnational temple theology of Paul. In Barnabas's words that need no further commentary:

> But let us inquire if a temple of God exists. Yes, it exists, where he himself said that he makes and perfects it. For it is written, 'and it shall come to pass when the week is ended that a temple of God shall be built gloriously in the name of the Lord' [cf. Dan. 9.24–27]. I find then that a temple exists. Learn then how it will be built in the name of the Lord. Before we believed in God, the habitation of our heart was corrupt and weak, like a temple really built with hands, because it was full of idolatry and was the house of demons through doing things which were contrary to God. 'But it shall be built in the name of the Lord' [cf. Dan. 9.24–27]. Now give heed, so that the temple of the Lord may be built gloriously. Learn in what way. When we received the remission of sins, and put our hope in the name, we became new, being created again from the beginning [cf. Mk. 10.6; Mt. 19.4; Eph. 2.15]; wherefore God truly dwells in us, in the habitation which we are. How? His word of faith, the calling of his promise, the wisdom of the ordinances, the commands of the teaching, himself prophesying in us, himself dwelling in us, by opening the door of the temple (that is the mouth) to us, who have been enslaved to death, into the incorruptible temple. For he who desires to be saved looks not at the man, but at him who dwells and speaks in him, and is amazed at him, for he has never either heard him speak such words with his mouth, nor has he himself ever desired to hear them. This is the spiritual temple being built for the Lord.
>
> (*Barnabas*, 16.6–10)

Chapter VIII

The Alexandrian Tradition II: Christianity Coming of Age: Clement and Origen

Clement and Origen are the early giants among the so-called Christian Platonists of Alexandria. They can be apologetical and polemical, but from anything but a defensive posture. For although they were in some ways quite different, Clement coming across more as a cultured gentleman comfortable in his world, and Origen coming across more as the severe ascetic yearning for martyrdom, they were quite alike both in their basic idea of what it means to be a Christian, and in their self-confident Christian intellectuality.

A. CLEMENT OF ALEXANDRIA

So Platonic in thought and so indebted to Philo is Clement of Alexandria (ca. 150–215) that one might call him a Christian Philo. But two things clearly separate him both from Philo before him and his own gnostic contemporaries: his faith in the Incarnation and his faith in the Church as the mediator and guarantor of the true, saving gnosis. The following headings indicate how rich is his theology of sacrifice: (1) Interpretation of Scripture; (2) Cult Criticism and the Idea of Spiritual Sacrifice; (3) The Sacrifice of Christ; (4) Christian Sacrificial Activity, and under that (4a) The Worship of the Gnostic, (4b) Universal Priesthood, (4c) Gnostic Martyrdom; (5) The Temple and the Altar. Implicit throughout his work is the threefold Pauline scheme: sacrifice of Christ, temple themes and Christian sacrificial activity.

1. *Interpretation of Scripture.* Quite in contrast with Irenaeus, Clement uses the noun *gnosis* and its adjectival and adverbial forms to refer to the true, spiritual meaning of Scripture:

> The sacrifice acceptable to God is unswerving abstraction from the body and its passions. This is the really true piety. Is not, then, Socrates correct in calling philosophy the practice of Death? . . . It was from Moses that the chief of the Greeks drew these philosophical tenets. For Moses commands holocausts to be skinned and divided into parts [cf. Lev. 1.6]. For the Gnostic soul must be consecrated to the light, stripped of the coverings of matter, separated from the frivolousness of the body and of all the passions which are acquired through vain and lying opinions, and divested of the lusts of the flesh.
>
> (*Stromata*, 5.11)

Allegory dominates; indeed, so much so that the Bible seems more like a symbolic poem than as the object of careful exegesis.

2. *Cult Criticism and the Idea of Spiritual Sacrifice.* Like Philo, Clement sees OT sacrifices as symbols of the soul's progress toward God; and like Barnabas, he rejects any literal understanding or validity of these sacrifices; but he does not rely solely on Scripture, for he has also clearly made his own the cult criticism of the pagan philosophers and poets. He also goes beyond the merely theoretical or negative to describe what the cult of the Christian or 'true Gnostic' should be:

> We ought to offer to God not costly sacrifices but such as he loves, and in that mixture of incense which is mentioned in the law. It consists of many tongues and voices in prayer [cf. Exod. 30.34–36], or rather of different nations and natures, prepared by the gift promised in the dispensation for 'the unity of the faith' [Eph. 4.13], and brought together in praise, with a pure mind, and just and right conduct, from holy works and righteous prayer.
>
> (*Stromata*, 7.6)

3. *The Sacrifice of Christ* is mentioned in a variety of ways: Christ as a whole burnt offering for us, as the Passover, as the Suffering Servant and Lamb of God, and also in developing the Isaac-Christ typology:

> Where, then, was the door by which the Lord showed himself? The flesh by which he was manifested. He is Isaac (for the narrative may be interpreted otherwise), who is a type of the Lord, a child as a son. For he was the son of Abraham, as Christ was the Son of God; and a sacrifice like the Lord, only he was not immolated as the Lord was. Isaac only bore the wood of the cross. And he laughed mystically, prophesying that the Lord would fill us with joy, who have been redeemed from corruption by the blood of the Lord. Isaac did everything but suffer, as was right, yielding the precedence in suffering to the Word. Furthermore, there is an intimation of the divinity of the Lord in his not being slain. For Jesus rose again after his burial, having suffered no harm, like Isaac released from sacrifice.
>
> (*Paedagogus*, 1.5; cf. also *Stromata*, 2.5)

The Incarnation thus provides the obvious background and foundation of Clement's understanding of Christ's sacrifice:

> For this also he came down. For this he clothed himself with man. For this he voluntarily subjected himself to the experiences of men, that by bringing himself to the measure of our weakness whom he loved, he might correspondingly bring us to the measure of his own strength. And about to be offered up and giving himself as ransom, he left for us a new covenant-testament: My love I give unto you.
>
> (*Quis dives salvetur*, 37. See also *Stromata*, 1.21; 5.6; *Paedagogus*, 1.6)

Within this incarnational thinking, the figure of Christ the high priest provides the specific model for Clement's understanding of Christ's sacrifice and Christian sacrifice. Three meanings of 'high priest' interplay: first, the high priest of the Hebrew scriptures, then, Jesus Christ, and third, the true gnostic or Christian:

> And he [the Levitical high priest] shall take off the linen robe, which he had put on when he entered into the holy place; and shall lay it aside there, and wash his body in water in the holy place, and put on his robe [Lev. 16.23–24]. One way, I think, of taking off and putting on the robe takes place when the Lord descends into the region of sense. Another way takes place when he [the Christian] who through him has believed, takes off and puts on, as the apostle intimates, the consecrated stole [cf. Eph. 6.13–17]. Thence, after the image of the Lord, the worthiest were chosen from the sacred tribes to be high priests. . . .
>
> (*Stromata*, 5.6)

The 'typological reversal' that is taking place in Clement is noteworthy. The Levitical high priest is no longer the archetype; Christ incarnate, and in him the Christian believer or true Gnostic, becomes the true archetype of the

Levitical high priests. When we look more deeply into this process of Chris-tologization, we find a passage that directly describes the sacrificial activity of Christ the high priest:

> If, then, we say that the Lord the great high priest offers to God the incense of sweet fragrance, let us not imagine that this is a sacrifice and sweet fragrance of incense but let us understand it to mean that the Lord lays the acceptable offering of love, the spiritual fragrance, on the altar.
>
> (*Paedagogus*, 2.8)

Significantly, this speaks mainly in the language of spiritual sacrifice. This is consistent with Clement's general tendency to minimize the human aspects of Christ's high priesthood, and his tendency to minimize – at least in contrast with other early Christian writers – the negative (i.e., atoning or sin-forgiving) aspects of redemption/atonement and sacrifice.

4. *Christian Sacrificial Activity.* Clement faithfully develops the early Christian understanding of the relationship between the sacrifice of Christ and the sacrifice of – i.e., by – the Christian. He does this under three headings: (a) the worship of the Gnostic, (b) universal priesthood, and (c) gnostic martyrdom.

(a) *The worship of the Gnostic* is suggestively referred to by Clement as 'gnostic assimilation':

> This is the function of the Gnostic who has been made perfect to have converse with God through the great high priest, and who is being made like the Lord, as far as possible, in the whole service of God which tends to the salvation of men through its provident care for us as well as through service, teaching, and the active ministry. The Gnostic even forms and creates himself; and he also, like God, adorns those who hear him, assimi-lating as far as possible the moderation which, arising from practice, tends to impassibility. He has, especially uninterrupted converse and fellowship with the Lord. Mildness, I think, and philanthropy, and eminent piety, are the rules of Gnostic Assimilation. I affirm that these virtues 'are a sacri-fice acceptable in the sight of God' [cf. Phil. 4.18]; Scripture alleging that 'the humble heart with right knowledge is the holocaust of God' [cf. Ps. 51.17, 19–LXX 50.19, 21], each man who is admitted to holiness being illuminated unto indissoluble union.
>
> (*Stromata*, 7.3)

The Christian becomes, like Christ, the offering itself: 'We have become a consecrated offering to God for Christ's sake' (*Protrepticus*, 4). This Chris-tian worship is also strongly communal; Clement calls it 'the sacrifice of the church':

> Breathing together is properly said of the church. For the sacrifice of the church is the word breathing as incense from holy souls, the sacrifice and the whole mind being at the same time unveiled to God ... Thus we should offer God not costly sacrifices but such as he loves. The mixture of

incense mentioned in the law is something that consists of many tongues
and voices in prayer, or rather of different nations and natures, prepared
by the gift bestowed in the dispensation for 'the unity of the faith' [Eph.
4.13] and brought together in praises, with a pure mind, and just and right
conduct, from holy works and righteous prayer.

(*Stromata*, 7.6)

Thus, where Justin, Irenaeus and Hippolytus may have had the Eucharist in
mind, it is clear that Clement, when speaking of the 'offering of the
church', is looking at the whole life of the gnostic as sacrificial worship, as a
'holding festival . . . in our whole life' (*Stromata*, 7.7). As is clear from the
whole context of Clement's treatment of the life of the Gnostic in *Stromata*,
7.11–16, the life of the Gnostic is both practical and contemplative: 'The
end of the Gnostic here is, in my judgment, twofold; partly scientific contemplation, partly action' (*Stromata*, 7.16).

(b) *Universal priesthood* is central for Clement, for the true Gnostic is 'the
kingly man; he is the sacred high priest of God' (*Stromata*, 4.25). In a long
passage in *Stromata*, 7.13, he points out that the apostles were chosen
precisely because, in the divine foreknowledge, they had been proven
worthy. He then states that the Gnostic is a presbyter not by reason of
ordination but by reason of virtue. Clement is aware of the tension
between this view and the existence in the church of a priesthood based
on ordination, but his resolution of the tension is not much more than a
graceful evasion. What we later came to call 'ecclesiology' was relatively
undeveloped at this time, but on one point Clement is very clear. He
clearly sees the Church as the guardian and guarantor of an orthodoxy
that comes from the proper interpretation of Scripture in accordance with
the apostolic traditions (see esp. *Stromata* 7.16). Gnosis means ecclesiastical gnosis, however difficult it may be for us to determine *precisely* what
he may have meant by this.

(c) *Gnostic martyrdom.* Without emphasizing it the way other early Christian
writers did, Clement sees both blood martyrdom and gnostic martyrdom as
sacrificial, as long as love towers over both:

The Lord says in the gospel, 'Whoever shall leave father or mother or
brethren', etc., 'for the sake of the gospel and my name' (Mt. 19.29), he is
blessed; not indicating simple martyrdom, but the Gnostic martyrdom [cf.
also *Stromata* 4.14], as of the man who has conducted himself according to
the rule of the gospel, in love to the Lord . . .

(*Stromata*, 4.4; cf. also 4.18)

5. *The Temple and the Altar.* In the way that Clement appropriates both Philo and
his already impressive predecessors there is, both in his theology and in the
inchoative ecclesiology that we can find in him, a richness and a depth that
goes far beyond what went before. He is the first to connect the idea of divine
indwelling with the temple-cleansing that prepares both a worthy abode for
God and a worthy place for offering Christian sacrifice. The Christian, the true

gnostic, is now not just the offering and the offerer, but also the place of worship. Clement is also the first Christian writer to see the reception of the Eucharist as enshrining Christ within us as in a temple:

> Such is the suitable food which the Lord ministers, and he offers his flesh and pours forth his blood, and nothing is wanting for the children's growth. O amazing mystery! We are enjoined to cast off the old and carnal corruption, as also the old nutriment, receiving in exchange another new regimen, that of Christ, receiving him if we can, to hide him within and to enshrine the savior in our hearts so that we may correct the affections of our flesh.
>
> (*Paedagogus*, 1.6)

We see Clement moving smoothly from traditional spiritualizing temple criticism, to the Church as temple, the gnostic as temple, the community as altar, and finally, both the individual soul and the assemblage of the elect as the altar from which rises the incense of holy prayer. The following passage is typical, but by no means unique:

> The altar, then, that is with us here, the terrestrial one, is the congregation of those who devote themselves to prayers, having as it were one common voice and one mind . . . Now breathing together is properly said of the church. For the sacrifice of the church is the word breathing as incense from holy souls, the sacrifice and the whole mind being at the same time unveiled to God.
>
> (*Stromata*, 7.6)

B. ORIGEN: CHRISTIAN LIFE AS SACRIFICE

Both in his own right and in terms of his massive influence on the great Fathers of both East and West, Origen (185–ca. 251), the great theologian of sacrifice, as Harnack called him,[18] represents not the end, but certainly the high point of the early Christian spiritualization of sacrifice. Like Clement, Origen had a basic openness toward Old Testament sacrifices. These he repeatedly used as the basis for spiritual or allegorical interpretations, interpretations that often move out into areas that have little to do with sacrifice in the text under discussion. But most importantly, as he pointedly emphasized in his *Treatise on the Passover*, his primary referent was not what happened in the past, but what is happening right now in the here-and-now life of the Christian who is still in the process of 'passing over' in and with Christ.[19]

Jesus is, of course, the central figure, the true Paschal Lamb that is led to the slaughter, who takes away the sins of the world, who by his blood reconciles us to the Father, who emptied himself, bearing our infirmities and chastisements out of love for us and obedience to the Father, who is the great and perfect High Priest,

---

18   Adolf von Harnack, vol. 1 of *Lehrbuch der Dogmengeschichte*, 4th ed. (3 vols; Tübingen: J.C.B. Mohr, 1909–10), 477. Harnack was taking his cue from Charles Bigg, *The Christian Platonists of Alexandria* (Oxford: Clarendon Press, 1886), 209–12.
19   See earlier in this chapter, at the end of Chapter V. on 'The Early Treatises on the Passover', pp. 82–84.

in fact both priest and victim in his perfect and unique offering to the Father, all this motivated by, embodying and carrying out the Father's love.

But despite this Christological richness, his primary referent was never historical, indeed not even the historical Christ, but rather how the Church, and its members, and indeed the whole world, now share in the sacrifice of Christ. For Origen, much more than for Clement, the privileged way of doing this was by martyrdom through which many others also receive blessings beyond description. Then, recalling that the Book of Revelation sees the martyrs standing next to the heavenly altar of sacrifice, Origen uses this recollection to introduce the eschatological perspective and thus to locate the ultimate meaning of sacrifice not in this world but in the heavenly mysteries, i.e., in the trans-temporal, meta-historical past – present – future of the Paschal Mystery.

Origen also develops even further what had already reached a significant high point in Clement of Alexandria: the use of the temple theme as an aid to seeing the whole of Christian life in terms of sacrifice.[20] He exhorts us to refuse to build merely lifeless temples; for our body is a temple of God, and the best of these temples is the body of Jesus Christ. The temple that has been destroyed will be rebuilt of living and most precious stones, with each of us becoming a precious stone in the great temple of God. As living stones we must also be active. For if, says Origen, I raise my hands in prayer, but leave hanging the hands of my soul instead of raising them with good and holy works, then the raising of my hands is not an evening sacrifice.[21] These and numerous similar passages show that Origen, in thus emphasizing the body, is remaining true to the central Christian mystery of the Incarnation. But he is also remaining true to his own strong spiritualizing instincts; he never tires of stressing the need for the proper internal dispositions for sacrifice. For, as he points out, truly celebrating a feast means serving God faithfully, living ascetically and prayerfully, and continually offering to God bloodless sacrifices in prayer. For it is by constant prayer that we become living stones from which Jesus builds the altar on which to offer spiritual victims.[22]

In contrast with those who went before him, and even in contrast with his kindred spiritualizing predecessor, Clement of Alexandria, it is noteworthy how little Origen's idea of sacrifice has to do with the Eucharist, liturgy or ritual. Although it is true that some of what he says makes sense only on the supposition that he conceived of the Christian liturgy as being in some way sacrificial, we must not forget that, like most of the New Testament writers, foremost in his mind when he thought of what Christians do when they offer sacrifice was not a liturgical rite of the Church, but rather the internal liturgy of the Christian heart and spirit by which one offers oneself and all one's prayers, works and thoughts through Jesus Christ to God the Father. Also noteworthy, in terms of the overarching Trinitarian

---

20 See esp. *Homilies on Leviticus*, 2.4; *Homilies on Joshua*, 2.1; *Commentary on the Psalms*, 49.5.

21 See esp. *Against Celsus*, 8.19; *Dialogue with Heraclides*, 20; *Homilies on Numbers*, 20.3.

22 See, among numerous other passages, *Homilies on Jeremiah* 18.10; *Commentary on John*, 6.52, 58 (37); *Homilies on Leviticus* 1.5, 4.8, 5.3–4; *Homilies on Numbers* 24.2; *Commentary on the Lamentations of Jeremiah*, Fragment 49; *Against Celsus* 8.17; *Commentary on the Psalms* (PG 12, p. 1428A–B); *Commentary on Romans* 8 (PG 14, p. 1132); *Exhortation to Martyrdom* 21.

picture that we sketched at the beginning of this book, is the absence of the Holy Spirit. Origen was writing a full century before the Church, especially through the early ecumenical councils, began to articulate with any consistency its doctrine of the triune God.

Chapter IX

Augustine of Hippo

With Augustine, we have moved fast-forward some 170 years from pre-Nicene Greek-speaking Alexandrian Christianity to post-Nicene Constantinopolitan Latin-speaking Roman North-African Christianity. Nevertheless, Origen and Augustine basically agree in their fundamental view on sacrifice. Paul's threefold scheme – sacrifice of Christ, temple themes and Christian sacrificial activity – is as helpful in summarizing Augustine's views on Christian sacrifice as it was for those of Clement and Origen. But there are significant differences. The first difference is that, unlike Origen, Augustine actually has a systematic treatment of sacrifice. It is a central theme in his larger discussion of the nature of true worship that occupies him in Book 10 of the *City of God*. Augustine begins (in terms reminiscent of the beginning of Aristotle's *Nicomachean Ethics*) by noting the universal human desire for blessedness. He then discusses approvingly the philosophical critique of sacrifice (God doesn't need it, etc.), moves on to express the close relationship, even identity, between the law of sacrifice and the law of love, and then gives his definition of Christian sacrifice, i.e., of Christian sacrificial activity:

> Thus, true sacrifice is every work which is done in order that we might be one with God in a holy society, i.e., a work which is related to that end of the good by which we can truly be happy.
> *Proinde verum sacrificium est omne opus, quo agitur, ut sancta societate inhaereamus Deo, relatum scilicet ad illum finem boni, quo veraciter beati esse possimus.*[23]

This is very different from what Origen would have written. It actually sounds more like the scholasticism still to come than the Platonism that Augustine had in common with Origen. We now summarize Augustine on sacrifice according to the threefold Pauline scheme:

A. SACRIFICE OF CHRIST

Compared with Origen, there is at least one notable difference. Origen sees the work of sacrificial redemption as having been completed by Christ only with his

---

23 Augustine, *On the City of God*, 10.6 [CC Ser Lat 47 (14/1), 278 lines 1–3].

'second baptism', i.e., when, after the resurrection, he returned to the Father to receive back his human soul which he had left in deposit with the Father while his body lay in the tomb.[24] Where Origen's focus had been on the heavenly realities of which sacrifices here are but the 'copy and shadow' Heb. 8.5), Augustine, by contrast, sees Christ's sacrificial redemptive work as having been completed *in this world*.

B. TEMPLE THEMES

Augustine agrees with Origen and the broad patristic tradition in seeing the individual and the community/Church as constituting the new temple. Whereas Origen occasionally used the Philonic and Neoplatonic categories of the ascent of the soul, and frequently spoke of the mind (*nous*) or soul (*psychê*) as well as the heart as the altar on which Christians are to offer true sacrifice to God, there is again, by contrast, a significant difference in Augustine. Despite his high respect for the Platonists, having called them the 'noblest of all philosophers',[25] Augustine seems to be resolutely distancing himself from Platonic categories in his insistence on speaking also of the human, bodily *heart* as the internal altar.

C. SACRIFICE BY CHRISTIANS

In seeing all Christian life and all truly Christian activity as sacrificial, Augustine is expressing what had become a common patristic insight. Actually, there is some likelihood that Augustine was actually influenced by Origen (but whether directly or indirectly cannot be determined) in his conception of Christ as both the priest and victim of his sacrifice, and of Christians themselves as the sacrifice that they, too, when united with Christ, offer to God. Nevertheless, despite the fairly obvious influence, Augustine is, again, very different. Where, for Origen, what is most significant in the sacrifices of Christians is what is taking place before the heavenly throne of God, Augustine's concept of the city of God has him attributing much more importance to what is taking place in this world. The 'holy society' he mentions in his definition of sacrifice (quoted earlier) includes both the blessed in heaven and the members of the Church here on earth. As co-citizens with the blessed in the city of God, Christians become, in performing their sacrificial works of love and mercy, the sacrifice itself which Christ the high priest offers to God. Compare and contrast Augustine's words with those of Origen:

> *Origen:*
> But we all have within ourselves our own burnt offering, and we ourselves ignite the altar of our burnt offering so that it will always burn . . . or 'if I deliver my body

---

24   See Robert J. Daly, S.J., 'Sacrificial Soteriology: Origen's Commentary on John 1:29', *Origeniana Secunda*, Quaderni di 'Vetera Christianorum' no. 15 (1980), 151–63 (159); also *Origen, Dialogue with Heraclides*, 6.22–8.21 and my comment on this in note 10 (pp. 105–6) in *Origen: Treatise on the Passover and Dialogue with Heraclides*, Ancient Christian Writers, 54; (New York/Mahwah, NJ: Paulist Press, 1992).
25   *On the City of God*, 10.1 (*Corpus Christianorum*, Series Latina 47 [14/1], p. 271, lines 14–15).

to be burned, having love' (cf. 1 Cor. 13.3), and if I attain the glory of martyrdom, I have offered myself as a burnt offering at the altar of God . . . and become myself the priest of my sacrifice.[26]

Augustine:
This he offered, in this he was offered, because it is in this way that he is the mediator; in this he is the priest, in this he is the sacrifice . . . [and] we ourselves are this whole sacrifice . . . this is the sacrifice of Christians: that we, though we are many, are one body in Christ. The Church celebrates this mystery in the sacrament of the altar, as the faithful know, and there she shows them clearly that in what is offered, she herself is offered.[27]

It is no accident that the last half of Augustine's text is quoted and highlighted by Joseph Ratzinger writing as the Supreme Pontiff, Pope Benedict XVI, in his 2007 Post-Synodal Apostolic Exhortation *Sacramentum Caritatis* no. 70.[28] For it shows that Augustine was beginning to do what Pope Benedict (and Catholic theology in general) is concerned to do: to connect all this with the Eucharist. For later in the *City of God*, Augustine seems to identify this 'sacrifice of Christians' with the Eucharist: 'To eat the bread, which in the New Testament is the sacrifice of Christians'.[29] Pope Benedict makes basically the same point, while, not surprisingly, being much more aware of the Trinitarian reality of Christian sacrifice than were the Church Fathers: 'The Eucharist draws us into Jesus' act of self-oblation. More than just statically receiving the incarnate Logos, we enter into the very dynamic of his self-giving'.[30]

D. CONCLUSION

To conclude this section, we highlight the way in which Augustine, in a way that became more or less normative for most of Christianity in the West, made a strong point of including earthly as well as heavenly members as citizens in God's city, and who, precisely in their role of being here-and-now earthly members of Christ's body, become one with him in being both the priests and the victims, those who offer and who are offered in the liturgy that is their Christian lives. Through all the devolutions and misunderstandings that have plagued so much of subsequent Christian thinking on atonement and sacrifice, this central Christian insight, though often pushed into the background, was never totally lost.

---

26 From Rufinus's Latin translation (possibly known to Augustine) of Origen's *Homily on Leviticus* 9.9 [GCS 29 (VI) 436.14–24 (trans. mine quoted from *Origen Spirit and Fire: A Thematic Anthology of His Writings* [Washington, DC: Catholic University of America Press, 1984], 291).
27 Augustine, *On the City of God*, 10.6 (PL 41, p. 284; CC Ser lat 47 [14/1], p. 279.
28 Quoted from the Vatican web site: <http://www.vatican.va/holy_father/benedict_xvi/apost_exhortations/documents/hf_ben-xvi_exh_20070222_sacramentum-caritatis_en.html>
29 'Manducare panem, quod est in nouo testamento sacrificium Christianorum' – *On the City of God*, 17.5 (*CC* Ser Lat 47 [14/1], p. 566, lines 157–58).
30 Pope Benedict XVI, *Sacramentum Caritatis*, no. 11.

Chapter X

Conclusion

When we began this chapter, we had found that the threefold Pauline division of sacrificial themes, sacrifice of Christ, the new temple and Christian sacrificial activity could be helpful in unveiling some sense of an overarching unity across the pluriform witness of the New Testament writings. Now, as we conclude this chapter, we have happily found that applying that threefold division to the even more pluriform witness of the patristic data was anything but a procrustean imposition. For first, and reassuringly, we found no instances of 'sacrificial data' that failed to relate comfortably to this division. Second, and indeed serendipitously, we found that in those instances where some aspect of this threefold division was lacking or only weakly witnessed, this very fact served as a handy heuristic for unpacking the development of sacrificial ideas among those witnesses. This is particularly revealing as one traces the development of the temple theme from the second-century writings up to the ecclesiologically more mature vision of an Augustine. Whereas, for example, Irenaeus seems to have picked up from Paul only the idea of the individual, but not yet that of the community, as the new temple, two centuries later, with Augustine, it is quite clearly not just the individual but the whole Christian community, the here-and-now, in-this-world Body of Christ that is the new temple in which, as 1 Peter 2.5 puts it, Christians are 'to offer spiritual sacrifices acceptable to God through Jesus Christ'.

PART TWO

ATONEMENT AND SACRIFICE: THE DISTORTING VEILS

In Part One, we laid out our fundamental Trinitarian understanding of Christian sacrifice. After that, we sketched out in three bridge sections the understanding of sacrifice (1) in the ancient world and in the Hebrew Scriptures, (2) in the Christian Scriptures and (3) in the early Christian writers. Now, in Part Two, our second and middle high point, we attend to those developments that, in the first millennium and a half of Christian history, cast a series of distorting veils over the authentic, Christian understanding of sacrifice. We do this in four chapters: (I) St. Paul and problems with sacrificial atonement; (II) Anselm, Abelard, Aquinas and Julian of Norwich; (III) the 'Sacrifice of the Mass' and (IV) sacrifice and the Reformation.

Chapter I

Paul and Problems with Sacrificial Atonement

A. PROBLEMS

There are several books and articles that provide much of the main background, and often much of the material itself, of what we are presenting in this section. Chief among them are Finlan's *Problems with Atonement* and my own extensive appropriation and development of this theme,[1] Heim's magnificently communicative *Saved from Sacrifice*,[2] and Nuth's important work on medieval soteriology.[3] The central insight that drives this section, an insight obviously shared with Finlan and Heim, is not only that problems with atonement are serious and real, but also that they coincide extensively with problems with sacrifice. There is painful irony in Heim's title, *Saved from Sacrifice*. It might, with even more painfully appropriate irony, have been called 'saved from atonement'. Nay more, there is

---

1   Stephen Finlan, *Problems with Atonement: the Origins of, and Controversy about, the Atonement Doctrine* (Collegeville, Minn.: Liturgical Press, 2005); Robert J. Daly, S.J., 'Images of God and the Imitation of God: Problems with Atonement', *Theological Studies* 68 (2007), pp. 36–51.
2   S. Mark Heim, *Saved from Sacrifice: A Theology of the Cross* (Grand Rapids, Mich.: Eerdmans, 2006).
3   Joan M. Nuth, *Wisdom's Daughter: The Theology of Julian of Norwich* (New York: Crossroad, 1992); idem, 'Two Medieval Soteriologies: Anselm of Canterbury and Julian of Norwich', *Theological Studies* 53 (1992), pp. 611–645.

also a serendipitous revelatory similarity in the very wording of the titles of these books: ***Problems*** *with Atonement* (Finlan), ***Saved*** *from Sacrifice* (Heim), and *Sacrifice Unveiled* (Daly). All three of us are deeply aware that we are engaged, first of all, in a remedial, revisionist theological task.[4] 'Atonement' and 'sacrifice' have not only been almost identified with each other in the course of Christian theological history, they also share the unhappy fate of having been massively misunderstood throughout much of that history.

Following the order I used in my 'Images of God' article,[5] this first section of Part Two will be arranged in the following order: (1) the relationship between the Incarnation and atonement theories, (2) the tension between authentic Christian doctrine and some of the theo-logical implications of the metaphors of atonement, (3) the problem of divine violence, (4) sacrifice and cult, (5) the pervasiveness of the legal and the judicial, especially in the West, (6) provisional conclusions.

B. Incarnation and Atonement Theories

The first point to be made and always kept in mind, is that 'the atonement' – especially when one means by that any particular theory of atonement – is not a central Christian doctrine. What is central, irreducibly central, is the Incarnation of Jesus Christ. Take away the Atonement, meaning the atonement theories developed in the Christian West, one still has the vibrant Christianity of the East that, although founded on the same biblical origins and patristic sources as that of the West, bases its theology of salvation, fully Trinitarian and fully incarnational, much more on theologies of theosis/divinization rather than on Western-type atonement theories. On the other hand, take away the Incarnation and there is, at least for mainline or Trinitarian Christianity, no Christianity left.[6]

Stated oversimply and in its most blatant stereotypical form, traditional Western atonement theory includes, or is ultimately reducible to the following affirmations: (1) God's honour was damaged by human sin; (2) God demanded a bloody victim – innocent or guilty – to pay for human sin; (3) God was persuaded to alter the divine verdict against humanity when the Son of God offered to endure humanity's punishment; (4) the death of the Son thus functioned as a payoff; salvation was purchased.[7]

If this, or this kind of, atonement theory is central to our idea of God and of salvation, we are indeed in deep trouble. In effect, it turns God into some

---

4　A revisionist agenda is also obviously present in the recent work of Erin Lothes Biviano, *The Paradox of Christian Sacrifice: The Loss of Self, the Gift of Self* (New York: Crossroad, 2007).

5　*Theological Studies* 68 (2007) 36–51. This article is extensively dependent on Finlan's arrangement and presentation.

6　Finlan expresses this as follows: 'It is incorrect to identify "Christianity" with atonement without remainder. Atonement is not an essential doctrine of Christianity but is in fact derivative. The more central doctrine is the Incarnation (see chapter 5.) [esp. Section 5.1: "The Incarnation Inerpreted through Secondary Doctrines"]. The Incarnation need not issue in the mythology of substitutionary atonement. God's participation in human life and God's indwelling of Jesus of Nazareth in particular did not make the Crucifixion inevitable or necessary' (Finlan, *Problems with Atonement*, p. 104).

7　As formulated by Finlan, *Problems with Atonement*, p 1.

combination of a great and fearsome judge, or offended lord, or temperamental spirit. It calls into question God's free will, or justice, or sanity (Finlan, pp. 97–98). It is incompatible with the central biblical idea of a loving and compassionate God. How, then, could such a notion have come to be regarded as Christian? Much of the explanation, not necessarily the blame but at least the beginning of an explanation, can be found in the Epistles of St. Paul.

For Paul, Christ is, simultaneously, the final scapegoat, the price of redemption, the long-promised Messiah, the reason for God's fostering of Abraham's descendants, and the leader who teaches the children to live by God's Spirit (Finlan, p. 50). When we ask what is achieved for us through this Christ-Messiah, the answer is: justification, reconciliation, adoption. When we ask further about the processes of achieving these, the answers are, respectively, judicial (justification), diplomatic (reconciliation) and familial (adoption). These processes that, almost immediately, were seen by following generations as transactions (susceptible, as subsequent developments show, to the residual overlay of archaic magical ideas) are expressed in a rich congeries, even wild range, of metaphors. These metaphors are cultic, economic, judicial, social, diplomatic and familial.

As we proceed, we have to remember that Paul was not a systematic theologian, at least not in any modern sense of that term. And we must also try to keep in mind not only the great range of metaphors with which Paul was groping to express something of the mystery of salvation, but also that he was quite possibly the first to try to do so in this way. We must pursue the implications of the way in which he combined, conflated and rapidly switched between these metaphors. This switching suggests his apparent awareness that no one metaphor or no narrow selection of them is normative. Pursuing this line of analysis makes us sensitive to the extent of the deformation that took place when theologians began to select just some of these metaphors and push them to their 'theo-logical' conclusions. For some of these conclusions are at odds not only with each other but also with the central biblical revelation of a loving and merciful God eager to save, rescue and forgive far beyond what the human mind and imagination often thinks is right and proper – and, significantly, at odds with what Paul himself was groping to express (Finlan, pp. 34 and 62). One can see this deformation already beginning to take place as early as the Pastoral Epistles and the Deutero-Pauline Letters where fidelity to right doctrine was increasingly seen as the sign of a true Christian (Finlan, pp. 39–62).

Increasingly, as atonement theories developed, an *interpretation* of Jesus' crucifixion, seen more and more as a *transaction*, indeed as a cultic, juridical and even quasi-magical transaction, became the core message, while the actual teaching of Jesus, that had little, if anything, to do with such an interpretation, 'became a secondary body of information' (Finlan, p. 57). It was a devolution, a reduction of atonement theory down to the idea that God deliberately intended Jesus' violent death (Finlan, p. 101, citing Walter Wink). Accompanying this devolution was a change in how one would talk about God the Father. For example, as all four Gospels attest, Jesus would talk about God not only as 'my Father' but also as '*your* Father'. But, as time went on, that locution shifted increasingly to talking about God as *Jesus'* Father (Finlan, p. 112). There was also a shift away from how Jesus used to speak and teach – which, in his mouth, seemed to be quite remarkably uncultic – and more towards a way of speaking about Jesus as a cultic sacrificial victim, and about his death as a cultic transaction (Finlan, pp. 113–15). As Christian teaching developed, at first in the common patristic tradition, and then, especially in its subsequent Western developments, atonement theory became the primary 'vehicle for conveying information about salvation and Incarnation' (Finlan, p. 120). However, as theologians are now increasingly aware, knowledge and information about the Incarnation does not need to be transmitted solely through atonement doctrine with its narrow focus on violent crucifixion as the central transactional moment. Or, put more positively, the Incarnation, Jesus' human life – that by which we are in fact saved – was not merely a lengthy prologue to the crucifixion (see Finlan, p. 123).

C. Metaphor and Doctrine

As already pointed out, many of Paul's metaphors, when pushed strictly and narrowly to their logical conclusions, have unacceptable 'theo-logical' implications. Does God's favour or forgiveness have to be *bought*? Does God's *anger* have to be *assuaged by sacrifice*? Is God a retribution-seeking, restitution-demanding judge? Is God a dishonoured lord whose honour needs to be restored? Atonement theories generally pick and choose among the metaphors, overlook both their range and complexity, and overlook the implications of how Paul would rapidly shift back and forth among them. Focusing on some of the implications of these metaphors, atonement theorists would turn them into doctrines. In doing so they would generally overlook Paul's actual teaching about a merciful God. For example, the metaphors sometimes imply a selfless Messiah *over against* a God who must be paid off. The metaphors sometimes imply an implacable Father *over against* a compassionate Son (Finlan, pp. 39–62). These were just some of the implications of some of Paul's metaphors rather than what he directly taught and, perhaps more significantly, rather than what he apparently was groping to communicate in those places where, apparently giving up on attempted 'theo-logical' exposition, he would break into song (e.g, see especially Rom. 11.33–36 and Phil. 2.6–11).

Excursus 4
Trinitarian Theology

The 'over-against' implications of the Pauline atonement metaphors, when they are turned into doctrine, logically introduce into the Trinity a tension that is at odds with what was (later of course) achieved in a mature Trinitarian theology. Such inner Trinitarian tension fails to appropriate the fundamental Christian faith-insight that, in sending the Son, the Father is actually sending himself. Despite the rhetoric, some of which is embedded in Scripture itself (e.g., Romans 8.32: 'He who did not withhold ["spare" – *ouk epheisato*] his own Son, but gave him up for all of us'), the Father was *not doing something to the Son*; the Father was giving/offering himself.[8] A significant factor in the history of this development is that the seeds of many of the theologically unacceptable implications of traditional atonement theory were planted relatively early in the patristic age, well before the full maturation of Trinitarian theology. Some of these unacceptable implications were already being superseded even as early as the theology of the late fourth-century Cappadocian Fathers, Gregory of Nyssa and Basil the Great.

For example, it was not until the post-fourth-century maturation of patristic theology, aided, of course, by the discussions and definitions of the early ecumenical councils, that it became even possible to articulate – as theologians are finally beginning to do – a Trinitarian theology of Christian sacrifice such as the following:

> First of all, Christian sacrifice is not some object that we manipulate, nor is it something that we do or give up. It is first and foremost, a mutually self-giving event that takes place between persons. It is, in fact, the most profoundly personal event that we can conceive or imagine. It begins, in a kind of first 'moment', not with us but with the self-offering of God the Father in the gift of the Son.
>
> It continues, in a second 'moment', in the self-offering 'response' of the Son, in his humanity and in the power of the Holy Spirit, to the Father and for us. And it continues further in a third 'moment' – and only then does it begin to become Christian sacrifice – when we, in human actions that are empowered by the same Spirit that was in Jesus, begin to enter into that perfect, en-spirited, mutually self-communicating personal relationship that is the life of the Blessed Trinity.
>
> In a nutshell, this is the whole story. Anything less than this, and especially anything other than this, is simply not *Christian* sacrifice. It might be something that Christians do, or it might be something that Christians think is sacrifice, but if it is not trinitarian in this sense, it is not *Christian* sacrifice.[9]
>
> END OF EXCURSUS 4

In other words, Jesus in his teaching seems to have a quite different instinct regarding God and access to God's mercy than does Paul – at least in contrast with the implications of some of Paul's metaphors. A sharply worded paragraph from Finlan highlights this striking contrast:

> Can we account for Paul's pessimism by saying that he is sensitive to the ever-present danger of human pride and sin? Is Paul, perhaps more savvy to human deceptiveness than is Jesus, and never speaks of open and free access to God by the pure in heart because most people will dishonestly convince themselves that

---

8   See Daly, 'Sacrifice Unveiled', p. 28.
9   Robert J. Daly, S.J., 'Sacrificial Preaching: The challenge of preaching sacrifice', *The Priest* 63 No. 9 (September 2007), p. 46, based on Edward J. Kilmartin, S.J., *The Eucharist in the West: History and Theology* (Collegeville, Minn.: Liturgical Press, 1998), pp. 381–82.

they are pure? Undoubtedly, Paul is perceptive on this point, but one can hardly say that he is more perceptive than Jesus, who could sniff out any scent of hypocrisy, or that Jesus' gospel is the result of naivety. We are dealing with two entirely different instincts about God and access to God. Jesus, with fully adult know-how and lack of illusions, is able to say that a sincere and childlike faith opens the portals of heaven. There really *are* some truth-hungering, merciful, and 'utterly sincere' people, who 'will be filled . . . will receive mercy . . . will see God' (Mt. 5.6–8)[10]

However, to be fair to Paul, if we take away the metaphors and look only at Paul's direct teaching and exhortation, we no longer see that strong tension between 'implacable Father and compassionate Son' (Finlan, p. 71). Further, when we attend to all that Paul is attempting to communicate, attend to his teaching and to the implications of his hymns as well as to the implications of *all* of his metaphors and models, we see that he is expressing not merely transactional ideas in metaphors that are cultic, economic and legal; he is also expressing spiritually transformative ideas. Notably – to jump ahead a millennium – it is especially the latter, the transformative ideas and implications, that Abelard (due perhaps to his heightened literary and imaginative sensitivity?) picks up and develops with his emphasis on moral influence (Finlan, pp. 74–75). Anselm, by contrast (more sensitive, perhaps, to at least some aspects of the 'theo-logic'?) focused more attention on the transactional aspect of the cultic, economic and legal metaphors.

D. DIVINE VIOLENCE

Anselm of Canterbury's *Cur Deus Homo – Why God Became Man* (CE 1098) has been called 'a master text of divine violence'.[11] Even those who disagree with it recognize it as perhaps the single most influential post-biblical text on the Atonement. Significantly, by the time atonement doctrine has developed (or devolved) to this point, it is no longer, as many patristic authors had thought, the devil who is the source of violence against humanity, but God the Father (Finlan, p. 72). What is laid out, even taken for granted here and in so many of the traditional atonement theories of the Western Church, is an inner divine 'scenario of divine violence restrained by divine mercy, but a mercy that had to be mediated through violence' (Finlan, p. 75). Hence the angry, punishing god of Calvin, or how Luther saw the Father as always severe, and the Son as always compassionate (ibid.), or how devout Catholics were schooled to make reparation to the Sacred Heart of Jesus. What all this does, whether consciously or subconsciously (and very much at odds with a mature Trinitarian theology as I indicated in the excursus a few pages earlier), is to locate violence and the negotiation of violence within the divine.

Underlying this whole line of development is the belief, or at least the fear, going back at least to Augustine, that all humanity faces damnation. Some of the

---

10   Finlan, p. 61. See Mt. 5.8 in J.B. Phillips, *The Gospels Translated into Modern English* (New York: Macmillan, 1961), p. 8.
11   Anthony W. Bartlett, *Cross Purposes: The Violent Grammar of Christian Atonement* (Harrisburg, Penn.: Trinity Press International, 2001), p. 76.

theories developed the idea that, to save humanity from condemnation, 'God preplanned the killing of the Son from the beginning of time' (Finlan, p. 76). Facilitating this development was the fact that, in contrast to much of the East, the idea of apocatastasis (universal salvation) was generally not even discussed in the West. More commonly taken for granted was the idea that God freely chose to save from damnation only some, and perhaps only the fortunate few. And if one did not have the good fortune to hear the gospel and be baptized, one had no chance at all. Nor was it only the churches of the Reformation that subsequently emphasized so strongly the fundamental depravity, the universal guilt of humankind. Jansenism, primarily a Roman Catholic phenomenon, could be just as negative in this regard. Saving humankind meant the transfer of divine wrath from us to the Son. 'Faced with such monstrous teachings' (Finlan, p. 78), theologians have desperately tried to make sense of it all. But as long as they remained bound within the framework of atonement theories that locate violence within the divine, they could not break out of a pernicious taking-for-granted of violence on all levels of existence, divine and human. Bad theology led to bad – that is, violent – morality.

As we will see in greater detail hereafter, René Girard, especially in his central major works, challenged the hegemony of this way of thinking, basically by exposing the violent mechanisms of sacrificial scapegoating, and by rejecting these mechanisms and the traditional (destruction-of-the-victim) idea of sacrifice as essential to Christianity. However, the theological appropriation of Girard's insights, that is, the development of a contemporary and authentically Christian (i.e., essentially non-violent) concept of God and Atonement remains a work in progress. Major contributions in this direction have come from the recently deceased Raymund Schwager, S.J. (d. 2004), especially in his *Jesus in the Drama of Salvation*[12] and *Banished from Eden.*[13] In these works, especially the latter, Schwager not only develops the concept of violence as the primordial sin, that is, seeing original sin as the common human tendency to reach for violent solutions, but also points out the 'natural' support for and indeed the 'natural' origin of, this concept in the findings of the contemporary biosciences.[14]

---

12   Raymund Schwager, *Jesus im Heilsdrama: Entwurf einer biblischen Erlösungslehre* (Innsbrucker theologische Studien, 29; Innsbruck: Tyrolia, 1990); ET: *Jesus in the Drama of Salvation: Toward a Biblical Doctrine of Redemption* (trans. James G. Williams and Paul Haddon; New York: Crossroad, 1999).

13   Raymund Schwager, *Banished from Eden: Original Sin and Evolutionary Theory in the Drama of Salvation* (trans. James G. Williams; London: Gracewing, 2005) = ET of *Erbsünde und Heilsdrama: Im Kontext von Evolution, Gentechnologie und Apokalyptic* (Münster: LIT, 1997). See the account of a panel discussion of this book, 'Celebrating Raymund Schwager': at the AAR Meeting in San Antonio, Texas, November 2004 in *The Bulletin of the Colloqium on Violence and Religion*, No. 26 (April, 2005), pp. 5–7.

14   Schwager arrives at this insight not by beginning with a traditional theology of original sin, and then asking how contemporary science relates to that theology. Rather, as far as possible, he begins with science itself. For example, he begins specifically with the finding that organisms at all levels, including the human psychic organism, have 'memories'. What the human organism has in its bio-psychic memory, from that critical evolutionary 'moment' that we call hominization, is the memory, encoded in our beings, that, when faced with the choice of spiritual self-transcendence, human beings generally chose to react in the (indeed tried-and-true) basically violent and instinctual ways that characterized the existence of their pre-human forebears. Influenced as he is by Girardian mimetic theory, Schwager suggests that this is a good way for us to begin to understand *peccatum originale originatum* – the original sin that continues to exist in us. Bridge 2C below (pp. 202–222) further expands on this theme.

Among the problems still needing adequate theological explanation is that of the residue of magical transactional thinking (see Finlan, p. 98) in Christian atonement doctrine (as well as in some popular understandings of the sacraments). Related to this is, for example, the persistence of seeing the Crucifixion as a kind of transaction that, ultimately or implicitly, calls into question the free will, or the justice, or the sanity, or the power of a supposedly benevolent God.[15] Similar to this transactional kind of thinking is the theological inconsistency of making the scapegoating of Jesus (an act of violence) a part of God's eternal plan (Finlan, p. 101). Similar also is the readiness to imagine magical power solutions (Hello, Harry Potter!) Is that far from the readiness to believe in miracles? All this seems to connect with the readiness to think of a violent God, or at least of the existence of some violence in God. It contributes both to the widespread human tendency to look for scapegoats (Finlan, p. 116), and to the widespread tendency to take violence for granted in human affairs.

Connected with all this is what seems to be a long-standing tendency to absolutize suffering. The popularity of Mel Gibson's film *The Passion of the Christ* is only a more recent example. In the suffering of Christ there is, undeniably, a transcendent sacredness. But there is no unconditioned absoluteness there in the suffering of Christ. For Christ did not *have* to suffer. There is no absolute divine necessity there. But there is – viewed from what I would insist is an authentic Christian point of view – absolute necessity in the *love* with which Christ suffered. For ultimately, it is not suffering but love that saves. In other words, as Cynthia Crysdale has observed, suffering and the violence that causes it is a consequence of union with God, not the cause of it or the means to it.[16]

E. SACRIFICE AND CULT

As we have been pointing out, problems with atonement generally also end up being problems with sacrifice. Sacrifice, along with atonement, is commonly perceived as an instance of divine violence. Emphasis on the once-for-all sacrifice of Christ can indeed spare Protestants from the problem their Catholic counterparts have in explaining how the Sacrifice of the Mass can be, as defined in 1562 at the Council of Trent, a 'true and proper sacrifice'.[17] But the problem still remains, whether located in a once-for-all past, or also in a continuing liturgical celebration, that the sacrifice of Christ ends up being an act of divine violence that God planned from all eternity.

In writing about Atonement Paul assumed the existence of, and familiarity with, already existing cultic patterns. He used several cultic metaphors and assumed

---

15   It is a common (and indeed often effective) pastoral strategy, when faced with the need to 'explain' evil and suffering, to point to the passion of Christ. This, however, does not solve the problem; it merely transposes it.

16   See Finlan's development of this theme on pp. 104–6. He acknowledges his dependence on Cynthia S.W. Crysdale, *Embracing Travail: Retrieving the Cross Today* (New York: Continuum, 1999), passim, but esp. p. 100.

17   'Verum et proprium sacrificium': *Enchiridion symbolorum, definitionum, et declarationum de rebus fidei et morum* (ed. Henricus Denzinger and Adolfus Schönmetzer; Freiburg im Breisgau: Herder, 1967, no. 1751) See also nos. 1743 and 1753: 'truly an atonement sacrifice – *sacrificium vere propitiatorium*'.

that salvation came from a cultic act (Finlan, pp. 44 and 51). But it is what happened after Paul that causes most of the problems I am struggling with here. For, as Christian reflection developed, the increasing emphasis on and blending together of ideas of penal substitution and the idea of death-as-payment caused sacrifice to become, for many, the dominant image of Atonement. This is obvious in the Epistle to the Hebrews. Subsequent patristic theologians then glued Paul's atonement metaphors onto the notion of a sacrificial and redeeming transaction (Finlan, pp. 65–66). This attachment filled the perceived need. For despite the inroads that the spiritualization of sacrifice had already made and was continuing to make in Greek religious philosophy, in late biblical Judaism, and in early Christianity, Christian antiquity was still a time when sacrifice in the traditional history-of-religions sense of that word, that is, an external cultic act involving the destruction of a victim,[18] was generally taken for granted as an essential part of religion. It was still a time when almost everyone assumed that a sacrificial death was required for a mediator or reconciler to appease God with a unique sacrifice (Finlan, pp. 70–71). We have to remind ourselves that this necessity for a sacrificial and redeeming transaction was perceived to be a necessity *in God*, or a necessity outside of God to which God was bound. Part of the problem is, of course, the apparent scriptural warrant for this necessity (e.g., Lk. 24.26: 'Was it not necessary that the Messiah should suffer . . .?'). This assumption of the necessity of Christ's suffering resulted in and/or went along with false ideas about God. Such false ideas about God and a consequent false morality are inevitable if the scapegoating death of Jesus is a necessary, divinely planned, transactional sacrificial event that God brings about like a puppet maser manipulating human events.

F. LEGAL AND JUDICIAL THINKING

From the outset, judicial metaphors were among the metaphors used to explain the Atonement. In the post-Pauline developments, the blending of penal substitution ideas with those of death-as-payment resulted in presenting redemption as sacrifice-dominant. Then the gluing of Paul's atonement metaphors onto the notion of a sacrificial and redeeming *transaction*, and the concomitant increasing emphasis on the logic underlying that atonement transaction, made recourse to legal thinking all the more necessary (Finlan, pp. 65–66 and 98–99). As a result, by the time of Augustine, ransom theory (with its subthemes of rescue, deception, mousetrap, etc.) was being increasingly trumped by legal theory (Finlan, p. 70). Then Gregory the Great, in his blending of legal and sacrificial motifs, and in his stressing of the need for a *proportionate remedy*, locked legal-logical thinking into the core of Western atonement thinking. Characteristic of Western theological thinking, generally, and even to this day, has been the fundamental importance of law, *even on the divine level.*

The significance of the adjective 'Western' in the previous paragraph is central to what I am trying to understand. Here, precisely here, may be the most

---

18   For a detailed exposition of how damaging this destruction-of-a-victim idea of sacrifice can be when applied to Christian sacrifice, see Robert J. Daly, S.J., 'Robert Bellarmine and Post-Tridentine Eucharistic Theology', *Theological Studies* 61 (2000), pp. 239–60. See also below, pp. 158–168.

significant fork in the road where the West went one way, understanding the Christian mystery of salvation primarily after the model of a legal transaction, and the East went another way, understanding the Christian mystery of salvation primarily as *theosis*, divinization.

These characteristically Western developments help explain why Anselm's theory was so influential. It was a social theory based on the feudal structure of his time. It involved a structural form of vengeance/reparation, all of which had to be governed by 'law' (see Finlan, pp. 70–71). This emphasis on law was consistent with the fundamental psychology of Atonement that I have already mentioned, namely, that it is based on a belief that nothing is free, and on the intuition that ritual establishes order (Finlan, p. 80). 'Law and order' may not be synonymous, but they are inseparable.

As René Girard has pointed out, Jesus exposes and repudiates the victimization mechanism by which atonement has been thought to work. Nevertheless, the need of human societies for social and other appropriate mechanisms remains as strong as ever. Take away the legal and the juridical, and one takes away human culture as we know it. We cannot prescind from the legal and juridical ways of thinking by which we live. But to project our human and thus inevitably flawed (at least inevitably finite) juridical thinking – or any kind of human-experience-based thinking – onto God, and then to take the resulting image of God as a model both for understanding God's actions and for us humans to imitate, is simply bad theology. It leads to bad, and sometime to very bad, morality.

G. Provisional Conclusions

Before moving on to the medieval developments, it may help to take stock of the point to which we have now come. We have come to a certain point of helplessness in outlining these 'problems with Atonement'. What can we do? Who, or what, can free us from this vicious circle?[19] Few indeed are the mystically graced who, like Julian of Norwich (as we shall shortly see) can transcend the limitations in the theology of an Anselm and begin to speak *with real knowledge* and experiential wisdom about her all-loving, all-merciful God.[20] The rest of us can only humbly – or at least with attempted humility, since humility is hard to maintain when indulging in the *Schadenfreude* of pointing out how so much previous theology has been wrong – attend to developments in the tradition that seem to point to a more authentically Christian understanding of the atonement. The first two developments that come to mind derive more from the East than from the West: apophatic theology and *theosis*.

Apophatic theology reminds us that all our projections onto God are just that: faulty human projections, and that developing a theology from the implications of such projections can, as we have seen and will continue to see, lead to disastrously mistaken results.

---

19 Notice the similarity to the aporetic cries of Paul: 'What then should we say . . . Who will rescue me from this body of death?' (Rom. 7.7 and 24).
20 See Joan M. Nuth, 'Two Medieval Soteriologies: Anselm of Canterbury and Julian of Norwich', *Theological Studies* 53 (1992), pp. 611–45; idem, *Wisdom's Daughter: The Theology of Julian of Norwich* (New York: Crossroad, 1991).

Theosis reminds us that salvation does not come about by anything like a transaction that can be adequately explained or imagined in human terms; salvation comes about by beginning to become one with the ineffable God. Good theology can proclaim *that* this 'divinization' is what is actually happening to us, but it is at a loss to explain *how* divinization comes about. On this point, however, we can at least be grateful for a highly significant ecumenical theological convergence among recent Christian writers. Both the atonement critic Stephen Finlan and the atonement (as traditionally understood) advocate Hans Boersma[21] have simultaneously, and apparently quite independently of each other, concluded their books by pointing to *theosis*/deification as probably the best possible solution to our Christian 'problems with Atonement'. The final chapter subheading of Finlan's book is '5.2 *Theosis*'; the final section of Boersma's book is 'Epilogue: The End of Violence: Eschatology and Deification' (Finlan, pp. 120–24; Boersma, pp. 257–61).

But then two more thoughts come to mind, and these are gifts that the West can also bring to the table. The first of these is the strong Western intellectual conviction that humans are capable of true knowledge and right thinking. We must not, however exaggerate this capability. It is in fact related to apophasis on the negative side, because it primarily serves to identify and eliminate what is bad theology. On the positive side, we can cautiously hope that our capacity for right thinking can also begin to point us in the right direction.[22] The second gift that the West can bring to this table is its modern development of critical biblical and historical studies. All the faulty theories of atonement (and/or sacrifice) that have developed in the Christian tradition characteristically have roots in this or that particular part or aspect of biblical revelation, but not in the whole of it. Modern biblical studies afford a balanced access to that whole; they provide an ability, not available to earlier ages, to contextualize the different parts of that whole. In addition, all of the faulty theories of Atonement, with their concomitant unbalanced ideas of sacrifice, that have developed subsequent to the Bible can also be contextualized, and thus deabsolutized, by locating them in their historical, intellectual, and cultural situations of origin.

---

21   Hans Boersma, *Violence, Hospitality, and the Cross: Reappropriating the Atonement Tradition* (Grand Rapids, Mich.: Baker Academic, 2004). Previously, but not wholly accurately, I had labeled Finlan as 'very Catholic' and Boersma as 'very Protestant'; since their theological positions correspond respectively to what is commonly thought to be typically – or perhaps stereotypically – Catholic and Protestant.

22   In an epoch that we call 'postmodern', it is countercultural to insist on our ability to attain true knowledge of things, to have assurance that some of the 'great stories' can be more true than others, or that we have the ability to cull out at least some truth from a variety of 'great stories'. We also need to remind ourselves that there probably has never been an epoch in which one or other part of the broad Church Christian has not leaned toward one extreme or the other – optimism or pessimism – on the question of our capacity to know the truth.

Chapter II

Anselm, Abelard, Aquinas and Julian of Norwich

Without attempting to touch upon all the details of the doctrinal-historical 'development' of the idea of Christian sacrifice, while nevertheless attempting, as we indicated at the beginning of this Part Two, to keep things in a broad historical context, we now take up what are commonly considered to be the high points of the medieval and scholastic theories of Atonement and sacrifice.

A. ANSELM OF CANTERBURY (ca. 1033–1109)

Throwing down the gauntlet, as it were, in the face of any who might want to gloss over the massive antinomies that characterize the differences in the ways in which Christians have understood Atonement and sacrifice, Anthony Bartlett characterizes Anselm's *Cur Deus Homo*, 'unquestionably the major single document in Western atonement doctrine,' as 'A Master-Text of Divine Violence'.[23] To be fair, Anselm's thinking is far more sophisticated and nuanced than the bare-bones outline of traditional Western atonement theory presented at the beginning of this section.[24] But also to be honest, Anselm cannot totally avoid being painted with the broad, caricaturing brush of this description. For example, a sympathetic summary of what Anselm accepted as doctrine and was trying to explain reads as follows:

1. The sin of Adam involved all members of the human race in its consequences. *As by one man sin entered into this world, and by sin, death, so death passed upon all men because all have sinned.*

(Romans 5.12)

2. God promised a Redeemer, (see Genesis 3.15) and in *the fullness of time . . . sent His Son . . . that He might redeem them who were under the law, that we might receive the adoption of sons.*

(Galatians 4.4–5)

3. This Redeemer is Jesus Christ, *who gave Himself for us, that He might redeem us from all iniquity . . .* (Titus 2.14, see also Ephesians 5.25–28). His offering of Himself is

---

23   Anthony W. Bartlett, *Cross Purposes*, p. 76.
24   (1) God's honor was damaged by human sin; (2) God demanded a bloody victim – innocent or guilty – to pay for human sin; (3) God was persuaded to alter the divine verdict against humanity when the Son of God offered to endure humanity's punishment; (4) the death of the Son thus functioned as a payoff; salvation was purchased.

free and voluntary: . . . *I lay down my life . . . No man taketh it away from me, but I lay it down of myself . . .*

(John 10.17–18)

4. The effects of Christ's redeeming acts – including His resurrection – are com-municated to Christians by baptism. *Know you not that all we who are baptized in Christ Jesus, are baptized in His death? For we are buried with Him by baptism into death, that, as Christ is risen from the dead by the glory of the Father, so we also may walk in newness of life.*

(Romans 6.3–4)[25]

This representation of Anselm's theological understanding of the atonement is somewhat idealized. For, the more closely one looks, even if only quickly reading the headings of the forty-seven chapters that comprise the two books of *Cur Deus Homo*, the more one discovers problems. By Anselm's time, some of the problems that had been caused by pushing a selection of biblical metaphors to their 'theo-logical' conclusions had been solved. The monks Anselm was trying to teach were no longer worried about 'the devil's rights' over the human race. They no longer thought the ransom of Christ was paid to the devil. As a positive replacement, Anselm offered the so-called 'satisfaction theory': payment is indeed made, and made in justice, but to God, not to the devil. But this solution only transferred the problem to another place. For, as Finlan (p. 72) trenchantly pointed out, it is now, in effect, not the devil but God the Father who seems to be the source of violence against humanity.

This satisfaction theory 'is built on the understanding of sin as the refusal to render to God what is due to Him' (Colleran, p. 44), namely, honour. This sets up an obligation to restore the honour. Failure to do so would introduce disorder into God's kingdom; supreme justice would be violated, and God's plans for the human race would be frustrated. To set all aright, satisfaction must be made, and made in proportion to the measure of the sin. But neither human beings nor angels can make satisfaction for sin, an insult against the honour of God. Only a God-Man can offer this satisfaction.

Objections to this theory are not only sufficient to call it into question, but also to identify the theory not just as a weak solution, but also as part of the problem, indeed as a major part of the problem. First and foremost, it is not scriptural. Proponents have indeed claimed that it is not contrary to Scripture, and that it merely, as do other traditional Christian doctrines, goes beyond what is explicitly revealed in order to attain a coherent theological explanation. But, as we will see shortly, in the face of a fairly obvious and authentic reading of Scripture, this claim turns out to be specious.

A common objection is that satisfaction theory is 'based on an analogy with Germanic law and is colored by a feudal notion of "honor" that is not worthy of God' (Colleran, p. 45). Now Colleran is not alone in claiming that Anselm's use of

---

25 James M. Colleran, *Why God Became Man and The Virgin Conception and Original Sin by Anselm of Canterbury* (Translation, Introduction and Notes; Albany, New York: Magi Books, 1969), Introduction, p. 42.

the notion of honour and satisfaction are thoroughly Christian. He does this primarily by appealing to the Trinitarian insight that, although 'divine justice requires satisfaction ... divine justice is identified, in God's self-contained and simple essence, with His mercy and omnipotence' (Colleran, p. 46). This Trinitarian insight may indeed begin to 'rescue' Anselm's atonement theory as inherently Christian, but it has had little effect on the satisfaction theory and atonement theory that lived on after Anselm with a life of its own, totally oblivious of the moderating force of Anselm's Trinitarian insight and of the love-filled monastic-contemplative context from which his work comes.

Another group of objections questions whether satisfaction theory might be projecting onto God ideas of necessity and lack of freedom. Once again, Anselm himself seems to be sufficiently nuanced to blunt the force of these objections. The popular understanding of the theory is, of course, another matter.

A further objection, one that Anselm cannot fully deflect from himself, because it was in the air as part of the world in which he lived and breathed and had his being, was the taken-for-grantedness of legal and judicial thinking in all aspects of life, and the concomitant projection of legal and judicial thinking onto God.[26]

Returning now to the question whether satisfaction theory is scriptural, if we are thinking of the integral and central meaning of Scripture, we can bluntly state that it is not. As Colleran, despite his desire to present Anselm in a favourable light, puts it:

> Perhaps the most basic and most telling criticism of Anselm's account of the redemption is that he does not seem fully to allow for the freedom of God in bringing about human reconciliation *in exactly the manner that has been revealed to us* [emphasis mine]. . . . He [Anselm] argues that if God were to remit sin without reparation or punishment, He would be letting a disorder pass in His Kingdom, and he would be treating the virtuous and the sinful alike.
>
> (Colleran, p. 46)[27]

This is Anselm projecting onto God human ideas of justice, fairness, and legality (see aforementioned under 'Legal and Judicial Thinking', pp. 107–108) in a way that seems contradictory to a central theme of overall biblical revelation that begins deep in the Hebrew Scriptures. For example, the famous Isaian 'My thoughts are not your thoughts, nor are your ways my ways, says the Lord' (Isaiah 55.8–11) seems to be a clear warning, against thinking that we are able to figure out how God does things. This commitment to what we later called an apophatic attitude towards our capacity to 'justify the ways of God to man' became a central feature of the teaching of Jesus. He seemed to go out of his way, repeatedly, to do

---

26   See my discussion of this in Section I of this chapter, pp. 107–8.
27   The reference here is to *Cur Deus Homo*, bk. 1, Chs. 12–13. Chapter 12 asks: 'Is it fitting for God to remit sin out of mercy alone, without any payment of the debt?' Within the chapter we read: 'There is another consequence, if an unpunished sin is remitted: one who sins and one who does not sin will be in the same position before God. And that would be unseemly for God.'

and teach things that simply did not make sense to our human way of thinking. Examples abound, some of them in direct teaching and action, like the Beatitudes, the repeated commands to unlimited forgiveness, and the promise of *immediate* paradise to a criminal being justly executed for his crimes (Lk. 23.43); and some of it in parables like that of the prodigal son and forgiving father (Lk. 15.11–32), or that of the workers in the vineyard who all get the same wage regardless of how long they worked (Mt. 20.1–16). This is not merely 'letting a disorder pass in His Kingdom,' to use the words of Anselm, it seems to be the actual way that the Kingdom of God works. Anselmian satisfaction theory, in the hands of sophisticated theologians,[28] may indeed be sufficiently nuanced to save it from outrightly contradicting authentic Christianity. However, it is difficult for us to defend it against two strong negative judgments: first, it seriously underplays the subjective side of the experience of atonement: and second, because of that, it gets us moving and thinking in the wrong direction.

B. PETER ABELARD (1079–1142/3)

Some four decades after Anselm, Peter Abelard tried to set atonement theory moving in a different direction. Bartlett astutely sums up the limitations of the Anselmian theory and introduces the somewhat opposite direction into which Abelard tried to steer atonement theory by exclaiming: 'At a certain level no one could believe that any true father would be "satisfied" by the execution of a beloved son, least of all when the preacher tells me that I brought about his death!'[29] Abelard is routinely characterized, in contrast with Anselm, as a proponent of a 'moral influence theory' or 'subjective theory' of Atonement. But looking beyond the labels, Dillistone sees Abelard as marking 'the transition from an outlook which saw God dealing with humanity *as a whole*, either through a legal transaction or through a mystical transfusion, to one in which the ethical and psychological qualities of *the individual within the community* begin to receive fuller recognition.'[30] In Abelard's own words:

> Now it seems to us that we have been justified by the blood of Christ and reconciled to God in this way: through this unique act of grace manifested to us – in that his Son has taken upon himself our nature and persevered therein in teaching us by word and example even unto death – he has the more fully bound us to himself by love; with the result that our hearts should be enkindled by such a gift of divine grace, and true charity should not now shrink from enduring anything for him.
>
> Wherefore, our redemption through Christ's suffering is that deeper affection in us which not only frees us from slavery to sin, but also wins for us

---

28 See, for example, Lisa Sowle Cahill, 'The Atonement Paradigm: Does It Still Have Explanatory Value?' *Theological Studies* 68 (2007), pp. 418–32; and the discussions in: John Sanders, ed., *Atonement and Violence: A Theological Conversation* (Nashville: Abingdon Press, 2006).

29 Bartlett, *Cross Purposes*, p. 86

30 F.W. Dillistone, *The Christian Understanding of Atonement* (Philadelphia: Westminster, 1968), p. 325.

the true liberty of sons of God, so that we do all things out of love rather than fear.[31]

In other words, the change that results from the loving death of Christ is not something that takes place in God; the change takes place in the subjective consciousness of sinners. Abelard may, as is routinely noted by books on the atonement, have presented an incomplete theory of Atonement, but what he did present is, at least to modern sensitivities, so obviously Christian, so obviously integral to an adequate theory of Atonement, that we have to ask why it seems to be so routinely dismissed by all but nineteenth- and early twentieth-century Protestant liberals?[32]

The answer may lie not merely in the Western weakness for legal and juridical thinking, nor simply in the widely held perception that Abelard's teaching, despite its obvious and needed theological insight, may be by itself insufficient to explain atonement. Much of the responsibility may lie in his reputation for maverick teaching and even heterodoxy. The 1121 Synod of Soissons had already censured him for various errors and had condemned his treatise *De unitate et trinitate divina*. Later, the Synod of Sens (1140 or 41) required him to renounce (without giving him the opportunity to defend himself) a series of propositions that Bernard of Clairvaux had excerpted from Abelard's works. Included among them are Trinitarian and other propositions that are – at least as Bernard formulated them – obviously heretical.[33] That, plus the fact that Abelard's insights were far in advance of his time, helped bring it about that it was only in the nineteenth century that they began to receive their due.

C. THOMAS AQUINAS (ca. 1225–74)

Another reason for this development, or non-development, was the sophistication with which, in the following century, Thomas Aquinas (ca. 1225–74) refined and advanced a basically Anselmian satisfaction theory that became the basic starting point for the way most subsequent theologians in the catholic tradition (broadly understood) tried to understand and explain the atonement. I here follow closely Colleran's outline of Aquinas's understanding of this mystery (the supposition, of course, is that God willed to free human beings from sin):

> 1. The death of Christ was not *absolutely* necessary for the salvation of human beings (*Summa Theologiae*, 3.46.2 c). In other words, the human life of Christ (with all its concomitant historical details) is *contingent*. It did not have to happen, nor did it have to happen in the way that it did.

---

31   Abelard, *Commentary on Romans*, LCC 10, *A Scholastic Miscellany: Anselm to Ockham* (ed. and trans. Eugene R. Fairweather; London: SCM, 1956), pp. 283–84, as cited in Robert H. Culpepper, *Interpreting the Atonement* (Grand Rapids, Mich.: Eerdmans, 1966), pp. 89–90.
32   See J. Denny Weaver, *The Nonviolent Atonement* (Grand Rapids, Mich.: Eerdmans, 2001), pp. 18–19.
33   DS 731–739: Heinrich Denzinger, *Enchiridion Symbolorum* 37th ed. (Freiburg im Breisgau/Basel/Rom/Wien: Herder, 1991), pp. 324–26.

2. It was not necessary in the sense of God having been forced by any extrinsic agent to require this death, or in the sense of Christ having been externally forced to endure it.

3. Hence it was still possible, simply or absolutely speaking, for God to free human beings from sin in some other way, than by the death of Christ.

4. The death of Christ, then, was necessary *on the supposition* that God required satisfaction proportionate to the sin, which only the death of the God-Man could provide.

(see *ST*, 3.46.1 c).

5. In other words, we can say it was impossible for God to free human beings in any other way, on the supposition that God had already decided not only on freeing human beings from sin, but on proportionate satisfaction in doing so.

(see *ST*, 3.46.2 c).

6. Although we can say that the justice of God required the death of Christ to atone for human sin, even this debt in justice depends upon God's Will to require proportionate satisfaction. If God willed to free human beings without any satisfaction, He would not be violating any justice, because He has no one superior to Him or independent of Him whose rights would be violated.

(see *ST*, 3.46.2 ad 3).

7. This method of liberation was the *most fitting*, however, because, besides freeing human beings from sin, it best manifested God's love for human beings and stimulated their love for God. It also gave us an example of obedience, humility, perseverance and justice. It not only freed us from sin, but merited grace and glory for us. By it, human beings are better stimulated to persevere in grace. This kind of redemption, involving the death of the God-Man, leads to a greater victory of humanity over the devil.

(see *ST*, 3.46.2 c)[34]

Colleran points out that Aquinas also brought the notions of 'mystical body' and 'vine and branches' into the description of the process of redemption in a way that Anselm never did. Whether for better or for worse, one of the effects of Aquinas's nuanced appropriation of the Anselmian satisfaction theory was to make it much more theo-logically acceptable, and thus ensure that it would remain, to this day, the starting point of most Christian theological reflection on the atonement.[35] This was the formidable situation that Julian of Norwich felt called to challenge.

---

34 Colleran, pp. 47–48.
35 A possibly helpful analogy can be found in the early history of modern political theory, in the way that John Locke appropriated the brutally harsh insights of Thomas Hobbes and made them more acceptable to Christian and humane sensitivities. This ensured that these insights, thus refined, would remain, to this day, the starting point of theorizing about modern liberal democracy.

D. JULIAN OF NORWICH (ca. 1342–after 1416)

The English spiritual writer, Julian of Norwich is a remarkable witness to the internal vitality of the Christian tradition that manages to shine through even in periods of apparent decline.[36] Because of the close relationship – indeed almost identity between 'sacrifice' and 'Atonement' – Julian's profound insight into the Atonement occupies a key position in this work. Whether by direct influence, or simply because of what was 'in the air' theologically in the late fourteenth century, she is, in her understanding of the Atonement, an heir to the theological achievements of her three medieval predecessors, Anselm, Abelard and Aquinas, especially Anselm. Julian, consciously faithful to the church teaching of her age, nevertheless appropriated it in a way that transcends it. For, in her significantly deeper understanding of the mystery of redemption, everything proceeds from and is explained by the overriding and overwhelming[37] love of God as the be-all and end-all of all human-divine interaction. In her own words:

> I was taught that love is our Lord's meaning. And I saw very certainly in this and in everything that before God made us he loved us, which love was never abated and never will be. And in this love he has done all his works, and in this love he has made all things profitable to us, and in this love our life is everlasting. In our creation we had beginning, but the love in which he created us was in him from without beginning. In this love we have our beginning, and all this shall we see in God without end.
>
> (86:342–43)[38]

Anselm, the monk, would not deny this; he'd agree with it. Theologically, however, this was not the vision that his work ended up communicating and bequeathing to subsequent generations of Christians. When we ask why this is so, we quickly come to the experiential starting points of their respective theologies. For Anselm, the starting point was the experience of compunction. For Julian, however, the starting point seems to have been an early mystical vision at a time when she thought she was dying. Whether or not it was something like what we now call a near-death experience, she described it as the experience of seeing everything in a point, of seeing things as God sees them, a God who sees sin with compassion rather than

---

36 In what follows, I am deeply dependent on the work of Joan M. Nuth, *Wisdom's Daughter: The Theology of Julian of Norwich* (New York: Crossroad, 1991) and 'Two Medieval Soteriologies: Anselm of Canterbury and Julian of Norwich', *Theological Studies* 53 (1992), pp. 611–45.

37 Words begin to fail, and even betray, as they always will when we use them to try to approach a central mystery of our faith. 'Overriding and overwhelming', to describe God's love can easily suggest a powerful force that eliminates human freedom and responsibility. It is in that suggestion that words fail and betray. For in Julian, as in all Christian groping to understand and communicate something of the divine mystery of love, authentic theology becomes inevitably apophatic. For the autonomy of human freedom and choice stands side-by-side with, but not overridden by, the overwhelming power of God's love that will finally and most certainly win out, but in a way that overwhelms the human capacity to understand. In faith we can be sure of this, as Julian was. But in reasoning about it, we are overwhelmed.

38 Quoted from *Showings*, Long Text, Chapter 86, pp. 342–43 of the critical edn by Edmund College, O.S.A. and James Walsh, S.J. (New York: Paulist press, 1978).

with blame, a God who sees like a mother who does not 'see' the sins of her children, but sees with loving compassion only the suffering that their sins cause. This is so because, in the sinner, God sees not the sinner but his own Son! This enables Julian not to deny – denial would not have been possible for a faithful daughter of the Church – but to transcend the inevitable dichotomies that human theological reasoning can never quite escape: the justice–mercy and justice–love dichotomies. Thus, when God is seeing sinful human beings, and in seeing them is seeing His Son, sin in the eyes of God is not something that human beings commit, sin is what human beings suffer from.[39] Here, according to Julian's vision into the mind of God, sin simply does not exist. For God, omniscient and omnipotent, who sees and knows all things, sees not the sin or the sinner, but Christ, His Son, who has identified himself with the sinner.

Julian spent twenty years reflecting on this, the twenty years that came between the 'Short Text' of her *Showings*, containing the first report of her visions, and the 'Long Text'. It is here, in the 'Long Text' that Julian shows her instinctive or natural talent as a theologian. It is here that she plays on the distinction between human and divine judgment, between God's eternal perspective and the human, historically conditioned perspective. She marvels at our common human inability to accept the self as lovable, as God does. She marvels at our perverse predilection for choosing to see God as a judge rather than as a mother. In her reflections, reflections that really are theology in the deepest sense, she is inviting us to transcend, with her, the limitations of Church teaching – which, by the way, she boldly classifies as human judgment – and to begin to enter with her into the mind of God and see things as God sees them.

One of the reasons why Julian's theological vision feels[40] so congenial to us in our own theological epoch at the beginning of the twenty-first century, is that it is not just incarnational but also Trinitarian. To be Trinitarian is unusual in the theology of the medieval West, but beyond that it is Trinitarian in a uniquely special way. Rather than seeing beatitude and fulfilment in heaven in the traditional way, namely that of our joy at partaking in the life of the Trinity, Julian, consistent with her visionary way of seeing things as God sees them, sees it the other way around. As Joan Nuth explains it:

> Heaven, for Julian, includes God's joy and delight in us. Humans are seen to give something to God, if not to God's essence, certainly to God's eternal rejoicing over human creation. . . . By the marvelous increase and fulfillment of human nature wrought by Christ, humanity becomes his glory and honor, and through him that of all the Trinity; 'the Father's joy, the Son's honor, the Holy Spirit's delight'.
>
> (51:278)[41]

---

39   This is a somewhat different twist on the common philosophico-theologico idea that sin/evil is not something positive, not something in itself, but is, rather, the absence of good. It is or has no substance as Augustine put it in *Confessions*, 7.18.

40   The verb 'feel' is chosen consciously because, quite in contrast with Anselm and Aquinas, and clearly more in line with Bonaventure, Julian's theology is an integration of thought and feeling; it is incarnational even to the extent of highlighting the place of sensuality in the Christian life.

41   Nuth, 'Two Medieval Soteriologies', p. 641, quoted from *Showings*, Long Text, Ch. 51, p. 278.

To conclude this brief and selective foray into the soteriology of Julian of Norwich, let me highlight its potential contribution to the development of an authentic Christian, i.e., Trinitarian, understanding of sacrifice such as we laid out at the beginning of this book. If that understanding of Christian sacrifice is valid, we can see that Julian's theology, because it is so profoundly incarnational and Trinitarian in the way it sees the divine–human relationship not as humans do but as God does, is a major contribution to that understanding. Christian sacrifice, as we explained, begins to become real when, in the power of the same Spirit that was in Jesus, we begin to enter into the perfectly loving and totally self-giving relationship of the Father and the Son. Julian's vision that the Father is not concerned with any satisfaction due from the sinner, because in the sinner the Father sees his own Son, fits in perfectly with our understanding of Christian sacrifice. This insight of Julian enables us to transcend the inevitable dichotomies of normal human theo-logic, and thus to see how humans actually do 'give something to God' (see quote earlier). This is not an encroachment upon the difference between human finitude and divine transcendence. Rather it is an attempt to draw the consequences of the fact that, via Incarnation, human beings are brought into and become, somehow, *in mysterio*, part of that transcendence.

But we began these concluding remarks by speaking of Julian offering a 'potential' contribution. Unhappily, It remained for centuries only a potential contribution, because what Julian the *woman* saw in vision and tried mightily to explain was, at least until recently, basically ignored by the theological *fraternity*.[42]

Chapter III

The Sacrifice of the Mass

In the course of the Middle Ages in the West, it had become common to refer to the Eucharistic liturgy as 'The Sacrifice of the Mass'. The theological and religious developments that account for this did not, of course, begin in the Middle Ages, nor did they end there. But the major elements of these developments that became so controversial in the controversies of the Reformation and post-Reformation, and that have also continued to this day to influence both traditional Roman Catholic thinking on the Mass and the controversies associated with that thinking, were in place well before the cataclysmic events of the Reformation. Because so much of this has to do with problematic misunderstandings of

---

42   The choice of the word *fraternity* is deliberate. It was only in the late twentieth century that theologians were challenged to acknowledge that mystical experience, even that (and perhaps especially that) of women, could be a legitimate source of theological reflection.

the atonement, this is where we will locate our basic treatment of the Mass as sacrifice.

Rather than attempt to survey the voluminous literature on this topic, we will simply call attention to the striking analogues in sacrificial themes in three of the 'most sacrificial' of Christian Eucharistic Prayers:[43] first, ICEL's[44] *Eucharistic Prayer I* and its original form in the traditional medieval Latin *Canon Missae*, then *The Third Anaphora of St. Peter*, commonly called *Sharar*, and finally, but much more briefly, *The Prayers of Sarapion*.

A. ICEL's EP I Translation/Adaptation of the *Canon Missae*

(This dates from late antiquity/early middle ages. It is presented here, except for the numbering of the lines, as adapted in the 1970 Roman Catholic *Eucharistic Prayer I*)[45]

1	We come to you, Father,
2	with praise and thanksgiving,
3	through Jesus Christ your Son.
4	Through him we ask you to accept and bless +
5	these gifts we offer you in sacrifice.
6	We offer them for your holy Catholic Church,
7	watch over it, Lord, and guide it;
8	grant it peace and unity throughout the world.
9	We offer them for *N.* our Pope,
10	for *N.* our bishop,
11	and for all who hold and teach the catholic faith
12	that comes to us from the apostles.
13	Remember, Lord, your people,
14	especially those for whom we now pray, *N.* and *N.*
15	Remember all of us gathered here before you.
16	You know how firmly we believe in you
17	and dedicate ourselves to you.
18	We offer you this sacrifice of praise
19	for ourselves and those who are dear to us.
20	We pray to you, our living and true God,
21	for our well-being and redemption.

---

43   The 'Eucharistic Prayer' or 'Anaphora' is that part of the Eucharistic celebration that comes between the *Sanctus* (Holy, Holy, Holy) and ends with the solemn doxology that customarily precedes the Lord's Prayer and Communion.

44   ICEL is the acronym for The International Commission on English in the Liturgy, the commission of bishops and scholars from the eleven world-wide English-speaking bishops conferences that has produced the current official liturgical texts of the Roman Catholic Church.

45   *The Sacramentary* (New York: Catholic Book Publishing Co., 1985), pp. 542–47.

22 In union with the whole Church
23 we honor Mary,

24 the ever-virgin mother of Jesus Christ our Lord and God,
25 We honor Joseph, her husband,
26 the apostles and martyrs
27 Peter and Paul, Andrew,
28 [James, John, Thomas,
29 James, Philip,
30 Bartholomew, Matthew, Simon and Jude;
31 we honor Linus, Cletus, Clement, Sixtus,
32 Cornelius, Cyprian, Lawrence, Chrysogonus,
33 John and Paul, Cosmas and Damian]
34 and all the saints.
35 May their merits and prayers
36 gain us your constant help and protection.
37 [Through Christ our Lord. Amen.]

38 Father, accept this offering
39 from your whole family.
40 Grant us your peace in this life,
41 save us from final damnation,
42 and count us among those you have chosen.
43 [Through Christ our Lord. Amen.]

44 Bless and approve our offering;
45 make it acceptable to you,
46 an offering in spirit and in truth.
47 Let it become for us
48 the body and blood of Jesus Christ,
49 your only Son, our Lord.
50 [through Christ our Lord. Amen.]

51 The day before he suffered
52 he took bread in his sacred hands
53 and looking up to heaven,
54 to you, his almighty Father,
55 he gave you thanks and praise.
56 He broke the bread,
57 gave it to his disciples, and said:

58 Take this, all of you, and eat it:
59 this is my body which will be given up for you.
60 When supper was ended,
61 he took the cup.
62 Again he gave you thanks and praise,
63 gave the cup to his disciples, and said:

64 Take this, all of you, and drink from it:
65 this is the cup of my blood,
66 the blood of the new and everlasting covenant.
67 It will be shed for you and for all
68 so that sins may be forgiven.
69 Do this in memory of me.

Let us proclaim the mystery of faith:

A. **Christ has died,**
   Christ is risen,
   Christ will come again.
B. **Dying you destroyed our death,**
   Rising you restored our life.
   Lord Jesus, come in glory.
C. **When we eat this bread and drink this cup,**
   we proclaim your death, Lord Jesus,
   until you come in glory.
D. **Lord, by your cross and resurrection**
   you have set us free.
   You are the Savior of the world.

70 Father, we celebrate the memory of Christ, your Son.
71 We, your people and your ministers,
72 recall his passion,
73 his resurrection from the dead,
74 and his ascension into glory;
75 and from the many gifts you have given us
76 we offer to you, God of glory and majesty,
77 this holy and perfect sacrifice:
78 the bread of life
79 and the cup of eternal salvation.
80 Look with favor on these offerings
81 and accept them as once you accepted
82 the gifts of your servant Abel,
83 the sacrifice of Abraham, our father in faith,
84 and the bread and wine offered by your priest Melchisedech.

85 Almighty God,
86 we pray that your angel may take this sacrifice
87 to your altar in heaven.
88 Then, as we receive from this altar
89 the sacred body and blood of your Son,
90 let us be filled with every grace and blessing.
91 [Through Christ our Lord. Amen.]

92   Remember, Lord, those who have died
93   and have gone before us marked with the sign of faith,
94   especially those for whom we now pray, *N.* and *N.*
95   May these, and all who sleep in Christ,
96   find in your presence
97   light, happiness, and peace.
98   [Through Christ our Lord. Amen.]

99   For ourselves, too, we ask
100   some share in the fellowship of your apostles and martyrs,
101   with John the Baptist, Stephen, Matthias, Barnabas,
102   [Ignatius, Alexander, Marcellinus, Peter,
103   Felicity, Perpetua, Agatha, Lucy,
104   Agnes, Cecilia, Anastasia]
105   and all the saints.

106   Though we are sinners,
107   we trust in your mercy and love.

108   Do not consider what we truly deserve,
109   but grant us your forgiveness.
110   Through Christ our Lord.

111   Through him you give us all these gifts.
112   You fill them with life and goodness,
113   you bless them and make them holy.

114   Through him, with him, in him,
115   in the unity of the Holy Spirit,
116   all glory and honor is yours, almighty Father,
117   for ever and ever. Amen.

In this most 'sacrificial' of the major EPs that, to my knowledge, are now in use,[46] there are, in this ICEL translation/adaptation of the traditional Latin *Canon Missae*, no less than 14 instances of sacrificial language or clear sacrificial reference, seven before and seven after the Institution Narrative. The two instances of *we offer* early in the prayer (Lines 5 and 6) translate one instance of *offerimus* in the *Canon Missae*. Similarly, the repetition of the word *offering* in Line 46 does not go back to the Latin. But this English expansion of sacrificial language is more than compensated by the fact that *this holy and perfect sacrifice* shortly after the Institution Narrative (Line 77) is a much 'quieter' rendition of *hostiam + puram, hostiam + sanctam, hostiam + immaculatam,* made all the more emphatic by the triple sign of the cross made by the priest over the offerings. Similarly, a few lines later *the bread*

---

46   Except for (1) the *Canon Missae* itself of the recently reinstated Tridentine Rite in the Roman Catholic Church, and for (2) *Sharar* which used to be – until the reforms of 1972 and 1992 – in occasional use in the mostly Lebanese Maronite (uniate) Church (see hereafter, pp. 125–135).

and wine offered by your priest Melchisedech (Line 84) is, in sacrificial terms, also a much 'quieter' rendition of *quod tibi obtulit summus sacerdos tuus Melchisedech, sanctum sacrificium, immaculatam hostiam.*

If one gets from this the impression that the original Latin *Canon Missae* is more sacrificial than its ICEL translation/adaptation as *Eucharistic Prayer I*, that is indeed correct. As **Table 4** shows, 21 total instances of 8 different Latin sacrificial words are translated into English by only 18 total instances of 6 different English words:

Table 4 Sacrificial terms in the *Canon Missae* and ICEL *EP I*

CANON MISSAE (NO. OF OCCURRENCES)		ICEL (NO. OF OCCURRENCES)	
sacrificium	(5)	sacrifice	(5)
offerre	(5)	offer (verb)	(5)
hostia	(4)	offering (noun)	(4)
oblatio	(2)	(no English equivalent)	
munera	(2)	(no English equivalent)	
dona	(1)	gifts	(2)
sacerdos	(1)	priest	(1)
altare	(1)	altar	(1)

But this relatively small verbal difference is only the tip of the iceberg. The sense of being involved in something sacrificial is much, much stronger in the *Canon Missae* than in its ICEL adaptation. This is reinforced by the rubrics of the *Canon Missae* prominently printed in red. In these rubrics, the word *hostia* (English: host) occurs 15 times and *oblata*/offerings once. (In the present *Sacramentary* of the Roman Rite in its ICEL adaptation, the rubrics mention 'host' just twice and 'offerings' once.) In ecclesiastical Latin, *hostia* is the word for the host, the bread wafer used at Mass. But even in ecclesiastical Latin, the word also means 'victim, sacrifice, offering',[47] and in the classical Latin that was the staple of traditional seminary education, *hostia* meant primarily 'a sacrificial animal, a full-grown victim'.[48] In addition, these rubrics directed the priest to make a sign of the cross over these sacrificial offerings no less than 20 times, 10 times before and 10 times after the Institution Narrative. In the current *Sacramentary*, these 20 signs of the cross are replaced by just one, at the very beginning of the prayer (Line 4). Among these 20 were 4 *triple* signs of the cross (see **Table 5**).

The combination of words and rubrics in the *Canon Missae* powerfully communicate – to the observer, and even more powerfully impregnate into the consciousness of the priest who would perform this rite every day – what used to be very strongly at the heart of Roman Catholic theology, piety and devotion: i.e., while celebrating Mass, *the priest is actively involved as the primary agent in a sacrificial action.* That explains why it was only in 2002 that the widely used Collegeville missalette hymnal finally got around to changing the words of a widely used offertory hymn. We used to sing:

47   See Leo F. Stelten, *Dictionary of Ecclesiastical Latin* (Peabody, Mass.: Hendrickson Publishers, 1995), p. 117.
48   P. G. W. Glare, ed., *Oxford Latin Dictionary* (Oxford: Clarendon Press; New York: Oxford University Press, 1982), p. 807.

Table 5 Rubrical signs of the Cross in *Canon Missae* and ICEL *EP I*

CANON MISSAE SIGNS OF THE CROSS *BEFORE* THE INSTITUTION NARRATIVE	IN ICEL
signat ter super hostiam et calicem simul dicens: *haec + dona, haec + munera, haec + sancta sacrificial illibata*	(Lines 4 and 5) . . . we ask you to accept and bless + these gifts we offer you in sacrifice
Quam oblationem tu, Deus, in omnibus, quaesumus, signat ter super oblata, bene + dictam, adscrip + tam, ra + tam, rationabilem, acctabilemque facere digneris	(Lines 44–46) Bless and approve our offering; make it acceptable to you, an offering in spirit and in truth
CANON MISSAE SIGNS OF THE CROSS *AFTER* THE INSTITUTION NARRATIVE	SIGNS OF THE CROSS IN ICEL
signat ter super hostiam et calicem simul dicens: *sancti + ficas, vivi + ficas, bene + dicis et praestas nobis*	(Line 77) this holy and perfect sacrifice
signat ter super hostiam et calicem simul dicens: *sancti + ficas, vivi + ficas, bene + dicis et praestas nobis*	(Line 113) you bless them and make them holy

> Lord, accept the gifts we offer
> at this eucharistic feast.
> Bread and wine to be transformed now
> *through the action of the priest.*

The offending fourth line is now sung:

> *through the work of Christ our priest.*[49]

Can it be surmised that the obvious lessening of sacrificial content and implication in ICEL's adaptation of the traditional *Canon Missae* into *EP I* is programmatic and intentional? A quick examination of the texts of ICEL's EP II, EP III and *EP IV* might support this surmise. For, counting the repetitions, there are almost twice as many instances of sacrificial language in just the text of the *Canon Missae* – without even mentioning the intensification of sacrificial affect brought about by the rubrics – than the total number to be found in ICEL's *EP II, III* and *IV* combined. However, before concluding to any programmatic intention in that direction behind the missal of Paul VI, one must recognize that other models of traditional anaphoras than the highly sacrificial *Roman Canon* were behind the 'new' *EPs II, III* and *IV*. And besides, *EP III*'s 'see the Victim' and *EP IV*'s almost totally unprecedented 'we offer you his body and blood'[50] suggest that perhaps even an opposite intention may have been at work.

---

49   Theologically, this is a vast improvement. It would be more accurate to attribute the transformation of the Eucharistic elements to the Holy Spirit, but that would ruin the rhythm and rime of the line.
50   Only *Addai and Mari* and *Sharar* (see hereafter) offer possible precedents for the sacrificial bluntness of this expression.

B. The Third Anaphora of St. Peter (*Sharar*) [51]

As Jasper and Cuming (p. 45) point out, this anaphora has a close relationship with *Addai and Mari*. They probably have a common ancestor. Many scholars hold that *Sharar* includes some readings that are earlier than the corresponding places in *Addai and Mari*. There are at least 12 obvious sacrificial references or passages, actually 28 of them if one enumerates them all thematically (see the statistics in **Table 6**, below p. 139). This makes it the only major EP (from our survey) still in use – at least until recently – that comes close to rivaling the *Canon Missae* in this respect. Also noteworthy is the very strong expiatory or propitiatory content of many of these references, especially as the prayer proceeds. Connected with this is the fact that this anaphora, like the *Canon Missae*, is predominantly epicletic or impetratory. In addition, after the *Sanctus*, like some other very early anaphoras, the whole prayer (apart from the apparent inconsistency at the end of Paragraph 11) is addressed to Christ. As Jasper and Cuming (p. 45) point out, the Trinitarian references in the preface and concluding doxology are probably later additions. But finally, as we will point out hereafter, in what is perhaps the most notable discovery in this line of our research, there seem to be some startling thematic similarities between the underlying theology of this anaphora and that of the *Canon Missae* and *Roman EP I*.

The numbers 1–12 in bold face in the right hand margin indicate the twelve obvious instances of sacrificial language and imagery.

Priest:

1. We offer to you, God our Father, Lord of all,   **1a**
an offering and a commemoration and a memorial in the sight of God,
living from the beginning and holy from eternity,
for the living and for the dead,
for the near and for the far,
for the poor and for travelers,
for the churches and monasteries which are here
and in every place and in all regions;
and for me, unworthy and a sinner,
whom you have made worthy to stand before you
(remember me in your heavenly kingdom);
and for the souls and spirits whom we commemorate before you,
Lord, mighty God,
and for this people which is in the true faith
and awaits your abundant mercy;
and for the sins, faults, and defects of us all,
we offer this pure and holy offering.   **1b**
People: It is fitting and right.

---

51 Text taken from R.C.D. Jasper and G.J. Cuming, *Prayers of the Eucharist: Early 2nd Reformed* (Collegeville, Minn.: Liturgical Press, 3rd rev. edn, 1987), pp. 46–50. I reproduce the Jasper and Cuming text exactly as printed, except for (1) reformatting it into approximate sense lines, and (2) numbering the paragraphs.

Priest: It is fitting and right, our duty and our salvation, natural and good.
Let our minds ever be lifted up to heaven, and all our hearts in purity.
People: To you, Lord, God of Abraham, Isaac, and Israel,
O King glorious and holy forever.

Priest: To you, Lord, God of Abraham, savior of Isaac, strength of Israel,
O King glorious and holy forever.
The Lord is worthy to be confessed by us and adored and praised.

(Here the priest blesses the people, and says a prayer relating to the incense and a number of commemorations, after which he begins the anaphora.)

Priest (bowing):
2. Glory to you, adorable and praiseworthy name
of the Father and of the Son and of the Holy Spirit.
You created the world through your grace
and all its inhabitants by your mercy
and made redemption for mortals by your grace.

3. Your majesty, O Lord, a thousand thousand heavenly angels adore;
myriad myriads of hosts, ministers of fire and spirit, praise you in fear.
With the cherubim and the seraphim,
who in turn bless, glorify, proclaim, and say,
let us also, Lord, become worthy of your grace and mercy,
to say with them thrice, 'Holy, holy, holy . . .'

(bowing)
4. We give thanks to you, Lord, we your sinful servants,
because you have given your grace which cannot be repaid.
You put on our human nature to give us life through your divine nature;
you raised our lowly state; you restored our Fall;
you gave life to our mortality;
you justified our sinfulness; you forgave our debts;
you enlightened our understanding, conquered our enemies,
and made our weak nature to triumph.

(aloud)
5. And for all your grace towards us,
let us offer you glory and honor   **2**
in your holy Church before your altar of propitiation . . .

(bowing)
6. You, Lord, through your great mercy,
be graciously mindful of all the holy and righteous Fathers,
when we commemorate your body and blood,
which we offer to you on your living and holy altar,   **3**
as you, our hope, taught us in your holy gospel and said,
'I am the living bread who came down from heaven
that mortals may have life in me.'

(aloud)
7. We make the memorial of your Passion, Lord, as you taught us.
In the night in which you were betrayed to the Jews, Lord,

you took bread in your pure and holy hands,
and lifted your eyes to heaven to your glorious Father;
you blessed, sealed, sanctified, Lord, broke,
and gave it to your disciples the blessed Apostles,
and said to them,
'This bread is my body,
which is broken and given for the life of the world,
and will be to those who take it
for forgiveness of sins and pardon for sins;
take and eat from it,
and it will be to you for eternal life.'

(*He takes the cup*)
8. Likewise over the cup, Lord, you praised, glorified, and said,
'This cup is my blood of the new covenant,
which is shed for many for forgiveness of sins;
take and drink from it, all of you,
and it will be to you for pardon of debts
and forgiveness of sins, and for eternal life.' Amen

9. 'As often as you eat from this holy body,
and drink from this cup of life and salvation,
you will make the memorial of the death and resurrection of your Lord,
until the great day of his coming.'

People: We make the memorial, Lord, of your death . . .

Priest:
10. We adore you, only begotten of the Father,
firstborn of creation, spiritual Lamb,
who descended from heaven to earth,
to be a propitiatory sacrifice for all men and to bear their debts voluntarily,   **4**
and to remit their sins by your blood,
and sanctify the unclean through your sacrifice.

11. Give us life, Lord, through your true life,
and purify us through your spiritual expiation;
and grant us to stand before you in purity and serve you in holiness
and offer that sacrifice to your Godhead,   **5**
that it may be pleasing to the will of your majesty,
and that your mercy, Father, may flow over us all. . . .

12. We ask you, only-begotten of the Father,
through whom your peace is established;
Son of the Most High, in whom higher things are reconciled with lower;
Good Shepherd, who laid down your life for your sheep
and delivered them from ravening wolves;
merciful Lord, who raised your voice on the cross and gathered us from vain
    error;
God, the God of spirits and of all flesh;
may our prayers ascend in your sight,
and your mercy descend on our petitions,

and let that sacrifice be acceptable before you;   **6**
we offer it as a memorial of your Passion on your altar of propitiation.
13. May it please your Godhead, and may your will be fulfilled in it;
by it may our guilt be pardoned and our sins forgiven;
and in it may our dead be remembered.
Let us praise you and adore you, and the Father
who sent you for our salvation, and your living and Holy Spirit now. . . .

14. By it may the glorious Trinity be reconciled,
by the thurible and by the sacrifice and the cup;   **7a**
by it may the souls be purified and the spirits sanctified
of those for whom and on account of whom it was offered and sanctified;   **7b**
and for me, weak and sinful, who offered it,   **7c**
may the mercy of the glorious Trinity arise, Father. . . .

(*The priest bows and says a prayer to the Mother of God.*)

15. We offer before you, Lord, this sacrifice   **8**
in memory of all righteous and pious fathers,
of prophets, apostles, martyrs, confessors, and all our patriarchs,
and the pope of the city of Rome and metropolitan bishops,
area bishops, visitors, priests, deacons, deaconesses,
young men, celibates, virgins, and all sons of holy Church
who have been sealed with the sign of saving baptism,
and whom you have made partakers of your holy body.

16. (*privately*) First and especially we commemorate
the holy and blessed and saintly virgin, the Blessed Lady Mary.

17. *Deacon*: Remember her, Lord God, and us through her pure prayers.

Priest (*bowing*):
18. Remember, Lord God, at this time the absent and the present,
the dead and the living, the sick and the oppressed,
the troubled, the afflicted, and those who are in various difficulties.

19. Remember, Lord God, at this time,
our fathers and brothers in spirit and in body;
and forgive their offences and sins.

20. Remember, Lord God, at this time, those who offer sacrifices,
vows, firstfruits, memorials: **9**
grant to their petitions good things from your abundant store.

21. Remember, Lord God, at this time,
those who join in commemorating your mother and your saints;
grant them recompense for all their good works;
and for all who communicated in this eucharist
which was offered on this holy altar;   **10**
grant them, Lord God, a reward in your kingdom;
and for all who have said to us, 'pray for us in your prayers before the
    Lord.'
Remember them, Lord God, and purge their iniquities.

22. Remember, Lord God, at this time,
my miserableness, sinfulness, importunity, and lowliness;
I have sinned and done evil in your sight consciously or not.
Lord God, in your grace and mercy pardon me
and forgive whatever I have sinned against you;
and may this eucharist, Lord,
be as a memorial of our dead and for the reconciliation of our souls.

23. Remember, Lord God, at this time,
your weak and sinful servant George, who wrote this,
and pardon him and forgive him his offences and sins,
and forgive his fathers. Amen.

24. (*kneeling*) Hear me, Lord (thrice), and let your living and Holy Spirit,
   Lord,
come and descend upon this offering of your servants,   **11**
and may it be to those who partake
for the remission of debts and forgiveness of sins,
for a blessed resurrection from the dead,
and for new life in the kingdom of heaven for ever.

25. (*aloud*) And because of your praiseworthy dispensation towards us,
we give thanks to you, we your sinful servants
redeemed by your innocent blood,
with eloquent mouth in your holy Church
before your altar of propitiation, now. . . .   **12**

FRACTION AND SIGNING
LORD'S PRAYER
PRAYER OF INCLINATION
ELEVATION

Priest:
26. The holy (thing) is given to the holy people
in perfection, purity, and holiness;
may we have a part and fellowship with them in the kingdom of heaven.

People:
One Father only is holy, one Son only is holy, one Spirit only is holy.
Glory to the Father, to the Son, and to the Holy Spirit.

THANKSGIVING FOR COMMUNION
BLESSING

1. *Commentary on* Sharar

First, some comments on each of the 12 'major' sacrificial references (as indicated by the bold numbers **1–12** in the right hand margins of the text repro-
duced earlier). While doing this we will be trying – just judging from the obvious
meaning of the text itself – to detect what concept of sacrifice might be behind
the text.

1. The very opening words in **Parag. 1** set the tone: *We offer to you,* . . . The first and third lines contain anamnesis: *Lord of all,* . . . *living from the beginning and holy from eternity.* But this brief anamnesis seems to be almost pro forma, for what then follows is twelve lines of earnest petition for just about all the things for which one needs to pray. The paragraph then concludes with: . . . *we offer this pure and holy offering.* But what do the verb *offer* and the noun *offering* actually mean here? The second line lists three things that are the object of the verb *we offer.* These are: *an offering and a commemoration and a memorial in the sight of God* (emphasis mine). Are *commemoration* and *memorial* basically synonymous with *offering?* Or is *offering* a thing or an action distinct from *commemoration* and *memorial?* One cannot escape the impression that, here in *Sharar,* the latter seems to be the meaning that is at least sometimes intended.

2. In **Parag. 5** – note that after the Sanctus in **Parag. 4**, the whole prayer is addressed to Jesus – we read: *let us offer you glory and honor in your holy Church before your altar of propitiation.* Is this perhaps simply using the sacrificial language of *we offer* in the sense of 'we give you' or 'we bring you'? But then one reads the immediately following *in your holy Church before your altar of propitiation.* The mention of *your altar of propitiation* might suggest that the primary meaning of *Church* might not be that of the Christian assembly but rather that of a church building, and that a physical altar in that building is intended. The pronoun *your* seems to point to the propitiating sacrifice of Christ as something distinct from what *we* offer.

But what is the meaning of the preposition *before* in *before your altar of propitiation?* This precise phrase with the same preposition is found in **Parag. 25** at the very end of the anaphora. However, earlier, at the end of **Parag. 12**, this phrase is found with a different preposition: *we offer it as a memorial on your altar of propitiation.* We are, at this stage, left wondering whether this is simply an inconsistency, or whether a significant difference is being expressed by *before* and *on,* or whether a plurality of meanings is either intended (or perhaps perceived by the hearers). When we seek clarity by asking what, in each case, is being *offered,* we find that in the first instance, in **Parag. 5**, what is offered is the spiritualized *glory and honor* that is being offered because of Jesus' (sacrificial) redemption. In the second instance of this in **Parag. 12**, the object of offer seems to be *our prayers . . . and . . . our petitions.* But when the next line adds *and let that sacrifice be acceptable before you,* we are again left wondering. Does *that sacrifice* refer to *prayers* and *petitions,* or does it refer – either exclusively or also – to the reconciling, delivering, redeeming work of the passion of Christ so forcefully appealed to just before this? We are left wondering, and also suspecting that those praying this prayer are comfortable with an at least implicitly intended plurality of meanings.

3. In **Parag. 6** we find one of the rare background supports for the startling – and for the most part quite untraditional – bluntness of the statement *we offer you his body and blood* found in the Anamnesis Offering Prayer of *Roman EP IV* (see aforementioned, p. 124). The Jasper and Cuming translation of *Sharar* reads . . . *when we commemorate your body and blood, which we offer to you on your living and holy altar.* This suggests that *commemoration* and *offering* in **Parag. 1** are not synonymous. It also suggests – or might suggest – that what is offered *on* the altar, i.e., the body and blood of Jesus, is different from what is offered *before* the altar: honor, glory, praise, prayers, petitions, etc.

4. In **Parag. 10** the incarnate Jesus is directly addressed as *a propitiatory sacrifice for all men* . . . To become this *propitiatory sacrifice* is declared to be the very purpose of the Incarnation that was achieved by way of sacrificial redemption: . . . *to bear their debts voluntarily, and to remit their sins by your blood, and sanctify the unclean through your sacrifice.* The words *propitiatory sacrifice* plus the threefold use of *your altar of propitiation* (**Parags. 5, 12, 25**) raise the question of the meaning of the words *propitiation* and *propitiatory.* Are they to be distinguished from, or are they basically synonymous with the *expiation* found in **Parag. 11**?[52]

5. Parag. 11 asks Jesus to *purify us through your spiritual expiation.* When *Sharar* then proceeds to ask that Jesus *grant us to stand before you in purity and serve you in holiness and offer that sacrifice to your Godhead,* . . . the logical meaning suggests that the words *offer that sacrifice* refer to the liturgical celebration itself. It would seem not to be logically consistent for the words *that sacrifice* to refer to the actual sacrifice of Christ, since that would mean offering Christ to Christ. However, early Eucharistic Prayers are known to have occasional inconsistencies, at least in the form in which they have come down to us. And indeed such inconsistencies are known to be not uncommon when one prays euchologically or with set formulas.

6. In **Parag. 12** we again find the words *that sacrifice,* apparently referring to *our prayers* and *our petitions* [or the liturgical celebration itself, as in **Parag. 11**] which *we offer* . . . *as a memorial of your Passion on* [see in our discussion of **Parag. 5**] *your altar of propitiation.*

7. Parag. 14 provides an example of this inconsistency. It begins by mentioning the Trinity, apparently in the third person; and then, although in a prayer that is consistently addressed to Jesus, it seems to end by addressing the Father. There are three sacrificial references here. First, praying that the Trinity be *reconciled* . . . *by it,* namely *by the thurible and by the sacrifice and the cup.* The pronoun *it* would seem to refer back to *that sacrifice* – i.e., the liturgical celebration – in **Parags. 11** and **12**. However, the appositional content of Line 2 suggests that the reference is to the actual gifts offered. The question arises: are the words *by the sacrifice and the cup* basically synonymous with *your body and blood* in **Parag. 6**? This would seem to be

---

52 In my early work – see esp. *Christian Sacrifice: The Judaeo-Christian Background before Origen* (Studies in Christian Antiquity, 18; Washington, D.C.: The Catholic University of America Press, 1978) and *The Origins of the Christian Doctrine of Sacrifice* (Philadelphia: Fortress Press, 1978) I carefully distinguished between propitiation as primarily a God-directed human action intended to influence or win favour with the divine, and expiation as primarily a human-directed divine action of forgiveness and reconciliation. This distinction enables me to ask the questions I ask here, but we cannot assume that such a distinction (helpful as it may be for what we are attempting to do) is associated with these euchological words either for those who wrote them or for those who then and/or now pray with them.

suggested by the fact that, in the phrase *by the sacrifice and the cup*, the preposition *by* is not repeated for the cup. The pronoun *it* (three times in this **Parag. 6**) clearly seems to refer to the means of the purification of the souls and the sanctification of the spirits *of those for whom and on account of whom it was offered and sanctified*, which is then followed by the rare first-person-singular reference: *and for me, weak and sinful, who offered it.*

Is Sharar simply confused and/or inconsistent? Or is Sharar, perhaps somewhat apophatically, deliberately suggesting a plurality of meanings? But that, of course, is asking the question (with twenty-first century presuppositions) from the point of view of the intention and meaning of the text itself. How is it understood/received when it is actually prayed by a living community, as it was until recently in the (uniate) Maronite Church? And then the further question: what is the meaning that is intended, and communicated, and received, when this anaphora is translated and prayed in different languages?

Excursus 5
Sharar and the Maronite Rite

In Fortaleza, Brazil, the day before the opening of the second meeting of the International Jungmann Society for Jesuits and Liturgy, 26 June 2006–1 July 2006, I mentioned to Lebanese Jesuit, Rooney el Gemayel, what I was discovering about the sacrificial similarities between the *Canon Missae* and *Sharar*. He pointed out that *Sharar* is no longer a live option in the Maronite Church. It did not survive the Maronite liturgical reforms of 1972 and 1992. Before those reforms, *Sharar* was sometimes used, especially on Good Friday. He said that he himself had experienced it only once. When I later asked el Gemayel why *Sharar* had been dropped – thinking perhaps that there may have been a desire to drop a prayer that had such primitive inconsistencies in it, and also because, contrary to most subsequent liturgical practice, it was addressed to Jesus instead of to God the Father – he replied that it was simply seen as part of an East Syrian heritage no longer relevant to the contemporary Maronite Church which, in any case still has Eucharistic Prayers that are addressed to Jesus.

But el Gemayel did resonate positively with my perception of *Sharar* as being aggressively (my word, not his) sacrificial, and, like the *Canon Missae*, as being very conscious of the special, actively sacrificial and almost 'proprietary' role of the priest in achieving or mediating sacrificial redemption. These are, of course, precisely the things that a modern liturgical reformer would probably want to de-emphasize. But at this writing I do not know whether that was a factor at all in the recent Maronite liturgical reform. To my knowledge, this leaves very open the question whether the apparently (or possibly) intended decrease in sacrificial emphasis in ICEL's translation/adaptation of *EP I* may also have been at work in the Maronite Church. In other words: was there at work in the Maronite Church anything analogous to the ecumenical motivation that can be perceived to be at work with (at least some) Catholics de-emphasizing aspects thought to be belligerently Catholic, and with (at least some) Protestants gradually (re)appropriating traditional elements they once branded as 'popish' or 'papist'?

END OF EXCURSUS 5

---

8. All this ambiguity remains when **Parag. 15** opens with: *We offer before you, Lord, this sacrifice in memory of* . . .

9. Parag. 20 with its *Remember, Lord God, at this time, those who offer sacrifices, vows, firstfruits, memorials: grant to their petitions* . . . expands even more the questions we have been raising. Up to now, *sacrifice* or *offering* seems to be referring to something that takes place in a church building and in a liturgical activity. But here *offer sacrifices* seems not to assume that at all. Logically, these words seem possibly to refer to just one (or to the first) of a series of good, meritorious works listed in the prayer.

10. In **Parag. 21** the words, *and for all who communicated in this eucharist which was offered on this holy altar* – especially since the paragraph ends with *Remember them, Lord God, and purge their iniquities* – clearly communicate a conviction that is also at the heart of the traditional understanding of the *Roman Canon*, namely, that offering sacrifice for the living and the dead is one of the principal purposes – if not indeed the principal purpose – of the priestly activity of celebrating Mass.[53] But note also the past tense of the verb in the phrase *which was offered on this holy altar*. The same past tense, *we offered* or *we also offered*, is found five times in *The Prayers of Sarapion* (see the comment on this hereafter, pp. 135–136, in my treatment of *Sarapion*).

11. Parags. 22 and 23 leave no doubt that (analogous to the *Canon Missae*) the forgiveness of sins is the major concern and purpose of this anaphora. Note also in **Parag. 23** the third-person mention of *George, who wrote this*. This rare insertion within an anaphora of a personal self-reference is something that would be quite at home in the psychology of priests schooled in the celebration of the traditional *Roman Canon*. In the current reformed Roman Rite, this can still be found in the first-person-singular 'Private Prayer of the Priest' inserted after the Fraction Rite before Communion. A general, contemporary awareness that these are indeed insertions can be inferred from the fact that these prayers in the Catholic

---

53   Witness the still living Roman Catholic custom of Mass stipends, especially for the repose of the souls of the deceased (see below in Chapter III of Bridge 2 A, pp. 184–188). Witness also what was communicated in the ordination ceremony in which, before the post-Vatican II reform of the rite, it was commonly thought that the ordaining 'moment' was the *porrectio instrumentorum*, the bishop placing a chalice and paten in the hands of the ordinandus with the words: '*Accipe potestatem offerendi sacrificium pro vivis et pro mortuis* – Receive the power of offering sacrifice for the living and for the dead.'

Sacramentary are usually not found in missalettes intended for the use of the Assembly.

All this is further confirmed in the Epiclesis in **Parag. 24**. The sacredness of the moment is heightened by the rubric (*kneeling*) and by the triple repetition of *Hear me, Lord*. Then, the first of the three purposes of this descent of the Holy Spirit *upon this offering of your servants* is declared to be *for the remission of debts and forgiveness of sins*.

12. Then, in **Parag. 25**, in the final words just before the elevation and communion, we find all this summed up by the words *before your altar of propitiation*. See our discussion of this phrase in our commentary on **Parag. 2** (above, p. 130).

2. *Conclusion of commentary on* Sharar

When we now step back from this kind of a detailed reading in order to get a 'big-picture' impression of this anaphora in the context of this ongoing study, a number of things stand out. The first, perhaps, at least in terms of structure, is the theme-setting function of the opening prayer just before the dialogue preface. This prayer (**Parag. 1**) is in the form of a sacrificial *inclusio*; the opening words of the first and the last lines are *we offer*. Within this *inclusio* we find an anamnetic-epicletic structure; but the anamnesis, at the beginning, is so brief as to seem almost pro forma. This emphasis on the epicletic/impetratory is then maintained throughout the anaphora, but largely because of the force of the opening prayer. I say 'largely because of the force of the opening prayer' because immediately after this prayer and up to **Parag. 10**, i.e., the first third of the remainder of the anaphora, we have clearly the kind of salvation-historical anamnesis culminating in the memorial of the institution of the Eucharist that is common in the classical patristic Eucharistic Prayers. However, even during this anamnesis, the epicletic/impetratory is kept in the foreground by the inclusion of such phrases as: *by your mercy* (**Parag. 2**), *become worthy of your grace and mercy* (**Parag. 3**), *we your sinful servants* (**Parag. 4**), *justified our sinfulness . . . forgave our debts* (**Parag. 4**), *before your altar of propitiation* (**Parag. 5**), *through your great mercy* (**Parag. 6**), and by the mention of *forgiveness of sins* and of *pardon for sins* in both the words over the bread and over the cup in **Parags. 7** and **8**. Then, in **Parag. 10**, returning to a fairly strong use of sacrificial language, we have:

> to be a propitiatory sacrifice for all men and to bear their debts voluntarily,
> and to remit their sins by your blood,
> and sanctify the unclean through your sacrifice.

These words in **Parag. 10** fairly clearly mark the end of the properly anamnetic, and transition to the properly epicletic, section of the anaphora. What now follows, with occasional supporting anamnetic elements, is a series of prayers that constitute a more detailed development of the petitionary needs mentioned in the body of the opening prayer (**Parag. 1**). Characteristic of these prayers is an intense focus on the need for reconciliation, forgiveness, atonement, expiation, propitiation, redemption, etc. I mention these many (sometimes synonymous) terms because, also characteristic of these prayers, as of the whole anaphora, is an apparently imprecise and 'sliding' use of the various terms and concepts of sacrificial redemption.[54]

Finally, as already indicated, there seems to be here in *Sharar* a striking affinity with the themes of sacrificial redemption, including the religious psychology of the traditional Roman Catholic priest-celebrant, that are found in the text and ritual performance of the *Canon Missae*. What is the nature of this relationship? Something of a source? Or just a mere analogue? Beyond the few indications in Jasper and Cuming, do we know anything of the rubrics of the ancient performance of this rite? Do the rubrics of those churches that, until recently, still used this anaphora shed any light? I have already pointed out how the rubrics of the traditional *Canon Missae* massively heighten its sacrificial tone and content. Does the same apply to this anaphora?

C. The Prayers of Sarapion

From immediately after the Sanctus to the end of the Institution Narrative the text reads:

> Full is heaven, full also is earth of your excellent glory, Lord of the powers.
> Fill also this sacrifice with your power and your partaking;
> for to you we offered this living sacrifice, this bloodless offering.

> To you we offered this bread, the likeness of the body of the only-begottten.
> For the Lord Jesus Christ, in the night when he was betrayed,
> took bread, broke it, and gave it to his disciples, saying,
> 'Take and eat; this is my body which is broken for you for forgiveness of sins.'
> Therefore we also offered the bread, making the likeness of the death.

> We beseech you through this sacrifice:
> be reconciled to us all and be merciful, O God of truth.
> And as this bread was scattered over the mountains,
> and was gathered together and became one,
> so gather your holy Church out of every nation
> and every country and every city and village and house,
> and make one living catholic Church. [Cf. *The Didache*]

> We offered also the cup, the likeness of the blood.
> For the Lord Jesus Christ after supper took a cup and said to his disciples,
> 'Take, drink; this is the new covenant, which is my blood
> that is shed for the forgiveness of sins.'

---

54   This imprecision seems, at least in our Jasper and Cuming translation, to extend, possibly, even to the Trinity. We read in Parag. 14: *By it may the glorious Trinity be reconciled, by the thurible and by the sacrifice and the cup* (see in our commentary on Parag. 14, above, pp. 131–132). The obvious orthodox interpretation refers, of course, to our reconciliation with the Trinity. However, can there not also be a suggestion here of the kind of inner-Trinitarian tension implicit in those atonement theories that conceive of a gentle, forgiving Son in tension with a severe, demanding Father?

Therefore we also offered the cup,
presenting the likeness of the blood.[55]

The dating seems to be mid-fourth century. For the questions we are asking, there
seem to be five significant points. (1) The total number of sacrificial references in
this relatively brief passage – at least six – is notable. (2) The past tense of the verb
we offered accounts for five of these. The past tense implies, as Jasper and Cuming
(p. 74) point out (thus indicating that the translation is indeed precise) that the
offering apparently took place before the anaphora.[56] (3) After the Institution
Narrative – in contrast with almost every other known anaphora – there is no
mention whatsoever of sacrifice or offering. (4) The emphatic location and repetition of *we offered*, introducing and concluding (thus forming a kind of *inclusio*) the
words over both the bread and the cup, is striking. (5) The repeated use of figurative language in such words as *the likeness of* does not imply a lack of realism.[57]

From these prayers we see that the Eucharistic celebration is both clearly and
emphatically thought of as a sacrificial offering. We also see that this offering is
associated with but clearly not identified with the words over the bread and the
cup. And finally, we find no indication that, as one might expect, either the Solemn Prayers of the Church after the Epiclesis, or for that matter the whole Eucharistic liturgy, were thought of as spiritualized offerings.

D. PROVISIONAL SUMMARY CONCLUSIONS, WITH SCHEMATIC TABLE

First, it needs to be humbly noted that the full range of critical scholarship relevant to this project has yet to be consulted. The questions raised and conclusions
drawn are necessarily provisional. Especially with the patristic material, for
example, consultation with available critical editions and with some recent studies
may result in the fine tuning, and perhaps not just the fine tuning, of some of our
questions and conclusions. Second, as Paul Bradshaw forcefully reminds us,[58]
there is the relatively fragmentary nature of our knowledge of early Christian
liturgical history. However, my long experience in working with this kind of
material assures me that my questions and provisional conclusions have at least
some merit. There is yet a third caution regarding the early material. We have, for
the most part, only the texts and few, if any, rubrics. We have very little to show us
how these texts worked as part of a living liturgy. This can be a vitally important
factor as we saw in the case of the traditional Roman *Canon Missae*.

---

55   Text, except for our arrangement of it into sense lines, as in Jasper and Cuming, p. 77.
56   In the current Orthodox liturgy there is a point where, in the preparation of the Eucharistic
elements, the deacon requests/signals to the celebrant to: 'perform the sacrifice', whereupon he
cuts into the bread in the form of a cross.
57   No more than a lack of 'realism' – can be inferred when the very realistic Ambrose refers to
this offering as the figure of the body and blood of our Lord Jesus Christ (Ambrose, *On the Sacraments*, 21
Jasper and Cuming, p. 145).
58   Paul Bradshaw, *The Search for the Origins of Christian Worship: Sources and Methods for the Study of
Early Liturgy* (New York: Oxford University Press, 2nd edn, 2002).

Finally, we must recognize that there is something inevitably arbitrary about lining up a dozen and a half Eucharistic Prayers from across cultures and millennia and comparing them closely, as the larger working paper from which this material is excerpted, has attempted to do.[59] These 18 Eucharistic Prayers, listed A to R as they are in **Table 6** (p. 139), are as follows:

A   The Didache
B   Roman Eucharistic Prayer I (ICEL translation/adaptation of the *Canon Missae*)
C   Roman Eucharistic Prayer II
D   Roman Eucharistic Prayer III
E   Roman Eucharistic Prayer IV
F   The Lutheran Great Thanksgiving
G   The Methodist Great Thanksgiving
H   The Presbyterian Great Thanksgiving
I   Anglican (see *Common Worship*)
J   The Liturgy of St. John Chrysostom
K   The Liturgy of Saints Addai and Mari
L   The Third Anaphora of St. Peter (*Sharar*)
M   The Byzantine Liturgy of St. Basil
N   The Egyptian Anaphora of St. Basil
O   The Liturgy of St. Mark
P   The Liturgy of St. James
Q   Hippolytus: The Apostolic Tradition
R   The Prayers of Sarapion

This inevitable arbitrariness is all the more true when, as here, we pull out just three of these (B, L and R) for more intensive comparison. For there are many things that we, from our vantage point in the twenty-first century, can notice and point out. But we cannot assume that the same things would have been even noticed or (even if noticed) considered relevant, by those in another time and place who were praying these texts as their living liturgy.

Taking a broad perspective, and applying a common-sense understanding of sacrifice, i.e., 'what any damn fool thinks is sacrifice', and focusing primarily on texts that use various forms of the words *offer* and *sacrifice*, we can classify some of our selected Eucharistic Prayers as very sacrificial, a few others as very little or not at all sacrificial, and most of the rest as somewhat in between. This leads to our attempt to begin to make the kind of table of classification of sacrificial meanings that has been implicitly developing in our mind in the course of this study. An initial threefold categorization suggests itself: Very Sacrificial – Not Sacrificial – Somewhat Sacrificial. This paper has focused on the EPs in the first of these categories.

---

59   See Robert J. Daly, S.J., 'Sacrificial Language and Rhetoric in the Church's Eucharistic Prayers: Ecumenical Considerations', in: Jesuits in Dialogue: Ecumenism East and West (The 19th International Congress of Jesuit Ecumenists, Lviv, Ukraine,15–20 July 2007; Roma, Prati, Italy: Secretariat for Interreligious Dialogue, Curia, S.J., 2007), pp. 4–54.

The first of these 'very sacrificial' Eucharistic Prayers, at least in the order of our presentation, is the traditional Roman *Canon Missae* and its somewhat mitigated – in terms of sacrificial language and meaning – translation/adaptation by ICEL as *Eucharistic Prayer I*. Next is *The Third Anaphora of St. Peter* (Sharar), and finally *The Prayers of Sarapion*. One is immediately struck by the variety of provenance of these three prayers. The *Canon Missae* was basically assembled from various sources in the course of late antiquity and the early Middle Ages (see Jasper and Cuming, pp. 159–161). Its strongest relationship of origin, if at all, would be with the Egyptian tradition and *The Liturgy of St. Mark*. But, in its final shape as perhaps the most 'aggressively' sacrificial of the Eucharistic Prayers here examined, it also has remarkable thematic and theological affinities with another of our 'very sacrificial' Eucharistic Prayers, that of Sharar from the fourth-century 'Syriac-speaking hinterland of the patriarchate of Antioch' (Jasper and Cuming, p. 45). The analogues between these two are striking, especially in terms of the need for sacrificial redemption and the provision for that in the very purpose of the Eucharistic liturgy, and the special, indeed almost 'proprietary' role of the priest-celebrant in carrying that out. But I am not aware of any evidence that suggests a relationship of cause or source between these two. Can such powerful analogues be merely fortuitous?

For the third Eucharistic Prayer in this 'very sacrificial' category we have, from fourth-century Coptic Egypt, *The Prayers of Sarapion*. What most stands out here is the unique way in which five of the six obvious sacrificial statements are in the past tense, in the words *we offered*. This suggests that the sacrifice was understood to have been carried out before the anaphora. Can this be analogous to the medieval Roman Rite's development of intense sacrificial language and imagery in the Offertory Rite? Or, has it any relation to what happens in the Orthodox Divine Liturgy when, while preparing the gifts, the deacon requests/signals the celebrant to 'perform the sacrifice' by cutting the bread in the form of a cross? Another point that stands out is the unique way in which four of these instances of *we offered* are used to form a *inclusio*, first in the words over the bread, and then in the words over the cup. However, if there are, beyond the obvious thematic and theological analogues, any actual, verifiable connections between any of these three Eucharistic Prayers, they are not presently known to me, nor to any of the liturgical scholars whom I have consulted on this.

In conclusion, we must keep in mind that, however much schematizing can help, it can never be totally objective and it can also mislead. For example, a numerical ranking in sacrificial reference of the prayers examined here would read:

28 Sharar
17 Sarapion
16 Roman EP I
 9 St. James
 6 Roman EP III
 6 Roman EP IV
 6 Anglican
 6 Addai and Mari
 6 St. Mark
 5 Methodist

Table 6 Sacrificial language and content in 18 Eucharistic prayers

	a	b	c	d	e	f	g	h	i	j	k	l	m	n	o		
A											1						
B	1			5	1	4	4						1				
C				1													
D				1		3				2							
E				2	1		1			1		1					
F		1															
G		1		1									1	1	1		
H				2									2				
I		2	1+1	2													
J			1	1									2		1		
K				2		2				1					1		
L		2		5	4	1+3	3	2	1			1		3	3		
M			1	1													
N			1	2								1			1		
O	1			1	1	1				2							
P				2			2	2					2		1		
Q				2						1							
R				6		6	5										

A = Didache
B = Roman EP I
C = Roman EP II
D = Roman EP III
E = Roman EP IV
F = Lutheran
G = Methodist
H = Presbyterian
I = Anglican
J = Chrysostom
K = Addai and Mari
L = Sharar
M = Byzantine St. Basil
N = Egyptian St. Basil
O = St. Mark
P = St. James
Q = Hippolytus/AT
R = Sarapion

a = sacrifice of Abraham and other biblical figures
b = sacrifice of Christ
c = offering your own from your own
d = offering the concrete elements (bread, cup, body, blood, etc.)
e = spiritualized offering (prayers, praise, thanksgiving, etc.)
f = offering in both realistic and spiritualized sense
g = the words 'we offer' ('we offered' only in *Sarapion*)
h = mention of the priest or others who offer
i = offering or sacrificial activity outside the liturgy
j = the Church is, or seems to be, the one offering
k = Eucharist referred to as sacrifice (*Didache* 14)
l = sacrifice offered for partic. purposes, people, intentions
m = offering ourselves (only Methodist and Presbyterian)
n = unworthy to offer (most explicit in Methodist and *Sharar*)
o = for purposes of forgiveness, atonement, etc.

5 Chrysostom
5 Egyptian St. Basil
5 Presbyterian
3 Hippolytus
2 Byzantine St. Basil
1 Roman EP II
1 Lutheran
? Didache

The schema, provisional as it is, does confirm my basic categorization into very sacrificial, not sacrificial, and somewhat sacrificial. But it also includes some anomalies.[60] In addition, the 'slice' from which this schema was made is limited not only by our choice of eighteen liturgies, but also by considering only the Eucharistic Prayers of those liturgies. But to come back to the main theme of this paper and to the question it raises: Can the striking analogues between *Sharar* and *Roman EP I*, especially its precedent in the *Canon Missae*, be merely fortuitous? The basic trajectory of my many years of work with this theme suggests that this cannot be merely, and in every respect, fortuitous. The qualification 'in every respect' is critical, because we may not have, and perhaps may not ever have enough critical historical evidence to settle the question in terms of possible direct influence. But it is quite possible, and indeed my scholarly 'nose' leads me to expect that the following scenario comes close to describing how these remarkable similarities came about.

If there had been influence from one of these prayers to another, it almost surely would have proceeded from the earlier prayers (*Sharar* and *Sarapion*) to the later (*Canon Missae*). But independently of that, one must assume that there probably were religious and psychological experiences of the need for sacrificial redemption in the formation of the *Canon Missae* that were similar to those that gave rise to such expressions in *Sharar* and *Sarapion*. That would probably be enough to explain these striking analogues.

To spell this out a bit, what seems strikingly common, and thus crying out for explanation, especially between the *Canon Missae* and *Sharar*, is the expression of the deeply felt need for sacrificial redemption, so deep that in these Eucharistic Prayers, this need seems to push anamnesis into the background and put great emphasis instead on (epicletic) impetration. A second striking similarity is the foregrounding of the special – seemingly personal and even proprietary – role of the officiating celebrant in bringing out this sacrificial redemption.

Exploring these probabilities and/or possibilities will make fascinating themes and questions for further study.

---

60 For example, the Lutheran EPs and *Roman EP II* receive the same low numerical ranking despite the fact that the Roman EP II is, without question, and especially in its context, vastly more sacrificial. Another statistical anomaly is that *Egyptian St. Basil* is given an equal or higher statistical ranking than either *Chrysostom* or *Byzantine St. Basil*, whereas, as a close reading reveals, the reality is quite different. One of the reasons for this is the criterion used in identifying the number of sacrificial references. A 'point' was given for each reference to one of the 15 sacrificial themes (a–o) in the schema, even if multiple thematic references were contained in just one, brief sacrificial reference, as happens to be the case with *Egyptian St. Basil*.

Chapter IV

Sacrifice and the Reformation

'Sacrifice', and most specifically the 'Sacrifice of the Mass' was one of the most neuralgic points in that pivotal sixteenth-century event in Western Christianity known as the Reformation. We will treat this event, at times sketchily, as is unavoidable in a book of this compass, under five headings: (1) background medieval problems, (2) Catholic abuses, (3) the reaction of the reformers, (4) the Catholic reaction to the Protestant reaction, and (5) the massive controversy over the idea of the Eucharist as sacrifice. Whether explicitly or just implicitly, but always in the background, the criterion against which we will be constantly measuring these reformation issues will be the Trinitarian concept of sacrifice outlined at the beginning of this book.

A. BACKGROUND MEDIEVAL PROBLEMS

It is important to note at the outset that what we now, in hindsight, look upon as 'problems' were not necessarily perceived to be problems by the Christians of the Middle Ages. These 'problems' or weaknesses were, for the most part, the fairly common patrimony of those who eventually ended up struggling against each other on the various sides of the sixteenth-century controversies. That sixteenth-century reformation goes down in history as perhaps the worst instance in which the Church's impulse to be constantly reforming itself went terribly awry.

1. Sacrifice and atonement

As we have already pointed out several times in this book,[61] we must not forget that, for all practical purposes, sacrifice was identified with Atonement, and Atonement with sacrifice. Among the many metaphors of Atonement that came from the Bible and the Fathers of the Church, the legal, transactional and commercial metaphors increasingly dominated and eventually turned into ideas that, especially from the time of Anselm, though not entirely due to him, became embedded in the development of Western atonement doctrine commonly known in the West as 'the atonement paradigm'.[62] These ideas also became embedded in Western ideas of sacrifice and hence also inseparable from ideas about the 'Sacrifice of the Mass'.

---

61   And at some length in the article, 'Images of God and the Imitation of God: Problems with Atonement', *Theological Studies* 68 (2007), pp. 36–51.
62   For a somewhat more positive, though still critical, reading of Anselm, see Lisa Sowle Cahill, 'The Atonement Paradigm: Does It Still Have Explanatory Value?' *Theological Studies* 68 (2007), pp. 418–32.

2. Loss of contact with the Bible

Although the great theology masters in the medieval universities devoted their prime-time morning lectures to the exposition of Scripture, and only in the afternoons turned to the treatment of *Questions* and the development of their great theological *Summae*, knowledge of Scripture did not, whether for better or for worse, become the principal heritage of medieval scholasticism. It was scholasticism, not biblicism, that, at least until the challenge of the Reformation, eventually won the day and dominated the theological heritage of Christianity in the West. The qualification suggested by the words 'for better or for worse' is due to the lack, at that time, of most of the positive developments of historical criticism. We are now, for example, sadly aware that the Bible, when it is read literally and without any critical hermeneutic, is anything but an unmixed blessing. *Sola scriptura*, especially in its extreme forms, brought new problems with which many Christians are still struggling. But *sola scriptura* was also, it must be admitted, a desperately needed attempt to remedy the situation of *nulla scriptura* that had come to characterize late medieval religious life.

3. Loss of contact with the tradition

It is common to describe lack of contact with the tradition as one of the characteristic weaknesses of Protestantism. Massive adherence to tradition is indeed one of the stereotypical characteristics of Catholicism, and massive rejection of tradition is one of the stereotypical characteristics of Protestantism. But those stereotypes veil as much as they reveal. For many of the best reformation theologians were deeply sensitive to the patristic traditions and to the theological value of a *consensus patrum* (patristic consensus). No, the problem was deeper than this stereotypical polemical difference. It was, as Edward Kilmartin put it, a general loss of contact with the first millennium. For all its differences and struggles, the first Christian millennium was generally characterized by an openness to a plurality of meanings that, in the West, tended to get lost as the scholasticism of the twelfth and thirteenth centuries became dominant and developed into a narrow splinter tradition.[63]

4. Lack of a sense of the 'Shape of the Liturgy'

In the words 'shape of the liturgy' liturgical scholars will recognize an allusion to the magnificent work of Dom Gregory Dix.[64] But I am using the phrase here, first, in an applied and somewhat broader sense, to refer, first, to the fundamental structure of Christian liturgical praying as addressed to the Father, through the Son, in the Holy Spirit, and then second, in a more particular sense, to refer to the basic structure of the Eucharistic Prayer, i.e., the central prayer of the Eucharistic

---

63 See Edward J. Kilmartin, S.J., 'The Catholic Tradition of Eucharistic Theology: Towards the Third Millennium,' *Theological Studies* 55 (1994) 405–457, and in greater detail in his *The Eucharist in the West: History and Theology* (Collegeville, Minn.: Liturgical Press, 1998).
64 Gregory Dix, *The Shape of the Liturgy* (London: Dacre Press, 1945), published also with additional notes by Paul Marshall (New York: Seabury Press, 1982).

celebration that the Eastern Orthodox refer to as 'the Divine Liturgy', many Protestants as 'The Great Thanksgiving', and Roman Catholics as 'The Canon' of the 'Sacrifice of the Mass'. The Eucharistic Prayer is commonly recognized as having the following basic elements and groupings:

A 1 introductory dialogue
    2 preface
    3 *sanctus*
B 4 post-*sanctus*
    5 preliminary epiclesis alternative or additional post-*sanctus*)
C 6 narrative of institution
D 7 anamnesis
    8 epiclesis
    9 diptychs or intercessions, which may be divided
E 10 concluding doxology

Practically all of the Eucharistic Prayers from the patristic period to those now in use in the main-line Christian churches seem to follow this basic order. Not all the elements 1–10 are always present, nor always in this order. But whatever the variations, something from each of the five groups A–E is invariably present. To this 'invariably' there are two major exceptions that prove the rule. The first is the absence of the narrative of institution/words of consecration from the ancient *Anaphora of Addai and Mari* that is still in use in the East Syrian family of liturgies (and that was recently formally recognized as a valid Eucharist by the Roman Catholic Church).[65] The second exception is the traditional Lutheran elimination of the whole Eucharistic Prayer with the exception of the narrative of institution, the consecrating words of Jesus, the *Verba Jesu.*

In the sixteenth century, neither the Catholic nor the Protestant theologians were explicitly aware of this structure. It is a Trinitarian structure that had survived even through centuries where hardly anyone was aware of it. Both the Catholics and at least the sacramentally oriented Protestants shared the conviction that the narrative of institution/consecrating words of Jesus were essential. No matter what variations there may have been, the words of consecration were always there, and generally considered to contain the essence of the Eucharistic celebration. The Catholic tradition's fixation on the 'moment of consecration' left it insensitive to the theological (Trinitarian) structure of the whole Eucharistic Prayer. For their part, the Lutherans, in their effort to eliminate everything that, as Luther put it 'smacks of sacrifice', drew one of the logical consequences of this and, from what had been an emphatically sacrificial prayer, they eliminated everything except the words of Jesus. Tragically, then, since no one seemed to be aware of its fundamentally Trinitarian 'shape', the traditional Roman *Canon Missae* that, properly understood, could have offered a solution to the Protestant–Catholic impasse, became instead one of its most intractable bones of contention.

---

65 See Robert F. Taft, 'Mass without the Consecration? The Historic Agreement between the Catholic church and the Assyrian Church of the East Promulgated 26 October 2001', *Worship* 77 (2003), pp. 482–509; idem, 'Mass without the Consecration?' *America* 188 (May 12, 2003), pp. 7–9.

5. The private Mass

There is little or no patristic precedent for it, but by the eighth century, and increasingly thereafter, the practice of a priest celebrating Mass privately, whether by himself or with/for a limited group of people, i.e., in the absence of a proper assembly, had become a taken-for-granted aspect of Western Christianity. Contemporary liturgical theology generally frowns on this practice[66] and especially on the many ideas and practices associated with it, for example, that the priest alone, rather than the whole assembly 'offers' the Mass, that the 'fruits' of the Mass are limited and therefore more Masses are better than fewer, that the priest alone has proprietary control over the fruits of the Mass, or at least over some of them, that the person for whom the Mass is specially offered need not participate in the celebration in order to receive its special fruits, that the priest has a right to a specific monetary stipend for offering a Mass for a specific intention, etc., etc. In the Middle Ages all this was taken for granted not just in the minds of the faithful, but also in the minds of the theologians. For example, the unquestioned legitimacy of the private Mass was apparently one of the things that Thomas Aquinas had in mind as he was expounding his theology of the Eucharist.

6. Emphasizing the Christological to the detriment of the ecclesiological

At first glance, this can seem puzzling. How can one possibly overemphasize Christ? The use, or misuse, of the axiom *in persona Christi* (in the person of Christ) can help clarify this point. It has been traditional, at least since Aquinas, to think of the priest celebrating Mass as acting *in persona Christi*. In traditional scholastic terms, God (Father, Son, Spirit) is obviously the ontological agent of what takes place in the Eucharistic celebration. But what can get veiled by a narrow use of the *in persona Christi* axiom is the fact that the primary *ritual* agent in the celebration of the Eucharist is not God, nor even the priest-celebrant, but the assembly. The axiom can mislead if it is not quoted in full: *in persona Christi capitis ecclesiae* (in the person of Christ the Head of the Church). Without the completion of the axiom in its reference to the Church, the axiom can be used to undergird a faulty theology of the individual power of the priest along with all the faulty emphases and practices associated with that and against which, legitimately for the most part, the Reformers reacted.[67]

7. The limitations of a schoolbook theology

The mere fact that a simplified – in many cases oversimplified – schoolbook theology dominated popular theology, preaching and catechesis was not a

---

66 The 'private Mass', however, is far from dead, and recent official Catholic instruction seems to be re-emphasizing it. See the 'Motu proprio "Summorum Pontificum" ' issued 7 July 2007 that re-establishes, alongside the 1970 Roman Missal promulgated by Pope Paul VI, what is basically the so-called 'Tridentine Mass', the 16th-century Roman Mass ritual (*Canon Missae*) promulgated by Pope St. Pius V.

67 This is a common theme among critical contemporary liturgical theologians. David W. Fagerberg speaks for many in the remarks he gathers under the heading 'The Underlying Ecclesiology' in *Theologia Prima: What is Liturgical Theology?* (Hillenbrand Books; Chicago/Mundelein: Liturgy Training Publications, 2nd edn, 2004), pp. 81–88.

problem particular to the late medieval period. Such is the fate of every period including, if we will admit it, our own. This is not an attempt to whitewash those faults and limitations of medieval Christianity that supplied the tinder that ignited in the Reformation. But it is a suggestion that looking at those limitations with more humble and less polemical eyes might enable us to look at them less defensively and with a greater prospect of learning from them. Let me focus here on one central theological development that, in its oversimplified, handbook form, played a central role in the Reformation controversies: the role of the Church in mediating grace and salvation within a sacramental dispensation or, in the rejecting words of the Reformers, the theology of works. As we are beginning to realize more than 400 years later – witness our growing convergence in liturgical theology, and witness the actual theological convergence on the theology of justification recently achieved by Lutherans and Catholics – both sides were *fundamentally* correct in their *basic* theological positions. As one Protestant liturgical theologian recently put it, referring to a scholarly discussion of contemporary Catholic liturgical theology: 'If we had only known this 400 years ago, we could have saved ourselves a lot of trouble'.[68]

As the historical work of Edward Kilmartin and Marius Lepin[69] has pointed out, the medieval and pre-Tridentine theological discussions about the role of the priest in presiding at the Eucharist and in performing the Eucharistic sacrifice were carried out at a daunting level of theological sophistication. Much of that theology, having been found faulty and misleading, has been superseded. But it was not precisely the weaknesses of that theology but rather its superficial oversimplifications that contributed to the Reformation. When popular preaching and teaching made the sacraments and other devotional practices to seem like magical transactions being carried out for a price by a very human Church, when that preaching and teaching made it seem that the Church was arrogating to itself the power to sacrifice Christ once again, it was not doing justice to the complexity of the late medieval theology of Church and sacraments. But it was reflecting on a popular level some of the practical consequences of the weaknesses of that theology. The Reformers were right to reject this as a faulty theology of works. They were definitely not reacting to something that did not exist. One way to test the adequacy of a theological position is to identify the popular forms and shapes with which it sells itself in the marketplace, and then try to articulate the theology that would be behind those forms and shapes. The results can be embarrassing. We may not have the humble clarity of vision to be able to do that accurately for our own present-day theology, but in the hindsight with which we can look back to the forms and shapes that late medieval theology took at the eve of the Reformation, we can see that they left much, very much, to be desired.

---

68   Hoyt L. Hickman, extemporaneous remark during a seminar (Eucharistic Prayer and Theology) meeting of the North American Academy of Liturgy.
69   Edward J. Kilmartin, S.J., *The Eucharist in the West: History and Theology* (Collegeville, Minn.: The Liturgical Press, 1998); Marius Lepin, *L'idée du Sacrifice de la Messe d'après les théologiens depuis l'origine jusqu'à nos jours* (Paris: Beauchesne, 1926).

B. CATHOLIC ABUSES

This is not the place to try to rehearse this vast and sorrowful history, but only to highlight a few of the more egregious abuses that relate to the subject of sacrifice. Viewed from a less-involved distance, these abuses could perhaps be regarded as being more of a structural, financial, political and practical nature than of a doctrinal nature. However, as suggested in the previous paragraph, such an idealistic and theoretical approach doesn't do honest justice to what actually happened. Yes, one can concede that the practical, on-the-ground abuses that cried out for reform may not have been *directly* connected to what the best theological minds of the Church were actually teaching. The more direct connection was with what was actually being practiced and preached in the marketplaces and parish churches. But those abuses, though perhaps not directly due to the admittedly faulty theology of the day, were, nevertheless, the kinds of abuses that could, and actually did, flow from that kind of theology. As I have pointed out earlier in this Part Two of this book, and elsewhere when dealing with sacrifice and atonement,[70] bad theology leads to bad morality.

The practice of stipend Masses and most of the customs associated with it, stand out as one of the major areas of abuse. 'Receive the power of offering sacrifice for the living and for the dead', proclaimed the bishop in the ordination rite as he handed over (*traditio insrumentorum*) to the deacon being ordained the chalice and the paten, the 'instruments' that the priest would use in offering the Eucharistic sacrifice. In Catholic thinking (that survives in popular forms even to this day), it was assumed that the priest received in ordination the *personal* power to carry out the Eucharistic sacrifice. This was thought of more as a personal, proprietary power adhering to his individual person rather than as a mandate or commission to lead the assembly in celebrating the Eucharist. There are some striking illustrations of how deep-rooted this consciousness was. There was the medieval 'case in conscience' about what to do if a renegade priest walked by and consecrated all the bread in a bakery. Since it was taken for granted that all that bread was now the Body of Christ, one of the central points of the case became one of justice and restitution, since the baker was no longer allowed to sell as bread what was now the Body of Christ. Another illustration was one that lasted to our very own day here in the twenty-first century. As already pointed out some pages ago (p. 124), until just a few years ago, a widely used missalette hymnal was still publishing a version of a popular Catholic hymn with the words: 'Bread and wine to be transformed now/*by the action of the priest*' (emphasis mine).[71]

The personal, individual, independent-of-the-assembly 'power of the priest' gave him certain rights over some of the particular fruits of the Mass that he could dispense according to his own will and pleasure, 'for the living and for the dead', as the ordination ceremony proclaimed (and indeed still proclaims in the current Catholic ordination ceremony). This gave the priest the right to receive a

---

70   See esp. 'Images of God and the Imitation of God', *TS* 68 (2007), pp. 36–51.
71   A further illustration, unforgettable in its grotesqueness to those witnessing it, was the experience, not uncommon just a few decades ago, of hearing a priest having extreme difficulty in pronouncing the words of consecration at Mass. Behind this was the neurotic fear that if he did not pronounce these words with the requisite precision, the Mass would not be valid.

monetary stipend for celebrating the Sacrifice of the Mass for a particular intention (see below, pp. 184–189). Just about all the imaginable abuses of this practice can be historically verified: priests celebrating multiple Masses in order to receive multiple stipends, accepting multiple stipend intentions for just one Mass, ordaining numerous 'Mass priests' with just enough education to 'read', however poorly, the Latin Mass, etc. But those were just the mercantile aspects of the abuse. Theologically, there was the problem of the obviously limited fruits of one individual Mass, or at least of the particular fruits or benefits of the Mass that the priest had under his personal control. One hundred – to say nothing of one thousand – Masses celebrated for a particular intention were considered to be more valuable, more 'effective' than just one Mass. This seemed inconsistent with the widespread Christian doctrine about the infinite merits of the unique and perfect Sacrifice of Christ. An additional problem connected with this was the practice of the granting – at times this was literally a selling – of indulgences. Behind this was the, in itself, legitimate theological idea of the relatively infinite merits of the Communion of Saints, that the Church possesses a relatively infinite and inexhaustible storehouse of merit that can be drawn upon to help make atonement for the sins of its members. But the step from this legitimate theological idea – in itself quite beautiful and consoling – to the abuse of selling indulgences, or seeming to be selling indulgences, was not far and was, all too often, a step actually taken. Behind all this, as we have already pointed out in our treatment of medieval atonement theories, was the deep-rootedness of mercantile and legal-transactional metaphors and ideas when thinking about grace and redemption. In effect, to a reform-minded Christian, the Church was turning into a dirty human business in which grace and salvation could be bought and sold; and the key and most valuable item being sold was the Sacrifice of the Mass.

C. The Reaction of the Reformers

Our deliberately provocative account of abuses connected with the Roman Catholic understanding of and practice of the Sacrifice of the Mass helps explain how visceral was Luther's rejection in his 1523 *Formula Missae et Communionis*: 'from here on [the Offertory] almost everything smacks and savors of sacrifice'.[72] The negative emotion that screams out from these words is one of the most critical factors in the sharpness and eventual radical rejection of everything 'Catholic' that characterized the reaction of the Reformers. This is not to minimize the major doctrinal differences that surfaced in the course of the Reformation, but only to point out that those differences might not have resulted in such radical separations if the emotional and cultural differences were not so strongly in play. What began as obvious reactions to obvious abuses, reactions that, at first, were not necessarily reactions against an authentic, genuine Catholicism, quickly morphed into a situation in which the baby – especially if one identifies the 'baby' as church

---

72   Cited from Jasper and Cuming, p. 191. In greater detail: '. . . That utter abomination follows which forces all that precedes in the Mass into its service and is, therefore, called the offertory. From here on almost everything smacks and savors of sacrifice. . . . Let us, therefore, repudiate everything that smacks of sacrifice, together with the entire canon and retain only that which is pure and holy, and so order our mass.' (ibid., 191–92)

unity rather than just traditional Catholic doctrine – got thrown out with the dirty bath water. It was for all practical purposes impossible for Protestants to see a value in church unity when it was being preached by ecclesiastics whom they perceived as propounding, or at least supportively tolerating, what they themselves experienced as abuses to be viscerally rejected. And, of course, what all too often followed was the demonizing of Catholics and the Catholic position and the energetic choice for the extreme opposite of whatever they perceived to be typically Catholic. Hence the quick development of the *sola* principle into such powerful and absolutizing battle cries: *sola scriptura* – Scripture alone, meaning a total rejection of all 'Catholic' tradition; *sola fides* – faith alone, meaning a total rejection of all 'works' (especially the specific works, practices and devotions of the Church) as contributing anything to salvation. With all the variations among the different Protestant movements a characteristically common trait among them was their rejection of or reservations about the traditional Catholic understanding of the sacramentality of the Church.

One of the tragic ironies of this sad history is that it is possible to argue that, in precisely what they were reacting against, the Protestants were being more Catholic than the Catholics. If one took away the 'Catholic abuses' against which the Reformers protested, there would have been very little, if anything, against which to protest. In other words, if one looks precisely at what was being attacked and defended, one can make the tragically ironic claim that the Reformation and the Counter Reformation were, for the most part, not fighting about authentic Christianity.

D. THE CATHOLIC REACTION AGAINST THE PROTESTANT REACTION

Our awkward repetition of the word 'reaction' is deliberate. In the recent past it became common to speak not just about the 'Protestant Reformation', but also about the 'Catholic Reformation'. There is a valuable insight there. But it should not be allowed to obscure the critically important fact that much of the work of the Catholic Reformation was, in fact, in reaction to Protestant developments. Catholics in general, and most specifically the bishops and theologians at the Council of Trent (1545–1563) were reacting to what the Protestants were doing and saying. This was normal in the sense that the agenda of church councils was generally set by the need to respond to the specific situations and challenges of the day. It is not surprising, therefore, that the Council of Trent did not attend directly to the heart, the soul, the essence of the Catholic tradition that it perceived the Protestants to be attacking. And actually, in the heat of controversy and with the limited resources then available to it, it might not have been able to do so even if it wanted to. In response to the Protestant attack on the traditional Catholic understanding of 'The Most Holy Sacrifice of the Mass', this, if we can reduce a complicated history to three 'moments', is how Trent reacted.

First, in a relatively early session (Session Thirteen in 1551), responding to the threat it perceived to the doctrine of the real presence of Christ in the Eucharist from the Lutheran attack on transubstantiation, Trent proceeded to shore up this aspect of the traditional Catholic understanding of the real presence of Christ brought about by the real change of the bread and wine into the body and blood of Christ.[73]

Second, in another session *a full eleven years later* (Session Twenty-Two in 1562), Trent, in a series of canons, defined that

> the Mass is a true and proper sacrifice offered to God' (canon 1: DS 1751). This sacrifice was instituted by Christ, who also instituted a priesthood ordered to the offering of his body and blood (canon 2: DS 1752). This sacrifice is propitiatory and can be offered for the living and dead, for pardon of sins, for satisfaction for sins, and as remedy for punishment due to sins, as well as for other necessities (canon 3: DS 1753). This sacrifice in no way detracts from the sacrifice of the cross (canon 4: DS 1754).[74]

Third – and this is most critical – Trent did not explain or define precisely what it meant or understood by 'sacrifice'. That, as we will see hereafter, was left for the theologians to argue about, Catholics defending the idea of the Mass as sacrifice, and Protestants attacking it. In addition, this defined doctrine, as Kilmartin has pointed out, leaves many questions unanswered.

> There is the matter of the relation of the Mass to the sacrifice of the cross. Is the sacrifice of the Mass an offering of the body and blood of Christ made by the Church as an additional offering subordinate to the sacrifice of the cross? The efficacy attributed to the sacrifice of the Mass leaves the question open as to how this efficacy is realized. Is it a matter of efficacy *ex opere operato,* or by way of intercession *ex opere operantis,* or both? Again, The Mass has the characteristic of thanksgiving and propitiation. But how are the two related? Is the Mass a propitiatory sacrifice for which thanksgiving is offered, or is it propitiatory because it is a thank-offering? Also, if the Mass is a true sacrifice does this mean that it is related only to the sacrifice of the cross, or also to the resurrection of Christ? Does a true sacrifice not include offer and acceptance?
>
> (Kilmartin, *The Eucharist in the West,* pp. 173–74).

If one's understanding of true Christian sacrifice is Trinitarian, as our whole book argues, then this last question is to be answered with a resounding affirmative. But this Trinitarian understanding of sacrifice was simply not available, at least not in any explicit way, to the Western theologians, whether Catholic or Protestant, of the sixteenth century.

---

73 ˙ Trent did this in the following two solemnly defining canons: 'Can. 1. Whoever should deny that in the most holy sacrament of the Eucharist, the body and blood together with the soul and divinity of our Lord Jesus Christ and hence the whole Christ is contained; but says rather that it is there [i.e., in that sacrament] only [as] in a sign or figure, or virtually: let them be anathema' – DS 1651. 'Can. 2. Whoever should say that in the sacrosanct sacrament of the Eucharist the substance of the bread and wine remains together with the body and blood of our Lord Jesus Christ, and [whoever] should deny that wondrous and unique conversion of the whole substance of the bread into the body and of the whole substance of the wine into the blood, while the appearances of bread and wine remain, which conversion the Catholic Church most aptly calls transubstantiation: let them be anathema' – DS 1652.

74 As summarized in Kilmartin, *The Eucharist in the West* 173.

But before we look back on at that unhappy polemical debate, we need to attend to the implications and consequences of the way, i.e., the order, in which Trent dealt with this topic. It has been noted that, in the basic theological orientation of the Tridentine council fathers, 'the sacrificial character of the Mass was thought to precede logically its relation to the sacrificial character of the event of the cross'. Nevertheless, they 'were not able to view the sacramentality and sacrificial character of the Mass as one reality, and to ground the sacramental character of the Mass in the sacrificial'. They had already, a full eleven years before they got to the question of the sacrifice of the Mass, excluded that possibility by defining both the somatic real presence of Christ in the Eucharist, and the Eucharist itself, as sacrament. Catholic theology had thus painted itself into a corner that the Protestants, theologically at least, found easy to attack: 'Both Christ and the forms of bread and wine had to be present in order that he might be offered to the Father. Hence each Mass is seen as a kind of new sacrifice related to the cross in which the priest and the victim [i.e. Christ] are identical with the priest and the victim of the cross'.[75]

E. EUCHARISTIC SACRIFICE AND THE 'DESTRUCTION OF A VICTIM'

A notable difference, indeed a chasm, often appears between what many liturgical scholars today agree is sound Eucharistic theology and the Eucharistic theology of several official documents of the Roman Catholic magisterium. Historical research suggests that Robert Bellarmine[76] is one of the 'messengers', if indeed not also one of the 'villains', of this unhappy story.[77]

The following summary can pass as a consensus position of contemporary liturgical theology that reflects recent developments: (1) The axiom *in persona Christi*, used to describe the role of the priest, is interpreted broadly; it is understood as including *in persona Christi capitis ecclesiae*, and also in tandem with the axiom *in persona ecclesiae*. Accompanying this is a growing emphasis on the ecclesiological (and not just Christological) aspect of the Eucharist, as well as on its Trinitarian dynamic and on the Holy Spirit's special role. (2) There is an awareness that the mystery of the Eucharist (the sacrament and the sacrificial action in traditional terms) is spread out across the whole Eucharistic Prayer and its accompanying ritual action, and that it cannot be atomized or located merely in one part, such as the Words of Institution. (3) There is an awareness that the dynamic of the Eucharistic action flows from Christ to the

---

75   Kilmartin, *The Eucharist in the West* 178.
76   Robert Bellarmine (1542–1621) was the leading Catholic controversialist of the late sixteenth century. His chief work was the *Disputationes de Controversiis Christianae Fidei Adversus Hujus Temporis Haereticos* (3 vols; Ingolstadt, 1586–93). A Jesuit, he was made a cardinal in 1599, canonized a saint in 1930, and declared to be a doctor of the Church in 1931.
77   The principal source and background for this historical research can be found in Kilmartin, *The Eucharist in the West*. Most of the material in the remainder of this chapter appeared first in *Theological Studies* 61 (2000) 239–60, and then in a more compact form in: Robert J. Daly, S.J., 'Robert Bellarmine and Post-Tridentine Eucharistic Theology', in: *From Trent to Vatican II: Historical and Theological Investigations* (ed. Raymond F. Bulman and Frederick J. Parella; Oxford: University Press, 2006), pp. 81–101.

Church to the Eucharist, and that the role of the priest is embedded in the Christ–Church relationship and not as something standing between Christ and the Church.

The following can pass as a description of the position, of the contemporary Roman magisterium: (1) The axiom *in persona Christi* is construed somewhat narrowly, eliminating, for the most part, the ecclesiological perspective and strongly emphasizing the Christological perspective, to the concomitant overshadowing of the Trinitarian aspect of the Eucharist and the special role of the Holy Spirit. (2) There is still a strong focus on the Words of Institution (formerly identified as the *forma essentialis* of the sacrament). (3) The dynamic of the Eucharistic action is conceived as flowing from Christ to the Priest to the Eucharist to the Church – thus leading to an overemphasis on priestly power, position and privilege against which many have protested.[78]

The discrepancy between these two views is striking. The late Edward Kilmartin, for instance, characterized this 'modern average Catholic theology of the Eucharistic sacrifice' as 'bankrupt' and 'without a future'.[79] The question, therefore for the historian of doctrine is: How did this discrepancy come about?

1. Modern average Catholic theology of the Eucharist

This phrase refers to a specific line of the teaching of the Roman magisterium from Pius XII's 1947 *Mediator Dei*[80] to John Paul II's 1980 *Dominicae cenae*[81] and the 1983 'Letter of the Congregation for the Doctrine of the Faith on the Subject of the Role of the Ordained Ministry of the Episcopate and Presbyterate in the Celebration of the Eucharist'.[82] The phrase 'specific line of the teaching' refers to an aspect, often the dominant aspect, of recent magisterial teaching that seems to circumvent or pass over in silence (and thus, at least implicitly, to reverse) some of the important developments of Vatican II's Constitution on the Liturgy, *Sacrosanctum concilium*, and the subsequent liturgical reform in the Roman Catholic Church.[83]

In *Mediator Dei* it is stated that: '[t]he priest acts for the people only because he represents Christ, who is head of all his members and offers himself for them. Thus he goes to the altar as the minister of Christ, inferior to Christ, but superior to the people'.[84] This is an obvious paraphrase from Robert Bellarmine (to whom

---

78   Kilmartin, *The Eucharist in the West* 346–47, 350–51.
79   Kilmartin, *The Eucharist in the West* 384. My task is not to substantiate Kilmartin's thesis. I assume that the force of his argument is strong enough to require serious attention by scholars. But before going on, we must acknowledge how difficult it is to write about the contemporary situation, since what we are referring to as traditional or official Catholic magisterial Church teaching on the Eucharist seems to be in transition. The recent writings of Pope Benedict XVI on the Eucharist and sacrifice – see esp. *Sacramentum Caritatis* (2007) – are much more nuanced and much closer to what critical liturgical theologians are writing than were the writings of his predecessor in the See of Peter.
80   *Acta apostolicae sedis* (=AAS) 39 (1947), pp. 521–600.
81   *AAS* 72 (1980), pp. 113–48.
82   *AAS* 75 (1983), pp. 1001–9.
83   See Kilmartin, *The Eucharist in the West*, pp. 187–201.
84   *AAS* 39 (1947), p. 553. The text is also found in DS 3850.

the encyclical's footnotes refer): 'The sacrifice of the Mass is offered by three: by Christ, by the Church, by the minister; but not in the same way. For Christ offers as primary priest, and offers through the priest as man, as through his proper minister. The Church does not offer as priest through the minister, but as people through the priest. Thus Christ offers through the inferior, the Church through the superior.[85]

On this Kilmartin pointed out: 'This theological approach . . . subsumes the ecclesiological aspect of the Eucharistic sacrifice under its Christological aspect. In other words, the priest represents the Church because he represents Christ the head of the Church who offers the sacrifice in the name of all the members of his body the Church.'[86] In other words, the dynamic line is not: Christ–Church–Eucharist, in which the role of the priest is embedded in the relationship Christ–Church, but rather, submerging the ecclesiological aspect under the Christological, and elevating the role of the priest: Christ–Priest–Eucharist–Church. That latter viewpoint is basically the position that is developed in *Mediator Dei*, as is clear from the following passage:

> For that unbloody immolation, by which at the words of consecration Christ is made present upon the altar in the state of victim, is performed by the priest and by him alone, as representative of Christ and not as representative of the faithful. But it is because the priest places the divine victim upon the altar that he offers it to God the Father as an oblation for the glory of the Blessed Trinity and for the good of the whole Church. Now the faithful participate in the oblation, understood in this limited sense, after their own fashion and in a twofold manner, namely, because they not only offer the sacrifice by the hands of the priest, but also, to a certain extent, in union with him. . . . Now it is clear that the faithful offer by the hands of the priest from the fact that the minister at the altar, in offering a sacrifice in the name of all his members, represents Christ, the head of the mystical body. Hence the whole Church can rightly be said to offer up the victim through Christ. But the conclusion that the people offer the sacrifice with the priest himself is not based on the fact that, being members of the Church no less than the priest himself, they perform a visible liturgical rite; for this is the privilege only of the minister who has been divinely appointed for this office; rather it is based on the fact that the people unite their hearts in praise, impetration, expiation, and thanksgiving with the prayers or intentions of the priest, even of the High Priest himself, so that in the one and same offering of the victim and according to a visible sacerdotal rite, they may be presented to God the Father.[87]

This is the line of teaching repeated and, in some respects, promoted even further by recent magisterial teaching. As is well known, Vatican II and its subsequent liturgical reforms took steps toward a much broader understanding of the Eucharist. But the Council did not in fact make a clean break from the

---

85 Robert Bellarmine, *Controversiarum de sacramento eucharistiae* lib. 6.6, *Opera Omnia* 4 (Paris: Vivès, 1873) p. 373.
86 Kilmartin, *The Eucharist in the West*, p. 190.
87 Pius XII, *Mediator Dei* (*AAS* 39 [1947]), pp. 555–56.

traditional, more narrow approach. In the Constitution on the Church, *Lumen gentium* no. 10, we read: 'In the person of Christ he [the ministerial priest] brings about the Eucharistic sacrifice (*sacrificium Eucharisticum in persona Christi conficit*) and offers it to God in the name of all the people.'[88] The Constitution on the Liturgy, *Sacrosanctum concilium*, also includes this line of thinking when it states:

> The Church, therefore, spares no effort in trying to ensure that, when present at this mystery of faith, Christian believers should not be there as strangers or silent spectators. On the contrary, having a good grasp of it through the rites and prayers, they should take part in the sacred action, actively, fully aware, and devoutly. They should be formed by God's word, and be nourished at the table of the Lord's Body. They should give thanks to God. Offering the immaculate victim, not only through the hands of the priest but also together with him, they should learn to offer themselves. Through Christ, the Mediator, they should be drawn day by day into ever more perfect union with God and each other, so that finally God may be all in all (no. 48).

There is indeed more emphasis on the participation of the faithful, but the traditional dynamic line of Christ – Priest – Eucharist – Church (rather than Christ – Eucharist – Church) remains intact, and there is no mention of the role of the Holy Spirit. A few years later, the *Missale Romanum* (1969) of Pope Paul VI made a significant advance by introducing an explicit epiclesis of the Holy Spirit, but in such a way (especially by placing it before rather than after the consecration) as to leave intact the traditional Western overemphasis on the Words of Institution. This is clear from the 'General Instruction on the Roman Missal' which, after speaking of the Eucharistic Prayer as 'the climax and the very heart of the entire celebration',[89] proceeds, under the heading 'The Institution Narrative and Consecration,' to say:

> Through the words and actions of Christ there is accomplished the very sacrifice which he himself instituted at the Last Supper when, under the species of bread and wine, he offered his Body and Blood and gave them to his apostles to eat and drink, commanding them in turn to perform this same sacred mystery.[90]

---

88   Vatican II translations are taken from *The Basic Sixteen Documents, Vatican Council II* (gen. ed. Austin Flannery, O.P.; Northport, New York: Costello, 1996).

89   Paul VI. *Institutio generalis missalis romani* no. 54, in *Missale Romanum* (Rome: Vatican Press, 1970) 39; also in *Enchiridion documentorum instaurationis liturgicae: Ordo Missae*, ed. Reiner Kaczynski (Turin: Marietti, 1976), no. 1449, vol.1, p. 488; also in *Vatican Council II: The Conciliar and Postconciliar Documents* (ed. Austin Flannery; Collegeville: Liturgical, 1975), p. 175.

90   Paul VI. *Institutio generalis missalis romani* no. 55 (d); Kaczynski, no. 1450 d, vol.1. p. 488; Flannery, *Vatican Council II*, p. 176. This basic position and emphasis, but now with more nuance, is repeated in the new (2002) General Instruction. See *A Commentary on the General Instruction of the Roman Missal* (ed. Edward Foley, Nathan D. Mitchell, Joanne M. Pierce; Collegeville, Minn.: Liturgical Press, 2008), pp. 176–78 and passim.

The result is that the Eucharistic Prayer and the communion of the faithful may still be considered as pertaining to the integrity of the liturgical rite, but, disappointingly, not to the integrity ('essential form' in traditional scholastic terms) of the sacrament or the sacrifice.

Before moving on to the subsequent development of magisterial teaching in John Paul II and the Congregation for the Doctrine of the Faith, it may be helpful to summarize how Kilmartin, under the headings 'Words of Consecration' and 'Representation of the Sacrifice of Christ', described this 'modern average Catholic theology of the Eucharist'. The core of this position is the theology of the 'moment of consecration'.

> In the Western tradition, the words of Christ spoken over the bread and wine are [also] understood to be the essential form of the sacrament. These words thus constitute the moment when the sacrament is realized, namely, when the bread and wine are converted into the body and blood of Christ. Thus, while the words are spoken by the presiding minister, they are understood as being spoken by Christ through his minister. This act is one accomplished only by the minister acting *in persona Christi* in the midst of the prayer of faith of the Church. . . . The representation of the death of Christ occurs with the act of conversion of the elements. The somatic presence of Christ and the representation of the sacrifice of Christ are simultaneously achieved in the act of the consecration of the elements.
>
> But what is meant by the idea that the death of Christ is 'represented at the moment of the consecration of the elements'? The post-Tridentine theories, which sought to find the visible sacrifice of the Mass in the separate consecration of the elements, proposed a 'mystical mactation' of Christ at the level of the sacramental signs. *Thus they espoused the idea of a sacrificial rite, the structure of which was the sacrifice of the self-offering of Christ in the signs of the food. This is a pre-Christian concept which is now generally discarded in current Catholic theology* [emphasis mine].
>
> Nowadays the average Catholic theology of the Mass . . . affirms that the representation of the sacrifice of the cross is a sacramental reactualization of the once-for-all historical engagement of Jesus on the cross. The idea that in the act of consecration a sacramental representation of the sacrifice of the cross is realized in the sense that the historical sacrifice is re-presented or reactualized also seems to be favored by official Catholic theology today. However, Pius XII in *Mediator Dei* did not attempt to settle this basic question.[91]

It should be noted that this idea of sacramental representation, although now quite characteristic of contemporary Catholic theology, is actually one of the weak points of that theology. For this theory – that the historical saving acts of Christ are 'metahistorically' made present to us – is not significantly supported by the biblical witness, nor by the Jewish background, nor by broad patristic evidence. Still more, it is also the kind of theory that creates further problems – i.e., one ends up with an explanation that still needs to be further explained – since

---

91   Kilmartin, *The Eucharist in the West*, pp. 294–95.

there is little agreement among scholars on how to explain what is being asserted.[92]

John Paul II in his 1980 Holy Thursday letter On the Mystery and Worship of the Holy Eucharist (*Dominicae cenae*), points out that the sacredness of the Eucharist is due to the fact that Christ is the author and principal priest of the Eucharist, and that this ritual memorial of the death of the Lord is performed by priests who repeat the words and actions of Christ, who thus offer the holy sacrifice '*in persona Christi* . . . in specific sacramental identification with the High and Eternal Priest, who is the author and principal actor of this sacrifice of his'.[93] Commenting on this, Kilmartin pointed out that here and throughout this letter,

> John Paul II limits himself to the typical scholastic approach to the theology of the Eucharist, passing over the trinitarian grounding of the holiness of the Eucharist. In modern Catholic theology, the sacred character of the Eucharist is grounded on more than just this christological basis. Its sacredness is not merely based on the fact of originating in a historical act of institution by Christ. Rather, what grounds the holiness of the Eucharist is the initiative of the Father: the self-offering by the Father of his only Son for the salvation of the world.[94]

John Paul II's description does not highlight the role of the Holy Spirit in the Eucharist suggested by Vatican II's *Sacrosanctum concilium* and subsequently implemented by the insertion of epicleses of the Holy Spirit in the new Eucharistic Prayers of the Missal of Paul VI. John Paul II's description of the role of the ministerial priesthood omits the pneumatological dimension. Rather, basing himself on Trent's decree on priesthood, canon 2, concerning the *potestas consecrandi* (DS 1771), the ministerial activity of priests is mentioned under the presupposition of its Christological grounding. Priests are said to be the acting subjects of the consecration: 'they consecrate (the elements of bread and wine)',[95] 'by means of consecration by the priest they become sacred species'.[96]

This neglect of recent magisterial and theological developments is characteristic of *Dominicae cenae*. Three more examples stand out. As first example one can note that appeal is made to Chapters one and two of the Council of Trent's Decree on the Sacrifice of the Mass: 'Since the Eucharist is a true sacrifice it brings about the restoration to God. Consequently the celebrant . . . is an authentic priest performing . . . a true sacrificial act, that brings men back to God.'[97] Also in the same number it is stated: 'To this sacrifice, which is renewed in a sacramental form . . .'[98] Kilmartin pointed out that this reflects the same kind of confusion as that caused by Trent using *offerre* to refer both to the historical sacrifice of the cross and to the (phenomenological, history-of-religions) liturgical-ritual sacrificial act of the Eucharistic celebration, not attending to the fact that sacrifice, in the

---

92　See Kilmartin, *The Eucharist in the West*, pp. 268–300.
93　*Dominicae cenae*, II 8 (*AAS* 72 [1980], p. 128).
94　Kilmartin, *The Eucharist in the West*, pp. 196–97.
95　*Dominicae cenae*, II 11 (*AAS* 72 [1980], p. 141).
96　Ibid., II 9 (*AAS* 72 [1980], p. 133).
97　Ibid., II 9 (*AAS* 72 [1980], p. 131).
98　'Ad hoc igitur sacrificium, quod modo sacramentali in altari renovatur . . .'

history-of-religions sense of the word, had been done away with by the Christ-event. The theological and terminological problem caused by Trent's failure to distinguish the historical self-offering of Christ and its ritual expression can be resolved, Kilmartin insisted, only by rethinking both the inner relation of the personal sacrifice of Jesus and his body the Church, and the outward form of the meal as its efficacious sign.[99]

A second example may be noted. *Dominicae cenae* follows Trent in viewing the Last Supper as the moment when Christ instituted the Eucharist and, at the same time, the sacrament of the priesthood.[100] But the pope also goes beyond Trent in teaching that the Last Supper was the first Mass.[101] This view was once favoured by Catholic theologians; but most now argue that the Church was constituted in the Easter-event, and that the sacraments are also Easter realities grounded on the sending of the Holy Spirit.[102]

A third and final example is available. *Dominicae cenae* also slips back into older and outmoded terminology when it speaks of the sacrifice of Christ 'that in a sacramental way is renewed on the altar (*in altari renovatur*)'.[103] It is hard to imagine that the pope wanted to take up again the infelicitous implications of the saying of Pope Gregory the Great that '(Christ) in the mystery of the holy sacrifice is offered for us "again" '.[104] One must presume that 'John Paul II did not intend to state anything more than that the newness of the Eucharistic sacrifice can only be ascribed to the repetition of the ecclesial dimension'.[105]

Two subsequent documents of the Congregation for the Doctrine of the Faith continued this narrow line of interpretation. The 'Letter of the Congregation for the Doctrine of the Faith on the Subject of the Role of the Ordained Ministry of the Episcopate and Presbyterate in the Celebration of the Eucharist' (1983) states the traditional teaching:

> For although the whole faithful participate in one and the same priesthood of Christ and concur in the oblation of the Eucharist, nevertheless only the ministerial priesthood, in virtue of the sacrament of orders, enjoys the power of confecting the eucharistic sacrifice in the person of Christ and of offering it in the name of the whole Christian people.[106]

Later on there is more detail regarding the representative function of the presiding minister:

---

99   Kilmartin, *The Eucharist in the West*, pp. 198–99.
100   Trent, session 22, canon 2; DS 1752.
101   *Dominicae cenae* (*AAS* 72 [1980], pp. 119–21).
102   Kilmartin, *The Eucharist in the West*, pp. 200–1.
103   *Dominicae cenae* II 9 (*AAS* 72 [1980]), p. 133, see also p. 131.
104   The sentence in which this phrase occurs reads: 'Haec namque singulariter victima ab aeterno interitu animam salvat, quae illam nobis mortem Unigeniti per mysterium reparat, qui licet resurgens a mortuis jam non moritur, et mors ei ultra non dominabitur (Rom. VI, 9), tamen in semetipso immortaliter atque incorruptibiliter vivens, pro nobis iterum in hoc mysterio sacrae oblationis immolatur' (Gregory the Great, *Dialogorum libri IV* 4.48 (PL 77, p. 425CD).
105   Kilmartin, *The Eucharist in the West*, p. 201.
106   CDF Letter of 6 August 1983, I 1 (*AAS* 75 [1983], pp. 1001–9 (1001). This letter conveniently contains footnote references to all the major statements of recent official teaching of the Roman magisterium on this point.

However those whom Christ calls to the episcopate and presbyterate, in order that they can fulfill the office . . . of confecting the eucharistic mystery, he signs them spiritually with the special seal through the sacrament of orders . . . and so configures them to himself that they proclaim the words of consecration not by mandate of the community, but they act ' "in persona Christi," which certainly means more than "in the name of Christ" or even "in place of Christ" . . . since the one celebrating by a peculiar and sacramental way is completely the same as the "high and eternal Priest", who is author and principal actor of this his own sacrifice, in which no one indeed can take his place.'[107]

The 'Declaration of the Congregation for the Doctrine of the Faith on the Question of Admission of Women to the Ministerial Priesthood' (1976) was obviously following this narrow line of teaching when it put special weight on the Christological argument to show that only men can represent Christ in the act of Eucharistic consecration: 'It is true that the priest represents the Church which is the body of Christ; but if he does so it is primarily because, first, he represents Christ himself who is head and pastor of the Church.'[108] In response to this Kilmartin had noted that the logical conclusion to this line of teaching is that, 'since the priest represents Christ in strict sacramental identity at the moment of consecration, the role must be taken by a man'.

Recent papal teaching, however, as in *Mane nobiscum Domine*, the 'Apostolic Letter of the Holy Father John Paul II to the Bishops, Clergy and Faithful for the Year of the Eucharist' (7 October 2004)[109] happily puts more emphasis on the transforming effects of the Eucharist in the lives of the faithful. This letter speaks of 'the impulse which the Eucharist gives to the community for *a practical commitment to building a more just and fraternal society*' (No. 28). But ultimately, this largely exhortatory document reverts to the same line of teaching whose weaknesses Kilmartin has exposed. It does so by explicitly referring its readers (see No. 3) to the teaching of *Ecclesia de Eucharistia*, the 'Encyclical Letter of His Holiness Pope John Paul II to the Bishops, Priest and Deacons, Men and Women in the Consecrated Life, and All the Lay Faithful on the Eucharist in its Relationship to the Church' (17 April 2003).[110] This document suffers from several additional theological deficiencies. The first is a biblical literalism, almost a fundamentalism, that is quite at odds with the Church's own official approval of the methods of modern historical criticism. The second is an embarrassing insertion of unscholarly personal piety into a formal teaching document when, for example, early on, the letter speaks of the Cenacle of Jerusalem (a building constructed in the Middle Ages) as the place where Jesus instituted the Eucharist. The third is the constant conflation of the existential and the historical when speaking of the relationship between the Eucharist and the Church. *Existentially*, the Eucharist is indeed the

---

107   Ibid., III 4 (*AAS* 75 [1983], p. 1006). The quotation which occupies the second half of this citation is from Pope John Paul II's *Dominicae cenae*, 8 (*AAS* 72 [1980], pp. 128–29).
108   *Inter insigniores*, 15 October 1976 (*AAS* 69 [1977], pp. 98–116 (112–13), as quoted by Kilmartin, *The Eucharist in the West*, p. 196.
109   English trans. available on the Vatican web site (www.vatican.va/phome_en.html).
110   Official text in *AAS* 95 (2003). English trans. available on the Vatican web site (www.vatican.va/phome_en.html).

source and summit, the centre and foundation of all that the Church is and is supposed to be. But *historically*, the Eucharist – if we mean by that what the Church now celebrates – came from the Church, not vice versa. It took the Church, under the guidance of the Holy Spirit, more than three centuries to learn how to celebrate and begin to understand the Eucharistic mystery as we now celebrate and understand it.[111]

So, if the consensus position of contemporary critical liturgical theology is basically correct, there is indeed an alarming divide – still not totally bridged by the more nuanced theological teaching of Pope Benedict XVI, for example, in *Sacramentum Caritatis* – between that position and contemporary magisterial teaching now exposed as being in need of renewal. I shall now try to contribute toward such a renewal by examining some of the sixteenth-century antecedents, eroded theological foundations, so to speak, of this contemporary magisterial teaching.

2. *The sixteenth-century antecedents*

Pius XII's *Mediator Dei* (1947) and, after that, subsequent magisterial teaching on the Eucharist appeals to Robert Bellarmine to support its typically Western emphases on the words of consecration and on the Christological aspects of the Eucharist to the neglect of its Trinitarian, pneumatological and ecclesiological aspects. In this sad story of division between the Church's teaching and that of its best liturgical theologians, is Bellarmine the 'villain' or just the 'messenger'? The answer, it seems is: a bit of both.

Marius Lepin[112] summarized the teaching of the theologians who formulated Trent's teaching on the Eucharist.[113]

> From all the preparatory discussions, several important facts stand out which it is important to underline.
>
> First, at no point in the Council's deliberations can one find a suggestion of the idea that the Mass contains any reality of immolation. No theologian and no [council] father pretended to find anything but a figure or a memorial of the immolation once realized on the cross. There is no trace of the theories one will see arising in the following years, theories that tend to require of the eucharistic sacrifice a change in the victim equivalent to some kind of destruction, as if, for a sacrifice to be real, there would have to be a real immolation.

---

111   For further details see Robert J. Daly, S.J., 'Eucharistic Origins: From the New Testament to the Liturgies of the Golden Age', *TS* 66 (2005), pp. 3–22.

112   Marius Lepin, *L'idée du Sacrifice de la Messe d'après les théologiens depuis l'origine jusqu'à nos jours* (Paris: Beauchesne, 1926). Marius Lepin (1870–1952), Sulpician, founder of the congregation Servantes de Jésus, Souverain Prêtre (1938), published prolifically on Modernism and the Eucharistic teaching of the Catholic Church. *L'idée du Sacrifice de la Messe*, honored by the Académie française, was his major work of enduring scholarly value (see *Dictionnaire de théologie catholique, Tables générales* [Paris: Letouzey et Ané, 1967], vol. 2, pp. 2972–73).

113   Contained specifically in the first two chapters of the *Doctrina de ss. Missae sacrificio* (DS 1739–43) and the first three canons of the *Canones de ss. Missae sacrificio* (DS 1751–53) of session twenty-two, 17. Sept. 1562 of the Council of Trent.

Second, the idea of the sacrifice of the Mass appears to be connected practically to three fundamental elements: the consecration, the oblation, and the representative commemoration of the past immolation.

If diverse theologians seem to place the formal reason of the eucharistic sacrifice in one or other of these elements apart from the others, they are the exceptions. The largest number of them, and the most important, tend to locate the formal reason of the sacrifice in the three elements together, i.e., in (1) the oblation of Christ, (2) rendered present under the species by the consecration, (3) with a mystical figuring of his bloody immolation. In doing so they seem to be recapitulating the best ancient tradition.[114]

To understand what developed later, one must remember that Trent never explained what it meant by sacrifice. That was left to the theologians to argue about. The Catholic theologians inherited Trent's confusing conflation of the self-offering of Christ and the ritual liturgical offering. And they joined the Protestants in looking first to the practice of sacrifice in the religions of the world, and in finding there that some destruction of the/a victim was essential to true sacrifice. In doing so both sides fatefully overlooked the fact that Christ's sacrifice had done away with sacrifice in the history-of-religions sense of the word; both sides tragically failed to look first at the Christ-event in order to understand the Eucharist. Destruction-of-the-victim thinking thus became the false touchstone in the debates whether and how the Eucharist could be, as Trent put it, a true and proper sacrifice. Inevitably, the Catholic theology of the Eucharist after Trent became extremely complicated. Lepin (pp. 346–415) distinguishes four major theories, most with subgroups, for explaining this destruction-of-the-victim idea of Eucharistic sacrifice.

Theory I: The sacrifice does not require a real change in the victim; the Mass contains only a figure of the immolation of Christ.

(Lepin. pp. 346–57)

This theory was explained in two different ways. First, for Melchior Cano, Domingo de Soto and others, the figure of the immolation of Christ is found outside of the Consecration.

Melchior Cano (1509–1560) saw neither the consecration nor the subsequent oblation as sufficient to constitute the sacrifice for which, following Saint Thomas, 'there must be a certain action exercised with the breaking and the eating of the bread understood as symbolic of the past immolation'. However, hardly anyone else placed this kind of significance on the breaking of the host.

Domingo de Soto (1494–1560) saw the essence of the Eucharistic sacrifice in three parts: the consecration, the oblation and the communion. But, like Cano, he needed to find an action exercised *concerning/around*, but *not on*, the sensible appearances of the Eucharistic Christ. This he finds only in the communion (he

---

114 Lepin, *L'idée du Sacrifice de la Messe*, p. 326 (my translation from the French). This 815-page study quotes extensively from theologians writing on this theme beginning with the ninth century and covering the next eleven centuries. It constitutes the indispensable and single most important scholarly work for this research.

did not mention the fraction). The Jesuits Louis de la Puente (1554–1624) and Pierre Coton (1564–1626) follow the reasoning of de Soto.

Secondly, for two Jesuits, Alfonso Salmeron and Juan de Maldonado, the figure of the immolation of Christ was seen to be found in the consecration. They followed in principle the lines developed by the Dominicans Cano and de Soto, but they concentrated the representation of the immolation of Christ wholly on the consecration itself.

Alfonso Salmeron (1518–1585) saw the immolation figured in the double consecration, in the separate species of body and blood. All that follows the consecration contributes to the perfection of the mystical signification and thus to the perfection of the sacrifice but not to its substantial truth. He found a 'death of a victim' to be 'represented' in the Eucharist; for he pointed out that the actual death of a victim is required only when the victim is present *in propria specie*, but not when present, as Christ is in the Eucharist, *sub aliena specie*. This became a very popular theological explanation.

Juan de Maldonado (1515–1583) found that what is called sacrifice in Scripture is not the death of the victim, but its oblation. The actual oblation of Christ on Calvary does not need to be repeated, for the Eucharist looks back to it, just as the Last Supper looked ahead to it.

Theory II: The sacrifice requires a real change of the material offered: in the Mass the change takes place in the substance of the bread and wine.

(Lepin, pp. 357–74)

This theory was held, for instance, by Michel de Bay [Baius], Francisco Torrès, Matthew van der Galen, Francis Suarez, Francisco de Toledo. In general, all the other theologians of the end of the sixteenth century agree in putting the idea of change into the definition of sacrifice. Many see this change only in the bread transubstantiated by the consecration. But since the bread and the wine are not the true victim offered to God, they are led practically to justify the Eucharistic sacrifice in some other way.

Michel de Bay, or Baius (1513–1589), in a small work in 1563,[115] claimed, with some equivocation (Lepin, p. 361), that the Eucharist is called sacrifice simply because it is the principal sacrament. He allowed that the bread and wine, as dedicated for change, are rightly called sacrifice, and the body and blood of Christ, as the term of the change, are rightly called sacrifice. However sacrifice is, properly, an act (of oblation); de Bay reduced it to a mere quality, the quality of victim.

The idea that sacrifice is a change affecting the bread and wine is presented in a form that is more orthodox – but theoretically hardly more satisfying – by the following:

Francisco Torrès (1509–1584) locates it in the change of the bread and

---

115 *De sacrificio, in Michaelis Baii, celeberrimi in Lovaniensi Academis theologi Opera, cum Bullis Pontificium, et aliis ipsius causam spectantibus . . . studio A.P. theologi* (Cologne, 1596), vol. 1, p. 160 (see Lepin, p. 359).

wine into the body and blood of Christ in the consecration as transubstantiation, which is seen as the sin-forgiving (and thus sacrificial) *opus operatum* work of Christ.

Matthew van der Galen (1528–1573), after building an elaborate definition of sacrifice from an analysis of a broad spectrum of ancient sources, and finding that the only change he could locate is in the bread and wine converted into the body and blood of Christ, he then, in effect, abandoned his elaborate theory and went back to the more constant tradition of the Church by finding the sacrifice in the oblation of Christ rendered present under the transubstantiated species.

The position of Francis Suarez (1548–1617), while more beautiful and more sophisticated, follows the same pattern as that of van der Galen. He built an elaborate definition of sacrifice that focused on change; but since, in the positive term of the change (*immutatio*), namely Christ, who is alone truly the host of our sacrifice, there can be no change, he ends up with a beautiful and profound interpretation of Eucharistic sacrifice that, however, had little to do with his own elaborate definition of sacrifice. Francisco de Toledo followed a very similar course.

Theory III: The sacrifice requires a real change of the material offered; in the Mass, the change affects Christ himself.
(Lepin, pp. 375–93)

A certain number of theologians actually took the 'logical' step in applying this change (*immutatio*) to Christ himself. These can be organized into three principal groups.

Group one (Jan Hessels, Jean de Via, Gaspar de Casal) argued that there was a change of Christ in the consecration. Jan Hessels. (1522–1596), following Ruard Tapper (1487–1559), stated for example that: 'The New Law . . . contains an image of what takes place in heaven where Christ, in exercising his priesthood, stands before God and intercedes for us in representing his passion to his Father and in consummating the sacrifice of the cross. . . . On the altar Christ does what he is doing in heaven'.

Jean de Via (d. ca. 1582) held a similar position, expressed with remarkable richness: 'But if his priesthood is eternal, so too should his sacrifice be eternal, not only in the effect that is produced but also in the function that is exercised, although in a different manner: in heaven in its proper form, here below by the mysterious action of a different minister (*in caelo in propria forma, in altari hic infra in aliena operatione arcana*) . . . in the Church militant, a new sacrifice is not made by the ministry of the priest, but it is the same sacrifice once offered which he continues to offer.'

Hessels followed Thomas Aquinas and Tapper in holding for a distinction between oblation and sacrifice, but he modified the Thomistic axiom that sacrifice is when a certain action is exercised with regard to/about the matter offered. His new formula read: 'Sacrifice occurs when the things offered are destroyed, (*consumantur*) in honor of God.' Thus, with destruction essential to the definition of sacrifice, he was unable to apply it satisfactorily to the Eucharist. All he can do is affirm that, above all, the Mass is an oblation, an oblation that is one with (and only formally distinguished from) the concrete reality of the consecration. 'The consecration . . . puts at our disposition the Body of the Lord so that we can offer it.'

Gaspar de Casal (1510–1585) combined two statements of Aquinas: (1) action with regard to/about the victim, and (2) an act done in honor of God in order to propitiate him (*ad eum placandum* [*ST* 3, q. 48, a. 3]) in order to come up with a definition of sacrifice which requires, essentially, a destruction. The 'immolation' he needed he found verified in the double consecration. Casal tried to go further, but each step he took only revealed further the difficulty or impossibility of trying to find a real 'destruction' or 'immolation' in the Eucharist.

The second group was led by Robert Bellarmine (1542–1621) who argued that the change of Christ occurs in the communion. Bellarmine saw the Mass as having two essential parts, the consecration and the communion. He failed to find the needed destruction in the consecration. For there the immolation is entirely mystical. The *real* destruction that constitutes the consummation of the sacrifice is the communion by the priest. For Christ suffers no diminishment in *acquiring* sacramental being (consecration), but in *losing* it (communion). As he pointed out from his analysis of the Old Testament, sacrifice requires a *real* destruction.[116] For their influence on later Catholic theology, Bellarmine's words are ominous: 'The consumption of the sacrament, as done by the people, is not a part of the sacrifice. As done by the sacrificing priest, however, it is an essential part, but not the whole essence. . . . For the consumption carried out by the sacrificing priest is not so much the eating of the victim [what the people do] as it is the consummation of the sacrifice. It is seen as properly corresponding to the combustion of the holocaust'.[117]

Bellarmine's influential and much repeated definition of sacrifice reads: 'Sacrifice is an external offering made to God alone by which, in order to acknowledge human weakness and confess the divine majesty, some sensible and enduring thing is consecrated and transformed (*consecratur et transmutatur*) in a mystical rite by a legitimate minister'.[118] He followed the Thomistic line in seeing the sacrifice as a mystical rite, as an action *circa rem oblatam*, apparently convinced that his whole theory was in accord with that of Aquinas. His great authority helped solidify the idea that true sacrifice requires a real destruction of the victim, but hardly anyone followed him in seeing that destruction in the sacramental consumption of the species.

Finally, a third group held composite theories that were more or less dependent on Bellarmine. Among these theologians were Henrique Henriquez

---

116 'Id vero probatur, primum ex nomini sacrificii . . . Secundo probatur ex usu Scripturarum . . . Et omnia omnino in Scriptura dicuntur sacrificia, necessario destruenda erant: si viventia, per occisionem; si inanima solida, ut similia, et sal, et thus, per combustionem; si liquida, ut sanguis, vinum et aqua, per effusionem: Lev., i et ii. Neque his repugnat exemplum Melchisedech . . .' (Robertus Bellarminus, *Disputationes de controversiis fidei* (Ingolstadt, 1586–1593; Paris, 1608], *De missa*, 1. V., c. xxvii, t. III, col. 792).

117 Bellarmine, *Disputationes de controversiis fidei*. col. 792–93.

118 Ibid., col. 792 (Lepin 383–84).

[Enríquez], Pedro de Ledesma, Juan Azor, Gregorio de Valencia, Nicolas Coeffeteau.

Henri Henriquez (1536–1608) modified Bellarmine's definition: 'Sacrifice is an external ceremony by which a legitimate minister consecrates a thing and, consuming it in a certain way, offers it cultically to God alone in order to appease him.'[119] Thus to Bellarmine's two essential parts of the Mass is added a third, oblation. But it is the consumption or destruction which transforms the victim pleasing to God, separates it from all other use and consumes its substance in order to attest the sovereign dominion of God over being and life. This is accomplished by the communion *of the priest!* (Lepin 388) But elsewhere Henriquez seems to speak of the priest's communion only as a 'more clear signification' of the death that has already been represented by the consecration under the two species (Lepin, p. 388).

Peter de Ledesma (d. 1616) spoke of a figurative immolation consisting in the separation of the species (Lepin, p. 389).

Gregory of Valencia defined sacrifice as: 'A function of an external order by virtue of which a man, particularly chosen for this purpose, offers something to God by way of confection or transformation – as when an animal is slaughtered or burned, or when bread is broken and eaten – in a certain ritual ceremony in recognition of the divine majesty and also in proclamation of the interior devotion of the man, i.e., his homage and servitude, towards the Sovereign Master of all things.'[120] One recognizes the language of Suarez and the ideas of Bellarmine. But in addition to Bellarmine's essential elements of consecration and communion he added a third, the fraction. But, like so many others, it is in the consecration that he saw the constitutive essence of the sacrifice.

Theory IV: The sacrifice requires a real change: nevertheless, there is in the Mass a change only in the species of the sacrament.

(Lepin, pp. 393–415)

A final group of theologians admitted that sacrifice requires a change in the material offered, and nevertheless placed the essence of the Eucharistic sacrifice elsewhere than in a real change in Christ. The resulting contradiction was ignored by some, while others tried to save the theory by restricting the rigor of its application to the Eucharist.

Some of these theologians such as William Allen, Jacques de Bay, and Willem van Est [Estius] were satisfied with a simple affirmation of the principle and of the fact. William Cardinal Allen (1532–1594) saw in the consecration a proper act of sacrifice simply because Christ is put to death there in (only) a figurative or sacramental manner (*mactatur sacramentaliter*). But he does not attempt to resolve the

---

119   Henricus Henriquez, *Summae theologiae moralis libri quindecim* (Salamanca, 1591; Moguntiae, 1613) 1. IX, c. III; 498b (Lepin, pp. 345 and 387).

120   Gregory of Valencia, *Metimnensis, De rebus fidei hoc tempore controversies* Lyons, 1591); *De sacrosancto missae sacrificio, contra impiam disputationem Tubingae nuper a Jacobo Herbrando propositam, atque adeo contra perversissimam Lutheri, Kemnitii aliorumque novatorum doctrinam* 1. I, c. II; 504a (Lepin 344 and 390–91).

contradiction with contemporary theories of sacrifice (including his own) which require a real change/destruction of the victim (Lepin, pp. 394–97).

Jacques de Bay [Baius] (d. 1614) also saw the Sacrifice of the Mass concentrated in the consecration (as did Salmeron) and, like Allen, left the contradiction unresolved (Lepin, pp. 397–99).

Willem van Est (1542–1613), when commenting on *The Book of the Sentences,* had similar contradictions. But when commenting on the Epistle to the Hebrews, he followed a more promising line that consisted in identifying (or at least associating) the sacrificial action of the Eucharistic Christ, with that which he accomplishes before his Eternal Father in heaven. Thus, the Eucharistic oblation and the heavenly oblation are one and the same: Christ, the High Priest, offering himself to his Father for his Church.

Other theologians such as Gabriel Vasquez and Leonardus Lessius attempted to reconcile the principle and the fact. Both of these Jesuits exercised considerable influence in the ages to follow.

Gabriel Vasquez (1549–1604) pointed out the 'absurdity' of the (à la Bellarmine) communion/destruction theory that the sacrifice takes place in the stomach of the priest. He also rejected the theory (of Suarez) that the Eucharistic sacrifice consists not in a change/destruction, but in a confection/production. He saw, with most of his contemporaries, the essence of sacrifice in the act itself of the change that takes place in the victim. He distinguished between an *absolute* sacrifice and a *relative* sacrifice (uniquely the Eucharist). He defined sacrifice as 'a mark or note existing in a thing, by which we profess God as author of death and life'.[121] This change, realized in the consecration of the two species is a *figurative,* or *mystical,* but not real immolation of the body and blood which represents/signifies the death of Christ. Vasquez's theory exercised great influence, but he too was unable to reconcile his theology of the Eucharist with his general theory of sacrifice. His idea of a *relative* sacrifice, unique to the Eucharist, did not catch on.

Leonard Lessius (1554–1623) defined sacrifice as 'an external oblation, offered to God alone, by a legitimate minister, in which a sensible substance undergoes a change, or even a destruction, in witness to the divine sovereignty and our servitude thereto.'[122] He was influenced primarily by Suarez's seeing the 'destruction' as a kind of *production* taking place in the consecration, and actually came to locate the whole essence of sacrifice in the consecration, seeing there a *virtual* or *mystical* *immolation* of Christ on the altar by reason of the *separate* consecration. In other words, 'under the species of bread is placed only the Body, not the Blood; under the species of wine only the Blood, not the Body.'[123] He also wrote that '[t]he

---

121   Gabriel Vasquez, *Commentarii ac disputationes in III^m partem S. Thomae* (Lyons, 1631), Disp. 220, c III n° 26; p. 394a (Lepin, p. 406).

122   Leonardus Lessius, *De sacramentis et censuris, praelectiones theologicae posthumae, olim in Academia Lovaniensi ann. 1588 et 1589 primum, iterum 1596 et 1597 propositae,* q. 83, art. I, no. 7. in *In divum Thomam, de beatitudine, de actibus humanis, de Incarnatione Verbi, de sacramentis et censuris, praelectiones theologicae posthumae* (Lovanii, 1645) p. 152 (Lepin, pp. 344–45).

123   Lessius continues, acknowledging his debt to Vasquez: 'Et hoc sufficit ad rationem hujus sacrificii, tum ut sit verum sacrificium (fit enim circa hostiam, dum sic ponitur, sufficiens mutatio, qua protestamur Deum habere supremam in omnia potestatem), tum ut sit sacrificium commemorativum, repraesentans nobis sacrificium crucis et mortem Domini. Qui plura hac de re desiderat, legat Gabr. Vasquez' (Leonardus Lessius, *Opuscula in quibus pleraque theologiae mysteria*

words of consecration are a kind of sword. The Body of Christ which is now living in heaven, is to be slaughtered here instead of a living victim. The Body, placed under the species of bread, and the Blood under the species of wine, are like the body and blood of a lamb now immolated.'[124] Like Aquinas, he did not insist on a change of the victim (*mutatio hostiae*), but on a *mutatio circa hostiam* – a change that takes place with regard to the host/victim, and insisted that this change suffices to assure the 'true and proper sacrifice' defined by Trent (Lepin, p. 414).

From this detailed outline of post-Tridentine theologies of Eucharistic sacrifice, Marius Lepin concluded finally:

> As we cast a retrospective eye over the half century since the Council [of Trent], we can see that the theologians follow one or the other of two clear tendencies.
>
> 1. The theologians of the first group propose in principle that sacrifice consists essentially in a destruction or real change of the victim. They are thus forced to find this real change (or destruction) in the Sacrifice of the Mass.
>
> No one found sufficient the pure and simple change of the bread and wine by transubstantiation. The idea of a simple acquisition by Christ of his sacramental essence (Hessels) also did not satisfy. Two theories received most of the attention: that of Casal, which sees the destructive change of Christ realized in the consecration itself; and that of Bellarmine, where it is accomplished in the communion [of the priest].
>
> 2. An equally large number insist, on the contrary, that the Eucharistic Christ *does not undergo any real change*, neither at the consecration, nor at the communion; there is only a figure of his past immolation and an appearance of death.
>
> Consequently, those who maintain that sacrifice in general requires the change (destruction) of the victim suppose that the Sacrifice of the Mass is an exception to the common rule. Salmeron and Jacques de Bay justify the exception from the fact that Christ is not rendered present under his own species. Vasquez justifies it by reasoning that the Mass is a relative sacrifice. The others are of the opinion that sacrifice can be conceived apart from a real change/destruction of the thing offered. Suarez replaces the idea of destruction with the quite opposite idea of *production*. Melchior Cano, Domingo de Soto, and Maldonado require, following Thomas Aquinas, a simple *action* carried out with regard to the sacrificial matter. Lessius, finally, with whom one can place van Est, holds on to the term 'change – *immutatio*' and, applying it to the same reality as the just-mentioned theologians, talks about change 'with regard to' the host/victim.
>
> (Lepin, pp. 414–15)

---

explicantur, et vitae recte instituendae praecepta traduntur: ab ipso auctore, paullo ante mortem, varie aucta et recensita [Antwerp, 1626], *De perfectionibus moribusque divinis* [1620], 1 XII, c. XIII, no. 97, p. 128) (Lepin, p. 413).

124   Lessius, *Opuscula in quibus* . . . no. 95 p. 128 (Lepin 413).

3. Bellarmine and the 'modern average Catholic theology of the Eucharist'

Returning to the question posed earlier, we can now see that Bellarmine was much more the messenger than the villain in mediating a decadent theology to some contemporary Catholic thinking. Catholic Eucharistic theology on the eve of Trent in the early sixteenth century was much broader and much more in continuity with earlier traditions than it was by the end of that century. None of the pre-Tridentine or Tridentine theologians suggested any *reality* of immolation in the Mass. But neither did any of them have a sense of the content and structure of the whole Eucharistic Prayer in its ritual context. But somewhat saving the day, at least for them, was their general understanding that, along with the consecration which always held pride of place, there were always two other essential elements in the Mass: the oblation and the representative commemoration of the past immolation. Most importantly, they generally refrained from reducing the Eucharist to just one of these essential elements.

Reacting against the Reformers, Trent defined that the Mass is a 'true and proper sacrifice – *verum et proprium sacrificium*',[125] but left it to the theologians, as we have seen, to argue over what sacrifice actually is. Trent's earlier definition about the reality of the change of the bread and wine into the Body and Blood of Christ,[126] inevitably freighted the whole discussion with heavily physical connotations that disrupted the fragile balance between the symbolic and the realistic that, up to this time, had never totally been lost. Further clouding the issue was the dawning of modern science. Both Protestant and Catholic theologians, in an ironic instance of ecumenical 'agreement', made the same fateful mistake of inductively analyzing the practice of sacrifice in the world's religions in order to establish a definition of sacrifice from which to examine the so-called Sacrifice of the Mass. They thus approached the matter backwards. Instead of looking first to the Christ-event and letting that define their thinking, both Protestants and Catholics first defined sacrifice phenomenologically and then applied that definition to the Mass. An awareness of the content and structure of the classical Eucharistic Prayers, which could have been a corrective, was no longer present in the Western Church. No one was conscious of what, after Gregory Dix, we now call the 'shape of meaning' of the Eucharist.

This massive methodological mistake was then matched by a content mistake that apparently, no one thought to question: namely, the idea, increasingly accepted by almost all involved, that a *real* sacrifice requires a *real* change or *destruction* of the victim, and then the application of this idea to the Mass. There was no clear awareness that the Christ-event had done away with sacrifice in the history-of-religions sense of the term. Theologians still dealt with the Old and New Testaments in a relatively undifferentiated way, i.e., without any historicizing or differentiating hermeneutic, applying to the Mass ideas of sacrifice taken from the Old Testament almost as if Christ never existed. Some Catholic polemicists came

---

125   Trent, Session 22, 17 Sept. 1562, canon 1 of *Canones de ss. Missae sacrificio* (DS 1751).
126   Trent, Session 13, 11 Oct. 1551, in the *Decretum de ss. Eucharistia*: cap. 4 *De transsubstantiatione* (DS 1642) and canon 2 of *Canones de ss. Eucharistiae sacramento* (DS 1652).

up with more or less workable understandings of the Eucharist, but none of them were able to do so in a way consistent with their own (unquestioned) definition of sacrifice as involving the destruction of a victim. The most successful theories were those that emphasized not a real, but a mystical or sacramental immolation. But often this 'mystical immolation' was described in terms so graphically realistic as to undercut the symbolic or mystical meaning. Jan Van Eyck's famous painting of 'The Adoration of the Mystical Lamb' is a graphic illustration of this.

By the beginning of the seventeenth century, with no one any longer following Bellarmine's idea that the Eucharistic sacrifice was consummated in the priest's communion, the only essential element that survived was the consecration carried out, as the infelicitous modern rendering (only recently beginning to undergo correction) of one of the classical Eucharistic hymns put it, 'by the action of the priest'.

In sum, the Eucharistic theology of Bellarmine and of the outgoing sixteenth century, to which Pope Pius XII's *Mediator Dei* and most subsequent magisterial teaching of the Catholic Church has continued to appeal, suffers from the following theological shortcomings:

1. Lack of Trinitarian perspective and massive overemphasis on the Christological perspective; no mention of the role of the Holy Spirit; no acknowledgment that the Eucharistic Prayer is addressed by the assembly and to the Father.
2. Neglect of the ecclesiological perspective. There is an allusion to the ecclesiological in the insistence that the rite is to be celebrated by a legitimate or properly ordained minister. This minister, however, is the sole essential performer of the action. He is not conceived as standing there as part of the Church, embedded in the Christ–Church relationship, but as standing between Christ and the Church.
3. Neglect of the role of the participating faithful. They are not even necessary for the essential integrity of the Eucharist. They take part in it only by a kind of association, by consenting to the action of the priest that is, in any case, essentially complete without them.
4. Minimal awareness of the ultimate (or eschatological) goal of the Eucharist, namely the reorienting transformation of the participants in the direction of the dispositions of Christ. So much emphasis was put on the real presence of the Body and Blood of Christ, so much emphasis put on verifying a real – or at least symbolic (but with graphically real descriptors) – destruction of the victim that the real goal and ultimate reality of the Eucharist – transformation of the assembly and its members into Christ – was effectively veiled.

This helps explain the embarrassing dichotomy between so much of the teaching of the contemporary official Roman magisterium on the Eucharist and that of most contemporary liturgical theologians. It is due to the magisterium's continued acceptance of some of the shortcomings of post-Tridentine Catholic Eucharistic theology. Thus, if there is to be movement toward a more broadly shared Catholic understanding of the Eucharist, the Roman magisterium will need to become less attached to explanations of the Mystery of Faith that are less than satisfactory. Theologians must do their part also. They must do a better job of pointing out that their attempts to provide the Church with a more adequate understanding of the Eucharist are not a challenge to but are in continuity with the fullness of the Catholic tradition.

FROM THE AFTERMATH OF THE REFORMATION TO THE PRESENT

These three sections can serve as a bridge between the Reformation and the present. The Reformation can be seen as the final phase of the Christian Middle Ages. It was the time when Western Christendom was beginning its often agonizing and sometimes even cataclysmic, transition into the modern period. It marked the end of a so-called 'age of faith' after which, having passed through what can be called an 'age of orthodoxy', Western civilization moved into an 'age of reason' or, as some would call it, the modern 'age of science'.

Painting with broad strokes of the brush, we will highlight three facets of this last half of the second millennium: first, the vastly contrasting poles represented by post-Reformation Christianity and scientific modernity; second, the relatively recent experience of liturgical renewal and ecumenism and third, the 'end-of sacrifice' kinds of questions raised by, among others, Girardian mimetic theory.

Bridge 2 A

Post-Reformation and Modernity: Two Contrasting Poles

This long period of transition, a transition that, for some, may still be incomplete, was characterized by two massively contrasting poles. These two poles were locked with each other in a kind of death struggle that, in many ways, is still going on (faith vs. reason, secularism vs. traditional religion, etc.). But it was a struggle in which, tragically, then as well as now, neither side took the other seriously enough to appropriate the strengths and learn from the weaknesses of the other, thus squandering the opportunity to transcend its own crippling weaknesses.

At one pole, post-Reformation Christianity, both Catholic and Protestant, was generally afflicted with faulty and, often, seriously distorted atonement theories, narrow and exclusive theories of salvation, and an authoritative, doctrinaire way of understanding and proclaiming its beliefs.

At the other pole, modernity basically dismissed as so much rubbish much of what traditional Christianity held most dear. Although they sometimes spoke and wrote cautiously and in a veiled way in order to avoid provocation, the new defenders of reason and science persistently struggled to liberate themselves from a dominative religious authority that dictated what one was to hold as true. The new ideal was to be free to dedicate oneself to what reason, science, and practical politics would reveal to be actually and usefully true.[1]

One of the earliest signs of this new age, this new way of thinking, was the work of Niccolo Machiavelli. His little book *The Prince* (1513) has become a foundational book for modern political science, and beyond that for the modern social sciences. The big change that was taking place was a shift of focus from how things, ideally – i.e., 'religiously' – *should* be done, to how (successful) things are *actually* done. This change legitimated giving priority attention not just to what is morally right, but above all to what actually works. In this dawning new age of 'modernity', as long as one covered one's backside – often by giving lip service to traditional values – it was becoming possible, not to let theory, religion or morality get in the way of what makes for success in politics and government. Moral and spiritual values, i.e., religion, could now be, and increasingly was, relegated to the individual and private spheres of life.

Helping to make this possible was a fundamental shift in the understanding of science, knowledge and truth. The new understanding was based on facts and experiential truth rather than on religious or on any other kind of doctrine or theory, or on any deduction therefrom. Machiavelli had laid this out quite clearly as early as 1513:

> Since it is my intention to write something of use to those who will understand, I deem it best to stick to the practical truth of things rather than to fancies [impractical ideals?]. Many men have imagined republics and principalities that never really existed at all [Plato's Republic?]. Yet the way men live is so far removed from the way they ought to live that anyone who abandons what is for what should be pursues his own downfall rather than his preservation; for a man who strives after goodness in all his acts is sure to come to ruin, since there are so many men who are not good.[2]

Almost a century later, Francis Bacon was extending this eminently *practical* principle to the realm of philosophy, especially to the understanding of knowledge and science:

> For all those before me who have applied themselves to the invention of arts have but cast a glance or two upon facts and examples and experience, and straightway

---

1 As indicated by the broad proliferation of books propounding the 'new atheism' – see, for example, the five articles on 'The New Atheism' featured in *America*, vol. 198 No. 15, May 15, 2008, pp. 11–29 – there is, at least for most of those now living in the contemporary Western world, little need to veil whatever anti-religious sentiment they might have. A residue of the now mostly victorious struggle against dominative religious authority is reflected in the common attitudes of educated intellectuals: they are anti-religious; or they are politely tolerant of a religion now seen as irrelevant and dying; or, if positively disposed towards religion, tend to relegate it to the private sphere.

2 Niccolo Machiavelli, *The Prince* (New York: Bantam, 1966) Chapter 15. The brackets in the text, both here and in the following quotes from Bacon and Hobbes, are my editorial insertions.

proceeded, as if invention were nothing more than an exercise of thought, to invoke their own spirits to give them oracles [traditional philosophical and theo-logical method?]. I, on the contrary, dwelling purely and constantly among the facts of nature, withdraw my intellect from them no further than may suffice to let the images and rays of natural objects meet in a point, as they do in the sense of vision; whence it follows that the strength and excellence of the wit has but little to do in the matter [i.e. let careful sense experience, not something that is already in your mind, tell you what is real]. . . . And by these means I suppose that I have established a true and lawful marriage between the empirical and the irrational faculty, the unkind and ill-starred divorce and separation of which has thrown into confusion all the affairs of the human family.[3]

A bit later, in 'The Plan of the Work', Bacon describes this in specifically religious, even liturgical terms: 'And thus I conceive that I perform the office of a true priest of the sense . . . [A]nd finally, I interpose everywhere admonitions and scruples and cautions, with a religious care to eject, repress, and, as it were, exorcise every kind of phantasm'.[4] At the end of this 'Plan of the Great Instauration', Bacon clothes his scientific method (his insistence on not projecting philosophical or religious ideas onto reality) with the rhetoric of religious mission:

And all depends on keeping the eye steadily fixed upon the facts of nature and so receiving their images simply as they are. For God forbid that we should give out a dream of our own imagination [i.e. our dogmatic beliefs] for a pattern of the world; rather may he graciously grant to us to write an apocalypse or true vision of the footsteps of the Creator imprinted on his creatures [i.e. the new Bible is to be written by scientists].

(Ibid., p. 44)

A few decades later, Thomas Hobbes applied this inductive/scientific method to his negatively critical views on the origin and nature of religion:

[11] And in these four things, [1]opinion of ghosts, [2]ignorance of second causes, [3]devotion towards what men fear, and [4]taking of things casual for prognostics, consisteth the natural seed of *religion*, which by reason of the different fancies, judgments, and passions of several men hath grown up into ceremonies so differ-ent that those which are used by one man are for the most part ridiculous to another.[5]

One of the effects of all this was to set up a new definition and understanding of real knowledge and truth as something that is scientifically, experientially, and ultimately (and necessarily) quantifiably verifiable. This was conceived as opposed to and as clearly replacing the more traditional, non-quantifiably

---

3 Francis Bacon, *The Great Instauration*, 'Preface' (London: Routledge/Thoemes Press, 1996 [repr. of the 1874 edn]), p. 9. The inserted brackets are mine.
4 Ibid., pp. 26 and 30.
5 Thomas Hobbes, *Leviathan* (ed. Edwin Curley; Indianapolis/Cambridge: Hackett Publishing Co., 1994), Part I, Chapter 12, no. [11]. pp. 66–67.

verifiable understandings of knowledge and truth. Interestingly, and to some extent also quite unfortunately, this scientific understanding of knowledge was eventually also accepted by many critically thinking theologians. One clear example of this was the assumption of these theologians that the existence of Jesus and his teaching had to be established and verified by the new 'scientific' canons of history. When this turned out to be impossible – since the Gospels are primarily faith-documents, not documents of scientific history – these theologians were faced with a painful dilemma. They could, on the one hand, adhering to the religious pole, continue to act and think as if the gospel truths of Christianity were scientifically verifiable, thus losing all credibility with intellectuals and scientists. (Note that this still fairly accurately describes the situation of contemporary fundamentalists and anti-evolutionary creationists.) On the other hand, they could adhere to the other pole, the pole of scientific modernity, draw the logical consequences of the new science and epistemology, and become, for that reason, atheists. Buckley has provided the definitive description of the development of this new kind of atheism in his book: *At the Origins of Modern Atheism.*[6]

All this, of course had its effect on the understanding of sacrifice. It set up a 'scientific' way of analyzing the phenomena and practices of religion, such as sacrifice. This has remained largely unchallenged up to our own day. (It is, for example, one of the main purposes of this book to challenge this way of thinking and proceeding.) As an example of the traditional methodology that I am attempting to correct in this book, take the opening words of the article on sacrifice in the first major 'modern' Catholic encyclopaedia to appear in English:

> By sacrifice in the real sense is universally understood the offering of a sense-perceptible gift to the Deity as an outward manifestation of our veneration for Him and with the object of attaining communion with Him. Strictly speaking, however, this offering does not become a sacrifice until a real change has been effected in the visible gift (e.g., by slaying it, shedding its blood, burning it, or pouring it out). As the meaning and importance of sacrifice cannot be established by a priori methods, every admissible theory of sacrifice must shape itself in accordance with the sacrificial systems of the pagan nations, and especially with those of the revealed religions, Judaism and Christianity. Pure Buddhism, Mohammedanism, and Protestantism here call for no attention, as they have no real sacrifice; apart from these there is and has been no developed religion which has not accepted sacrifice as an essential portion of its cult. We shall consider successively: I. Pagan Sacrifice; II. Jewish Sacrifice; III. Christian Sacrifice; IV. Theory of Sacrifice.[7]

---

6 Michael J. Buckley, S.J., *At the Origins of Modern Atheism* (New Haven: Yale University Press, 1987).

7 Pohle, J. 'Sacrifice', *The Catholic Encyclopedia* (New York: Robert Appleton Company, 1912), vol. 13, pp. 309–21 (309).

Everything that is said or claimed in this descriptive definition of sacrifice is more or less accurate. It is a more or less 'scientific' summary description of what was known about sacrifice by representative Catholic scholars at the beginning of the twentieth century. One can find here that mistaken emphasis on the destruction of the victim that was pointed out at the beginning of this book and discussed further in the final section of Part Two. Definitions, such as this result from analyzing the available data scientifically, i.e. inductively. In other words, one analyzes the practice of sacrifice in the various religions of the world, and inductively draws from this analysis the essential characteristics of sacrifice. Then, with that result in hand, one moves to examine the phenomenon and practice of Christian sacrifice.

Of course, the contemporary reader can also find in this descriptive definition the typical bias of traditional Catholic attitudes towards sacrifice, especially in the way it speaks of sacrifice and/or the lack of it in the other religious traditions, especially Protestantism. Contemporary readers can more easily notice this bias because they are living in a 'postmodern' age, an age that is much more self-critical regarding matters of bias, an age that is instinctively skeptical of any large cover story that attempts to offer a key to explaining present and ultimate reality.[8]

This typical post-modern suspicion of big cover stories must also, in all fairness, be applied to the big cover story with which this book begins and which guides its whole development, namely that authentic Christian sacrifice is something quite different from what was descriptively defined in the paragraph quoted on the previous page. True Christian sacrifice is, rather, a profoundly interpersonal event. It begins with the self-offering of the Father in the sending of the Son. It proceeds, in a second 'moment', through the en-Spirited human response of the Son to the Father and for us. And then it begins to become 'real' – recall the phrase 'sacrifice in the real sense' in the first line of the above descriptive definition – only when the faithful, in the power of the same Spirit that was in Jesus, at least begin to enter into that Trinitarian relationship. As we have been pointing out, it is the main purpose of this book to make this specifically Trinitarian idea of sacrifice the starting point and the center – the 'source and summit' so to speak – of the authentic Christian understanding of sacrifice.

Two further comments on this question of bias, this post-modern suspicion of big cover stories: First, there is a well-recognized consensus position in contemporary hermeneutics that points out that there is no such thing as a position or starting point that has no bias. On that matter, there is simply no choice. But one does have a choice about whether or not, or about the degree to which, one will recognize one's bias and open it up for critical examination. My second comment about bias, about which there is not full agreement, concerns whether or not it is possible to examine the relative adequacy of this or that bias. Some claim that once one has identified someone's basic presuppositions, once one has arrived at the pre-discursive, imaginative world view within which and from which someone is living and acting, one can go no farther. One can only agree or disagree.[9]

---

8 See hereafter, the chapter: 'Grand Narratives in a Postmodern Age' in Bridge 2 C, below, pp. 206–207.
9 For an exposition of this position, see David Kelsey, *The Uses of Scripture in Recent Theology* (Philadelphia: Fortress, 1975).

Others, however, such as Bernard Lonergan and those who follow him in applying the theological functional specialty that he calls 'Dialectic',[10] insist that one can make at least some judgments, judgments that are true and reliable, about the relative truth, the relative adequacy, the relative authenticity of this or that position.[11]

This is not the place to try to develop this further. But it does alert the reader to the background and presuppositions from which we will now examine what has been going on regarding the idea of sacrifice in the time between the Reformation and the present. Another way of putting this is to ask: Why was the Trinitarian 'cover story' with which we started this book not part of the data that was 'scientifically' analyzed in order to come up with the traditional Catholic or Christian definitions of sacrifice that prevailed unquestioned a hundred years ago, and still remain largely unquestioned to this day? The main reason seems to be that our Trinitarian cover story – the bias, if you will, from which this book is being written – was, especially in the West, simply not available. We now look briefly at the ideas and understandings that were available in order to see how effectively they cast an obscuring veil over any authentically Christian understanding of sacrifice.

Chapter I

Sacrifice among the Writers of Late (Post-Enlightenment) Modernity

A. SACRIFICE IN SECULAR MODERNITY

We have already sketched the basic modern understandings of science, knowledge and religion in some early modern writers: Machiavelli, Bacon and Hobbes. (Descartes, had we looked into him, would have revealed a somewhat similar trajectory.) Now let us look to the (basically secular/religious) understanding of sacrifice in some of the post-Enlightenment writers: Georg Wilhelm Friedrich Hegel (1770–1831) and Sigmund Freud (1856–1939). First, a few passages from Hegel's *Reason in History:*

> Freedom is itself its own object of attainment and the sole purpose of Spirit. It is the ultimate purpose toward which all world history has continually aimed. To this end all the sacrifices have been offered on the vast altar of the earth throughout the long lapse of ages.

---

10 Bernard J.F. Lonergan, S.J. *Method in Theology* (New York: Herder and Herder, 1972), esp. pp. 235–66.
11 See, for example, Charles Hefling, 'Lonergan on Development: *The Way to Nicea* in Light of His More Recent Methodology' (diss.; Boston College, 1982), pp. 305–57.

But in contemplating history as the slaughter-bench at which the happiness of peoples, the wisdom of states, and the virtue of individuals have been sacrificed, a question necessarily arises: To what principle, to what final purpose, have these monstrous sacrifices been offered?

To say that an individual 'has an interest' in something is justly regarded as a reproach or blame; we imply that he seeks only his private advantage. Indeed, the blame implies not only his disregard of the common interest, but his taking advantage of it and even his sacrificing it to his own interest.

The particular in most cases is too trifling as compared with the universal; the individuals are sacrificed and abandoned. The Idea pays the tribute of existence and transcience, not out of its own funds but with the passions of the individuals.

We might find it tolerable that individuals, their purposes and gratifications, are thus sacrificed, their happiness abandoned to the realm of [*natural forces and hence of*] chance to which it belongs; and that individuals in general are regarded under the category of means. Yet there is one aspect of human individuality that we must refuse to take exclusively in this light even in relation to the highest, an element which is absolutely not subordinate but exists in individuals as essentially eternal and divine. I mean morality, ethics, religion.[12]

A similar understanding of sacrifice is found in Freud, in, of course, the typical Freudian context:

The final outcome should be a rule of law to which all – except those who are not capable of entering a community – have contributed by a sacrifice of their instincts, and which leaves no one – again with the same exception – at the mercy of brute force.

But civilization demands other sacrifices besides that of sexual satisfaction.

If civilization imposes such great sacrifices not only on man's sexuality but on his aggressivity, we can understand better why it is hard for him to be happy in that civilization.[13]

It is not hard to see here obvious instances of the general, secular idea of sacrifice that we outlined in the opening pages of this book.

B. THE CHRISTIAN SCENE

All well and good; but what was developing during this time in the specifically Christian religious context? The situation here was anything but good. It was not good because of two ironically contrasting and quite infelicitous developments

---

12 G.W.F. Hegel,. *Reason in History* (trans. Robert S. Hartman; The Library of Liberal Arts; Indianapolis/New York: Bobbs Merrill, 1953), pp. 25, 27, 28, 44.
13 Sigmund Freud, *Civilization and Its Discontents* (1929) (trans. James Strachey; New York: W. W. Norton & Company, 1961), pp. 42, 55, 62.

within Christianity. First, Christianity during this period was counter-culturally out of step with what was going on in intellectual modernity. This was tragic in the sense that modern Christianity remained mostly out of touch with or in antagonistic tension with the exiting new intellectual developments, and thus unable to appropriate their positive aspects. A huge amount of Christian intellectual and spiritual energy was turned inwards. A huge amount of this energy was squandered in Christian infighting, i.e., in controversy with other Christians instead of engaging with the exciting new scientific and intellectual developments of modernity. Christianity, most specifically the Christian churches, made themselves largely irrelevant to the scientific and intellectual developments of this age.

But second, there was one aspect in which Christian thought was actually in step with modernity. As we pointed out a few pages ago, Christian thinkers, including Christian theologians, generally accepted the new epistemological criteria for knowledge and certitude, namely, experience-based quantifiability and measurability. With regard to sacrifice, one gathered (as we have already pointed out several times) data from the practice of sacrifice in the various religions of the world. This allowed one to come up with a historically-scientifically based idea of sacrifice which one could then use as a matrix in trying to understand Christian sacrifice.

The writers of post-Enlightenment modernity cannot be faulted for not including in their scientific inductions, even if they had wanted to, a Trinitarian/liturgical idea of Christian sacrifice. As I have already indicated, such a theological construct was simply not available, at least not explicitly, even to Christian thinkers, writers and preachers of the time. What was available to them? One can get a stunningly eloquent and sadly revelatory sense of what devout Christians thought about Christian sacrifice from Chapter I, 'Distorting Mirrors' of Philippe de la Trinité's *What is Redemption?*[14] We see here the tragic effects of Anselm's doctrine of objective atonement when it is pushed logically – which Anselm and the best medieval theologians never did – to its religious and devotional extremes.

C. DISTORTING MIRRORS

De la Trinité's opening chapter, appropriately entitled 'Distorting Mirrors', reads like a horror-story description of precisely what Christian sacrifice and redemption is not. This horror story pushes to the extreme the kind of 'bad theology' of atonement that I described above at the beginning of Part Two. The 'whipping boys' de la Trinité parades before us are mostly a series of French Catholic writers; but the distortions they preached were typical of many Christian writers and preachers across Christianity. Apart from some brief reference to Luther and Calvin, I quote no Protestant writers, but colleagues from the Reformation churches assure me that I would easily find the same distortions, if not worse,

---

14 Philippe de la Trinité, O.C.D., *What is Redemption?* (trans. Anthony Armstrong, O.S.B.; Twentieth Century Encyclopedia of Catholicism, 25; New York: Hawthorn Books, 1961).

among their preachers and spiritual writers. For this was an age in which penal-substitution atonement theories achieved the status of creedal orthodoxy in traditional Protestantism, something that Catholic orthodoxy, at least in its official teaching and among its best theologians, managed to avoid.

However, any attempts to parcel out blame, Protestants vs. Catholics or vice versa, would be an evasive quibble. For while both Luther and Calvin, in contrast to authoritative Catholic sources, taught an atonement theory of penal substitution,[15] this theory was also enthusiastically embraced by a whole host of widely read Catholic authors who assume, like their Protestant counterparts, that it is a matter of belief beyond discussion. While thinking that they are presenting the true faith, they present penal substitution with an outrageous grossness that would be hard to match by anyone, and that, from the perspective of authentic Christian theology, does not merely border on, but at times actually crosses the line into outright blasphemy. A few quotations will amply illustrate this:

Chardon (ca. 1595–1651)
It seems to me that Simeon's words contain, as it were, a refusal on God's part to accept the sacrifice which Mary offers him. Mother! That head is too small for the crown of thorns which I have prepared for it. Those shoulders are not strong enough to support the heavy burden of the cross. There is not enough blood in those veins to satisfy my justice. Those hands are too small for the large nails which must pierce them. Those arms and legs would not fit the length and breadth of the cross. The whole of that body offers insufficient surface for the blows of the whip which must lacerate it. Take that child away and, when he shall have reached the size and proportions necessary if I am to exercise my justice to the full, then will be the time to bring him and present him to me.[16]

Massillon (1663–1742)
He would undoubtedly have expired, such was the severity of these trials, had not the justice of his Father been keeping in reserve for him longer torments and a finer sacrifice. Righteous Father! Was more and yet more blood still necessary in addition to this interior sacrifice of your Son? Is it not enough that it should be shed by his enemies? And must your justice hasten, as it were, to see it shed? See how far this God, whom we believe to be so good, carries his vengeance against his own Son whom he beholds carrying our sins.[17]

Bossuet (1627–1704)
It was necessary that all in this sacrifice should be divine; a satisfaction worthy of God was necessary, and it was necessary that a God should make it; that

---

15   E.g., Luther, *In Epistolam Sancti Pauli ad Galatas Commentarium, Opera Lutheri*, XL (Weimar Edition) p. 435; Calvin, *Institutio christianae Religionis*, cap. 16 (as cited by de la Trinité, pp. 16 and 21).

16   Louis Chardon, *La Croix de Jésus* (Paris: Lethielleux, 1895), vol. 1, pp. 154–55 (quoted from de la Trinité, p. 17).

17   Jean-Baptiste Massillon, *Oeuvres de Massillon*, (Paris, 1843), vol. 1, pp. 518 and 520 (quoted from de la Trinité, pp. 18–19).

there should be a vengeance worthy of God, and that God himself should take it. . . .[18]

It is an unheard-of prodigy that a God should persecute a God, that a God should abandon a God; that an abandoned God should complain, and that an abandoning God should prove inexorable: but it is to be seen on the cross. . . . Jesus suffers the disdain of God, because he cries out, and his Father hears him not; and the wrath of a God, because he prays, and his Father answers him not; and the justice of a God, because he suffers, and his Father is not appeased. He is not appeased for his son, but he is appeased for us. When an avenging God waged war upon his Son, the mystery of our peace was accomplished.[19]

Josefa Menendez (1890–1923)

(Christ says) I offered myself to achieve the work of redeeming the world. At that moment I saw upon me all the torments of the passion, the calumnies, the insults. . . . All these pains forced themselves on my sight, together with the hordes of offences, sins and crimes which would be committed down the ages . . . Not only did I see them but I was clothed in them . . ., and, under this burden of disgrace, I had to present myself before my most holy Father and implore his mercy. Then I felt breaking over me the wrath of an offended and irritated God,: and I offered myself as a scapegoat, I, his Son, to calm his rage and appease his justice.[20]

Bourdaloue (1632–1704)

Strike, Lord, strike now: he is ready to receive your blows; and, without considering that he is your Christ, see him only to remember that he is ours, that is, that he is our victim and that, in immolating him, you will satisfy that divine hatred you have for sin . . . Not at the last judgement will our irritated and offended God satisfy himself as God; nor is it in hell that he declares himself authentically to be the God of vengeance; Calvary is the place he has chosen: *Deus ultionum Dominus.* On Calvary his vindictive justice is free to act without restraint, untrammeled, as it is elsewhere, by the smallness of the subject who is made to feel it: *Deus ultionum libere egit.* All that the damned will suffer is but a half-revenge for him; all that gnashing of teeth, those groans and tears, those inextinguishable fires, all that is nothing, or almost nothing, compared with the sacrifice of the dying Jesus Christ.[21]

Le Camus

Jesus had insensibly bowed his head to the ground under the crushing burden which he was making his own. But suddenly the infuriated countenance of God,

---

18   Jacques-Benigne Bossuet, *Oeuvres oratoires de Bossuet* (Lille–Paris, 1891), vol. 3, p. 379 (quoted from de la Trinité, p. 22).
19   Ibid., vol. 4, pp. 286–87 (quoted from de la Trinité, p. 22).
20   Josefa Menendez, *Un appel a l'amour, Le message du Coeur de Jésus au monde et sa messagère Soeur Josefa Menendez* (Toulouse: Apostolat de la Prière, 1944), p. 402 (quoted from de la Trinité 25–26).
21   The reference given in de la Trinité, p. 28 n. 30 is '*Op. cit.*, x, pp. 157, 159–61' The section heading is *Bourdaloue*, but there is no prior reference to him. Louis Bourdaloue was a prolific seventeenth-century Jesuit preacher.

of which he just catches a glimpse, shatters his soul. He can bear it no longer and, rising, cries: 'Father, if it be possible, and with you all things are possible, let this chalice pass from me!' This, then, has nothing to do with Satan. It is with his Father alone that Jesus wishes to drive the hideous bargain. Will divine justice deduct nothing from the overflowing chalice?[22]

Perroy

He (Jesus) was born to ascend Golgotha, and to ascend it as a victim; for was he not first and above all, the Victim of Expiation? He knew this, he felt it in every fibre of his being, he had willed it, and his heavenly Father so regarded him. The foremost reason for Christ's earthly existence, his chief role, was to satisfy the justice of God, to repair the outrage offered to God, to cherish God's honour. It would seem, almost, as though the salvation of mankind came second.[23]

D. COMMENT ON THE DISTORTIONS

Above, in the early pages of Part Two, I outlined a stereotypical description of Western Christian atonement theory in the following four points: (1) God's honor was damaged by human sin; (2) God demanded a bloody victim – innocent or guilty – to pay for human sin; (3) God was persuaded to alter the divine verdict against humanity when the Son of God offered to endure humanity's punishment and (4) the death of the Son thus functioned as a payoff; salvation was purchased.[24] We then went on to point out that, in effect, this theory logically turns God into some combination of a great and fearsome judge, or offended lord, or temperamental spirit. It calls into question God's free will, or omnipotence, or justice, or sanity. Behind it is an image of God that is fundamentally incompatible with the central biblical self-revelation of God as loving and compassionate. One may have suspected that this criticism was an exaggeration. But the passages I have quoted in the last few pages suggest that, if anything, it was more like a whitewashing understatement. Ideas like these distortions are widespread, even rampant, even to our own day, in the minds of many Christians. No need to search to see where Mel Gibson in his film *The Passion of the Christ* got his idea of a Christ suffering far, far more, as doctors have pointed out, than any human being could suffer and still be alive. And it explains why that film's grotesque exaggerations could have been the cause of a moving religious experience in so many of the film's viewers. It simply fed on their own ideas of a severe, relentlessly judging God being appeased, for our sakes, by the suffering of his Son.

---

22   In: *Soixante-quinze Méditations sur la Passion de Notre-Seigneur Jésus Christ* (Tournai: Casterman, 1925), p. 389 (quoted from de la Trinité, p. 30. The author was, apparently, Émile-Paul-Constant-Ange Le Camus [1839–1906]).

23   Louis Perroy, *La Montée du Calvaire* (Paris), p. 7. English translation: *The Ascent of Calvary* (New York, P.J. Kenedy & Sons, 1922), p. 6 (quoted from de la Trinité, p. 32).

24   As formulated by Finlan, *Problems with Atonement*, p. 1.

Ultimately, there is something inherently un-Christian, even deeply pagan, in these ideas about the sacrificial death of Christ. We marvel that so many could seem to be so blind to this. Take, for example, Bousset's statement quoted two pages ago:

> It is an unheard of prodigy that a God should persecute a God, that a God should abandon a God, that an abandoned God should complain, and that an abandoning God should prove inexorable: but it is to be seen on the cross . . . When an avenging God waged war on his Son, the mystery of our peace was accomplished.

What is so telling about this is that it is not at all 'unheard of'! By no means! It is precisely the kind of thing we find in the stories about the gods in the ancient pagan mythologies and cosmogonies. Thus, what is at work here is, ultimately, and embarrassingly, not a Christian idea of God but a pagan idea of God. It is an idea of God that makes a shambles of the central biblical self-revelation of God as a God of love. It is an idea that takes violence, calculating violence, a primordial human sin and projects it into the Trinitarian life and relationship of the Father and the Son. If this is not blasphemy, then what is? To take such ideas of calculating vindictive justice and vengeance, ideas we tend to classify as monstrous when we find them present in human behaviour, and then to predicate these ideas of God?!? This is indeed outrageous and monstrous.

Although we can hope that the extremes I have been excoriating are more the exception than the rule, it cannot be denied that some kind of thinking like this is fairly characteristic of what most people think is Christianity. To return to the metaphor with which we began this chapter, to say nothing of these ideas being poles apart from an authentically Christian image of God, they are poles apart from the rational, enlightened, scientific thinking of modernity. Is it any wonder that in our contemporary, and at least historically Christian, Western society, the more educated one is, the less likely it is that (s)he will be religious? And indeed, if being religious means adhering to anything like the monstrous images of God that we have been excoriating, can we honestly continue to claim that choosing to be an atheist, or at least somewhat agnostic, is not, at least sometimes, choosing the better part?

Chapter II

Moment-of-Consecration Theology

One of the clearest signs of the 'bankruptcy' of the 'splinter tradition' that 'has no future',[25] that characterizes most of the (especially, but not exclusively) Roman Catholic Eucharistic theology of the second millennium in the West,[26] and that also sets this theology at opposite poles from the more scientific ways of thinking that characterize modernity, is the view that locates the centre, the essence and indeed the fullness of the Eucharistic sacrifice in the consecration, the Eucharistic words of institution. The recent official Roman Catholic recognition of the validity of the liturgy of the Assyrian Church of the East, which still uses the ancient East Syrian *Anaphora of Addai and Mari*, an anaphora that does not include the words of institution, put the last nail into the coffin of this erroneous and now officially discredited theory.[27]

Nevertheless, the idea of a moment of consecration – 'magic moment' in the polemical language of modernity – remains strong in the mind of most Catholics. Indeed, the performative rubrics of the current Roman Rite (the Epiclesis over the gifts inserted *before* the consecration, the detailed rubrics for handling the species to be consecrated, the genuflection and the elevation of the bread and cup after each consecration, the acclamations of the assembly immediately after the consecrating words, etc.) still dramatically reinforce moment-of-consecration thinking. Thus, a few words about the history and the deleterious consequences of this theology are in order.

But first, stepping back, and looking at the matter positively, two interrelated transformations, both brought about by the power of the Holy Spirit, can be identified as taking place during the Eucharistic celebration. The more important of these, for this is the whole goal and purpose of the Eucharistic celebration, is the ongoing, deepening transformation of the worshipping assembly into the Body of Christ. Subordinate to that transformation, and for the purpose of more effectively achieving it, is the transformation of the bread and wine into the body and blood of Christ for the spiritual nourishment of the assembly in Holy

---

25 The 'scare quotes' indicate phrases that occur passim in Kilmartin's *The Eucharist in the West* and in his 'The Catholic Tradition of Eucharistic Theology: Towards the Third Millennium', *Theological Studies* 55 (1994), pp. 405–57.

26 This moment-of-consecration theology had its counterparts in classical Lutheranism which eliminated the entire Eucharistic Prayer except for the Lord's words of institution, and in Anglicanism which developed rubrical instructions to the effect that, should the consecrated Eucharistic elements be found to be insufficient, one needed to repeat only the words of institution over additional elements in order to remedy that situation.

27 See Robert F. Taft, 'Mass without the Consecration? The Historic Agreement between the Catholic Church and the Assyrian Church of the East Promulgated 26 October 2001', *Worship* 77 (2003), pp. 482–509; idem, 'Mass without the Consecration?', *America* 188 (May 12, 2003), pp. 7–9.

Communion. In other words, the transformation of the elements does not take place simply to have Christ become present upon the altar but rather, first and foremost, to have Christ and his virtuous dispositions become present in the hearts, minds, wills and lives of the members of the Eucharistic assembly. If this transformation is not at least beginning to take place, the transformation of the gifts becomes meaningless. One is then forced to ask – at least from the standpoint of modern philosophical thinking that tends to equate meaning with reality – whether the transformation of the gifts has actually taken place, since the whole meaning and purpose of the transformation of the gifts is to bring about the transformation of the assembly. Quite obviously, the transformation of an assembly, or of any of its members, into the Body of Christ is not something that does or can take place in anything resembling a 'magic moment'. Such a transformation can, at best, only begin in the here-and-now, and it can become complete only at the Eschaton.[28]

But looked at negatively, how did this discredited moment-of-consecration theology come about? In practical, methodological terms, the sad story can be easily traced, along with its pervasive and still operative deleterious consequences, by following up the 15 references to 'Moment of consecration' in the subject index of Kilmartin's *The Eucharist in the West*. The story begins in Chapter 4 with Kilmartin's treatment of the 'High Scholastic Theology of the Eucharist' in the twelfth century and continues, passim, right up to the contemporary situation discussed at the end of his book. By the middle of the twelfth century, and this represents the state of the question later assumed by Aquinas, the basic questions had become:

(1) What are bread and wine? (2) What change takes place with the bread and wine? (3) How is the change to be conceived? (4) When does the change take place? (5) By what instrumental cause does the change take place? . . . By the close of the early scholastic period, . . . there was agreement: (1) that the change takes place at a single moment within the scope of the Eucharistic Prayer; (2) that the words of Christ contained in the liturgical narrative of institution of the Eucharist constitute the essential form of the consecration of the elements of bread and wine; (3) that the presiding priest, reciting these words of Christ, acts as the minister of Christ insofar as Christ himself exercises a theandric act, i.e., an act accomplished by the person of the Word in and through his humanity, which serves as sacrament of the purely divine act by which the conversion of the eucharistic elements is effected.[29]

Kilmartin immediately goes on to point out that we have here 'the three elements which constitute the kernel of the later scholastic orientation in Eucharistic theology': the identification of the exact moment of consecration (i.e., the exact moment of the sacrifice), the essential form of the Eucharistic liturgy (i.e., of the Sacrifice of the Mass) and the attribution of the consecration of the elements

---

28   See my 'Sacrifice Unveiled or Sacrifice Revisited: Trinitarian and Liturgical Perspectives', *Theological Studies* 64 (2003), pp. 24–42 (39–40).
29   Kilmartin, *The Eucharist in the West*, p. 128.

exclusively to the presiding priest (i.e., identification of the presiding priest as the principal agent in the offering of the sacrifice). In the mind of the priest-celebrant (which also means in the mind of the theologian, since practically all theologians were, in fact, priests) this was massively reinforced both theologically and psychologically in the ordination rite when the ordaining bishop handed over to the deacon being ordained the sacred instruments of the Eucharistic sacrifice, the cup and the paten, with the words: 'Receive the power of offering sacrifice in the Church on behalf of the living and the dead, in the name of the Father and of the Son and of the Holy Spirit'. The Council of Florence was only making explicit what everyone had long since assumed to be the case when it identified this as the 'form' of the sacrament of ordination to the priesthood, and the words of consecration as the 'form' of the sacrament of the Eucharist.[30]

To be fair, it must be pointed out that the medieval theologians were often much more sophisticated and nuanced than my broad-brushed description would imply. But nuance inevitably gets lost in practice. The late medieval theologians, especially Scotus and Biel, accurately taught the nuance that Christ was the principal active subject of the consecration of the Eucharistic elements, and that the Church, represented by the priest, was the subject of the offering of the Eucharistic sacrifice. But by the time that the Council of Trent had come and gone, this nuance was lost. The ecclesiological reality of what was taking place had receded far into the background and Christ alone was identified as the principal active subject of both the consecration of the elements and the offering of the Eucharistic sacrifice.

> As a consequence of this, the moment of the consecration of the eucharistic elements through the proclamation of the words of Christ contained in the liturgical formula of the narrative of institution of the Eucharist was also identified as the moment of the reactualization of the liturgical self-offering of Christ.[31]

In the popular mind, however, this had long been anticipated, actually since the end of the twelfth century, in the ritual celebration by the attention given to the elevation of the host at the moment of consecration.[32]

Bad theology has bad consequences. Among the unhappy consequences of this moment-of-consecration theology was the elimination of the meal aspect of the Eucharistic celebration. 'The ritual act of Holy Communion is not considered to be an essential part of the Eucharistic sacrifice'.[33] In other words, the role of the assembly, to say nothing of its transformation, becomes superfluous. Nor is it any longer necessary to see the Eucharistic celebration as an activity of the Church, let alone the high-point of the Church's being and activity. It can be seen

---

30 In the A.D. 1439 *Decree for the Armenians*, (DS 1326 and 1321). For further details, see Kilmartin, *The Eucharist in the West*, pp. 127–43.
31 Kilmartin, *The Eucharist in the West*, p. 151.
32 Ibid., pp 151–53.
33 Ibid., p. 365; see also p. 200.

as something that takes place privately between just the priest and Christ. Even the Holy Spirit can be bracketed out. It thus also supports a Mass-stipend theology (see below) and tends to enhance not a sense of kenotic ministry, but rather a sense of priestly power and proprietary privilege. Angelus Häussling expresses it trenchantly:

> It leads to the elevation of the priest, because he speaks the words of Christ in the account of institution according to 1 Corinthians 11 and the Synoptic Gospels, to the role of the one acting *in persona Christi*, (and finally representing the person of Christ himself . . .) in such a way that he is no longer, as the rite clearly shows, receiver with and in the celebrating assembly (which is the church) and so remains and must remain. Otherwise, as the logical consequence, a sacramentalistic clericalism results that works destructively.[34]

In addition, by reinforcing the erroneous impression that the Last Supper was the first Mass, it veils the obvious fact that it took the Church, under the guidance of the Holy Spirit, several centuries to arrive at something approaching the 'classical' form of the Eucharist that we now celebrate,[35] thus further marginalizing the Eucharistic celebration as an ecclesiological event.[36] Finally, moment-of-consecration theology demolishes any pretence of equilibrium between *lex orandi* and *lex credendi*. For the theology that ignores the theological content and dynamic of the whole Eucharistic Prayer and that fixates only on the words of Christ as the essential form of the Eucharist is a 'dogma' that is found only 'within the splinter theology of the Western scholastic tradition'.[37]

Chapter III

Mass-Stipend Theology: Theology in Transition

Why devote any space at all to an apparently declining practice and theology that seems to be relevant only to a limited sphere of devotional Roman Catholicism? The answer flows from the second half of the title of this chapter: 'theology in

---

34   Angelus Häussling, 'Odo Casel – Noch von Aktualität? Eine Rückschau in eigener Sache aus Anlass des hundertsten Geburtstages des ersten Herausgebers', *Archiv für Liturgiewissenschaft* 28 (1986), pp. 357–87 (377) (as quoted by Kilmartin, *The Eucharist in the West*, pp. 350–51).
35   See Robert J. Daly, S.J., 'Eucharistic Origins: From the New Testament to the Liturgies of the Golden Ages', *Theological Studies* 66(2005).
36   'In fact, before the liturgy of the Eucharist of the Church could be realized, the whole Christ-event had to take place: the death, the resurrection, and glorification of Jesus, and the pentecostal sending of the Holy Spirit to establish the Church and draw its members into the earthly body of Christ' (Kilmartin, *The Eucharist in the West*, p. 367).
37   Ibid., p. 350.

transition'. Attending to what is here in transition, and why, is not only consonant with the 'bridging' function of this part of our book, it also brings us back to the fundamental Trinitarian understanding of Christian sacrifice that is the heart and soul of what we are attempting to communicate.

The straightforward meaning of the word stipend' (Latin: *stipendium*) is that it is a fixed sum of money, or 'offering' paid for services or to defray expenses. In the religious context it refers to the specific fee paid to a minister for the performance of specific religious services. Here, it refers not simply to the (usually) prearranged fee that a guest or visiting priest would receive for leading a parish community in one of their regularly scheduled Eucharistic celebrations, but most specifically to the additional fee that a priest would receive for 'offering Mass', whether publicly or privately, for a specific intention. First, some history, and then the specific state of the question that reveals that we are dealing with a theological issue that is in transition.[38]

> The practice by which the faithful make offerings in connection with the eucharistic celebration as a particular mode of active participation in the eucharistic sacrifice has a long history. Such offerings are the symbolic expression not only of one's spiritual union with the sacrificial worship of Christ, but also of one's membership in the celebration of the faith of the hierarchically organized local Catholic community.[39]

Probably originating in the Roman provinces of North Africa as early as the third century, was the offertory procession, an extension of the earlier custom by which the faithful brought bread and wine from which the presider selected what was needed for the Eucharistic celebration, the rest being distributed to the poor and the needy. The basic idea and theology, which quickly spread across the Western Church, was that of a *communal* co-offering of the faithful with and through the presiding bishop or presbyter. By the fifth century, however, other gifts of value, in addition to just bread and wine, were being added. 'Whereas the original communality of gifts signalled a communal act in which the differentiation of the offerers is not expressed, the new practice of offering a variety of gifts underscored the individuality of the offerers'.[40] Eventually, this emphasis on the individuality of the offerer or donor supplanted the idea of communal co-offering. Where the old Roman notion of gift-giving as not entailing reciprocity prevailed, the priest was 'considered to be bound in charity – but not, strictly, in justice – to remember the donor's intention. But in the Frankish territories of northern Europe, the gift was instinctively understood to imply reciprocity. There was at first resistance to this idea of specific reciprocity with its concomitant juridical and even commercializing implications, but:

> In the end [i.e., by the eleventh century], and under very precise conditions for such transactions, including their juridical consequences, and with the full

---

38 For much more detail on all this, see Kilmartin, *The Eucharist in the West*, pp. 109–15, 165, 167–68, and esp. Chapter 8 'The Practice and Theology of the Mass Stipend', pp. 205–37.
39 Ibid., pp. 109–10.
40 Ibid., p. 110.

approval of ecclesiastical authorities, the practice of celebrating distinct Masses for distinct intentions of individual donors of offerings became the rule everywhere.[41]

Accompanying this were also significant developments in the understanding of the role and power of the priest and the people in the celebration of the Eucharist. At the 'moment of consecration' (see the preceding sub-section), 'the priest is said to be placed precisely *on the side of Christ vis-à-vis* the liturgical assembly and to act in the name of Christ'.[42] In other words, the distinction between priest and people was becoming more sharply defined. The laity were understood to act not as active participants but as 'hearers' and to participate by reason of their spiritual devotion. They contribute *by their devotion* (rather than by active participation) to the spiritual benefits that derive from the Mass.

Selectively summing up the historical development, one can say that by the thirteenth century, things had fairly clearly shaken out in such a way that:

1. The people were no longer understood as active subjects of the offering of the Eucharistic sacrifice. The contributions to the priest for doing this were thus, appropriately, called 'stipends'.
2. The practice of celebrating Mass for just one donor, excluding other intentions, seemed to imply a special propitiatory or impetratory value intrinsic to the Mass prior to any consideration of the subjective devotion either of those participating in the Mass, or of the offerers/donors, or of those for whom the Mass is offered.
3. The fact that such Masses can be repeatedly offered for the same intention seemed to imply that the special fruit derived from the application of the Mass is somehow limited.[43]

This was the basis of what can be called the 'classical scholastic thesis' that undergirded most Roman Catholic practice and thinking from the Middle Ages up to our own day. At present, however, it garners little support from theologians who have recently written about it, and less than enthusiastic support even from the official magisterium of the Catholic Church. This thesis states

> that a special fruit, intrinsic to the Mass itself, independently of any consideration of those actually participating in the Mass, accrues to the intention of the person in whose favor the priest applies this special fruit.[44]

It is easy to see why contemporary theologians are reluctant to defend this thesis, especially in this its blatant and un-nuanced formulation; and also why the Church itself is now reluctant to appeal directly to this thesis to shore up the waning

---

41   Ibid., p. 113.
42   Ibid., p. 114.
43   Ibid., p. 115.
44   Ibid., p. 231.

but still widespread practice of the Mass stipend. But there is a grain of truth contained, or at least pointed towards, in this scholastic thesis, a truth that both the theologians and the magisterium are eager to defend. Kilmartin expresses it as follows:

> What must be held, as doctrine guaranteed by the instinct of the faithful, and by the teaching of the magisterium, is the conviction that fruit derives from the Mass for the whole Church, and the world, and individuals for whom the Church prays in the eucharistic sacrifice; and especially for those who actively participate in the celebration as well as for those in favor of whom the eucharistic sacrifice is celebrated. This is especially witnessed by the liturgy of the Eucharist itself.[45]

One detects a sense of apophatic reserve in the way this is expressed. What is absent from this is any sense of the Eucharist being a juridical act of the Church, any sense of juridical or measurable reciprocity due to an individual (as opposed to communal) offerer/donor, any sense of 'commerce' in things spiritual, any attempt to calculate a specific value of the Eucharistic sacrifice. What is present here is a reverent, while being bold, openness to a Trinitarian understanding of the event that is taking place in the celebration of the Eucharist. The Trinity is so much at the heart of this 'mystery' that it seems just to explode from Kilmartin's pen within a sub-section unpromisingly entitled 'Treasury of the Church':

> Above all, in the Eucharistic Prayer the Church intercedes in union with Christ for the whole Church, for the world, and for individuals. The Church appeals to the salvific will of God in virtue of the value of the redemptive work of Christ. This prayer makes manifest that, in the economy of salvation, the Father offers himself to be loved through the twofold self-communication of the incarnate Word and Spirit, and that the answering response of love is possible in union with Christ's once-for-all-response of love. Moreover, according to the ontology of love, the divine offer of love necessarily includes the capacity of receiving the love of creatures; for by its very nature love is fulfilled in mutually exercised self-communication. When this love of the father is expressed with reference to love for the Father's children by praying for their salvation, the Father is 'moved' to hear this prayer of intercession.[46]

In contrast to the polemical positions that characterized the Christian pole of post-Reformational modernity, this is a theology whose beauty and power and (ultimately) simple profundity could so easily have united rather than separated Christian minds and hearts, and could so easily have offered, in humility, an acceptable invitation to those at the other pole so enamoured of their new-found freedom from a dominative religious authority. But it is a theology that was tragically not yet

---

45 Ibid., p. 231.
46 Ibid., p. 229.

available to the theologians of that time. Due to the developments of liturgical renewal and ecumenism, we are now, happily, in transition to a stage when such a theology is beginning to become available to Christians eager to communicate to others the gifts that they have received.

Liturgical Renewal and Ecumenism

The original outline for this book had one full chapter dedicated to liturgical renewal and another to ecumenism. However, analogous to the insight that had come to me several years ago when I changed the title of a course from 'The Eucharist in Ecumenical Context' to, simply 'The Eucharist,' so too, I have come to recognize that to treat 'liturgical renewal' and 'ecumenism' as separable would now imply an embarrassing tautology. Just as there is no way to do an adequate study of the Eucharist other than in an ecumenical context, so too, there is no way to study liturgical renewal adequately other than ecumenically.

What has liturgical reform and renewal to do with Christian sacrifice? The answer should already be fairly clear to readers of this book. In the Roman Catholic mind, 'sacrifice' and the 'Mass' tend to be identified. When, for example, back in the 1960s, people heard that Bob Daly was working on 'Christian sacrifice', they routinely assumed that I was working on the Eucharist. For, from time immemorial, and also from well before the Reformation when it unhappily became an object of bitter controversy, Western Christianity generally referred to the Eucharist with such titles as 'The Sacrifice of the Mass', or the 'The Holy Sacrifice'. *Sanctissimum Sacrificium* or *Sanctissimum Missae Sacrificium* or sometimes just simply *Sanctum sacrificium* were the official Latin terms.

However, that traditional Catholic naming of the Church's central act of worship and the eventual Protestant rejection of that naming and concept is by no means the whole story. Recent liturgical reform and renewal, to which all the main line Christian churches have in various ways contributed, has enabled us to move beyond the polemical oppositions that characterized most Catholic and Protestant attitudes towards sacrifice from the time of the Reformation until very recently. For Catholics, liturgical renewal has enabled them to recognize in the classical Eucharistic Prayers realities and understandings of sacrifice that they did not realize were there all the time. For Protestants, liturgical renewal has enabled them to re-appropriate many of these same (for Catholics rediscovered) realities and understandings after having seemingly totally distanced themselves from them in their reformational opposition to Catholic abuses. Catholics now more frankly recognize the limitations of some of their traditional doctrinal formulations and practices that provoked the Protestant reaction, and Protestants, for their part, more frankly recognize that the polemical heat of battle may have caused them to reject more than just some obvious abuses.

We have already seen a great deal of this in those parts of this book where we attended specifically to the sacrificial content of the classical Eucharistic Prayers. Now, however, it is time to take note of the religio-cultural context of modern and contemporary liturgical renewal. This renewal has been to a significant extent taking place in the context of the intrusive thrust of so-called modernism into literature and the arts, and into culture in general. Much of this was happening in the aftermath of the first World War. It was a time when:

> ... late romantics like Jean Sibelius and Sergei Rachmaninoff flourished simultaneously with Igor Stravinsky and Arnold Schoenberg. Likewise, William Butler Yeats and Robert Frost ['romantic' types] wrote contemporaneously with T.S. Eliot and Ezra Pound [decidedly unromantic, 'modernist' types].[1]

However, it must be noted that even these modernist types who seemed to be debunking the tradition really had a great interest in it and were at heart profoundly traditional. They were desperately interested in recovering the riches of the past. History was very important to them. Thus it is neither accidental nor surprising that the great liturgical scholars in the first half of the twentieth century were also primarily historians.[2]

For all that, however, they were also men of their own age. Just as their 'scientific' contemporaries in the history of religions were attempting to discover the basic idea or basic model of sacrifice, they too were attempting to discover the basic 'shape' or model of the liturgy. Their search was for 'some elusive apostolic model from which all later liturgies developed.'[3] Gregory Dix gave this its (now) classical expression:

> The outline – the Shape of the Liturgy – is still everywhere the same in all our sources, right back into the earliest period on which we can yet speak with certainty, the earlier half of the second century. There is even good reason to think that this outline – the Shape – of the Liturgy is of genuinely apostolic tradition.[4]

We have learned much from Dix's magisterial work, but subsequent liturgical historical studies[5] have proven illusory his hopes of recovering an apostolic model. It needs to be pointed out that, until quite recently, most scholars assumed that there were some authentic 'original' liturgical models, just waiting to be discovered in order to guide us in our contemporary renewal efforts. Only recently did this cease being a dominant assumption in liturgical studies. Complicating the communicative aspects of our main project is the fact that this assumption of the existence of some original model still seems to be the dominant assumption among people not familiar with the cutting edge of current developments in the history of the liturgy.[6]

---

1 Frank C. Senn, *Christian Liturgy: Catholic and Evangelical* (Minneapolis, MN: Fortress, 1997), p. 609.
2 Ibid., p. 610.
3 Ibid., p. 10.
4 Ibid., p. 10, quoted from Gregory Dix, *The Shape of the Liturgy* (New York: Seabury, 1982), p. 5. (Originally published in London: Dacre Press, 1945).
5 See esp. Paul F. Bradshaw, *The Search for the Origins of Christian Worship:Sources and Methods for the Study of Early Liturgy*, 2nd ed. (New York: Oxford University Press, 2002).
6 See, e.g., Robert J. Daly, S.J., 'Eucharistic Origins: From the New Testament to the Liturgies of the Golden Age', *Theological Studies* 66 (2005), pp. 3–22.

From the outset, and indeed through much of the twentieth century, liturgical studies went hand-in-hand with patristic studies. And these mostly historical studies did contribute much that, in the Western churches, has been taken up into current liturgical practice, things like the altar facing the people, the offertory procession, the prayer of the faithful, etc. However, there was also a healthy resistance to the idea that good liturgy meant simply reinstating practices from the past. Some of this was also resistance to the perception – it was indeed a genuine danger – that liturgical reform was an elitist movement. To some extent, it must be frankly admitted, it sometimes actually was elitist. The fact that it, for the most part, successfully resisted devolution into merely something for the elite – into merely 'smells and bells,' to put it derogatively – the fact that it actually became a major movement of practical reform involving a wide spectrum of Christian churches, this fact constitutes one of the more glorious achievements in all of church history.

Chapter I

The Monasteries

Critically, important parts of this history were brought into being by the monasteries, especially some Benedictine monasteries in Belgium, France and Germany. However, what is considered to be the first significant moment in this history of the modern monastic contribution to the liturgical movement – while constituting an important part of the background that made later developments possible – did not originate the actual trajectory that led to contemporary liturgical renewal. That first moment is associated with the name of Dom Guéranger and the monastery of Solesmes, France in the nineteenth century.[7] That movement sought a recovery of medieval ritual. In significant contrast to that, what characterizes the trajectory that characterizes the contemporary liturgical movement in the Western Christian churches has been 'a recovery of the corporate character of the liturgy as "the work of the people".'[8]

The fact that Benedictine monasteries should take the lead in liturgical renewal was, of course, not surprising. They were centres of learning with great library resources. They were by tradition and commitment deeply concerned with worship. And – a critically important enabling condition – they enjoyed a significant amount of self-rule, especially concerning practices of worship within the monastery. This relative independence from the ordinary governing structures of the local church gave them a certain amount of freedom to experiment. Their

---

7   Dom Prosper-Louis-Pascal Gueranger, O.S.B. (1805–1875) is credited with being primarily responsible for the modern recovery and renewal of Gregorian chant. However, he vigorously sought to suppress all local liturgical practices that were not in line with the official liturgy of the Roman Rite. Thus, much good was lost along with the bad.

8   Senn, p. 612.

responsible use of this freedom gave valuable impetus to many of the things we now take for granted in the celebration of the liturgy.

The monastery of Maria Laach in northwest Germany assumed a leadership role in this development. For example, in 1914, the Dialogue Mass (the *Missa Recitata*)[9] first came into practice there, sending shock waves across Catholic Germany. Today, except for those few who have been longing for the – now officially sanctioned as an alternative option[10] reinstatement of the Tridentine Rite, most Western Roman Catholics would find it hard to imagine the liturgy being celebrated any other way. Ninety years ago, even with everything still in Latin and nothing else changed, the Dialogue Mass was perceived as a shocking innovation. But the obvious spiritual and pastoral success of this 'innovation' proved to be a critical foundation moment in the Catholic and High Church liturgical movement. It demonstrated for all to see and to experience that the Middle Ages was not the primary place in which to look for practical guidance in liturgical renewal.

Chapter II

Mystery Theology

'Mystery Theology' or 'The Theology of the Mystery' provided the theological glue that enabled liturgical reform, especially on the theological and academic level, to move ahead as an irresistible ecumenical reform movement. Mystery theology enabled the liturgical theologians of the main line Christian Churches to arrive at a commonly acceptable theoretical, i.e., theological, way of understanding the Eucharistic mystery and, along with that, the Eucharist as sacrifice. That common theological understanding has allowed Catholic and Protestant scholars to devote most of their energy to working with rather than against each other.

The precise critical point in this all-important development was the question of the relationship between the historical saving action of Jesus Christ and the current celebration of the Eucharist. In other words, what is the relationship between, as Catholics would put it, the Sacrifice of Christ and the Sacrifice of the Mass? Or, as Protestants generally prefer to put it, between the Last Supper of the Lord and the Lord's Supper we celebrate today? How bridge the gap between Jesus' act in the past and the innumerable celebrations of the Eucharist in the present? Protestants, in reacting to what they perceived to be Catholic

---

9   In a Dialogue Mass or *Missa Recitata*, the whole congregation, and not just the servers on the altar, recited aloud all the responses.

10   See the 7 July 2007 Apostolic Letter 'Motu proprio data' of Pope Benedict XVI, 'Summorum Pontificum' (http://www.summorumpontificum.net/2007/07/summorum-pontificum-english.html) concerning the use of the Roman liturgy prior to the reform of 1970.

teaching and practice, stressed, indeed massively emphasized, the fact that the sacrifice of Christ was a unique, all-sufficient and unrepeatable once-for-all event. No reputable Catholic theologian had ever denied this, at least not in principle. However, what Catholics commonly taught and preached, and above all how and what they practiced (especially, e.g., the private-Mass and the stipend-Mass system) did give the impression that they were contradicting this fundamental Christian truth. The way Catholics tried to express the real relationship – 'identity', they seemed to be saying – between Jesus' sacrifice and the Sacrifice of the Mass inevitably made it sound like they were teaching (blasphemously to Protestant ears) that Jesus' sacrifice was being repeated and that therefore it wasn't once-and-for-all and all-sufficient. Even worse, Catholic teaching and practice made it sound (again blasphemous to Protestant ears) as if the Eucharist were a work of the Church, the performance of which was meritorious for salvation.

One cannot dismiss the Protestant reaction as mere polemical overreaction. Overreaction there may have been, but the reaction itself was more than amply justified. For example, Pope Gregory the Great, writing around AD 594, expressed himself on this in a way that then sounded quite 'natural' to traditional Catholic ears but that, today, would be considered blatantly irresponsible: '(Christ) in the mystery of the holy sacrifice is offered for us again.'[11] Similar lack of nuance can still be found in contemporary Catholic teaching and preaching, especially when it is not taking place in an ecumenical context. However, the contributions of many scholars, especially the Swedish Protestant scholar Bishop Yngve Brilioth and the German Benedictine Dom Odo Casel have enabled us to get beyond this impasse.

> Brilioth explored four major strands of eucharistic meaning that are rooted in the institution of the Lord's Supper and are more or less constantly present throughout the history of eucharistic celebration: [1]*thanksgiving* (eucharistia), [2]*communion* or *fellowship* (koinonia), [3]*commemoration* or *memorial*, and [4]*sacrifice*. To these he added the dimension of *Mystery*, 'which embraces and united all the others, and bridges the gap between the one act of the savior and the innumerable eucharists in which that act is apprehended in the experience of faith, and its benefits appropriated'[12] [Emphasis and superscript numbering added]

In terms of our theme *Sacrifice Unveiled*, Senn emphasizes the significance of Brilioth's work, accomplished well before the ecumenical advances of the recent decades, by pointing out that, for Brilioth:

> Sacrifice is the self-offering of the church when it assembles to celebrate the

---

11 Gregory's words are: *iterum in hoc mysterio sacrae oblationis immolator* – *Dialogorum libri iv* 4.48 (PL 77.425CD). See Edward J. Kilmartin, *The Eucharist in the West* (Collegeville, MN: Liturgical Press, 1998) 22. See above, pp. 155–56.
12 Yngve Brilioth, *Eucharistic Faith and Practice, Evangelical and Catholic* (Abridged and trans. A.G. Herbert; London: S.P.C.K., 1965), p. 17. [First published in Swedish in 1926; first English edition published in 1930.] As quoted by Senn, pp. 615–16.

eucharist, expressed through its offering of gifts. It is surprising even now to find Brilioth, a Protestant, understanding sacrifice in this way; but it shows that he derived his theology of the eucharist from the liturgical data.[13]

In line with this, we note that among contemporary Eucharistic Prayers, it is in the typically Protestant Great Thanksgivings, i.e., the Methodist and Presbyterian prayers, that the idea of the self-offering of the assembly is most explicitly expressed. This idea, that would seem to be an essential element in a well-rounded 'sacrificial' Eucharistic Prayer is not found, at least not explicitly, in most other Eucharistic Prayers. Although the assembly offering the Eucharistic elements of bread and cup *and* the self-offering of the assembly would *both* seem to be essential elements of a well-rounded Eucharistic Prayer, no single EP presently in official use seems to include both of these sacrificial themes in an explicit way.[14]

A. ODO CASEL AND MYSTERY THEOLOGY

At about the same time that Brilioth was writing, Dom Odo Casel (1886–1948) on the Catholic side was developing the idea of the 'mystery presence' of Christ in the Eucharist. He used the German word *Vergegenwärtigung* to express this presence. The closest we can come to this in English is the hyphenated neologism 're-presentation'. This word, a noun, denotes the action of 'making present'. It can therefore be made to carry the meaning of real presence, in contradistinction from the non-hyphenated 'representation' in which the reality represented is usually not understood to be really present. Put in an oversimplified way and in a few words, Casel's theory claims that the sacrifice of Christ, the saving action of Christ, is really, but 'trans-historically' or 'meta-historically – i.e., in 'mystery', made present to us in our celebration of the Eucharist. It is very much worth noting that the word and concept 'mystery' is used by both Brilioth and Casel to point toward both the 'that' and the 'how' of Christ's presence in the Eucharist. This also seems to correspond to the more apophatic way in which the Eastern Orthodox understand and refer to the presence and activity of the Trinity in the celebration of the Divine Liturgy.

With this theory, with this 'theology of mystery', As Senn and numerous others have pointed out,[15] we are dealing with one of the most significant Christian ecumenical breakthroughs of the twentieth century. It was now possible, when thinking of the celebration of the Eucharist, to speak of the real presence of the once-for-all sacrifice of Christ, along with its saving benefits, without at the same time suggesting that the sacrifice of Christ was somehow 'repeated' as a work of the Church. Years later, in the early 1980s, this was amply confirmed in the publication of a bilateral Roman Catholic/German Lutheran study whose title, if translated into English, would read: *The Sacrifice of*

---

13 Senn, p. 616.
14 See above, pp. 136–40.
15 Ibid., loc. cit.

Jesus Christ and Its Presence in the Church: Clarifications on the Sacrificial Character of the Lord's Supper.[16]

Curiously, and against the expectations of some of its earlier enthusiastic proponents, mystery theology, as liturgical theology moved on, has proven to be anything but a permanent achievement. However, it did the job that needed to be done. It brought about what seems to be a lasting good effect. It made it easier for Catholic and Protestant theologians to recognize in each other a common Eucharistic faith that is stronger and deeper than the various theologies that this or that group will use to try to understand and explain it. If theology is 'faith seeking understanding', there is now an experiential awareness that faith can be one, even if the understandings of it, its 'theologies', are somewhat different.

As a theological explanation, however, mystery theology leaves much to be desired. Although it offers formerly divided Christians a common way to understand the reality of the relationship between the sacrifice of Christ and the Eucharistic celebrations of the Church, it is not directly grounded on biblical revelation; nor, contrary to claims made by some of its early proponents, is it supported by a significant consensus in the teaching of the Fathers of the Church. Finally, and tellingly, it is a theory that claims to be an explanation, but there is no significant agreement among theologians and philosophers about how to explain the explanation. This suggests that theologians are not only free to keep looking for a better explanatory solution, they are indeed obliged to keep looking.[17] In recent years, as we have already pointed out, there has been a convergence among some prominent liturgical scholars in suggesting that we should be thinking not in terms of the Christ-event being made present to us, thus locating the 'action' (i.e., the effect of the action) in what happens to Christ. Rather, we should be thinking in terms of we/the assembly being made present to the Christ-event, thus locating the 'action' (i.e, the effect of the action) in what happens to us.[18]

---

16 *Das Opfer Jesu Christ und seine Gegenwart in der Kirche. Klärungen zum Opfercharakter des Herrenmahles* (ed. Karl Lehmann and Edmund Schlink; Dialog der Kirchen, 3; Freiburg/Göttingen: Herder, 1983).

17 See Edward J. Kilmartin, S.J., *The Eucharist in the West: History and Theology* (Collegeville, MN: Liturgical Press, 1998), pp. 268–300.

18 Among these theologians can be mentioned three Jesuits: Edward Kilmartin (see previous note) Hans Bernhard Meyer, *Eucharistie, Geschichte, Theologie, Pastoral. Gottesdienst der Kirche* (Handbuch der Liturgiewissenschaft, Teil 4; Regensburg: Pustet, 1989); idem, 'Odo Casels Idee der Mysteriengegenwart in neuer Sicht', *Archiv für Liturgiewissenschaft* 28 (1986), pp. 388–95; and Cesare Giraudo, *Eucaristia per la chiesa: Prospettive teologiche sull'eucaristia a partire dalla 'lex orandi'* (Aloisiana, 22; Rome: Gregorian University/Brescia: Morcelliana, 1989).

Chapter III

Liturgical Conferences, Institutes, Academies, and Societies

The academic liturgical societies are among the most powerful engines that have been driving forward the ideas of liturgical reform and renewal. They were, from the outset, strong in Belgium, Germany, Austria and France, and subsequently also in North America, but weak in England, and almost totally absent in Spain and Italy. In England, this weakness was due to the fact that English Catholicism was primarily a survival from and expression of pre-Reformation Christianity. In Spain and Italy, the lack of liturgical reform seems to have been due largely to a culturally dominant Catholicism that was not significantly threatened or challenged by any other cultural forms. Absent ecumenism, or at least a potentially ecumenical context, liturgical renewal does not seem to flourish.

From England, however, we have the magisterial work of Dom Gregory Dix, *The Shape of the Liturgy*. Recognizing that the lack of early Christian liturgical texts did not allow one to discover on a textual basis the elusive authoritative apostolic model that he sought, Dix proposed to derive this from analysing the fundamental ritual 'shape' of all Christian liturgy that, as everyone agreed, traces its origins back to the ritual action of Jesus, namely:

- *Taking* bread and wine
- *Giving thanks* over them
- *Breaking* the bread
- *Giving* the elements to the disciples

Although Dix's fundamental assumptions have now been superseded, generations of liturgical scholars cut their teeth on his work. This clearly suggested that sound liturgical studies could no longer be responsibly undertaken solely within the confines of a narrow confessional orientation. Anglicans, Protestants and Catholics have all learned from Dix. Now, as a matter of course, they routinely learn from each other.

In the United States and Canada, the Liturgical Conference became the primary mediator of liturgical renewal, primarily for the Catholic Church, but also with beneficial service to the other churches.[19] St. John's Abbey and University in Collegeville, Minnesota have been doing for North America what Maria Laach and the other Benedictine monasteries did for Europe. Centres for the study of liturgy have been established at Notre Dame University and the Catholic University of

---

19   Beginning in Chicago in 1940, The Liturgical Conference sponsored a series of well-attended annual 'liturgical weeks', held in a different city each year. See Keith F. Pecklers, S.J., *The Unread Vision: The Liturgical Movement in the United States of America: 1926–1955* (Collegeville, MN: Liturgical Press, 1998), pp. 147, 198–200.

America. Important liturgical scholars, both Catholic and Protestant, have held chairs at major universities like Duke, Yale and Emory. Many leading Protestant liturgical scholars have done their doctoral studies at, for example, Catholic Notre Dame, and some of the professors of liturgy there are not Roman Catholic. On the other side of the coin, some leading Catholic liturgical scholars have done their doctoral studies at non-Catholic universities like Emory, Yale and Duke, where (just as at Notre Dame the professors are not all Catholic) the professors of liturgy are not always Protestant.

One of the strongest signs of the developing maturity of the liturgical movement and liturgical studies has been the North American Academy of Liturgy (NAAL) with some 400 active members who come from all the major Christian church bodies (plus a few also from Judaism) and major universities and seminaries. This academy was founded in 1975 as an ecumenical academy whose members learn from each other as they contribute to the ongoing liturgical development of the Church both in general and in their own particular religious bodies. This is where much of the thinking takes place that has contributed to, and will continue to contribute to, the best in what has been taking place and will eventually be taking place in North America in terms of renewed and revised liturgical practices. For example, in recent years, representatives of the United Methodist Church Task Force on Holy Communion commissioned to come up with a theological state-ment on this subject for their church have consulted with the Eucharistic Prayer and Theology Seminar of the NAAL. This seminar happens to have been chaired in recent years by Roman Catholics. But its working members are Anglican, Meth-odist, Presbyterian, Lutheran and United Church of Christ, as well as Roman Catholic. In other words, most liturgical scholars, when working for their own churches, don't want to be making theological statements regarding the liturgy without first running them by members of the other Christian churches. And for our own special subject, Christian sacrifice, this particular NAAL seminar has been hearing from me about my work on this subject for almost two decades, and I have been learning from the feedback of its members.

What the NAAL has been doing on the North American scene, the *Societas Liturgica*, founded 1967, has been doing on the international scene. When it meets – every two years in a different part of the world – its working structure, like that of the NAAL, is totally ecumenical. In other words, the ritual and liturgical differences between the Christian churches that, for some 400 years, were an occasion of polemical division, are now, increasingly, being experienced as mutual enrichment.[20]

---

20 For a detailed treatment of this theme, see the magisterial chapter by Geoffrey Wainwright: 'Ecumenical Convergences', in *The Oxford History of Christian Worship*, ed. Geoffrey Wainwright and Karen Westerfield Tucker (Oxford: University Press, 2006), 721–54.

Chapter IV

A High Point of Restorationism: The New Worship Books

One would expect that this situation of ecumenical cooperation would have an effect on the structure and content of the worship books of the various Christian churches. This has, in fact, been the case. Over the past few decades, the Anglicans/Episcopalians, the Lutherans the Methodists, the Presbyterians, the United Church of Canada (and this is not an exhaustive list by any means) have all produced new or revised worship books and or hymnals that obviously demonstrate the effects of this ecumenical collaboration. For example, one striking example of this can be found in the Eucharistic Prayers/Great Thanksgivings in the current worship books of the North American Methodists[21] and Presbyterians.[22] When ordinary Catholics look at or hear these prayers, they think that they are experiencing Catholic prayer. When liturgical scholars examine them, they are aware of encountering something that seems to be more Catholic than what they find in the official Roman Catholic Sacramentary (– the official missal used in the Catholic celebration of the Eucharist). The reason for this is that, as Kilmartin has demonstrated, the Mass of the Roman Rite is the product of a relatively narrow splinter tradition of the Universal Church. In addition, the present Catholic Sacramentary was put together (and indeed somewhat hastily) some 40 years ago before Catholics and Protestants had much experience in learning from each other. In contrast to the Catholic Sacramentary, the main line Protestant churches have generally been more free to appropriate the wealth of the Christian tradition both from the past, especially the patristic age, as well as from the East. Because they are of more recent vintage, these worship books have had more opportunity to appropriate the advances of recent ecumenical liturgical scholarship. A striking example of this kind of development is the new hymn and worship book of the United Church of Canada.[23] This hymnal and worship book, for the first time in these basically evangelical, free-church communions, is organized liturgically, i.e., according to the structure of the Church's liturgical year.

All of this might lead one to expect that the new Catholic Sacramentary, now in preparation, would become a glorious exemplification of the developments I have been expounding. But, alas, the opposite now seems, at this writing, to become more likely. The original draft of the revised Sacramentary prepared by the International Commission for English in the Liturgy (ICEL) did indeed give much

---

21   *The United Methodist Book of Worship* (Nashville, TN: The United Methodist Publishing House, 1992).
22   *Book of Common Worship*, prepared by The Theology and Worship Ministry Unit for the Presbyterian Church U.S.A. (Louisville, KY: Westminster/John Knox Press, 1993).
23   *Voices United: The Hymn and Worship Book of the United Church of Canada* (Etobicoke: The United Church Publishing House, 1996).

promise of being such a glorious exemplification. But Vatican authorities rejected this draft, dismantled the ICEL membership that had produced it, and replaced the then operative translation principle of 'dynamic equivalence' with an insistence that everything be translated very literally from the Latin *editio typica*. Anything that was not an exact translation of that Latin text, for example some magnificent new collects that would make use of language and imagery that the Assembly was about to hear from the readings of the day, was eliminated. The proposed new Sacramentary even goes as far as to introduce unilaterally new formulations for the acclamations and other parts to be spoken by the people, thus reversing and running roughshod over those remarkable ecumenical convergences by which most of the main line Protestant churches had, for the sake of unity in praying, adopted the Roman Catholic way of saying things. At this writing, these unilateral Roman Catholic changes – recall how just a few decades ago no one would have questioned the appropriateness of such unilateral action – have not been totally finalized, but the struggle over them is bitter. All this points out that, although ecumenical liturgical reform may indeed have already come a long, long way, the road that lies ahead is probably still beset with obstacles and more than just speed bumps.[24]

Chapter V

The Constitution on the Sacred Liturgy of Vatican II

The second Vatican Ecumenical Council met in four sessions beginning on 11 October 1962 and ending on 8 December 1965. Representatives from more than 40 Anglican, Baptist, Congregationalist, Disciples of Christ, Lutheran, Presbyterian and other churches and groups were present as delegate-observers. They did not take part in the voting, but they freely participated in the discussions and committees that met between the official voting sessions.

The first document to be produced by the council was *Sacrosanctum Concilium*, the Constitution on the Sacred Liturgy. The early stages of the modern liturgical movement had prepared the way for this. Note this assessment by a sympathetic Lutheran observer:

---

24   Some indication of the complexity and bitterness that can be involved in this process can be gleaned from the following articles: Peter Jeffrey, 'A Chant Historian Reads Liturgiam Authenticam', *Worship* 78, no. 1 (January, 2004), pp. 2–24; no. 2 (March, 2004), pp.139–64; no. 3 (May, 2004), pp. 236–65; no. 4 (July, 2004), pp. 309–41; Nathan D. Mitchell, 'The Amen Corner', *Worship* 81, no. 2 (March, 2007), pp. 170–84; Donald W. Trautman, 'How Accessible Are the New Mass Translations?' *America* 196, no. 18 (May 21, 2007), pp. 9–11. The most comprehensive, summarizing treatment is probably that of Maxwell E. Johnson, 'The Loss of a Common Language: The End of Ecumenical-Liturgical Convergence?', *Studia Liturgica* 37 (2007), pp. 55–72.

The constitution was a political document that shows the tendency of the Roman church to evolve teachings without repudiating what was taught previously. For example, the statement in I, 9 that the liturgy does not exhaust the entire activity of the church recalls the teaching of Pope Pius XII at the Assisi conference in 1956; yet it also prepares the way for the statement that 'the liturgy is the summit toward which the activity of the church is directed' and 'the fountain from which all her powers flow' (I, 10). The Constitution was not only a pastoral statement; it was also a juridical document emanating from the highest authority in the church – an ecumenical council convened by the pope. Thus it not only called for the 'full and active participation by all the people' in the rites of the church (I, 14); it also dealt with the education of liturgy professors (15), liturgical instruction in the seminaries (16) and in religious houses (17), the continuing education of clergy who were already serving in the ministry (18), and the instruction of the laity necessary to promote their full and active participation in the liturgy.[25]

This document is credited with being the authorization for the remarkable reform of the Roman Rite that has taken place over the past 40 years.[26] Most of that period experienced the promulgation and acceptance into practice of what might seem to be a whole new set of sacramental ritual practices, but which, in fact, were logical changes, fully in line with the tradition and designed to move liturgical practice toward the goal of 'full and active participation by all the people'. The past decade, however, has experienced something of a restorationist dynamic in which some are claiming that the reforms have gone too far. As indicated at the end of the previous chapter, it remains to be seen whether this is merely a bump in the road, or the harbinger of a significant change of direction in the course of Roman Catholic liturgical renewal.

Chapter VI

Liturgical Work in an Ecumenical Context

Senn points out that the ecumenical movement made appreciative contact between the churches possible at a time when, increasingly, common cultural challenges required common pastoral strategies. For example, both Protestants and Catholics have the same religious/cultural goals of combating modern individualism and social disintegration. In the early stages of this cooperation and collaboration between the churches, a great deal of liturgical experimentation took place. Thirty-five or so years ago was an age of 'paperback liturgies'. That the

---

25   Senn, pp. 629–30.
26   An inside view into just how remarkable was the early history of this Roman Catholic liturgical reform can be found in Archbishop Piero Marini, *A Challenging Reform: Realizing the Vision of the Liturgical Renewal 1963–1975*, ed. Mark R. Francis, C.S.V., John R. Page, and Keith F. Pecklers, S.J. (Collegeville, MN: Liturgical Press, 2007).

present age sees much less overt experimentation is due both to the emergence of far more adequate 'official' liturgies and to a more widespread knowledge and understanding of the basic, classical 'shape' of the Christian liturgy. But also putting a damper on experimentation is the rise, in some church communities, of conservative and restorationist tendencies. At the moment, these seem to be strongest in the Roman Catholic Church.[27]

However, a great deal has been achieved. Not the least of these achievements, and in the long term possibly the most important, has been the widespread adoption of the 'common lectionary', a three-year cycle of Sunday and feast-day readings from across both testaments of the Bible. With relatively minor variations, this 'common lectionary' has been in use now for several decades across the main line Christian churches. Thus, for the first time, the people in these churches are celebrating the Eucharist[28] in basically the same way, and with basically the same theological-background understanding, and are hearing basically the same selection of biblical readings in the preceding Liturgy of the Word. The eventual ecumenical effect of this, its eventual unifying power, is only beginning to be felt. Will this one day bring about the sudden crumbling of the already shrinking walls of separation that still divide the Christian churches, perhaps in a quietly prepared-for but also seemingly sudden event like the 1989 dismantling of the physical barriers between Eastern and Western Europe? Time alone will tell. In the meantime, we work and pray towards the realization of that blessed event. However, other factors suggest that rapid unification of all the churches cannot realistically be hoped for. A common (or at least similar) lectionary and a common theology are indeed, like a hidden, leaven, working for unity among the main line Eastern and Western churches. However, the 'non-sacramental' churches and the free churches that do not follow a regular lectionary have remained relatively marginal to this dynamic. This is where the ecumenical divide is at its widest and where the ecumenical challenge is the greatest, although, even here, use of a lectionary is beginning to make inroads. For, as we notice that some of these churches are beginning to discover the liturgy, and that some of their scholars are more and more discovering the riches of the patristic age, there is more than a glimmer of hope. The 'exciting times' in which we are living may well turn out to be more of a blessing than a curse.

---

27 A clear indication of this would be the recent reinstatement of the Tridentine Rite as an available parallel option for Roman Catholics (documentation above in Note 10). See also my comments on the preparation of the new Sacramentary in the preceding chapter.

28 At least when they do celebrate the Eucharist. In many churches, monthly rather than weekly Holy Communion is the normal practice.

Bridge 2 C

Sacrifice and Girardian Mimetic Theory: The End of Sacrifice?

In this final 'bridge' section, before wrapping things up in a summary conclusion, we find ourselves reaching back to the question of the meaning of sacrifice that we raised at the beginning of this book. Both the liturgical theologian, Edward Kilmartin, the source of the fundamental insight on which this book is based, and the mimetic theorist, René Girard, whom I explicitly draw on here for the first time, have, in the late twentieth century written about sacrifice in ways that suggest what we might call 'the end of sacrifice'. Kilmartin speaks of 'the fact that "sacrifice" in the history-of-religions sense was abolished with the Christ-event'.[1] Reading that, I feel I am reading something that might also have been written by René Girard. For as is well known, key to Girard's theory of cultural and religious origins is mimesis, the effective 'good mimesis' that keeps culture going by means of underlying sacrificial mechanisms.[2] However, as Girard has repeatedly, and ever more clearly pointed out, Christianity unveils the deception with which the sacrificial scapegoat mechanism works, thus rendering the mechanism progressively ineffective. I hear that as saying more or less what Kilmartin was expressing when he wrote about the Christ event doing away with sacrifice in the history-of-religions sense of the word. They are approaching, or groping to express, fundamentally the same insight, but from different directions: Kilmartin, as we have seen, by way of Trinitarian theology, Girard, to whom we now turn, more by way of phenomenology.

Chapter I

General Introduction to Girardian Mimetic Theory

The claim can be made, and indeed began to be made shortly after the appearance of his groundbreaking *La violence et le sacré*,[3] that René Girard is one of the

---

1 Edward J. Kilmartin, S.J., *The Eucharist in the West: History and Theology* (ed. Robert J. Daly, S.J.; Collegeville, Minn.: The Liturgical Press, 1998), p. 182.
2 See James G. Williams, *The Bible, Violence, and the Sacred: Liberation from the Myth of Sanctioned Violence* (HarperSanFrancisco, 1992), p. 261 n.17.
3 René Girard, *La violence et le sacré* (Paris: Bernard Grasset, 1972). ET: *Violence and the Sacred* (trans. Patrick Gregory; Baltimore: Johns Hopkins University Press, 1977).

seminal thinkers of the late twentieth century. He provides what might be called a unified field theory on the issue of religion and violence. One quick way to illustrate Girard's significance is to compare his contribution with that of Sigmund Freud.

> Until Freud, an impressive list of human phenomena remained fundamentally mysterious to the inquiring human mind: for example, the meaning of dreams, infantile sexuality, the activity of the subconscious, hypnosis, hysteria, and humor. Freud provided a coherent, rational explanation for all these things. Of course, not all agree with everything he finds, no more than do all who follow Girard agree with every detail of his theory; but no one can deny that Freud's insights have changed the face of Western cultural history.[4]

This, in effect, was also the claim made by the philosopher Paul Dumouchel more than two decades ago:

> Beginning from literary criticism and ending with a general theory of culture, through an explanation of the role of religion in primitive societies and a radical reinterpretation of Christianity, René Girard has completely modified the landscape in the social sciences. Ethnology, history of religion, philosophy, psychoanalysis, psychology and literary criticism are explicitly mobilized in this enterprise. Theology, economics and political sciences, history and sociology – in short, all the social sciences, and those that used to be called moral sciences – are influenced by it.[5]

There may well be many who would scoff at this claim, just as there are some who scoff at the insights of Freud while, nevertheless, still living in a world that has been shaped by Freudian insights. The comparison with Freud is particularly helpful for the way that Girard provides a coherent, rational explanation for the pervasive presence of violence not only throughout human history but also, and most especially throughout the Bible, throughout both Testaments – something that traditional biblical theologies fail to do – and throughout Christian history. A few years ago, while attempting to discuss the theme of 'Violence and Institution in the History of Christianity', I came up with the following quick list, since then somewhat expanded, of what might be called world-historical events within the history of Christianity:

1. The biblical foundation of Christianity in the Hebrew Scriptures.
2. The pervasiveness of violence in the Bible.
3. The Christian Scriptures presenting themselves as a gospel of peace.

---

4   Robert J. Daly, S.J., in the 'Foreword' of Raymnd Schwager, S.J., *Must There be Scapegoats? Violence and Redemption in the Bible* (trans. Maria L. Assad; Gracewing; A Herder & Herder Book; New York: Crossroad Publishing Company, 2000), p. v. This book, one of the better and more accessible introductions to Girardian mimetic theory, first appeared as *Brauchen wir einen Sündenbock?* (Munich: Kösel, 1978, and was first published in English by Harper & Row, San Francisco in 1987.
5   Paul Dumouchel, *Violence and Truth* (Stanford, Calif.: Stanford University Press, 1988), p. 23, as cited in Gil Bailie, *Violence Unveiled: Humanity at the Crossroads* (New York: Crossroad, 1995), p. 6.

4. Jesus and non-violence.
5. Early Christians and non-violence.
6. The early Christians and the military.
7. The 'Constantinian turn'.
8. Caesaro-papism.
9. The relegation of Christian pacifism to religious and monastic life.
10. The just war theory.
11. The medieval Christian taken-for-grantedness of violence.
12. The Crusades.
13. Medieval Christian peace movements.
14. Christians and heretics. The Inquisition. See [11] above.
15. Christianity and the witches. See [11] above.
16. The Reformation.
17. The Radical Reformation and the Peace Churches.
18. St. Bartholomew's Day Massacre (August 1572).
19. The religious wars.
20. Absolutism.
21. Modernity.
22. The Quakers – Religious Society of Friends.
23. The Enlightenment and Modernity.
24. Christianity and world mission; Christianity and colonialism.
25. Slavery.
26. Christianity and the 'war' against native cultures.
27. Christianity and the First World War.
28. The Second World War.
29. The Holocaust.
30. Christianity and the modern peace movement.
31. Christians and the 'seamless ethic of life'.
32. Christianity and International Communism.
33. Liberation theology.
34. The liberation of women.
35. Christianity and the resurgence of tribal and nationalist violence.
36. Christianity and human rights.
37. The violent ethic of the American Christian right.
38. The violent apocalyptic imaginings of the Left Behind books.[6]

This list is by no means exhaustive. It is, also, unfortunately, capable of almost indefinite expansion. But whether one reads this list as understated or overstated, as one-sided or even reasonably objective, one cannot escape the conclusion that the history of Christianity cannot be separated from the history of human violence. Normatively, i.e., in terms of its preached ideals, Christianity is a religion of peace and non-violence. Descriptively, however, Christianity has had, and often still has, a history of violence, a violent history that begins in the Bible and courses

---

6 See Robert J. Daly, S.J., 'Violence and Institution in Christianity', *Contagion, Journal of Violence, Mimesis, and Culture* 9 (Spring, 2002), pp. 5–6.

throughout the Bible, especially – at least on the level of the written text – in the Old Testament.[7] How can we explain this? Christian biblical theologians have generally sidestepped the issue, using allegory and other devices to explain away violence rather than attempt to explain why it is there. Girard gives us a way to begin to understand violence, to begin to explain it; it is precisely on that point that he can be compared to Freud.

Girardian mimetic theory can seem forbiddingly complex. Those who have thought that they can quickly figure it out by thumbing through, for example, *The Girard Reader*,[8] know this quite well. Raymund Schwager, however, helpfully suggests that its fundamental insights can be summed up in a few points:

1. Fundamental human desire is of itself not oriented towards a specific object. It strives after the good that has been pointed out as worthy of effort by someone else's desire. It imitates a model.
2. Imitating the striving of another person (who is also one's model) inevitably leads to conflict, because the other's desire aims at the same object as one's own desire. The model immediately becomes a rival. In the process, the disputed object is forgotten. As desire increases, it focuses more and more on the other's desire, admires and resents it together. The rivalry tends finally toward violence, which itself begins to appear desirable. Violence becomes the indicator, and hence worthy of imitation, of a successful life.
3. Since all human beings have a tendency toward violence, living together peacefully is anything but natural. Reason and good will (social contract) are not enough. Outbreaking rivalries can easily endanger the existing order, dissolve norms, and wipe out notions of culture. New spheres of relative peace are created however, when mutual aggressions suddenly shift into the unanimous violence of all against one (scapegoat mechanism).
4. The collective unloading of passion onto a scapegoat renders the victim sacred. He or she appears as simultaneously accursed and life-bringing. Sacred awe emanates from him or her. Around him or her arise taboo rituals and a new social order.
5. The sacrifices subsequently carry out in strictly controlled ritual limits the original collective transfer of violence onto a random scapegoat. Internal aggressions are thus diverted once again to the outside, and the community is saved from self-destruction.[9]

---

7   This is undeniably true, at least on the level of the written text. There are more than 600 biblical passages that contain accounts of violence, often massive violence. As Schwager has pointed out in *Must There Be Scapegoats?* (p. 47) no other 'activity' is as frequently mentioned in the pages of the Bible as violence.
8   *The Girard Reader* (ed. James G. Williams; New York: Crossroad, 1996).
9   Schwager, *Must There Be Scapegoats?* pp. 46–47.

Chapter II

Grand Narratives in a Postmodern Age

In a postmodern age, an age of deconstruction, we quickly learn that it is politically correct to be mistrustful and suspicious of any and all 'grand narratives', those big, broad-ranging, broad-brushed cover stories that claim to explain the way things are (or are supposed to be), the way things work (or are supposed to work). Some of the more influential of these grand narratives from the age of Western modernity are associated with the following figures:

Thomas Hobbes (1588–1679)
John Locke (1632–1704)
Jean-Jacques Rousseau (1712–78)
Georg Wilhelm Friedrich Hegel (1770–1831)
Karl Heinrich Marx (1818–83)
Sigmund Freud (1856–1939)
Friedrich Wilhelm Nietzsche (1844–1900)

In addition, there are two additional grand narratives to which we accord special attention in the present study:

Judaism and Christianity
René Girard and Mimetic Theory

In the present age we all, at least to some extent, buy into the hermeneutics of suspicion. We are suspicious of the pretensions of these grand narratives. And while we may accord special status to the grand narratives of Judaeo-Christianity and of our mentor René Girard, we are suspicious of their narratives too, or at least of the way that some of their followers understand these narratives. Now this is not simply because it is 'cool' to be suspicious. It is also because we've learned that grand narratives tend to get superseded or modified by other grand narratives that do a better job of telling the big story – or at least tell it in a way that is more congenial, more politically or intellectually 'correct' for those living in a different age. Nevertheless, it is also clear that we also continue to learn from many of these grand narratives. Even if we reject them, or consider them hopelessly outmoded, we really do stand on their shoulders.

The grand narrative of Christianity, as cannot be denied by any clear-sighted observer, is filled with ambiguity. Descriptively, and in its actual history, Christianity is, just like any other grand narrative, subject to post-modernity's critique. Normatively, however, in the authentic teaching and example of Jesus, and in the way that this is lived out in the lives of those we revere as saints, Christianity transcends this critique. But even at their best, Christians are always only striving towards that point of transcendence. And even the saintly heroes of the past, those who seem to have achieved or at least approached this transcendence have often done so with theological presuppositions that we now, from a more developed Christian standpoint, and even without being patronizing, must categorize as inadequately or even inauthentically Christian. Girardian and mimetic theory illustrates this ambiguity, this being still just 'on the way' to the full, authentic story.

To jump now right into the middle of Girardian mimetic theory, notice the central role played in it by *desire*. Recall the first two of the five points (quoted above) with which Schwager summed up Girard's theory:

1. Fundamental human desire is of itself not oriented towards a specific object. It strives after the good that has been pointed out as worthy of effort by someone else's desire. It imitates a model.

2. Imitating the striving of another person (who is also one's model) inevitably leads to conflict, because the other's desire aims at the same object as one's own desire. The model immediately becomes a rival. In the process, the disputed object is forgotten. As desire increases, it focuses more and more on the other's desire, admires and resents it together. The rivalry tends finally toward violence, which itself begins to appear desirable. Violence becomes the indicator, and hence worthy of imitation, of a successful life.

Chapter III

Desire

'Fundamental human desire' are the words with which Schwager begins his capsule summary of Girardian mimetic theory. This is absolutely central. It flows from, but does not totally depend on the accuracy of Girard's particular version of the 'great story' of the origins of human culture outlined in *Violence and the Sacred*. A striking illustration of this can be found in Gil Bailie's imaginative and revelatory account of a nursery scene:

> Imagine a scene. A small child is sitting alone in a nursery that has a couple of dozen toys scattered about it. He sits there rather dreamily, exhibiting only a casual interest in the toy that just happens to be nearby. Another child comes into the nursery and surveys the room. He sees the first child and a great number of toys. There will come a moment when the second will choose a toy. Which of the toys will he most likely find interesting? The first parent you meet will be able to tell you. It will likely be the toy with which the first child seems to be interested, although the first child's interest is yet only a casual one. The second child will no

doubt be more interested in the first child than in any of the toys, but this interest will almost instantly be translated into a concern for the toy for which the first child has shown some interest. Dealing with the resulting squabbles is an almost constant aspect of child-rearing. We joke about it. We shrug our shoulders. We even try to exploit it in order to elicit the behavior we want. But we almost never ask what this familiar phenomenon tells us about *desire*, and about the little bundle of it that we like to call the *self*.

Imagine, now, what most parents would predict. The second child becomes interested in the toy for which the first child has shown an interest. The second child reaches for the toy. What happens? The first child's nonchalance vanishes in an instant. Suddenly, he clings to the toy for dear life. Extremely vexed, the first child says, 'I had that!' His intense reaction arouses in the second child a desire for the toy vastly more powerful than the rather mild one with which he had first reached for it. The two children simply feed each other's desire for the toy by demonstrating to each other how desirable it is. Each further intensifies the desire of his rival by threatening to foreclose the possibility of possession. As the emotions rise, the opportunity for parental compromise declines rapidly. Each child treats the suggestion that he take turns playing with the toy as a betrayal by the adult who makes it . . . As long as the conflict remains unresolved, the suggestion that both children bear some responsibility for the squabble will be resolutely rejected. Each child will be certain that the other is the sole cause of the conflict.

Already in the children's nursery, therefore, we have the basic dynamic of scapegoating fully manifested . . . the same dynamics – writ large – that operate in religious or ethnic or nationalistic conflicts.[10]

Many other examples can be adduced to show that *mimetic* desire (not just desire pure and simple) is fundamentally central to who and what we are, and to how we act as human beings. With this point made, with what has been thus far 'unveiled', we can now look to what is undeniably central to Judaeo Christianity: the Ten Commandments.

Notice how the Ten Commandments culminate in the prohibition of desire. Whereas the previous commandments in the second half of the Decalogue all prohibit acts of violence against one's neighbour: You shall not kill . . . not commit adultery . . . not steal . . . not bear false witness against your neighbour,

the tenth and last commandment is distinguished from those preceding it both by its length and its object: in place of prohibiting an *act* it forbids a *desire*.

You shall not covet the house of your neighbor. You shall not covet the wife of your neighbor, nor his male or female slave, nor his ox or ass, nor anything that belongs to him.

(Exod. 20.17)[11]

---

10   Gil Bailie, *Violence Unveiled*, pp. 116–17.
11   René Girard, *I See Satan Fall Like Lightning* (Maryknoll, New York: Orbis), p. 7.

Girard, relying apparently on the research of Williams,[12] points out that the Hebrew term, *chamad*, translated as 'covet' means, just simply, 'desire'. Williams had previously pointed out that the final commandment articulates, as a kind of *conclusio*, the ethical principle underlying the four previous commandments.[13] But now, before we go on to speak of original sin as disordered desire, we alert the reader to the way that we will return to the centrality of this concept of desire when, turning to the positive, we speak of the phenomenology of redemption (i.e. sacrifice) in the final two chapters (VII and VIII) of this section Bridge 2 C.

Chapter IV

Original Sin as Disordered Desire

Traditional (especially Western) Christian theology distinguishes between two aspects of original sin: first, original sin at its origin, the primordial sin, and second, the effects of that sin in all (subsequent) human beings, i.e., the proneness or susceptibility to sin that characterizes the human condition. The primordial sin in the narrative of biblical revelation is the sin of Adam and Eve recounted in Genesis 3. Sean Fagan is reflecting a consensus position of modern Christian (at least non-fundamentalist) theology when he writes:

> It is now recognized that Genesis 3 is not a literal description of an historical first sin but an ingenious psychological description of all sin, telling us nothing of what happened at the beginning of human history, but reminding us of what is happening all the time in our sinful existence. It needs to be read not in the past tense but in the continuous present.[14]

When we read Genesis 3 in this way, we find ourselves asking: what is it, then, that God wants to forbid to Adam and Eve, that God wants to forbid to human beings? God can give everything to human beings *except* that they don't owe. We *are* receivers of gifts. We cannot deny that. (And actually, if one takes that away entirely, we simply don't exist.) We cannot deny that, cannot deny what we are except by sinning. Original sin, therefore, is the sin of non-receptivity. It is denying

---

12 Girard is himself not trained as a theologian and is sometimes hesitant to draw theological conclusions or spell out the theological implications of his position. But, over the years, he has shown an ability to learn from the theologians (among whom I modestly include myself) who have been learning from him. Here, the theologian in question is James G. Williams, *The Bible, Violence, and the Sacred*, pp. 108–13. Williams points out that the final commandment articulates the ethical principle underlying the four previous commandments.
13 Ibid., 112–13.
14 Sean Fagan, S.M., 'Original Sin' in: *The Modern Catholic Encyclopedia* (ed. Michael Glazier and Monika K. Hellwig; Collegeville, Minn.: Liturgical Press, rev. expanded edn, 2004), pp. 597–99 (598).

what one is and wanting to be, *desiring* to be (or desiring to have) something else, which brings us back to the prohibition against desiring that we find at the end of the Decalogue.

Notice how this is not just an interpretation of the text. It is a reading of, an uncovering of what is actually there. 'You will be like God, knowing good and evil' the serpent temptingly promises in Genesis 3.5. What incredibly perverse irony! – since Genesis 1.26 has proclaimed from the outset that humankind, male and female, has been created in the image and likeness of God. They already are *like* God! But they desire more. They want to *be* God. The use of the Hebrew *chamad* in the Adam and Eve story (Genesis 2.9 and 3.6) is telling. As we have already pointed out, that is the word that is translated *covet* in the last of the Ten Commandments. 'The verb seems usually to express a desire that strongly impels one towards acquiring the object of attraction'.[15] That's what is going on 'when the woman saw that the tree was good for food, and that it was a delight to the eyes, and that the tree was to be *desired* (*chamad*) to make one wise' (Genesis 3.6).

All this suggests that *our* sin, here and now, is the sin of *non-receptivity*, the sin of *coveting*, the sinful condition of what Girardians call *acquisitive mimesis*: wanting to be like God; wanting to be like those who have what we want; wanting to have what they want and have – and willing to do whatever may be necessary, to kill if necessary, in order to get it. And indeed, the next episode in this 'ingenious psychological description of all sin' is the story of the first murder: Cain killing his brother Abel. Notice the summarizing statement of Genesis 6.11–13, that 'the earth was filled with violence'. God is going to fix that. But the solution – the divine solution, let's not forget – was also violent. For this is the beginning of the Noah flood story.

Let's now modulate this tune, change perspective, and look at this from a modern, scientific point of view. Take our human nature: we seem to be inherently sinful, or, in more neutral, modern terms, all messed up. We are in a constant struggle to keep from killing each other, for, most of us most of the time seem to be willing and ready to use whatever force may be necessary to be number one. Are we sinning as we engage in that struggle? Or, are we merely the top dogs in the food chain, perhaps even occupying some unique position there, as the 'moderns' (Hobbes, Locke, Rousseau, etc.) have conditioned us to assume? *Or*, are we above that? Or at least called to be above that? The Girardian story of human origins begins to answer that question in a sober, but basically optimistic way. This is how Gil Bailie puts it:

> Jesus' whole life, ministry, and death had the effect of restoring to their senses those who had eyes but could not see and ears but could not hear. If the healing of disease or the curing of afflictions involves a suspension of the 'laws' of nature, softening the human heart or refashioning the human self requires that social and psychological reflexes relied upon and reinforced 'since the foundation of the world' be overridden. So tenacious are these reflexes that they have

---

15 Williams, *The Bible, Violence, and the Sacred*, p. 112. Williams cautiously notes that there could be some question about this precise meaning.

often enough been thought synonymous with 'human *nature*.' Transcending these reflexes, or suppressing their influence, is at least as arduous a feat as manipulating objects in the material order, and vastly more spiritually significant.[16]

Remember *Hobbes*'s story of the human state of nature in which all were equal because even the weakest, if he would just wait for the right opportunity, could kill the strongest. Recall how accurate it seems to be as a possible history of the origin of human civilization, and how much it can still explain what might still happen, for example, in Iraq and in other hotspots in the Middle East in 2009, if there is no power strong enough to impose order and peace. Girard's basic story is structurally quite similar. It too is insightful as a revelation to us of our self-destructively violent human condition, and of how human culture manages to survive, specifically via the culture-saving function of the scapegoat mechanism, i.e., when self-destructive violence threatens to get out of hand, you:

- find a convenient victim (at first, this can happen by accident, serendipitously),
- gang up on him/her,
- discover that this results in peace/harmony,
- and then, sense/see something 'sacred' in this victim, something even 'divine',
- in the next crisis, this process repeats itself,
- thus, the ganging up on a convenient victim happens again, and again a measure of peace results,
- this gets repeated, and eventually it is just ritually repeated with surrogate victims (animals instead of humans).

It works! But it involves a deception. *It depends on the participants believing in the guilt of the victim.* Whether or not the victim is actually guilty is irrelevant, as long as people *believe* that the victim is guilty, or *assume* that the victim is guilty, or assume that the victim has little or no value except to function as the needed victim … or … whatever they believe about the victim, *they believe that this process works.*

Hence the title of Gil Bailie's book, *Violence Unveiled.*[17] What does 'unveil' mean? Remember the film *The Wizard of Oz*? Once the wizard is unveiled, his power is gone. In our case, the unveiling that is going forward brings it about that *the scapegoating mechanisms on which culture depends become less and less effective.* As horribly widespread as these mechanisms still are, they seem to be on the wane. Now, in the story that we Christians tell – remember, there is no such thing as not having a story – who or what is the center of our story? It is Jesus Christ, a victim. So, from what point of view, from whose perspective, do we tell our story? *From the perspective of Jesus Christ the victim!!!*

---

16 *Bailie, Violence Unveiled*, p. 216.
17 *Violence Unveiled*, the book whose title inspired the title of our own *Sacrifice Unveiled*, is probably the best book available for mediating to a wide readership the insights of Girardian mimetic theory. *Sacrifice Unveiled* tries to 'unveil' for a wide readership the meaning of authentic Christian sacrifice.

- Do we believe in the guilt of Jesus Christ the victim?
- Is it irrelevant whether or not this victim, Jesus, is guilty or innocent?
- Can we believe, or assume, that Jesus Christ is guilty?
- Or, even regardless of all that, should this have happened to him?

What, now, is our 'instinctive' attitude towards victims, our instinctive attitude towards an underdog? Doesn't this attitude still hold, at least to some extent, even if the victim is actually guilty? Is not this 'instinctinve' identification with the underdog, the persecuted, the oppressed, the abused, largely due to the influence of Christianity? The claim here, a claim based on careful observation and reflection, is that this 'instinct' is a learned and specifically (though perhaps not exclusively) Christian response. In other words, take away Christianity and that instinct is not there, or at least not there as strongly as it is now. And conversely, take away that instinctive siding with the victim, and Christianity is eviscerated. Hence, the intensity of the reaction of so many people in our basically Christian society to the institutional Church's insensitivity to the victims in the recent clergy sex-abuse scandals. Whether or not they are able to articulate it, people know 'in their gut' that such insensitivity, such non-siding with victims is profoundly un-Christian.

In other words, and to repeat for emphasis, the effectiveness of the scapegoat mechanism – the channelling of acquisitive, conflictual, self-destructive mimesis onto a convenient victim, and thus being saved from self-destructive violence – that effectiveness depends on the innocence of the victim remaining veiled. Unveil the victim, identify with the victim, and culture is in crisis:

- In the Cold War, Americans needed communism to unite them, give them 'someone' to gang up on.
- With communism no longer a threat, is the West now replacing it with radical Islam?
- Conversely, radical Islam needs the evil Americans to gang up against.
- Homophobic people need gays to gang up against.
- The Christian middle ages needed infidels (hence the Crusades) to gang up against.
- The Nazis needed the Jews to scapegoat.
- Red Sox fans need the Yankees (notice the similarity between Red Sox Nation referring to the Yankees as 'the evil empire' and President George W. Bush referring to Iraq/Iran/North Korea as the 'axis of evil'.
- And, of course, Boston College needs Notre Dame, Harvard needs Yale, etc., etc.

The list could go on indefinitely, for we are talking about a fundamental human mechanism that extends from the sublimely important down to the everyday trivial. Characteristic of all these instances, and in order for the mechanism to have its unifying, culture-forming and culture-preserving effect, the innocence, or at least the non-guilt of the scapegoated victim has to remain veiled.

The authentic Christian story (of course, there are many inauthentic Christian stories) is a story that is being told from the point of view of the victims, especially from the point of view of the primary victim, Jesus Christ. In other words, stated directly and succinctly, *authentic Christianity identifies with Jesus and strives to imitate the desire of Jesus.*

Chapter V

Original Sin: A Scientific View

In *Banished from Eden*,[18] Raymund Schwager offers an illuminating scientific reconstruction of original sin that can be helpful to us in understanding the depth of the challenge we face in our attempts to overcome violence. Methodologically, Schwager is also suggesting a model of how theologians should deal with data from the natural sciences. Ordinarily, theologians (and not just preachers) would begin with a doctrine or a theological position, and then, reactively, look to see how this position is supported by or challenged by scientific data, evidence or claims. Put simplistically, theologians working according to this model are not looking to science as a primary source of knowledge or understanding, but only to see whether and how science fits in with their already established theological position. Schwager suggests that we should instead, or at the very least also, work the other way around, i.e., we should *first* try to understand the findings of the sciences on their own scientific terms, and then, only then, try to see what light those findings might shed on religious or doctrinal data. In other words, start by taking science seriously on its own terms.

One of the findings of modern biology and microbiology, Schwager reminds us, is that all organisms, from the most simple to the most complex, have memory. Nothing that happens to an organism is ever completely 'forgotten'. It remains in a kind of memory bank influencing the later life of the organism. Whether or not this is significantly verifiable for the most minute of micro-organisms – though it clearly explains why antibiotics work at first, and then later don't work – it is clearly one of the most obvious characteristics of the higher organisms. And since Freud we are acutely aware of how true this is for the super-complex organisms that human beings are. When we, then, in the context of Girardian mimetic theory, take this scientific finding of contemporary evolutionary biology as the starting point of an attempt to understand original sin, some excitingly illuminating results suggest themselves.

In pursuing this, we are, of course, crafting another hypothetical 'great story'. And, like all great stories, its usefulness will have to be judged by the extent to which it offers an improved explanation of our past (how we humans came about

---

18   Raymund Schwager, *Banished from Eden: Original Sin and Evolutionary Theory in the Drama of Salvation* (trans. James Williams; Leominster, Herefordshire: Gracewing, 2006) = the ET of *Erbsünde und Heilsdrama: Im Kontext von Evolution, Gentechnologie und Apokalyptik* (Münster: Lit Verlag/Thaur: Verlagshaus Thaur, 1997).

and evolved), our present (the challenges with which we are now faced) and our future (how we might work to make things better). As for the past, the focal point is the 'moment' or process of hominization, This is the term that philosophers, theologians and evolutionary thinkers, among others, give to the process of 'the development of the higher characteristics that are thought to distinguish [humans] from other animals'.[19] In traditional philosophical terms, it was the process of moving from animal instinct as the principal source of action, to human reason as the preferred principal source of action. In traditional theological terms, it was the process of becoming a free subject capable of relating to the transcendent. How long this process took, and whether its critical transitional points were focused in a relatively short period of time, or spread out over a long period of time, is not the point at issue here. The point is, to build on scientific data that we do have, and then, relying on the insights of mimetic theory, to reconstruct the 'event' of human origins; and then to ask critically whether that hypothetical reconstruction has heuristic value in helping us to make sense of our human past, present and future.

Schwager invites us to imagine the critical point of hominization, whether we consider it as a kind of knife-edge event, or as a long, ongoing process extending over thousands of generations, even continuing into our own day and beyond, and to imagine it in this way: it is the point where, however inarticulately, the now-becoming human being becomes aware of him/herself as capable of acting in a way that transcends animal instinct. The now-becoming human being has choice. Instinct will no longer suffice to preserve and protect the human being the way it does the other higher organisms. The human being now must choose, must decide, how to live, how to survive. How does the human being now do this? Does the human being choose the spiritual, the transcendent, or does the human being now do by choice that which the animals continue to do by instinct? From all that we can reconstruct from our prehistoric past, to say nothing of the fairly consistent message we get from the prehistoric myths, our human forebears most often chose violence: survival of the fittest, might makes right, etc., etc. In other words, hominization, both in its origin and in its continuation in human history, has been the process of human beings receiving the gift/offer of self-transcendence and, more often than not, turning it into self-assertion. This is the process of *acquisitive mimesis*. At this point in the reconstruction, it matters little what particular 'great story' we follow, whether that of a Thomas Hobbes postulating an inherently violent, might-makes-right human being whose life was 'nasty, brutish, and short'[20] until, by some kind of social contract a magistrate was given enough power to impose order by violent force ... or perhaps we follow a René Girard who envisions our forebears serendipitously discovering that they can escape their mutually destructive violence by offloading it onto a convenient scapegoat. It doesn't matter. Whatever great story we follow or reconstruct for ourselves, if the story deals with the reality of human history, it is a story of violence.

---

19   S.v. 'hominization' in: *The New Shorter Oxford English Dictionary* (Oxford: Clarendon Press, 1993), p. 1252.
20   Thomas Hobbes, *Leviathan* (ed. Edwin Curley; Indianapolis/Cambridge: Hackett Publishing Co., 1994), Chapter 13, no. 9, p. 76.

This brings us back to Schwager reminding us about all organisms having memory. An integral part of our historical and psychosocial memory is a memory of violence. The choices that our human forebears made, the choices that first constituted them as human, distinct from the animals, the choices by which they managed to survive and come down to this day, the choices by which we human beings manage to survive in this present world, the choices that we will probably continue to make as we move into our future, are, characteristically, violent choices. As human beings, we are conditioned to violence. We are conditioned to rely on the violence of the scapegoat mechanism to save our skins. Violence is our original sin. But that violence is being unveiled. The culture-saving scapegoat mechanism is becoming less and less effective. We are, therefore, increasingly in crisis. Can we be healed of the violence (sacred, sacrificial violence in the Girardian great story) that used to save us, but, increasingly unveiled, will now destroy us?

Serendipitously, in February 2007, just as I was about to finish working on the first draft of what has become this section of this book, the most recent issue of *Contagion* arrived with an article that, totally independent of the work of Raymund Schwager on this point, powerfully undergirds what I have been attempting to say here.[21] At this point, I can only quote the 'Summary' with which the author, Scott Garrels, concludes each of the two main parts of his article. To conclude his section on 'Imitation in Developmental Psychology and Neuroscience', he writes:

The combined efforts of developmental psychology, neurophysiology, and cognitive neuroscience have produced a dramatic array of data elucidating the role and mechanisms of imitation. This brief survey is admittedly selective and schematic; however, the implications are revolutionary in regard to the social sciences. The above research demonstrates the profound significance of reciprocal imitative phenomena at both neural and behavior levels. Imitation is no longer seen as a mindless act expressing simple mimicry, but rather a fundamental and inherently positive mechanism stimulating the individual mind to develop through its relationship with another mind. The congruence of such reciprocity of minds, along with the ability to delay imitation, is understood as the basis for the emergence of more diverse and complex behaviors and representations, including human language and the development of a theory of mind.[22]

To conclude his section on 'Convergence between Mimetic Theory and Imitation Research', he writes:

While mimetic scholars have long stressed the primordial role of psychological mimesis in human motivation and social relations, it is only recently that empirical research has been able to account for and support such reciprocity of experience, even at a level as basic as that of individual neurons. Taken together,

21   Scott R. Garrels, 'Imitation, Mirror Neurons, and Mimetic Desire: Convergence between the Mimetic Theory of René Girard and Empirical Research on Imitation', *Contagion: Journal of Violence, Mimesis, and Culture* 12–13 (2006), pp. 47–86.
22   Garrels, 'Imitation, Mirror Neurons', etc., p. 68.

imitation research, still in its infancy, alongside mimetic theory, provides a complementary set of theories, which inevitably lead to greater clarity and explanatory depth on human mimesis, which is not found in Girard's work alone or in the work of those who have advanced his ideas. In addition, the developing fields of developmental psychology and cognitive neuroscience are influenced by and dependent upon disciplines such as anthropology, philosophy, literary analysis, and theology, all of which approach similar or unique questions from differing sources and points of view. Without these other disciplines, neuroscience would not be able to ask the questions that it does, or apply its findings in a meaningful preexisting framework of knowledge. For example, the broader implications relevant to mimetic theory did not originate within the empirical sciences but from literary, anthropological, and historical investigations. At the same time, Girard's entire corpus of work rests on the primacy of human imitative behavior, the significance of which must be measured against the unfolding and revolutionary research in the fields of developmental psychology and cognitive neuroscience.[23]

Garrels then concludes his article with the following prognostication:

When imitation research is viewed through the lens of mimetic theory, one sees not only the building blocks of relatedness, mindfulness, and meaningfulness but also the mechanisms of distortion, disillusionment, and violence. If a reciprocating feedback loop between mimetic scholars and imitation researchers can be established – and I believe wholeheartedly that it is inevitable – the social sciences may begin to better appreciate and understand the incredible nature of human life, culture, and religion, an appreciation that is essential in transforming human culture and relationships through infinitely more imaginative and non-violent ways of learning.[24]

All this provides critical support and validation for the attempt (see below, Chapter VII, pp. 219–21) to begin to articulate a phenomenology of redemption, of the way, ultimately, that Christian sacrifice 'works' in the process of atonement. But first, a few words about René Girard as a Christian theorist.

---

23   Ibid., 79–80.
24   Ibid., 80.

Chapter VI

René Girard as Christian Theorist

One of the striking things about the history of Girardian mimetic theory was that, in its initial formulations in the mind of Girard, it was not consciously Christian. Looked at from the outside, it seems to have become increasingly more Christian as time went on, and indeed quite strongly Christian in Girard's recent 2001 (French 1999) *I See Satan Fall Like Lightning*. But looked at from the inside, Girardian mimetic theory did not *become* Christian in the course of time. Rather, in the course of time, it discovered how profoundly Christian it was all along. *La Violence et le sacré* (ET: *Violence and the Sacred* [1977]), the definitive theoretical articulation of the theory in 1972, was published well after Girard himself had discovered how profoundly Christian his thinking actually was. That book, however, did not emphasize this fact. This can be verified not only bibliographically, but also biographically.

Girard published four books in the 1970s, but two of them stand out. The first was his highly acclaimed *La Violence et le sacré* in 1972. The second was his somewhat controversial *Des choses chachées depuis la fondation du monde* in 1978.[25] It was controversial because it did something that, for many people in the intellectual world, was not politically correct. It placed the Bible and Christian revelation at the very heart of things. As James Williams put it, speaking of this book:

> [T]he heart of the book, right at the center of its format and central to its argument, is the thesis that the biblical revelation, the disclosure of 'things hidden since the foundation of the world,' is the key to understanding human violence, human history, and human knowledge. What had been hidden in culture and its formation through the sacred was the violence done to victims and camouflaged in prohibition, ritual, and myth. The sacred as violence is demythologized in the tendency of biblical narratives to side with the victim against the persecuting community and in the biblical witness to the God of victims. This exposure of sacred violence and affirmation of the God who sides with victims is fully realized in the Gospel texts, in which Christ is the perfect revelation of the innocent victim.[26]

A glance at Girard's bibliography reveals that, subsequent to the 1978 publication of *Des choses chachées/Things Hidden*, Girard has indeed turned his attention increasingly to biblical and Christian theological themes.

---

25 René Girard, *Des choses chachées depuis la fondation du monde*, with Jean-Michel Oughourlian and Guy Lefort (Paris: Grasset, 1978) ET: *Things Hidden Since the Foundation of the World* (trans. Stephen Bann and Michael Metteer; London: Athlone/Stanford: Stanford University Press, 1987). See Matthew 13.35 which in the final part of the verse, a reworking of Psalm 78:2, provides the title of this book: 'I will open my mouth to speak in parables; I will proclaim what has been hidden from the foundation of the world'.

26 James G. Williams in the Foreword to René Girard, *Resurrection from the Underground: Feodor Dostoevsky* (ed. and trans. James G. Williams; New York: Crossroad, 1997), p. 9.

But there is also biographical evidence. A significant part of this came to light in a public way at the 2–5 June 2004 meeting of the Colloquium on Violence and Religion – COV&R[27] at Ghost Ranch, in Northern New Mexico. This meeting began with a symposium tribute to the recently deceased Innsbruck Professor, Raymund Schwager, S.J. Father Schwager was recognized as the premier theological mind among the Girardian scholars who constitute the international membership of COV&R. The biographical aspects of this posthumous tribute to him help explain why. When Schwager, a young Swiss Jesuit theologian, read *La violence et le sacré* when it first appeared in 1972, he immediately recognized its theological implications. He made contact with Girard, and the two quickly developed a close personal and especially intellectual relationship that lasted until Schwager's death more than three decades later.

For Schwager, this intellectual encounter and friendship meant that mimetic theory became the leitmotiv of his subsequent voluminous theological work.[28] What Girard had been discovering and expressing in literary, psychological and anthropological terms was what Schwager had been learning and spiritually appropriating as a Jesuit schooled in the Spiritual Exercises of Ignatius of Loyola. For Girard, this encounter with Schwager meant a significant confirmation of the intellectual-plus-religious conversion to catholic Christianity (catholic in the broad, ecumenical sense) that had already started more than a decade earlier.[29] That conversion, both intellectual and religious, was something that had not yet been fully expressed in Girard's academic writing. That is what took place in the 1978 *Des choses cachées/Things Hidden from the Foundation of the World*. In other words, the insights that Girard had been uncovering in the world's great literature and in philosophy and the social sciences, the insights that sparkle from the pages of his acclaimed 1972 *La Violence et le sacré/Violence and the Sacred* were now publicly proclaimed as being profoundly Christian. Hence, the consternation of those who, like Girard himself just a few years earlier, assumed that real scholarship is not supposed to be influenced by biblical faith or any other kind of faith.[30] This

---

27 The Colloquium on Violence and Religion – COV&R – is the international English-speaking organization of some 400 members, half European and half North American, that is dedicated to the study of mimetic theory and the works of René Girard. It has a 3-day annual meeting, usually alternating between North America and Europe, publishes an annual journal called *Contagion, Journal of Violence, Mimesis, and Culture* and a twice-a-year *Bulletin*. Extensive information is available via the web site (http://theol.uibk.ac.at/cover/) that also contains all but the current copies of the journal and the bulletin. COV&R is far and away the most interdisciplinary academic organization known to this author. Law, Education, Psychology and Psychiatry, Anthropology, History, Sociology, Political Science, Environmental Studies, Ethnology, Economics, Spirituality and Pastoral Studies as well as Philosophy and Theology are among the disciplines represented by its various members.

28 One of the first of these works was the 1978 publication of the book translated into English under the title: *Must There Be Scapegoats? Violence and Redemption in the Bible* (1987) that we pointed to above at the beginning of our treatment of Girard.

29 For Girard's own description of this conversion experience, see 'Epilogue: the Anthropology of the Cross: A Conversation with René Girard' in: *The Girard Reader*, pp. 262–88 (283–88).

30 'In France he was a *cause célebre* or a *bête noire*, because his argument for a universal anthropological theory, combined with the position that the deepest insights of Western culture stem from biblical revelation, shocked and alienated those who held to the assumption of the all-encompassing nature of language and who tended to ignore Christianity or view it with contempt' – James G. Williams, 'René Girard: A Biographical Sketch' in: idem, ed., *The Girard Reader*, p. 4.

development obviously made Girard something of a controversial figure, something that he has had to deal with for the rest of his life. And, that Girard himself may have been struggling with the implications of his conversion is suggested by the fact that the steady stream of his publications seems to have been noticeably lighter in the years between the first appearance of *Violence and the Sacred* in 1972 and the appearance of *Things Hidden since the Foundation of the World* 6 years later.

To round off this section on René Girard as Christian theorist, let me point out the striking parallel between Girard's evolution from a non-religious (or at least a-religious) theorist to a Christian theorist, and Bailie's words as he concluded his book:

> This began as a book about the present anthropological, cultural, and historical crisis, analyzed in the light of the remarkable work of René Girard. At the outset, I had no intention of ending it, as I have, on such a confessional note. It has ended that way because writing it has drawn me ever deeper into the mysterious power of the Christian revelation, and it would be silly to put on a wooden face and pretend otherwise . . . I have come to realize the degree to which his [Girard's] groundbreaking work is part of what Andrew McKenna has called 'the legacy of the crucifixion narrative'.[31]

Chapter VII

A Phenomenology of Redemption: Imitate the Desire of Jesus

A quote from René Girard:

> Jesus is not there in order to stress once again in his own person the unified violence of the sacred; he is not there to ordain and govern like Moses; he is not there to unite people around him, to forge its unity in the crucible of rites and prohibitions, but on the contrary, to turn this long page of human history once for all.[32]

A quote from Jesus:

> I still have many things to say to you but you cannot bear them now. When the Spirit of Truth comes he will guide you into all the truth; for he will not speak on his own, but will speak whatever he hears and he will declare to you all the things that are to come.
>
> (John 16.12–13)

---

31   Bailie, *Violence Unveiled*, p. 275.
32   René Girard, *Things Hidden Since the Foundation of the World*, p. 204, as cited in Bailie, *Violence Unveiled*, p. 217.

This chapter would be disappointingly incomplete if it described only the crisis that Girardian mimetic theory unveils. What hope can it offer for the future? The beginning of an answer is to point out that mimetic theory begins to articulate a phenomenology of redemption.[33] 'Phenomenology of redemption' is basically synonymous with 'phenomenology of atonement' which in turn, as I have been pointing out, is practically synonymous with 'phenomenology of Christian sacrifice'. By this I mean a description, in social-scientific terms, of the process, or of the effects of the process of what we theologically call redemption, or atonement, or Christian sacrifice. The inner essence of redemption/atonement/Christian sacrifice is, of course, an action or event in the spiritual realm of divine grace. As such it transcends the capacity of human concepts or words to describe it. But redemption/Christian sacrifice is also something that is taking place in human, this-world space and time. These effects, therefore, that are taking place in observable space and time, are patient of social-scientific, i.e., phenomenological analysis. One can also argue – but this, of course is where it begins to get 'sticky', that it is also possible for us to reach back at least somewhat towards the cause of these effects.

From at least the golden age of patristic writings untold volumes have been written, and are still being written, about the practical, spiritual and sometimes mystical experiences of conversion and the life of grace. Preachers, spiritual writers and theologians are constantly talking about what it means to be 'saved'. But they have generally been doing this on a devotional, non-scholarly level, or, if scholarly, then inevitably in school-theological terms that have little or no connection with contemporary thought. Most theologians don't get around to asking about what is happening phenomenologically, i.e., psychologically, sociologically, anthropologically, culturally, economically and politically, when people are experiencing salvation.

One of the central phenomenological facts we are dealing with is that human beings are by nature ineluctably mimetic beings. Thus, mimesis is integral not only to that from which we need to be saved but also integral to the process that we hope will save us. If Girard's analysis of the phenomenon (or congeries of phenomena) that we human beings are is an analysis that is anywhere close to the mark, if, in other words, we, precisely as human beings, are ineluctably by nature imitating someone's desire, then the mimetic activity by which, through which, in which we will be saved is the activity of imitating the desire of Jesus. In Chapter V above, 'Original Sin: A Scientific View', we spoke of hominization as the process by which human beings, in receiving the gift/offer of self-transcendence characteristically turned it into self-assertion, the process of acquisitive mimesis inevitably characterized by and committed to violence. What we (i.e., our forebears) then rejected, and what we now need more and more to accept, is the gift/offer of transformative mimesis. We must reject acquisitive and conflictive mimesis, and embrace receptive and transformative mimesis. In other words, we must look to

---

33 I am drawing on remarks from my essay 'A Phenomenology of Redemption?' to appear in a René Girard Festschrift entitled *Essays in Friendship and Truth* (ed. William A. Johnsen; Michigan State University Press, 2009), pp. 101–109.

Jesus as the one perfect image of God, and see him inviting us to imitate, not him precisely, but his desire.[34]

Chapter VIII

A Post-Scientific Epilogue

Imitate the *desire* of Jesus? As I try to explain what this means, I am conscious of sliding – or should I say 'rising'? – from one literary genre to another, from theological exposition towards (Christian) preaching. I put 'Christian' in parenthesis because, although the preaching that I do will be Christian, and specifically Catholic Christian, I try to do it in a way that will not be narrowly or exclusively Christian. For God promises and actually offers salvation to all, not just to Christians. Further, not everyone who is inspired by Girardian mimetic theory is Christian, and therefore the way in which they 'preach' the non-violent message that I preach will not be specifically Christian. However, as a Christian, it is primarily Christian preaching that I will be doing.

So we come to the question: How can we imitate the *desire* of Jesus? Doesn't that imply imitating, or putting on the *mind* of Jesus? And isn't this what Paul was groping to express (actually much more successfully than most) in Philippians 2 when he says: 'Make my joy complete' (Philippians 2.2) or, in colloquial terms: 'Make my day!' and then goes on:

> Be of the same mind, having the same love, being in full accord and of one mind. [3]Do nothing from selfish ambition or conceit, but in humility regard others as better than yourselves. [4]Let each of you look not to your own interests but to the interests of others. [5]*Let the same mind be in you that was in Christ Jesus,*
>
> [6]who, though he was in the form of God,
>   did not regard equality with God
>   as something to be exploited,
> [7]but emptied himself,
>   taking the form of a slave
>   being born in human likeness. Etc.
>
> (Philippians 2.2–7)

Verse 5 (italicized for emphasis) is the key: *the same mind that was in Christ Jesus*. In other words: think like Jesus! This, of course, means *desire* like Jesus. If you go along with this, if this makes sense to you and you buy the basic argument that

---

34   This was the main *theological* point of my article: Robert J. Daly, S.J., 'Images of God and the Imitation of God: Problems with Atonement', *Theological Studies* 68 (2007), pp. 36–51, the substance of which is included above in Part Two, Chapter I, 'Paul and Problems with Sacrificial Atonement'.

I have been developing, then we have something like what Bernard Lonergan would call an intellectual conversion; i.e., one has achieved basic understanding of what the issue or problem is.[35] Moral conversion goes further. It involves a personal commitment actually to live that way. That's quite a bit. But we're still not there. For we can be convinced that this is the right way to think about the problem of violence, and we can be committed to live and act accordingly, but we're still not home safe. However impressive intellectual and moral conversions might be, they are still relatively easy. Because we can still be – and most of us probably are – where Paul was when he agonizingly exclaimed: 'I do not understand my own actions. For I do not do what I want, but I do the very thing I hate . . . I can will what is right, but I cannot do it. For I do not do the good I want, but the evil I do not want is what I do' (Rom. 8.15, 18–19). Paul seems to be saying that he was not yet *religiously* converted.

We can easily illustrate that from our attitudes towards the problems of poverty and malnutrition. We have the scientific and technological know-how to eliminate extreme poverty and malnutrition throughout the world. We can call that intellectual conversion: we *know* how to solve the problem. We also seem to be morally committed to do that: practically all the moral and moralizing rhetoric that we can respect seems to flow in that direction. We can call that moral conversion. But we don't do it, we don't act on it, we don't make it real. Scientifically, technologically, we are able to, but we don't take the steps to do it. We are not willing to pay the price, not willing to make the 'sacrifices' (using the general, secular meaning of the word) to do it. We are not, in other words, religiously converted.

So, how do we get to religious conversion? Oh, be careful now! Most of us don't really want that. We don't really want to pay the price or make the sacrifices that would involve. Following the analysis we've tried to lay out here, we can get to religious conversion, or at least expose ourselves to it, by associating with and identifying with victims. I'm not sure there is any other way. The affluence of most of those who will be reading this book generally shields them from the victims of society. We, who are affluent, know instinctively that if we want a comfortable, secure, safe life, we must insulate ourselves from victims. But if we are Christians, when we are doing that, we will be insulating ourselves from Jesus Christ, the victim. We can't have it both ways.

But, if we want to be happy, truly happy, with a happiness that will not be illusory, then it will be a happiness that does not try to protect itself by hiding behind a veil of violence.

In other words, if we want to begin, in this life, to see the face of God, then we must look into the face of victims. True Christian sacrifice will then 'naturally' follow.

---

35 I am referring, of course, to one of the central points of Bernard J.F. Lonergan's magisterial *Method in Theology* (New York: Herder and Herder, 1972).

PART THREE

UNVEILING SACRIFICE: A JOURNEY OF DISCOVERY

In this final section, we will do the expected summing up of our conclusions, taking stock of where we are and looking ahead to what the future might have in store. We will structure this primarily by way of what will basically be autobiographical narrative. For what has been laid out in the preceding pages has really been the result of a lifetime of work, a veritable voyage of theological, spiritual and pastoral discovery. Although reactions to what I have thus far produced make me confident that the results portrayed in this volume transcend the significance of any one particular life, particularly my own, I have also learned, and not just from my experience in preaching, that telling a story is vastly more effective than attempting to explain something. The reader will notice, in addition, that while the book as a whole has the title *Sacrifice Unveiled*, the title of our conclusion is 'Unveiling Sacrifice'. This is not a job that can be done once and for all; it is an ongoing journey of discovery.

Chapter I

Beginnings

Born in 1933 of second-generation Irish and French Canadian immigrant parents in south suburban Boston, and nurtured in the ghetto-like atmosphere of working-class neighbourhood and Catholic family life, I early on ambitioned to become a priest. Remarkably, what was at first only a typically childish boyhood ambition – priests were really looked up to in the culture of those days – gradually matured into a real religious vocation. As a small boy, I wanted to be a priest because I naively thought that 'priests don't go to hell' – hell being a very real and very threatening reality in the religious mind and imagination of those days. A bit later, as an idealistic adolescent, I aspired to become a heroic missionary priest. But as adolescence faded, I began to have doubts about whether I really had the 'right stuff' for the demanding life of a missionary. But that doubt providentially coincided with my studying under the Jesuits at Boston College High School. Unsure of what kind of priest I was cut out to be, and noticing that Jesuits seemed to have their fingers in all kinds of priestly work, I figured that if they'd take me they'd find something for me to do. Happily, they took me. Barely seventeen, I entered the Jesuit novitiate at Shadowbrook in Lenox, Massachusetts.

In many ways I was still a child, an avid, long-suffering fan of the Boston Red Sox (long, long before they finally got to win it all) and lover of sports in general. Sports were my primary source of fun and joy. I was good at the books and liked to read, as long as it didn't interfere with sports. But ultimately, study was not a joy, it was only a duty. I had not yet discovered that I had a mind and that using it was to become central to the meaning of my life. By the time I hit twenty, however, I was beginning to discover the joys of art and literature, indeed so much so that English literature, instead of my earlier fascination with physics, became my 'special discipline' (Jesuits in training were expected to develop expertise in some particular academic discipline). For the next decade, English literature, in addition to a Jesuit's regular training in philosophy and theology, was my special academic focus. In line with that, I spent a year and a half in 1959–60 at The Catholic University of America getting a masters degree in medieval English literature. The success of those studies resulted in the provisional plan that, after finishing my regular Jesuit theological training, I would work for a doctorate in the literature of the Renaissance, most likely at the University of North Carolina.

However, shortly before ordination, in response to requests from my Jesuit superiors and teachers, I discovered that I would be quite happy in shifting my academic focus to theology itself. 'Dogmatic theology' was what we then called it. So after a final year of spiritual and pastoral training in Florence, Italy, I found myself in Mainz, Germany, apprenticed under Professor Doktor Johannes Betz, and planning to write a dissertation that investigated the idea of the value of suffering in the early Christian centuries. Serendipitously, I soon discovered that my Doktorvater thought I was working, not on that topic, but on the idea of sacrifice. Having learned to be adaptable, I thought to myself, 'Well, why not?' Especially since Prof. Betz was enthusiastic about the idea and I was not yet strongly wedded to my own assumptions. Thus, in the Fall of 1965, there began my lifelong engagement with the idea of Christian sacrifice.

In these few paragraphs, I have already recounted a number of significant changes and discoveries. Such changes and discoveries have happened again and again in my academic life, most of them bringing me closer and closer to producing what is appearing in this book. Ten years ago, I thought that such changes and discoveries would long since have ceased to be a part of my life. But they are still happening. And now, in my seventy-sixth year, I have given up assuming that changes and discoveries are a thing of the past.

Chapter II

Early Work on Christian Sacrifice

The first plan for my dissertation was to study the topic of sacrifice in the writings of the early third-century Christian writer, Origen of Alexandria. After 2 years, I had methodically worked through these writings, collated the relevant texts, and worked through most of the secondary literature. The dissertation was ready to be written. But not so fast! In the course of this research, I had failed to discover a reliable historical-critical study of sacrifice in the Bible that I could use as background for studying how Origen, the first great Christian biblical theologian, had dealt with sacrifice. I could indeed write the dissertation with what I already had in hand, but without the historical-critical work on the biblical background, it probably would have had no lasting scholarly value.

There was bullet there to be bitten. Being young and still full of energy, and also with the generous support of the New England Province of the Jesuits—they didn't seem to be worried that the job would now take a few extra years—I bit it. This accounts for most of the research (from my dissertation years, 1965–71) that I have summarized in the following sections of this book: Bridge 1 A: 'Sacrifice in the Ancient World and in the Hebrew Scriptures'; Bridge 1 B: 'Sacrifice in the New Testament'; and Bridge 1 C: 'Sacrifice in the Fathers of the Church'. But in the process of doing this research, another 'change' was taking place. Setting up the background for studying sacrifice in Origen took so much time that, although I eventually produced some half dozen articles on sacrifice in Origen, I never got to write the major monograph on that subject that I had thought was going to be my dissertation.

For the purposes of rounding off this book, I can summarize in a few broad strokes the major findings of this early research that had the effect of establishing me, at least in the eyes of some, as an expert on Christian sacrifice. First, from the Old Testament/Hebrew Scriptures, I discovered overwhelming evidence that atonement, the assumed primary function and purpose of sacrifice, is primarily and most emphatically not a human activity or achievement. It is not something that humans do; it is not even something that humans *can* do. For atonement was increasingly revealed in the Hebrew Scriptures as a human-directed activity of God, really a gift from God. 'Propitiation', on the other hand, was indeed something that humans did, or at least thought they could do. For propitiation was thought of as a God-directed human activity by which the human agent 'propitiated', i.e., assuaged, bought off, etc. an alienated or offended God. Such ideas are, of course, clearly found in the Bible, but mostly in the earlier, less theologically developed sections. The later phases of Hebrew biblical revelation were increasingly purified of propitiatory ideas.

Second, from the New Testament/Christian Scriptures, I was able to establish critically, and not just intuitively or by way of homiletic projection, that the primary idea of Christian sacrifice, i.e., sacrifices that Christians perform, is ethical, not cultic. Christian sacrifice, at least as far as the New Testament is concerned, is not something that happens in a temple, or church building, or in some place; it is primarily the virtuous activity of Christians incarnating in practical action the love of God that has been poured out into their hearts through the Holy Spirit that has been given to them (Rom. 5.5).

Third, while searching for a consistent thread of meaning as I worked through the New Testament, I found that the threefold Pauline division of the theology of sacrifice into (1) temple themes, (2) the sacrifice of Christ and (3) Christian sacrificial activity turned out to be not just that sought-for thread of meaning, it also provided a helpful matrix for making sense of the various Christian sacrificial themes present in the early Christian writers.

Finally, I also found that the theme of spiritualization, along with its associated and/or contrasting themes of 'Christologizing', 'incarnationalizing' and 'institutionalizing', also provided a similarly helpful model structure for making some sense of the pluriform witness to sacrifice found across these early writings.

But soon another change was in the process of taking place. When I had finished my dissertation at the university of Würzburg in Germany, and had begun my teaching and – all too soon – administrative career in theology at Boston College, I had been planning, unrealistically assuming, as it turned out, that I would build my academic career on the production of a series of historical-doctrinal monographs on Christian sacrifice, from the Bible to the present. It was a series that was to culminate in a great systematic work that brought everything together in a definitive work on Christian sacrifice. However, only a modest few pieces of that ambitious historical-doctrinal work have been achieved. I now find myself no longer able to realize that dream, but I also find myself beginning to discover that I have things to say about Christian sacrifice that seem to be excitingly revelatory, and not just to theologians and scholars.

The present book is my attempt to communicate these findings to a wide reading public. I dream that this will become a book that is not only a 'must-read' for my theological and scholarly colleagues, but also a 'can-read' for the well-educated and determined reader, especially pastors, teachers and preachers. For, as the readers of the journal *Theological Studies* already know, the central scholarly-theological findings undergirding this book are already available to and appreciated by a small circle of highly trained theologians. The remaining great need is to communicate them to a much wider circle of people.

Chapter III

Christian Sacrifice:
Liturgical and Phenomenological

The next major changes, ones that took place starting in the mid to late 1980s, were my discoveries of liturgical theology and, shortly after that, of what one might call 'theological phenomenology' in the form of Girardian mimetic theory. First, liturgical theology. My Jesuit brothers, who were already members of the North American Academy of Liturgy (NAAL), invited me to come to their 1985 annual meeting, in Philadelphia that year, to talk to them about Christian sacrifice. No group had ever invited me to speak to them about my work, so, of course, I did that. I then stayed to attend the full NAAL meeting as a guest, sitting in on the meeting of the Eucharistic Prayer and Theology Seminar. What a discovery! These were people who not only knew about my work, they also wanted to talk with me about it. I quickly discovered that liturgical theology, and not just biblically grounded systematic-sacramental theology and/or patristic theology as I had previously thought, was where I really belonged. As a result of this discovery I also became an active member in the international Societas Liturgica, cutting back necessarily, on my participation in the biblical and patristic associations. It is largely through work done in relationship with these two liturgical societies that I have produced what is summarized in several parts of this book.[1]

Second, 'theological phenomenology' – i.e., Girardian mimetic theory. Shortly after this, in the early 1990s, I came in contact with mimetic theory in a way remarkably similar to the way in which I came into contact with liturgical theology. The members of the Colloquium on Violence and Religion, an international group of scholars and practitioners studying the work and the implications of the work of René Girard, invited me to speak with them about my work on Christian sacrifice. Unless one has become overwhelmingly famous, or too old and tired to care any more, a scholar never passes up a chance to talk about his or her work. In the course of my, eventually many, meetings with this group, I discovered them, first, to be the most fascinatingly interdisciplinary group I had ever met. But second, and theologically very very important, I discovered that mimetic theory seemed to gave me an entrance into what I would call – at least in layman's terms, for I am definitely not a phenomenologist – a phenomenology of grace. By that I mean a phenomenology, i.e., social-scientific analysis of the external effects of the internal, spiritual workings of redemption/atonement, and hence, of sacrifice. In other words, if atonement, if the salvific effects of sacrifice are real in our time-space human world, then these effects must in some way be approachable or

---

1   Part One, Chapter III: 'The Sacrifice of the Mass'; Part Two, Chapter III: another treatment of 'The Sacrifice of the Mass' and Chapter IV: 'Sacrifice and the Reformation'; Bridge 2 A, Chapter II: 'Moment-of-Consecration Theology' and Chapter III: 'Mass-Stipend Theology: Theology in Transition'; and the whole of Bridge 2 B: 'Liturgical Renewal and Ecumenism'.

analyzable by the social sciences. Theology alone cannot do this, but phenomenology, the social sciences – as long as they resist being reductionistic – can. What I make of this has been summarized in this book as Bridge 2 C: 'Sacrifice and Girardian Mimetic Theory: The End of Sacrifice?' (pp. 202–222).

Chapter IV

The Trinitarian Insight

One cannot have read through, or even skimmed through, this book, or any of my recent writings without repeatedly encountering the fact that the central and overwhelming insight now governing all my thought, work and writing on Christian sacrifice is Trinitarian. How this came about is the story of yet another discovery in my life, this one a profound intellectual and theologically transformative change. It is a change that began to take place just in the past decade, in the late 1990s, at a time when I had, again naively, assumed that by then – I was in my mid sixties – the time for any kind of a change like this was long past.

It began with the premature death in June of 1994 of the great liturgical theologian, Edward J. Kilmartin, S.J., a man who in 1964 had been my first teacher in the theology of the Eucharist. Somewhat by serendipitous default, I became Kilmartin's literary executor. Among what he left behind was a canvas folder with some 2 dozen obsolete Word Perfect diskettes that, after some adventurous technological updating, were revealed to contain the substantially mature, but in style and form still very rough, draft of what was his magnificent final work; *The Eucharist in the West.* Aware that I was barely worthy to lace up his bootstraps, I postponed my own plans to do at least some of my originally planned historical-doctrinal study of Christian sacrifice, and took on the task of preparing this work for publication. To that task, I devoted my entire sabbatical year of 1996–97. In the course of that year, what I thought was going to be a duteous self-effacing work of piety turned out to be the occasion of the most transformative change in my theological career. I, who thought of myself, by then, as a recognized expert on Christian sacrifice, discovered that I had, until then, totally missed the central point.

The central reality of Christian sacrifice is that it is a profoundly interpersonal Trinitarian event. It is an event that begins, as I now never tire of repeating, with the self-offering, self-giving, self-communicating gift of God, the Father in the sending of the Son. It continues in a second 'moment' with the totally free self-giving, self-communicating 'response'[2] of the Son, in his humanity, and in the

---

2   The scare quotes around the words 'moment' and 'response' are to remind us of the inherent inadequacy of language to do justice to the mystery of the Trinity and of divine–human relationships. In the inner Trinitarian relationships there is nothing of the temporality that can be suggested by 'moment', nor is there in the relationship between the Son and the Father anything of the over-against otherness that can be suggested by the word 'response'.

power of the Holy Spirit, to the Father and for us. And it continues, and only then does it begin to become actualized as authentic Christian sacrifice in a so-to-speak third 'moment' when human beings, by the power of the same Spirit that was in the human Jesus, and by the ways in which they actively love and give themselves to other human beings, begin to enter into that profoundly interpersonal reality that is the life of Father, Son and Spirit.

Along, presumably, with many other Christian theologians, I probably already had an inchoative inkling that this was so. But so far was this from my conscious understanding that it was only towards the end of that year devoted to editing Kilmartin's book that it began to take shape in my conscious mind. Maybe it wasn't all that clear in Kilmartin's mind either, for the passage that finally triggered it into the open in my own consciousness is found less than two pages before the very end of his book:

> For sacrifice is not, in the first place, an activity of human beings directed to God and, in the second place, something that reaches its goal in the response of divine acceptance and bestowal of divine blessing on the cultic community. Rather, sacrifice in the New Testament understanding – and thus in its Christian understanding – is, in the first place, the self-offering of the Father in the gift of his Son, and in the second place the unique response of the Son in his humanity to the Father, and in the third place, the self-offering of believers in union with Christ by which they share in his covenant relationship with the Father.[3]

There is delicious irony in this reference to 'the New Testament understanding'. Edward Kilmartin had occasionally mentioned to me that he had learned from me what that 'New Testament understanding' was. Maybe that was why it took me so long to become aware of how much further Edward Kilmartin had brought all this. After all, as I thought, he was learning from me. What did I have to learn from him?

---

3   Edward J. Kilmartin, S.J., *The Eucharist in the West: History and Theology* (Collegeville, Minn.: Liturgical Press, 1998), pp. 381–82. As the great Austrian liturgical theologian, Hans Bernhard Meyer pointed out in his review of Kilmartin's *Christian Liturgy: Theology and Practice, I. Systematic Theology of Liturgy* (Kansas City, MO: Sheed & Ward, 1988), Kilmartin was the first Western theologian to expound a theology of liturgy from a consistently Trinitarian perspective (for further details, see Part One, n. 12). This was, doubtless, among the more important things that Kilmartin learned during those 15 years in the 1970s and 80s when he was intensely involved with the Roman Catholic–Eastern Orthodox theological dialogue.

Chapter V

The Final Turning

It is with hesitation that I use the word 'final'. For all that I can now be sure of is that this is the most recent turning, the most recent change – and indeed so recent that it is probably still going on – in this more than 40-year journey of discovery into the meaning of Christian sacrifice. It represents, in my present awareness, the coming together of three different moments in this journey.

The first of these moments is primarily a homiletic moment that began as I became aware of the challenge of trying to communicate my Trinitarian understanding of Christian sacrifice to non-theologians. The massively negative – for many people overwhelmingly negative – associations and feelings aroused in them by the very mention of the word sacrifice make this from the outset a particularly difficult pastoral-theological challenge. With theologians and with analytically trained scholars and readers, one can perhaps use a 'frontal' approach and hope that some of them might stay with you long enough to get what you are saying. But for people not so trained, you are not likely to get them past the negative connotations, associations and feelings that will be aroused by the mere mention of the word 'sacrifice. This can lead to the suggestion that we delete the word, at least at the beginning, from our homiletic vocabulary. For, in terms of what most people think is sacrifice, in terms of what they think is Christian sacrifice, we do need to be, in the words of S. Mark Heim, 'saved from sacrifice'. But this word is so embedded in traditional Christian thinking that it is impossible to prescind from it. Somehow or other, sooner or later, we cannot avoid facing, in the words of Erin Lothes Biviano, 'the paradox of Christian sacrifice'. 'The question of sacrifice' to use the words of Dennis King Keenan, is simply not going to go away. Concomitantly, there is no easy way to get rid of those 'problems with atonement' that Stephen Finlan so graphically describes.[4]

A way out of this impasse came with the realization that most people, in fact, already know, and indeed know by personal experience, what I am talking about in that third Trinitarian 'moment' of Christian sacrifice, that 'moment' when human beings, in the power of the same Spirit that was in the human Jesus, begin to enter into that perfect relationship of loving, mutual self-giving that is the life of God, Father, Son and Spirit. What I am able to tell them, as I will explain in more detail a few pages further on, is that the self-giving love that they have already experienced, and to which they know themselves as challenged to respond, that

---

4   See S. Mark Heim, *Saved from Sacrifice: A Theology of the Cross* (Grand Rapids, Mich.: Eerdmans, 2006); Erin Lothes Biviano, *The Paradox of Christian Sacrifice: The Loss of Self, The Gift of Self* (A Herder & Herder Book; New York, Crossroad, 2007); Dennis King Keenan, *The Question of Sacrifice* (Bloomington and Indianapolis: Indiana University Press, 2005); Stephen Finlan, *Problems with Atonement: The Origins of, and Controversy about, the Atonement Doctrine* (Collegeville, Minn.: Liturgical Press, 2005).

dynamic of love that makes them who they are as human beings, is their already actual knowledge and experience of Christian sacrifice.

The second moment or high point in this most recent turning of my journey towards understanding Christian sacrifice became crystallized at a meeting of the Boston Theological Society in December 2007. This was the second of four meetings in Academic year 2007–08 devoted to the theology of non-violence. Four persons: first, Gordon Kaufman, a Mennonite, then, Robert Daly, a Roman Catholic, third, S. Mark Heim, a Baptist, and fourth, Roger Johnson, a Lutheran, were asked to set up discussion of their respective positions on non-violence not just by expounding that position (which I did with my Bridge 2 C: 'Sacrifice and Girardian Mimetic Theory: The End of Sacrifice?'), but also and especially by contextualizing it in personal autobiographical narrative, as I am doing now at the end of this book.

For me, the most exciting part of the discussion of my position that evening was Gordon Kaufman's statement that he discovered that my thoroughly – and indeed 'aggressively' – Trinitarian understanding of Christian sacrifice was speaking to him in terms of his own non-Trinitarian understanding of God and of the divine–human relationship as 'serendipitous creativity'.[5] This powerfully reinforces the validity of what has been a deepening awareness during this journey of discovery, namely, that what is most true, most profound and most transcendent in the Christian experience of God, or, in the language of this book, what is most true, most profound and most transcendent in Christian sacrifice, is definitely not restricted to Christians. It is, in whatever different ways it may be articulated in different religions and cultures, the universal human experience, indeed the universally humanizing experience, of discovering that one is being loved, and the attempt to respond to that love.

The third 'moment' or high point in this most recent turning of this journey of discovery begins with my reaction to a comment made by one of the editorial readers of this manuscript for T&T Clark of the Continuum International Publishing Group, a comment to the effect that the Trinitarian character of this book might limit its readership. My reaction is to exclaim: *au contraire!* My experience in discovering that the most telling examples (stories) I can find to illustrate my understanding of Christian sacrifice are drawn from human experiences that are universally human, and then the experience of hearing a decidedly non-trinitarian theologian (Gordon Kaufmann) say that my Trinitarian theology was reminding him of his own 'serendipitous creativity', these experiences are telling me that my decidedly Trinitarian approach to understanding Christian sacrifice is limiting only in terms of the technically theological aspects of the insight. In terms, however, of my attempts to communicate this insight in experiential terms, the trajectory is very much both from and toward what is universally human.

---

5   See hereafter, p. 234, footnote 11 for the references.

Chapter VI

The Journey Ahead

For the past 10 years, my primary mission in life has been not just to deepen and solidify in my own mind this understanding of Christian sacrifice but also, and increasingly, to communicate it to as many people as possible. I consciously express this in terms of 'mission' and 'vocation' because, in fact, this has become the primary assignment given to me by the Jesuit order of which I have been a member for the past fifty-eight years. But in terms of the journey ahead, one of the first things that I have noticed in attempting to communicate this understanding of Christian sacrifice is that it does not communicate well or easily on the purely theological level. Not at all surprising, considering how long it took me, a supposed expert on the subject, to, finally, 'get it'.

I remember a standing-room-only gathering at a Catholic Theological Society of America meeting around the year 1998. It was announced as my presentation of the findings of Edward Kilmartin's posthumous and about-to-be-published *The Eucharist in the West*. People dutifully and respectfully listened, but I wasn't at all sure, especially from the questions that came up after my presentation, that the message was getting across. Similar, too, was my experience of explaining this to the Eucharistic Prayer and Theology seminar of NAAL. These were people, Protestants and Catholics, already associated with me in this journey of discovery. But as I droned on with my explanation, I noticed that eyes would begin to glaze over. But that changed in the following year when I shifted the point of discussion and the question being asked. I began to put it this way: if Kilmartin is right, then it should have such and such practical effects in the way that we celebrate the Eucharist. If Kilmartin is right, then the Eucharist should be celebrated and prayed, not as we are now doing it, but in the following, for example, kinds of ways. As soon as the question was put this way, the interest and understanding, indeed the excitement, became intense. I was beginning to learn how to communicate this Trinitarian understanding of sacrifice.

By now, in the early years of the third millennium, I was seizing the opportunity to talk about this to any group that would listen, not just the two liturgical societies/academies already mentioned, but also, among others, to the Catholic Theological Society of America and to the local ecumenical Boston Theological Society. The positive, usually enthusiastic response I received emboldened me to the next step. In the summer of 2002, while on a 'working vacation' at Sankt Georgen, the Jesuit-run seminary and research institute in Frankfurt, Germany, I postponed (once again) what was left of my original plan to work on the history of the doctrine of sacrifice in order to write an article on what I had been discovering. I was surprised at how easily it came. The subject had become so much a part of me that the article almost wrote itself. Michael Fahey, S.J. and the editorial readers of *Theological Studies* seemed to be smitten with what I had written, for the article appeared in that journal just a few months later.[6] The positive response to that article told me that the central thesis and insight behind this book was indeed sound.

Increasingly aware that I had a message that cried out for a wider audience, I submitted a popular version of that article to the weekly journal, *America*. The editors there were of the same mind, and this shorter and more accessible presentation of my findings appeared just a month later.[7] The success of this article was key to what later developed as the goal of this present book. Edward Foley, O.F.M., asked me to present this material as a specific aid to preaching on the subject. This was a different kind of challenge, but one very much in line with what I was now discovering to be the mission and vocation of my life. The result was an article in the journal *Preach. Enlivening the Pastoral Art*.[8] I was beginning to get 'on a roll'. The next step was a further refinement of these articles that I used as the text of a 'Short Communication' for some 45 of the participants at the August 2005 meeting of the Societas Liturgica in Dresden, Germany. The enthusiasm with which this was received was overwhelming, indeed exciting and energizing. I was now determined more than ever to produce a book that would lay all this out for a wide range of readers.

What I had been discovering was not only a style of exposition more accessible to a readership wider than that of a scholarly theological journal. I was also discovering how to connect my central vision of a Trinitarian understanding of sacrifice to a broad range of human experience. This began in the 'Sacrificial Preaching' article, was developed further in the 'Short Communication' in Dresden just mentioned, and developed further still in an article that appeared in *The Priest* magazine.[9] I have also successfully tried it several times in preaching, and many more times in serious conversation. The key to doing this successfully has been to point out or evoke real experiences in people's lives in which they have actually – though without knowing it in the technical, theological sense – experienced Trinitarian Christian sacrifice, experiences with which they can at least imaginatively identify.

An important first step, as already mentioned, is to avoid using the word 'sacrifice' before you have evoked the powerful recollection of these experiences. Otherwise your readers/hearers might be overwhelmed with the predominantly negative understandings commonly associated with 'sacrifice'.[10] One might hope that the 'frontal approach' of theological exposition can work successfully with the trained theologian, but that may be too much to expect from less analytical readers and listeners. They'll hardly ever get past or beyond the negatively laden word 'sacrifice' in order to arrive at the profoundly and exhilaratingly liberating

---

6   Robert J. Daly, S.J., 'Sacrifice Unveiled or Sacrifice Revisited: Trinitarian and Liturgical Perspectives', *Theological Studies* 64 (2003), pp. 24–42.

7   Robert J. Daly, S.J., 'Sacrifice, the Way to Enter the Paschal Mystery', *America* 188 (May 12, 2003), pp. 14–17.

8   Robert J. Daly, S.J., 'Sacrificial Preaching', *Preach. Enlivening the Pastoral Art* (January/ February, 2005), pp. 26–29.

9   Robert J. Daly, S.J., 'Sacrificial Preaching: The Challenge of Preaching Sacrifice', *The Priest* 63/9 (September 2007), pp. 41–48, 33.

10   Recall Chapter I 'The Many Meanings of Sacrifice' in Part One, pp. 1–5.

Trinitarian insight. And, let me also repeat that this insight is not just Trinitarian, and not even exclusively Christian in any narrow or excluding sense of the word. For example, as I've already mentioned a few pages earlier, Prof. Gordon Kaufman of Harvard Divinity School, in reading and discussing my work, heard it speaking to him of the 'serendipitous creativity' that has been the central insight of some of his most recent theological work.[11] In other words, a Trinitarian understanding of sacrifice is *actually* – and not just by way of a convenient example or illustration – grounded in a broad range of universal human experience.

This is quite a claim. How do I substantiate it? Actually, quite simply, once one gets the point. The practical strategy that I am proposing is based on the theological conviction, supported by sociological observation, that anyone listening to a sermon, anyone listening to someone attempting to explain what I am talking about, has already had some experience of Christian sacrifice. They have already at some time, perhaps many times, been the recipients of self-giving love, whether from parents, spouse, guardians, siblings, relatives, teachers, colleagues, friends or whomever. Theoretically, i.e., theologically, the key is the fact that *all* acts of genuine self-giving love, regardless of whether one is Christian or not, are participations in the self-giving love of God. For God is love. One consequence of that is that all genuine acts of love, i.e., genuinely self-giving, self-communicating acts of love are from and of God, participations, as theology tells us, in the self-giving, self-communicating love that is the life of the Blessed Trinity. People know that, not necessarily in technical theological terms, but at least, virtually, implicitly, instinctively. It is the job of the preacher, the teacher, the one explaining this to them, to bring this knowledge, this experience, to the surface, to invite people to become aware that the self-giving love of God – the ultimate reality of Christian sacrifice – is already at work in their lives.

People, and once again, not just Christian people, already have this knowledge and experience of Christian sacrifice. Ask anyone what perfect happiness is. Lead them deep into themselves, past all the sometimes quite powerful desires for wealth, power, success and pleasure. What do you come up with? You come up with the hope and the dream of being in love. Whether one conceives it sexually, or Platonically, or anything or everything in between, it is the dream of being loved by someone totally, unconditionally and eternally, the dream of being able to return that love totally, unconditionally and eternally, and along with that dream, not just the trust or the hope, but the unconditioned knowledge and absolute assurance that that love will never fade and never be betrayed.

If you've got that, then wealth, power, success and pleasure have been transcended in this perfect and permanent ecstasy of mutual self-giving love. This dream is everyone's dream because it grows from and indeed is the actual desire for God implanted within each one of us. As Augustine so unforgettably put it at the beginning of his *Confessions*, God's image and likeness within us will not let that desire lie still.

---

11 Gordon D. Kaufmann, *In the Beginning . . . Creativity* (Minneapolis, Fortress Press, 2004), esp. Chapter 2: 'On Thinking of God as Serendipitous Creativity'; idem, *Jesus and Creativity* (Minneapolis: Fortress Press, 2006).

We are talking about union with God; we are talking about heaven, about beatitude; we are talking about the working of 'God's love [that] has been poured out into our hearts through the Holy Spirit that has been given to us' (Rom. 5.5). We are also talking about every true love story that we have ever read or seen on TV or film. It is implicitly behind even that endless succession of seemingly mindless TV situation comedies to which so many are addicted. We are talking about the essence of Christian sacrifice.

But is this realistic? Is it concrete and real? Actually, nothing is more humanly real. For this is precisely what makes us human. Try to imagine taking this away. What you've got left might conceivably be a magnificent animal, but it certainly won't be a human being.

Alright then, it is a beautiful dream, a magnificent ideal. But does it really work? Well, take the story of a man (or woman – change the sex and the concomitant details and the story works the same way) who is a totally selfish, self-absorbed person. He's smart. He knows how to use people to get what he wants, to make life better and easier for himself. He may even seem to belong to some religion or church, but that is also just something else that he uses, for his real gods are wealth, power, success and pleasure.

But one day, to his great surprise, he finds himself beginning to fall in love. And because the roots of God's image and likeness never totally die out, even in the worst of us, and because he's smart, he begins to figure out what is facing him. He knows his beloved is willing to give herself to him totally and unconditionally. She'll do for him or with him whatever he wants. He knows that he can use her, he knows that it can be useful to him to 'play the game', to let people around them think that the both of them are really in love. But he knows, too, that he is ready to drop her whenever it suits him.

But his old world, the world that he controls, is beginning to crumble. For he senses a call to begin to return that love. He knows that if he begins to do this, the life that he knew he could control for his own ends, the life in which there would never be any doubts about who is 'number one', will be over. He'll be turning his back on his trusted gods of wealth, power, success and pleasure. He'll be asking for trouble by making himself vulnerable, by exposing himself to suffering and victimhood instead of shielding himself from it. He'll be turning away from his trusted gods that have served him so well in order to reach for something – true happiness – that he thought never even existed, except in the minds of romantic, unrealistic fools. People across all cultures and religions are faced with this kind of choice, for the call to face it is what distinguishes us from the animals. God's love is so powerful that sometimes people actually make the choice facing this man. They begin to accept the self-offering of another. They begin to offer themselves in return.

Homiletically, this works. I told this story as part of a brief homily preached at an ecumenical Eucharistic liturgy for about 40 people at the close of the July 2007 meeting of the Colloquium on Violence and Religion at the Kontakt der Kontinenten center in Soesterberg, near Amsterdam. I had begun with my three-'moment' understanding of Christian sacrifice, and then illustrated it with this story, after which I sat down and invited the participants to add to the homily, if they wished. One man did so, testifying that the story I had told was the story of what had happened to him about 15 years before. Afterwards a number of others, in word, or in writing, or in email, mentioned that this brief homily had given them a glimpse of what the whole conference – and life itself – was really all about.

However, making the choice to respond to love almost inevitably leads to suffering. Suffering is bad. Suffering is to be avoided. But letting yourself fall in love means not avoiding suffering but walking right into it. In the end we have no choice, of course. Even the self-centred young man in our story knows that we're all going to suffer and die. Nothing is more absolute than that. But to keep it at a distance as long as possible. That, he used to think, was the only way to get to that limited pleasure that might be possible in life.

However, to step back from our story and reflect on its implication, none of the particular ways in which we suffer and die are absolute. They are, as the philosophers say, contingent. They don't have to happen. They don't have to happen in the way that they do. But the love with which we live, suffer and die, that is not contingent. And that's where we do have a choice. In choosing love we are choosing something absolute, something divine. For ultimately, as St. Paul's magnificent hymn about love in 1 Corinthians 13 so eloquently teaches, it is love, not suffering in and of itself that is holy. It is love, not human achievement, not suffering, not anything else, but only love that is transcendently and eternally sacred.

This leads us to look at the suffering of Christ or, in the terms of our subject, the sacrifice of Christ. In terms of a strategy of pastoral communication, we are finally coming to use the S-word. We need to look very carefully here, for some traditional ways of looking at the sacrifice of Christ – almost synonymous with atonement[12] – actually veil, and veil horribly, rather than reveal the mystery of God's love.

For every detail in Christ's life, in the same way, indeed, as every detail in every human life, is contingent. None of these details had to have happened. None of them had to have happened in the way that they did. This does not in any way undercut the absoluteness and centrality of the Incarnation, of the life, death and resurrection of Jesus Christ as the central Christian doctrine. It does not in any way undercut that we have in fact been saved by the historical life, death, resurrection and Spirit-sending of Jesus Christ. But it does point out that there is a certain contingency in these events. Contrary to some strains of Christian theorizing, there is no absolute necessity for them to have happened, or to have happened in the way that they did. Simply put, God could have done it differently.

However, what definitely is not contingent, what definitely could not have been done differently is the love with which the Father offered himself in the sending of His Son, the love with which the incarnate Son, in the Spirit, loved 'in return' and the love 'poured into our hearts' (Rom. 5.5) with which we begin to respond to that divine love in the love that we experience from parents, spouse, guardians, siblings, relatives, teachers, colleagues, friends or whomever.

In other words, although we have in fact been 'redeemed by the blood of Christ', as the traditional Christian formulation puts it, it was not, in the most precise sense, the suffering of Christ that saved us. Rather, what saved us is the love with which he suffered. And so, too, it is not precisely the suffering involved in our

---

12   As we saw earlier in the Subsection of Bridge 2 A: 'Distorting Mirrors', pp. 176–79.

Christian sacrifices through which God is working our salvation that contributes to our salvation. Rather, it is the love with which we respond to the love we receive from parents, spouse, guardians, siblings, relatives, teachers, colleagues, friends or whomever – it is that love that saves us.

My years of working on the idea of Christian sacrifice have been, indeed increasingly, as the years went on, exciting and fulfilling. In preparing this book, and especially here at the end as I try to sum up its meaning and talk about the challenge of communicating it to a wide circle of readers, I am aware that the conventional borders between analysis, exposition, vision, hope, preaching and prayer, too, have begun to dissolve. So be it. Lord have mercy! Lord have mercy! Lord have mercy!

BIBLICAL INDEX

SUBJECT INDEX

INDEX OF NAMES

Lightning Source UK Ltd.
Milton Keynes UK
UKOW06f0632220116

266918UK00006B/73/P